How Photography Became Contemporary Art

How Photography Became Contemporary Art

Inside an Artistic Revolution from Pop to the Digital Age

Andy Grundberg

Yale University Press
New Haven and London

For Merry

Published with assistance from Furthermore: a program of the J. M. Kaplan Fund.

Furthermore:
a program of the J.M. Kaplan Fund

yalebooks.com/art

Designed by Jeff Wincapaw
Set in Adobe Text Pro and Akagi Pro
Printed in Singapore by 1010 Printing International Limited

Library of Congress Control Number: 2020942545
ISBN 978-0-300-23410-7

A catalogue record for this book is available from the British Library.

This paper meets the requirements of ANSI/NISO Z39.48–1992 (Permanence of Paper).

10 9 8 7 6 5 4 3 2 1

Jacket illustration: Louise Lawler, *Life After 1945 (Faces) (adjusted to fit)*, distorted for the times. 2006/2007/2015. Dimensions variable. Courtesy of the artist and Metro Pictures, New York.

For the book's jacket, Lawler's work *Life After 1945 (Faces) (adjusted to fit)* has been reproduced with a digital distortion filter, making the media circulation of this work "distorted for the times."

Contents

Acknowledgments

First, thanks to all the artists whose work I discuss; they have provided the material that shapes my narrative as well as a central reason my life has been so full and rewarding. Also, to the critics, writers, and editors of my generation who have endeavored to explain why art matters and which art matters more than most. I am blessed to have experienced firsthand such a disputatious and energetic era in the history of art, thanks to you.

This book includes my own recollections, which lack the fabled veracity of still photographs, so I have relied on my peers and on much recent scholarship to confirm as many of them as possible. Among the many individuals who supplied their own memories of the period to supplement mine, and who submitted to my interrogations in person, I am indebted to Janet Borden, Roger Bruce, Charles Hagen, Marvin Heiferman, Harold Jones, Jane Livingston, Lisa Spellman, Carol Squiers, Charles Stainback, Helene Winer, and Ealan Wingate. Deborah Bell, Philippe Garner, Michael Klein, Rosalind Krauss, Laurence Miller, and others also supplied key details when asked. Joan Simon supplied valuable feedback on some early drafts.

I have benefited over the years from the support of colleagues, editors, and friends far too numerous to mention, but here are a few: at *Art in America*, Elizabeth C. Baker and Joan Simon; at the *Soho Weekly News*, Gerald Marzorati; at the *New York Times*, Eva Hoffman, Michael Kimmelman, William McDonald, Marilyn Minden, Claiborne Ray, Constance Rosenblum, Le Anne Schreiber, Jack Schwartz, and Rebecca Sinkler; at the *Washington Post*, John Pancake. My faculty colleagues at the Corcoran College of Art and Design, especially Dorothea Dietrich, Frank DiPerna, Muriel Hasbun, and Susan Sterner, helped inspire me to develop and expand the course that was the basis for this book.

Julia Scully, former editor of *Modern Photography*, was my most important influence at the start of my career; she introduced me to a world of photography I might never have known and to writing about it with passion and compassion. Art historians Rosalind Krauss, Robert Rosenblum, and Irving Sandler I got to know but briefly in my years in New York, but their sagacity and openness to new art set a standard for art writing I deeply admire. In the photography world, in addition to those already mentioned, I am fortunate to have shared my formative years as a critic with gallerists of exquisite visual refinement, including Bonni Benrubi, Evelyne Daitz, Jeffrey Fraenkel, Peter MacGill, Marcuse Pfeifer, Julie Saul, Daniel Wolf, and Virginia Zabriskie—

some of whom sadly are not here to share in my memories. They, along with many talented museum curators, made my decision to take up reviewing seem wise.

Thanks to the George Washington University, which, after absorbing the Corcoran College, saw fit to make me an emeritus professor and thus entitle me during my research to use its extensive library resources, online and in the stacks at the Gelman Library, and to Marisa Bourgoin of the Archives of American Art, who helped me navigate its rich collections of artist and gallery archives. Helene Winer let me browse in the gallery records at Metro Pictures.

Many artists, artist estates, and galleries generously cooperated in supplying images for the book, and many went so far as to allow me permission to reproduce artwork without paying their usual reproduction fees. To them, sincere thanks for helping to make this book richly illustrated and economically feasible. For their cooperation and assistance with multiple requests, I am especially indebted to Lisa Ballard at the Artists Rights Society, Catherine Belloy of Marian Goodman Gallery, Jane Crawford and the Estate of Gordon Matta-Clark, and the William Wegman Studio. And a special thank you to Louise Lawler, who provided the perfect picture for the book's cover, producing a new art object in the process.

At Yale University Press, my editor, Katherine Boller, has kept me from my worst excesses and shepherded me through drafts and readers' reports. I also thank Sarah Henry, Raychel Rapazza, and Kate Zanzucchi. Copy editor Alison Hagge efficiently fixed my grammatical lapses and corrected my facts, and proofreader Julia Ridley Smith and indexer Krister Swartz supplied much needed finishing touches. (Despite their due diligence, any errors that remain to be discovered are entirely mine.) Jeff Wincapaw made the book as beautiful as it is, and Dan Cohen rounded up the illustrations and their permissions. I take great pleasure knowing that the Press is nurturing such a high standard of publishing. And I owe a true debt to my agent, Martha Millard, and Lord Literistics, who placed me in such good hands. Martha's enduring faith in me as an author even after a long fallow period is truly remarkable, and appreciated.

And to Merry Foresta, who insisted that I write this book. She not only gladly suffered through three years of my self-induced preoccupation with my past, but also provided valuable guidance and feedback all along the way.

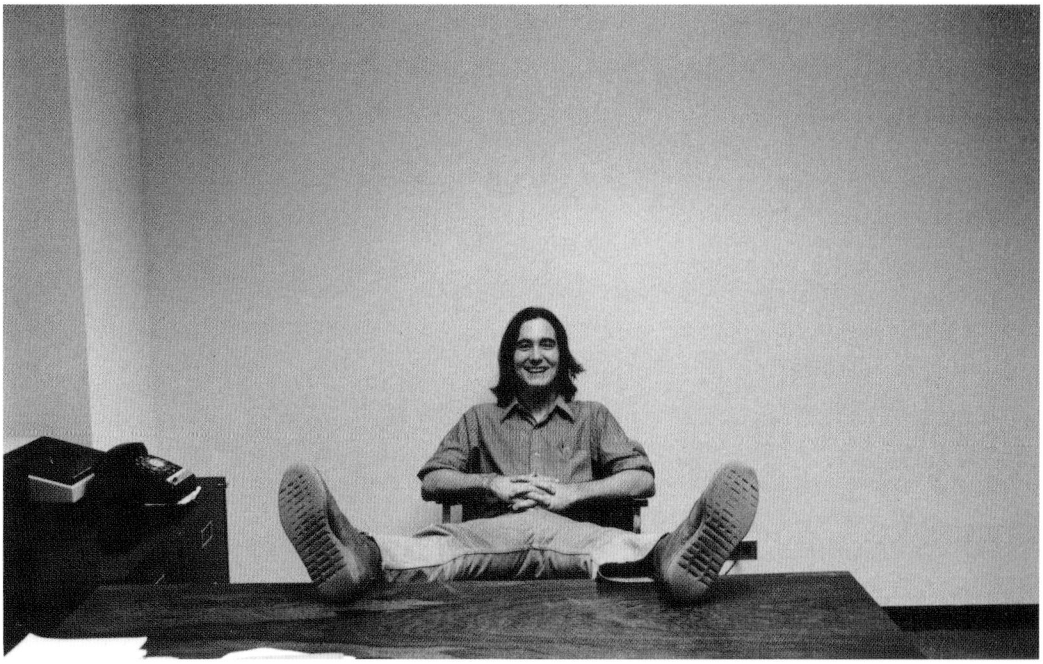

Introduction

That's one of the central problems of history, isn't it, sir? The question of subjective versus objective interpretation, the fact that we need to know the history of the historian in order to understand the version that is being put in front of us.

—Julian Barnes, *The Sense of an Ending*, 2011

This book recounts the remarkable rise of photography from the margins of art to its vital center, all within a span of twenty-five years. It is told from a point of view that is formed in part from my eyewitness perspective and in part from researching and writing about the interactions of art and photography in the three decades since I lived in New York. The story cuts two ways: From one perspective, it is the fulfillment of photographers' long and embattled quest to have their medium fully accepted as a form of art. From another, it is a revolutionary tale in which contemporary art, once the rarified province of abstract painting and sculpture, becomes broader, vastly more popular, and more engaged with the world and the ways that cameras represent it. In the years since photography entered the art world, contemporary art has replaced Impressionist and Old Masters painting as the most sought-after, collected, exhibited, and expensive segment of the art market.

Photography's near omnipresence within contemporary art is, historically speaking, new. At the midpoint of the twentieth century, anyone venturing into a gallery or museum would have been hard-pressed to find any photographs on view among the displays of paintings, drawings, prints, and sculpture. Only a few select museums in major cities—New York, Chicago, San Francisco—considered photographs to be something worth collecting and exhibiting. When photographs were exhibited as works of art, they were far more likely to be found on the dusky walls of coffeehouses and bars than hanging in the white expanses of commercial galleries. Nor, despite their important presence in magazines like *Life*, *Look*, and *National Geographic*, did they much figure on the pages of art magazines or of the few newspapers that could afford to employ art critics.

Scholarly and academic attention was equally nearly nonexistent. When I wanted to take a photography class as an undergraduate at Cornell

The author at his first job with the *Herald*, a short-lived weekly Manhattan newspaper, c. 1972.

University in the late sixties, I went to the fine-art department office and asked what was available. "Nothing" was the answer, "We don't consider photography a fine art." Confoundingly, the only class on offer was taught in the college of agriculture, which had one intro course. I enrolled. As for the history of the medium, the art-history department provided no help either. The art-history survey course I took as a sophomore made no mention of photography. The course textbook, H. W. Janson's *History of Art*, did not even list photography in its index.[1]

Flash ahead fifty years. One would need to search hard to find a contemporary gallery or museum that does not include photography. Not only photographs, but also video, which has largely replaced film as the preferred medium for making and presenting moving images. Photography is now the subject of headliner shows at major museums, of PhD theses in art-history departments and of MFA degrees in studio art programs (including Cornell's), of books of art criticism that liberally quote from some of the important thinkers of the past century, including Roland Barthes, Walter Benjamin, Michel Foucault, and Susan Sontag. Original black-and-white prints that magazine editors once routinely discarded after using them to make halftone reproductions now command prices at auction of tens if not hundreds of thousands of dollars.

Similarly, the art world itself has been transformed. While paintings can still be found hanging discreetly on many walls, and sculpture commanding the floors, museum and gallery visitors will just as likely encounter rooms filled with video projections, displays of color photographs as large as any paintings by Jackson Pollock, assemblages of unprepossessing materials that constitute artists' installations, or an artist performing her art by sitting in the gallery and staring intently at visitors one by one, as Marina Abramović has done. Moreover, there are now more galleries showing contemporary art than those devoted to the entire rest of art history, a sign of its growing and pervasive popularity. Sales at auction houses have followed the same trend, a sign of contemporary art's financial appeal. As strange and inchoate as its forms can appear, contemporary art is no longer confined to a small vanguard of true believers; instead, it has developed into a worldwide phenomenon that engages the attention of a broad young audience. Pictures that come from cameras are a large part of the reason why.

How this dramatic shift occurred, how contemporary art broadened as photography went from its margins to its center, is a textured and multifaceted tale, one I endeavor to tell in subsequent chapters. But the gist is this: Artists, seeking to move beyond the Modernist primacy given to painting and sculpture, first began to use photography primarily as a documentary device for recording a range of new art practices, and this interest led them to reimagine what might constitute art making. Photographers, meanwhile, began to see the medium's potential for individual expression as its most interesting feature, forsaking the printed page for the gallery wall just as the marketplace for picture magazines entered a steep decline. This happened as the *subject* of photography itself, its functions as both a product and producer of cultural attitudes, became a central preoccupation for critical theorists who were trying to understand how, exactly, the language of photography communicated its messages in the territories of advertising, entertainment, politics, family dynamics, and individual identity. Together, these forces moved photography onto center stage.

Existing accounts of photography's flowering in the seventies and eighties focus almost exclusively on the establishment of institutional structures designed to support it: museum curators and collections, photography-specific galleries like Witkin, Light, and Lunn, auction-house sales at Sotheby's and Christie's, tenured university positions for teaching photography, supportive National Endowment for the Arts programs, niche publications focused on photography as a fine art, and space within general-interest newspapers and magazines for photo-specific reviews. (I took advantage of the new interest in writing on photography, cutting my teeth at *Art in America* before becoming a contributor to the *Soho Weekly News* and, for most of the eighties, the *New York Times*.) But as important as these developments were, they are symptoms and not causes; what changed contemporary art was art itself and the artists who made it. And while the lexicon still distinguishes photography and art, and photographers and artists, in the context of contemporary art such distinctions now are moot: photography is art, and photographers are artists (notwithstanding the few diehards who reject the term).

For the record, I am not saying that photography's claim to be art, and the medium's interaction with the territories of painting and drawing, originated in our times. From the medium's very beginnings, starting in 1839, photographers had sought to have their work recognized as art. Indeed, the modern history of photography has been written as a kind of pilgrim's tale, a major plotline of which is a progressive discovery of the medium's unique artistic nature following a series of unsatisfying imitative encounters with the arts of painting and drawing.

In the words of William Henry Fox Talbot, one of the two principal inventors of photography, the new medium was no less than a "new art," yet he called his process "the art of Photogenic drawing," not photography. The first newspaper report in Paris about the discovery made by the medium's other credited inventor, Louis Jacques Mandé Daguerre, begins by saying "this discovery . . . will revolutionize the art of drawing." The writer then refers to Daguerre's images as "beautiful drawings," in part because the eponymous term for them had yet to be coined.[2]

Yet for many early observers, the comparison of photography to the work of artists of the pen or brush shortchanged the medium. It fell to commentators like Lady Elizabeth Eastlake, who wrote an influential essay in the British journal *Photographic Notes* in 1857, to argue that photography's value should be measured not by existing aesthetic standards but by its own. Lady Eastlake's article was the first to advance what in the twentieth century came to be seen as a Modernist aesthetic—that photography could be an art by following its own unique characteristics and abandoning influences and standards from other visual arts, specifically painting and drawing. Rather than compete in terms of flattering depictions of its human subjects, for example, it could excel by providing near infinite detail, which Eastlake noted was one of its native talents.[3]

The idea that the art of photography is determined by photography itself justified the creation of independent histories of photography written more or less without regard for contemporaneous histories of art. The earliest of these focused more on technological progress than on the makers of outstanding pictures,[4] but Beaumont Newhall's 1937 *The History of Photography*, the first real American attempt, inverted that emphasis, placing individual pictures and picture makers at the center of its narrative even as it recapitulated the notion that scientific and technological breakthroughs helped propel aesthetic ones. Little was said about painting.

This was the history enshrined at the Museum of Modern Art, where Newhall led a department of photography established in 1940, and the one I read when I was getting seriously interested in photography. It was an account revivified in the sixties by John Szarkowski, then the director of the photography department at the Museum of Modern Art, who essentially mixed Lady Eastlake's argument for photography's uniqueness with the Modernist imprimatur of critic Clement Greenberg. In the exhibition/book *The Photographer's Eye* (1964/1966), Szarkowski listed five essential characteristics of the medium: the thing itself, the detail, the frame, time, and the vantage point. Contemporary photographers hoping to enter the aesthetic discourse of photographic practice produced work that reflected on these characteristics and, more generally, on "the photographic," the idea that whatever else a photograph is about, it ultimately is about the nature of photography itself.

Photography also developed its own independent exhibition system, arguably of necessity since it was excluded from the nineteenth-century salons, with only one exception, the Paris Salon of 1859.[5] As a result, by the end of the century photographers had established their own salons to present their work to the public as art. In England, an association called the Linked Ring started an annual photographic salon in 1893; similar juried exhibitions happened in Vienna and Paris around the same time, as a new generation of photographers with artistic aspirations replaced the medium's pioneers. The style they created, photography's first international aesthetic movement, came to be known as Pictorialism.

The Pictorialists made their case for photography being an art by producing photographs that looked as if they had been made by hand. The only trouble was, art itself—the kind of advanced art centered in Paris that became known as *avant-garde*—was changing so rapidly at the turn of the century that these photographers' efforts came to seem *retardataire*. Among those caught in the middle was Alfred Stieglitz, a German-born New Yorker who is often credited with single-handedly promoting the acceptance of the idea of photography-as-art in the first half of the twentieth century. The young Stieglitz was a wholehearted Pictorialist, a leader of a largely American Pictorialist group called the Photo-Secession, until a trip to Paris with Edward Steichen in 1907 introduced him to truly modern artists like Auguste Rodin, Paul Cézanne, Pablo Picasso, Constantin Brancusi, and Henri Matisse. At his modest gallery on Fifth Avenue, called the Little Galleries of the Photo-Secession when it opened in 1905 and later known as 291, he alternated new European art with Pictorialist photography shows.

By 1910 an older and presumably wiser Stieglitz virtually stopped showing Pictorialist photography and became a promoter not just of new European art but also of young American artists who responded to Cézanne, Picasso, and the others: Arthur Dove, Marsden Hartley, John Marin, and, starting in 1916, a year before the gallery closed, Georgia O'Keeffe.[6] Two months before O'Keeffe's first appearance at 291, Stieglitz mounted the gallery's final photography show: the work of Paul Strand.

Strand's photographs, especially his close-in, near-abstract pictures of porch shadows and bowls, revived Stieglitz's interest in photography because they seemed to make it modern. Like Lady Eastlake before him and Szarkowski after, Stieglitz came to believe that the art of photography could only be understood in terms of photography. In Strand's work Stieglitz found "no tricks" of the sort that Pictorialists used in printing to emulate the atmospherics of a James McNeill Whistler painting; it was "pure" and "direct" in the sense that its appearance, even when abstract, could be readily recognized as photography.

But there was a small catch to Stieglitz's ambition for modern photography: there was little or no market for photographs. This led artists like Strand's friend the Precisionist painter Charles Sheeler to minimize or even renounce the importance of photography in their work. In the early thirties

Sheeler's gallery dealer told him to stop showing his photographs, lest his paintings be seen as copies of them. The dealer's interests were clearly financial, but they also reflect what was a long-standing prejudice against photography in the art marketplace. Photographs could be seen but not sold.

What might be called the Modernist apartheid system for photography was not entirely hegemonic. In Europe during the period between the world wars, photographs *were* a big deal, as a number of vanguard art movements incorporated the medium into their fold, Russian Constructivism, European Dada, and Surrealism among them. At the German Bauhaus László Moholy-Nagy was at the center of an art and design revolution in which the camera was seen as a powerful tool for reorganizing consciousness. What Moholy-Nagy explicitly called "the new vision" became a central part of Bauhaus teaching.

The Surrealists Max Ernst, Man Ray (Emmanuel Radnitzky), and Maurice Tabard had their work included in a large 1929 exhibition called *Film und Foto,* in Stuttgart. That show is legendary because it brought together new and experimental photography from throughout Europe with some from the United States, with contributions by Imogen Cunningham, Edward Steichen, Ralph Steiner, and Edward and Brett Weston.[7] Photography, as Suzanne Pastor has said, became a part of "the modern chic" of the twenties,[8] and it also represented, for many, the radical new future for the visual arts. Photographs also played a role, albeit minor, in the 1936 exhibition *Fantastic Art, Dada, Surrealism,* organized by Alfred H. Barr Jr. at the Museum of Modern Art in New York, which mixed them together with paintings, drawings, and films.[9]

Sadly, the rise of the Nazis in Germany and World War II brought an end to these essentially experimental art movements and consequently an end to photography's budding status within the art world. The migration of artistic talent to the United States included Moholy-Nagy, Ernst, Man Ray, and many of the European artists in *Film und Foto,* but unless they worked as magazine photographers their photographs were largely marginalized. After the war the aesthetic momentum shifted to Abstract Expressionism and "the triumph of American painting," in the words of art historian and critic Irving Sandler.[10] Photography was consigned largely to the printed page, in the form of picture magazines, fashion magazines, and newspapers. When it was exhibited it was often as a nostrum of conventionality and commonality, as in the wildly popular 1955 show *The Family of Man,* organized by Steichen at the Museum of Modern Art. The role photography played in Dada and Surrealism and at the Bauhaus was largely overlooked until, like a recovered memory, it was recouped amid the growing interest in photography in the seventies and eighties, which are the decades in which I enter the story.

Photography's rise within contemporary art—and contemporary art's simultaneous rise to prominence—encompasses a period coincident with my own life. I was a child of an amateur photographer and a member of the first generation of Americans to grow up with television. I learned to dance by watching Dick Clark's *American Bandstand*; *Father Knows Best* and *The Adventures of Ozzie and Harriet* provided aspirational models for measuring my upbringing. Waiting my turn at the barbershop, I would devour dated copies of *Life* magazine, and my interest in visual experience developed alongside my attraction to literature and writing.

I arrived in New York City in 1971 prepared to be a proverbial penniless poet, although I had achieved some résumé cred by working part-time as a newspaper photographer at the end of my graduate writing program in North Carolina. The most famous photographer of the moment, Diane Arbus, committed suicide in her apartment at Westbeth in the West Village at about the same time that I moved into my first apartment on the Upper West Side, but I would encounter two of her peers, street photographers Garry Winogrand and Lee Friedlander, prowling midtown in search of telling moments in the human comedy. They were famous, at least in my mind, for being shown at the Museum of Modern Art. Arbus was about to have her posthumous retrospective there. And a new breed of galleries had just sprung up, devoted to selling photographs as works of art.[11]

Visiting friends downtown, I discovered a whole other world: in Soho, artists my age or slightly older were making art that I could barely recognize as such, filling old industrial spaces with tree trunks and piles of dirt and creating a scene in which any manner of activity—rappelling headfirst down the side of a building, cooking, masturbating, talking to oneself—could count as an artwork. Much of what was happening was recorded with cameras, producing photographs, films, and (soon enough) video. The art world was in ferment, reconfiguring itself to a new age, assimilating a new generation, my generation.

It wasn't only the art world in upheaval. The later sixties and early seventies were full and fraught with political, social, and cultural unrest, marked by the civil rights movement, the war in Vietnam, a growing feminist awareness, and a consciousness-changing youth movement that coalesced around rock music, sex, and drugs. Some of this I experienced firsthand, going to Bob Dylan, Rolling Stones, and Janis Joplin concerts, traveling to anti–Vietnam War "mobilizations" in Washington, D.C., visiting San Francisco during its 1967 "Summer of Love," inhaling illegal botanicals. But much of it I assimilated through photographs.

I saw images of black protesters in Birmingham being sprayed by high-pressure fire hoses, a Marine dying in the Khe Sanh mud with his blood recorded in living color, a Vietnamese girl running naked and burned from her napalmed village, and, on the May 18, 1970, cover of *Newsweek*, a distraught young woman on the campus of Kent State University kneeling next to the body of a student killed by a bullet from the Ohio National Guard. These stills were part of a broad, essential-seeming media environment, novel then but now exponentially denser, that included not only film, television, and picture magazines but also rock album covers, psychedelic concert posters, and R. Crumb underground comics.

In one instance, my firsthand experience and an iconic photographic image coincided directly. The Pulitzer Prize–winning news photograph of 1970, taken by Steve Starr of the Associated Press in 1969, showed a group of my college classmates leaving the campus student union with long guns in their hands and bandoleers of bullets across their shoulders. All were black, and they had been protesting on-campus discrimination; purportedly they armed themselves after some white students threatened to forcibly end their occupation of the building. Unfortunately, the mere sight of weapons played into some people's fear that civil rights might lead to horrible and violent outcomes, even on bucolic college campuses.

I reacted differently. I knew not only that the image was laden with fraught symbolic significance, but also that the students depicted were mostly suburban kids who did their best to look fierce but barely knew a rifle's sight from its safety. I recognized then, if I hadn't before, that photographic meaning was contingent rather than absolute.

The assassinations within a five-year span of President John F. Kennedy, Robert Kennedy, Malcolm X, and the Reverend Martin Luther King Jr. had added more grizzly images to my generation's memory bank, no doubt troubling our ability to fit into the existing order of things as much as they instilled an appreciation of life's tragic dimension. That art in all its forms—visual, written, performed—would be radically altered in this convulsive climate should have come as no surprise. What *was* surprising, at least at the time, was the starring role that photography, and its younger partner, video, would come to play in this transformation.

It is no exaggeration to say that photographs snuck into view in contemporary art, starting in the sixties. They were first seen as paintings, in the silkscreens of Robert Rauschenberg and Andy Warhol, or as documentation, in a wide range of new and transgressive art styles such as Earth Art, Conceptual Art, and Performance Art. Artists who relied on photographic documentation and then their dealers and collectors began to notice that photographs were interesting in and of themselves; they searched the medium's history and discovered figures like the nineteenth-century photographer Eadweard Muybridge, whose action studies fit Conceptual Art's interest in seriality like a glove. Plus photographs could be easily made, exhibited, and reproduced, something that couldn't be said for earthworks or performances.

It helped, too, that photographs were part of what was fast becoming an overwhelming domain of camera images, an "image-world," in Susan Sontag's phrase, that encompassed movies, television, magazine picture essays, advertisements, and everyday snapshots and threatened to replace firsthand reality. In the seventies theorists, critics, and artists all started to look at the medium with a fresh interest, recognizing it as a medium not just for making pictures but also for making meaning. It wasn't long before contemporary art galleries were exhibiting photographs and video as a regular part of their schedules.

As photography took center stage as a subject for art, photographers were engaged in tossing off the constraints of past attempts to make photographs function as art. At the time the art of photography was best represented in the public imagination by glorious prints of glorious nature made by the likes of Ansel Adams, but it also encompassed street photography and other modes of factual documentation. The new photography was different. Another photographer named Adams, Robert, showed us landscapes filled with suburban houses. John Pfahl, another of the new generation, made beautiful color pictures of what he called "altered landscapes," altered because he put objects into the scene to produce amusing optical conundrums, like a hayrick that was visually transformed by a well-placed skein of rope into an outsized ice cream cone.

James Casebere, David Levinthal, Cindy Sherman, Laurie Simmons, Sandy Skoglund, and others started staging their pictures in studios and on tabletops, taking cues from commercial studio photography and Hollywood scenography while rebelling against the belief that good photographs were unmediated slices of reality. Most radically, there were artists who decided to take photographs of photographs. Sherrie Levine and Richard Prince impertinently claimed the results as their own, leading to much umbrage among older photographers and many lawsuit-threatening letters from copyright lawyers. The point of their appropriations wasn't theft, however, but to point out how overburdened we are with images, to the extent that we don't often recognize what they are selling us, or why.

By the eighties' end, the distinction between what was photography by artists and art by photographers no longer seemed to matter. What *did* matter was the impact that photography and video were having on the very conception of what contemporary art was. No longer a prisoner of formal proscriptions about what it should look like, contemporary art had become more diverse, more open to a variety of voices, and more reflective of cultural concerns, including, but not limited to, the experiences of women, gays and lesbians, African Americans, Latinxs, and first- and second-generation immigrants. For many, photography and video were ideal tools for expressing the complexities of their lives. For others, lens-based media were the harbingers of a new media culture, one now fully realized in the inescapable twenty-first-century environment of the digitally networked image.

In writing this account of the period I have come to recognize how fortunate I was to have landed in New York when I did, because I had a front-row seat as the curtain came up on photography's transformation from a minor role to a lead actor in the drama of twentieth-century art. When I started paying attention, art and photography were separate domains, and when I began writing for the *New York Times* I was assigned to cover photography exhibitions and books while the paper's other art critics covered everything else. My territory initially was a small enough world that I got to meet and interact with many of the major players of an older generation—Berenice Abbott, André Kertész, Russell Lee, Helen Levitt, W. Eugene Smith, Ansel Adams himself—and to rub elbows with Peter Campus, Ralph Gibson, Nan Goldin, Duane Michals, Cindy Sherman, Carrie Mae Weems, and scores more contemporary artists, many of whom appear in the narrative to come.

Given my participation in the events of the era I describe, this book is not a conventional or comprehensive art-historical text, in the manner of Irving Sandler's admirable *Art of the Postmodern Era*.[12] At heart mine is a critic's account, based on my experience during my years as a working reviewer. My narrative focuses on the New York art world specifically and American art more generally, largely ignoring activity on other continents that retrospectively has proved important. Closer to home, because of my scope, many artists working on the margins of the gallery system at the time remain underrepresented here as well. This includes many African American artists and other artists of color, some of whom appear relatively late in my story. Their recognition, and the slightly earlier recognition of women artists, does not mask the reality that the art world I describe at the beginning of the book was overwhelmingly white and largely male.

Neither does my account have autobiography as its primary propellant, as in the published first-person accounts of the same period by Douglas Crimp, Keith Richards, and Patti Smith. I would hope this book is a useful hybrid of these two approaches, art history and memoir, a narrative that gives texture and nuance to the developments in art that I witnessed. Best case, it might serve as an impetus for a reconsideration of how art history might be written in an era when storytelling has become paramount.

The eradication of photography's separate-but-not-quite-equal status within the art world—its triumph as an art, if you will—is central to the story that I tell, but equally important is the crucial position that photography and other lens-based media have come to occupy throughout our culture, not only by representing it but also in large part by producing it. Given that camera images are practically inescapable and incalculably influential, is it any wonder that many of the most creative artistic talents of the past fifty years have devoted themselves to showing us not only the medium's aesthetic possibilities but also its paradoxes and peculiarities?

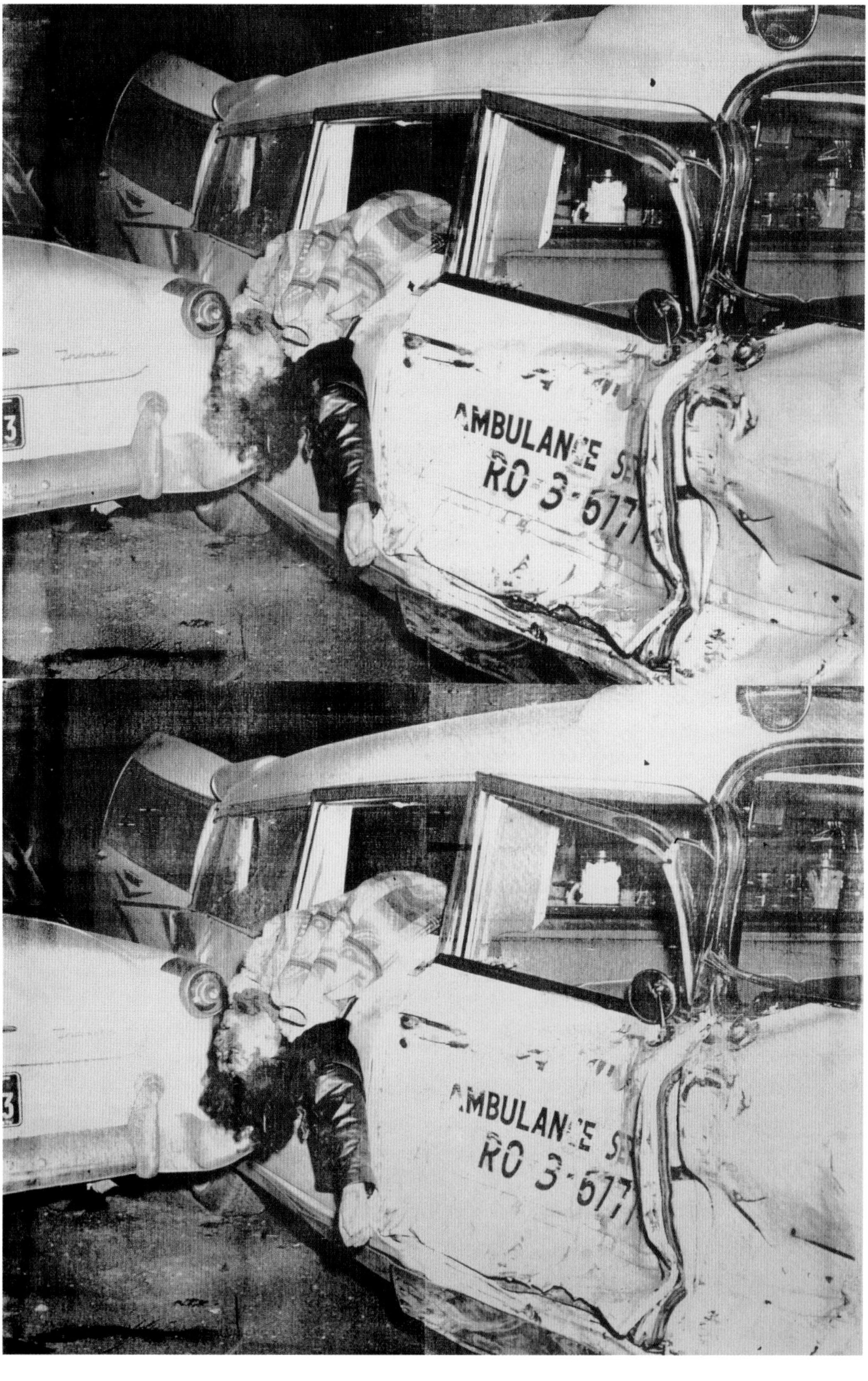
AMBULANCE
RO 3-677

CHAPTER 1

Prelude, 1962

In the fall of 1962—when the United States and the Soviet Union were flirting with nuclear Armageddon over the Cuban Missile Crisis and the Beatles were recording "Love Me Do" at Abbey Road Studios with their new drummer, Ringo Starr—the artists Robert Rauschenberg and Andy Warhol met for the first time. The encounter had been organized by Henry Geldzahler, then an assistant curator of American art at the Metropolitan Museum of Art, and included Ileana Sonnabend, who previously had been married to Rauschenberg's dealer, Leo Castelli, and was about to open her own gallery in Paris.

The meeting did not go well at first. According to the art historian Thomas Crow, the older and better-known Rauschenberg was initially standoffish, but he warmed to Warhol when he saw the new photo silk-screen paintings that Warhol had begun making that summer, including the artist's first portraits of Marilyn Monroe, who had just died in August.[1] Warhol, who was in the midst of transforming his reputation from that of commercial illustrator to artist, basked in Rauschenberg's enthusiasm. Before long, his work would be shown at Sonnabend's eponymous gallery.

Within a month of visiting Warhol, Rauschenberg used the same silk-screen technique to transfer newspaper and magazine photographs, his own photographs, and other camera-generated images to canvas, producing a kind of pigment collage that was understood then, as now, as a form of painting. One of his earliest efforts, *Crocus* (1962), is typical of the disjunctive effects Rauschenberg was able to achieve: the vertical canvas reads like a totem pole, with an image of an Army truck atop a reproduction of Diego Velázquez's *Rokeby Venus,* which itself is atop a sequence of pictures of a mosquito and another fragment of the Velázquez painting. Rauschenberg could not resist adding paint, including a dripping white cross or plus-mark across the middle of the picture.

Using photographs as source material for his art made perfect sense for Rauschenberg, who as a student, first at the Kansas City Art Institute and then at Black Mountain College, devoted a considerable amount of energy to photography. He made casual portraits of friends and was fascinated by textures and signage he encountered in the outside world, producing an

Andy Warhol, *Ambulance Disaster*, 1963–64. Silk-screen ink on linen.

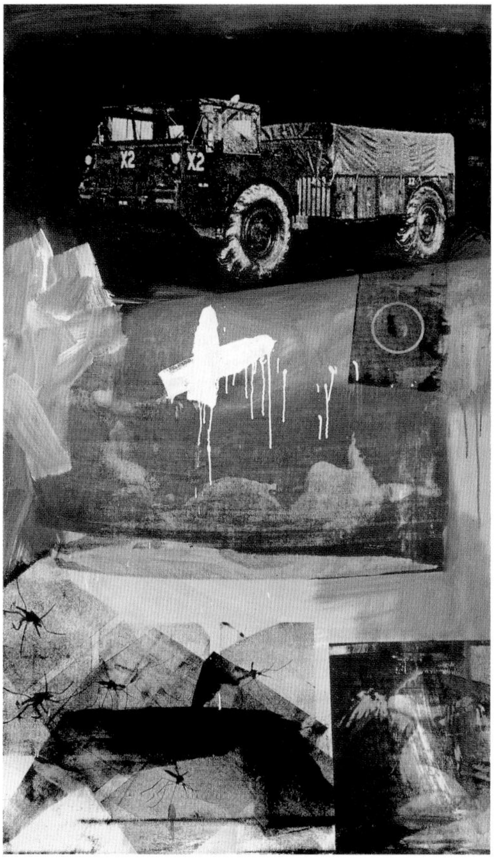

Robert Rauschenberg, *Crocus*, 1962. Oil and silk-screen ink on canvas.

extensive series of black-and-white images in North Carolina and while he was in Italy with fellow student Cy Twombly. He briefly toyed with becoming a photographer.

Black Mountain, begun in 1933 in the hills of North Carolina, was arguably the most progressive and sophisticated place to study art in the country. It was known for its experimental approach to the arts, thanks in large part to its faculty of Bauhaus refugees, most notably Josef and Anni Albers. Both emphasized the use of available materials, without regard to their "art" status, and encouraged collage as a method of assembly. Rauschenberg took these messages to heart.

The school also was known for bringing in major art stars, visual and otherwise. Buckminster Fuller perfected and built his first geodesic dome there; John Cage put on his first performance there; poets Robert Creeley, Robert Duncan, and Charles Olson were among the writing teachers. Significantly, the school also included photography in its visual-arts purview. Historian Beaumont Newhall visited, and photographers Harry Callahan, Arthur Siegel, and Aaron Siskind taught there in the summer of 1951. Callahan and Siegel were full-time teachers at a second Bauhaus outpost in

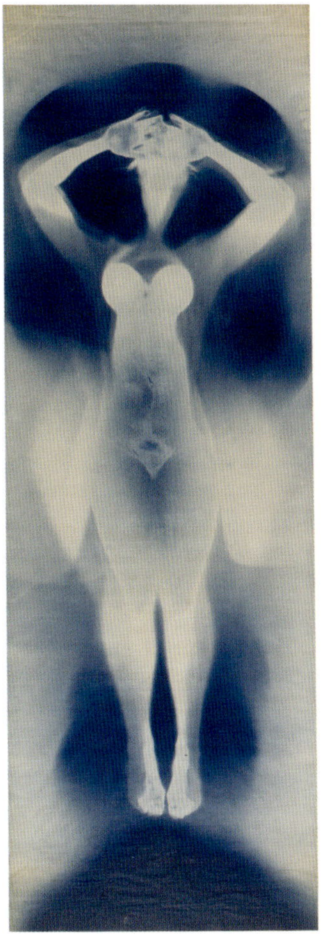

Robert Rauschenberg and Susan Weil,
Female Figure, c. 1950. Cyanotype.

America, originally called the New Bauhaus but rechristened the Institute of Design, in Chicago; Siskind would join them a year later. They were part of the heady stew of influences that Rauschenberg imbibed with gusto.

Together with Susan Weil, his wife and fellow student, he produced a remarkable series of life-size female figures using blueprint paper (what photographers call cyanotypes). Essentially they were photograms: the model would lie on the paper and Rauschenberg and Weil would shine flood lamps on them from above. What resulted looked like imprints of classical sculpture or, with the addition of flowers, a Pre-Raphaelite fantasy. The prints were impressive enough that they were published in *Life* magazine in 1951.[2]

At some point at Black Mountain, though, Rauschenberg realized that his creative interests exceeded a single medium, and he proceeded to paint, sculpt, dance, and perform as a kind of all-purpose art student. Today interdisciplinarity of this sort is almost de rigueur, but in the mid-twentieth century it was rare, even in New York, where Rauschenberg would soon make his reputation.

Warhol came to photography by a different route. He studied graphic design at Carnegie Institute of Technology in Pittsburgh and spent more than a decade in New York working as an illustrator for fashion magazines and clothing stores. In 1960 he turned his attention to art and started painting, at first re-presenting comic strips and then Campbell's Soup cans, which he painted by hand.

The soup-can paintings were his entry ticket into the Sidney Janis Gallery's now-legendary show *New Realists,* in the fall of 1962, which marked the public arrival of a new category of art, christened "Pop" by the critic Lawrence Alloway. Jim Dine, Robert Indiana, Roy Lichtenstein, Claes Oldenburg, James Rosenquist, George Segal, and Warhol were featured in the show. Warhol's contribution, descriptively titled *200 Campbell Soup Cans,* was painted in acrylics but appeared almost to have been machine made, like the actual cans of soup (and like the actual soup, for that matter).

If the *New Realists* show was, as many art historians have written it, the American birth of the Pop Art movement, it was also a marker of the end of the reign of Abstract Expressionism and an enthusiastic opening up of art to the visual vocabulary of a broad, popular cultural arena pejoratively known as "kitsch," the supposed opposite of high culture. In protest of the exhibition, Adolph Gottlieb, Philip Guston, Robert Motherwell, and Mark Rothko—all first-rank, first-generation abstract painters in Janis's stable—resigned from the gallery.

In truth, the dominion of Abstract Expressionist painting had been crumbling even before the *New Realists* show, thanks in large part to Rauschenberg and the painter and sculptor Jasper Johns. As roommates and (briefly) partners downtown starting in the fifties, they shared a fondness for ordinary objects and an urge to include cultural baggage in their art (a flag, a beer can, a stuffed goat wearing a tire, a picture of the Yankees baseball team). Their work predated and presaged the fascination that Pop artists had with comics, billboards, and commercial advertising of all sorts—an influence that could not have escaped Warhol's attention.

But by the time of the *New Realists* show, Warhol had realized that the photo silk-screen process allowed him to indulge his appetite for repetition with much greater efficiency than drawing and painting everything a line or brushstroke at a time. Assistants could perform much of the work, further distancing Warhol's "artistic hand." Although the process of squeezing ink through a screen naturally produced small variations from image to image, he could achieve near-photographic replication of his subjects, leading to works that repeated publicity-still portraits of celebrities or news shots of car crashes multiple times on a single canvas (or, occasionally, linen). The repetition of the images, like all repetitions, simultaneously emphasizes the subject of the image and deflates it.

Regardless of how they are ultimately ranked in the canon of art history, Warhol and Rauschenberg were key in helping inject photographic images into the bloodstream of postwar contemporary art. For them, the camera was a battering ram with which to breach the rarified domain of abstraction. Abstract painting after 1962 was merely an option for young artists, and ten years later it would come to reside near the bottom of a long list of career possibilities. But the photographic nature of their silk-screen works seems to have largely escaped critical notice at the time; the photographs were, after all, inked onto canvas, and the galleries that sold them and the collectors who bought them had no doubts that they were buying and selling paintings. Photography's contemporary-art coming-out party would have to wait.

That the adoption of photo silk-screen painting fundamentally changed the aesthetics of contemporary art became a linchpin of the idea of Postmodernism, argued most powerfully by the critic Douglas Crimp, whose 1977 show *Pictures* marked a turn to a new generation of young artists fascinated by photographs. In a 1980 essay in the journal *October,* "On the Museum's Ruins," he wrote:

> While it was only with slight discomfort that Rauschenberg was called a painter throughout the first decade of his career, when he systematically embraced photographic images in the early sixties it became less and less possible to think of his work as painting. It was instead a hybrid form of printing. Rauschenberg had moved definitively from techniques of production (combines, assemblages) to techniques of reproduction (silkscreens, transfer drawings). And it is that move that requires us to think of Rauschenberg's art as postmodernist.[3]

For Crimp, as for Walter Benjamin four decades before him, the change from individual production to mechanical reproduction represents a watershed development in the history of art (for Benjamin, it was art's "aura" that disappears in the age of mechanical reproduction).[4] It is a view that privileges photography as a medium of both theoretical and practical currency, and as the essential if not defining character of Postmodernism, and it bears returning to at length in a later chapter. But to be art-historically accurate, Rauschenberg and Warhol had company in heralding this shift. Other, less well-known and arguably more radical artists were waiting in the wings.

In 1962 on the West Coast another graphic-designer-turned-artist, Edward Ruscha, launched an ambitious if quixotic project: he would photograph twenty-six gasoline stations on the side of the highways between his studio in Los Angeles and his hometown of Oklahoma City. Ruscha's idea

Edward Ruscha, *Phillips 66, Flagstaff, Arizona,* 1962. From the book *Twentysix Gasoline Stations,* 1963.

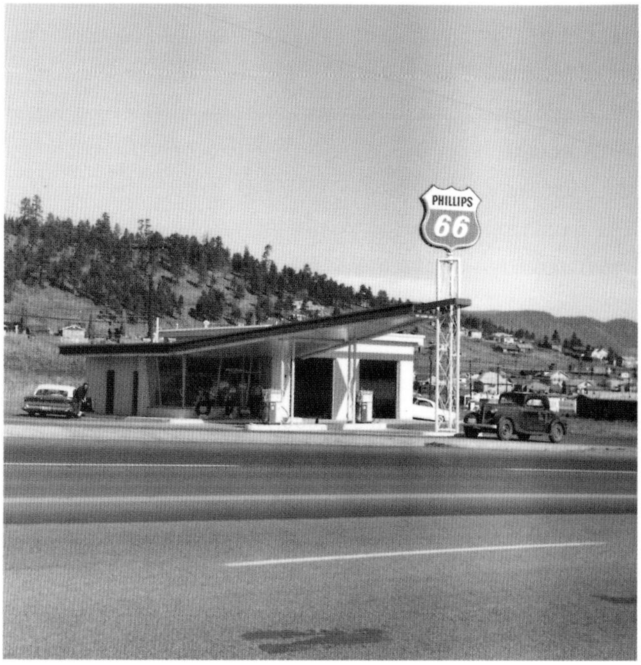

was to produce a small book with the title *Twentysix Gasoline Stations,* the number having been predetermined because it sounded right in the artist's mind.[5] The result has since become a classic exemplar of a new generation of artist's books—cheap, conceptual, photographic, and unpretentious.

Twentysix Gasoline Stations first appeared in 1963 in an edition of four hundred copies, printed on a high-speed offset press of the kind used for commercial printing. Its twenty-six black-and-white photographs are straightforward and undramatic, verging on snapshot-like; most show that they were taken by a photographer standing across the road from the subject at hand. The layout follows a well-trod format: usually one picture per right-hand page, with white borders all around and an identifying caption on the left, although a few images span two pages or are grouped two to the page. The printing itself is similarly mundane; no effort seems to have been spent to give the photographs a high-quality sheen or otherwise seem aesthetically interesting. The entire book is in black and white except for the cover, which uses red ink for its title: "Twentysix / Gasoline / Stations."

How such a modest and peculiar chapbook came to be considered one of the most innovative works of contemporary art is a long story, but suffice it to say that, one, its use of photography was unprecedented at the time; two, it represented a new kind of artist's book, one without the pretensions of hand-set type, deluxe bindings, and other markers of earlier artistic productions; and three, it can be considered a pioneering example of Conceptual Art, having been created according to a procedure that the artist devised in advance of its execution. While Ruscha was also engaged in painting at the time (and still is), *Twentysix Gasoline Stations* helped instigate a transition away from an aesthetic based on hand skills to one rooted in the quality of an artist's thought processes.

Twentysix Gasoline Stations was followed by sixteen photo books Ruscha produced between 1963 and 1978, including *Some Los Angeles Apartments* (1965), *Every Building on the Sunset Strip* (1966), and *Nine Swimming Pools and a Broken Glass* (1968). While some of the books feature attractive color photos, all are presented in deadpan fashion, and the editions were sold at the time for a few dollars apiece. (Today, copies of the first edition of *Twentysix Gasoline Stations* go for more than $10,000.)

Ruscha's work, as groundbreaking as it was, did not emerge from nowhere; he was a fan of Rauschenberg's work, as well as that of Jasper Johns and Roy Lichtenstein. While Ruscha was working on *Twentysix Gasoline Stations* one of his paintings was included in a West Coast Pop Art show organized by the curator Walter Hopps at the Pasadena Art Museum. Rauschenberg was not in the show, but Lichtenstein and Warhol were. *New Painting of Common Objects,* as the show was titled, coincided with the Sidney Janis *New Realists* show on the East Coast, suggesting that the California art scene was keeping close tabs on new developments in New York. Indeed, the first show of Warhol's paintings of Campbell's Soup cans took place at Los Angeles's Ferus Gallery about the same time that Ruscha was busy photographing gas stations.

The art world did not fall from its axis in 1962 because of exhibitions of Pop Art, or because Rauschenberg and Warhol began to silk-screen photographs, or because Ruscha began work on a new form of art using photography. Indeed, art criticism throughout the sixties barely registered photography's presence within contemporary art, and photographs were rarely presented in most galleries and museums devoted to art. Painting remained the central preoccupation of most collectors, with sculpture increasingly of interest as a new style, called Minimalism, came to the fore. Even though some radical young artists like Ruscha pioneered new forms of art and, in doing so, came to rely on photographs to document them, the idea that photographs could function as fully independent works of art was for the most part accepted only in the domain of photographers and their supporters, who comprised a separate-but-equal (or would-be-equal) photography world.

The centrifugal center of this photography world in 1962 was the Museum of Modern Art in New York. Uniquely for its time, the Modern had created a department of photography in 1940, first led by Beaumont Newhall, whose legendary *History of Photography* grew out of a 1937 exhibition he had assembled for the museum. By the sixties MoMA was not alone;

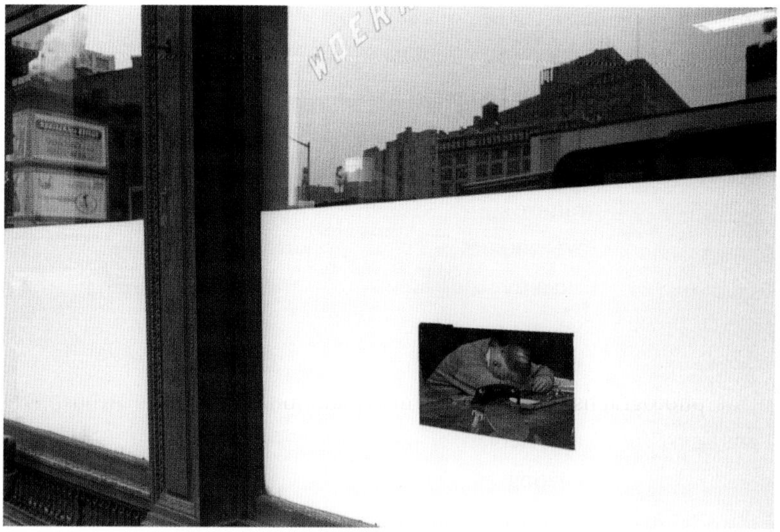

Lee Friedlander, *New York City*, 1964.

museums in Chicago and San Francisco also had started to pay attention to photographs and to collect them, but MoMA, being in New York, brought the medium the most attention.

The MoMA photography exhibition schedule in 1962 began with a two-person exhibition of work by Harry Callahan and Robert Frank, organized by the department's then-director, Edward Steichen, followed by a smaller one-person show devoted to near-abstract color photographs by Ernst Haas. (Color at the time was a novelty in photography, at least as far as its artistic aspirations were concerned.) But the state of the museum's photography program, and with it the state of the art of photography, was about to change dramatically.

That summer, the museum made what turned out to be a watershed announcement: John Szarkowski, a photographer with a budding reputation in the Midwest, would become the new director of the photography department, replacing the then eighty-three-year-old Steichen. Under Steichen, the museum's photography program seemed aimed more at achieving popularity than critical rigor, as typified most obviously by the celebrated exhibition *The Family of Man* (1955), which toured the world for eight years and was seen by millions. Steichen produced other popular thematic shows, like *Power in the Pacific* (1945), which hinged on patriotism rather than aesthetics. When not organizing blockbusters, Steichen developed smaller group shows about focus, motion, and other photography-specific subjects.

Szarkowski had no interest in harnessing the medium to social causes or ideals, or indeed in continuing Steichen's legacy of wildly popular thematic shows. His interest in social documentary photography of the thirties, for example, was not directed at the Farm Security Administration as a national project that involved a dozen photographers documenting poverty, but at the work of a singular FSA photographer he deeply admired, Dorothea Lange. And while paying his respects to the great names of the history of photography, he found vernacular photography in some ways equally interesting. Snapshots, commercial photographs done by small-town studios, and everyday portraiture appealed to him because he believed, as he would posit in a 1964 show called *The Photographer's Eye,* that the everyday uses of photography form a tradition from which the art of photography arises and finds sustenance.

Szarkowski's complex and sometimes perplexing notions about what made photographs works of art, his championing of Diane Arbus, William Eggleston, Lee Friedlander, and Garry Winogrand, and his elegant and authoritative writings and lectures—not to mention his post as gatekeeper at a powerful museum—together made him a figure of unmatched influence for three decades. (He retired in 1991.) His writing, in particular, seemed to give photography an intellectual heft that had heretofore been lacking, and as a result the medium seemed to grow in importance and to attract the attention of critics, curators, and others from outside its customary precincts.

Throughout his career Szarkowski maintained that the art of photography resided within the traditions and historical capabilities of the medium itself, not with its interactions with painting, drawing, or any other art medium. It was, he insisted, "a different kind of art."[6] This essentially Modernist idea of a medium's autonomy, much like that promoted by Clement Greenberg in regard to painting and sculpture, put Szarkowski in the mainstream of thinking about modern art at the time. But it also allowed photography to remain isolated from the larger art world, an independent but relatively underprivileged branch of the visual arts. Separate, as the Supreme Court had acknowledged several years earlier, was not equal.

That isolation had a downside, inasmuch as photography was small fry compared to the other arts, with no viable market and few support structures within academe or museums. Those connected to photography outside of New York tended to huddle together for support. In November of 1962 Nathan Lyons, the associate director at the George Eastman House, a museum of photography in Rochester, New York, organized a conference of teachers of photography in higher education throughout the United States. All of some thirty people attended, including Beaumont Newhall, who had become the director of the museum at the George Eastman House, and Szarkowski, the newly installed director of photography at MoMA.

The conference, which focused on defining issues confronting the teaching of photography within an academic setting, led directly to the founding of the Society for Photographic Education a year later.[7] Lyons was savvy to recognize that teachers of photography within higher education faced myriad issues. As the new kids on the block within their departments, they had to confront faculty and student prejudices against photography as an art form. As pioneers of a new rank of teaching, they had little in the way of precedents for their curricula. And they lacked a substantial literature beyond the technical manuals that Eastman Kodak and other manufacturers then supplied. The Society, or SPE as it since has become known, mounted annual conferences starting in 1963 that allowed photography teachers to share their teaching methods, swap war stories about the politics of their departments, and bathe for a few days in an atmosphere where photography was taken seriously as a form of art. Membership at first was by invitation only.

The recognition of photography as a subject of higher education, which began postwar with the creation of a few studio programs within art schools and art departments of colleges and universities, and later spread to art-history departments, can be measured by the growth of SPE's membership from the thirty-some attendees at the beginning of the sixties to more than 1,500 by the end of the eighties. The number of colleges in which photography is taught swelled as well; even Cornell, where I had sought with little luck to study photography in the late sixties, now includes photography as part of its undergraduate and graduate studio-art programs.

The development of a curricular approach to teaching the art of photography coincided with a growing popularity of museum exhibitions devoted to the medium and with a small but growing practice of critical writing. Thanks in part to the evangelical efforts of complex thinkers like Szarkowski and Lyons, a small community of serious photography practitioners and admirers began to band together and shed its fear of being mistaken for yet-another camera club. Although cameras had long been available to anyone with a few dollars, and photographs remained most influential in the form of news and magazine picture stories, the notion that photographs could be viewed as art snowballed throughout the sixties.

And not just art like any other, but "a different kind of art," as Szarkowski put it. He meant this distinction to signify the medium's independence and uniqueness from other forms of picture making—it is analytic, not synthetic, in conception, he argued—but he could also be interpreted as claiming that photography was superior, a modern art form with a particular currency that the more ancient picture-making methods of painting and drawing lacked. In this regard, and perhaps only in this regard, he aligned himself with the influential Frankfurt School theorist Walter Benjamin, who earlier had made an argument for photography as a radical, game-changing form of art.

Both Szarkowski and Lyons, who were in their thirties in 1962, were crucial to the growing critical and popular acceptance of photographs as works of art worth hanging on a wall. They also were hugely influential on my boomer generation—Szarkowski, through his exhibition program at MoMA and his eloquent writing, and Lyons, through his teaching at the experimental school he started in 1969, the Visual Studies Workshop in Rochester. Both were also photographers before and after assuming their positions, and kept that distinction as a badge of pride.[8] Soon enough, though, those making some of the most radical contributions to the future of photography as an art had little to no training as photographers. They were a different breed: contemporary artists.

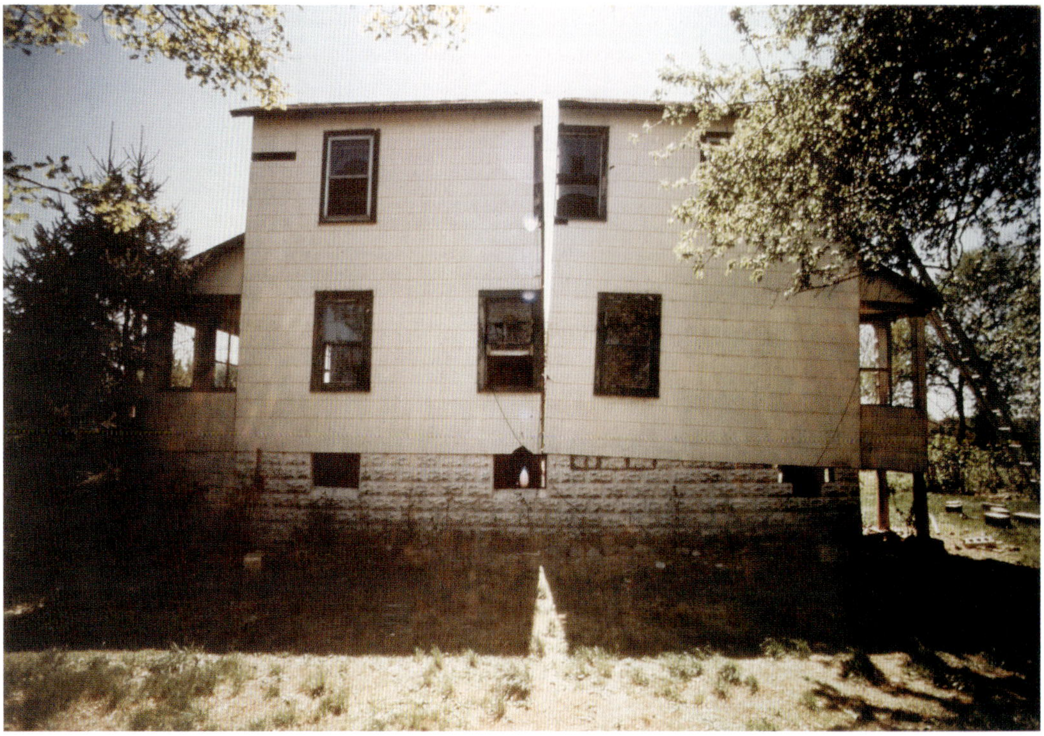

CHAPTER 2

Arrival

When I landed in Manhattan in the hot August of 1971 something remarkable was happening downtown: the transformation of a square-mile, nearly emptied commercial neighborhood into a thriving center for contemporary art. I am of course speaking of Soho, the area south of Houston Street roughly bounded by West Broadway on the west, Lafayette Street on the east, and Canal Street on the south—although plenty of artists I knew lived on the downscale fringes of this territory, especially in what soon became known as Tribeca, the "triangle below Canal."

This transformation of a place that once had been a busy center for small manufacturing into a cultural mecca was a once-in-a-lifetime event, for my generation but also for New York City itself, since it has never been repeated. Visitors to today's Chelsea art neighborhood may want to dispute this claim, but they would miss what made Soho a real art neighborhood as opposed to a shopping center. For starters, the first people interested in Soho were not gallerists but young artists, who discovered that the open floors of the solidly constructed cast-iron buildings that once held heavy equipment were ideal for their studios and, although it was technically illegal, could serve as comfortable places to live as well. And the buildings were relatively cheap; a hot artist who managed to sell out a show or two could buy a whole building, as Donald Judd did in 1968. Alternatively, three or four artists or artist couples could pool resources to share a building, each with their own floor.

The studios and residences led to artist-run exhibition spaces like 112 Greene Street, founded in 1970, and to commercial galleries, starting with Paula Cooper in 1968 and followed shortly thereafter by OK Harris (in the person of Ivan Karp), [Leo] Castelli, [Ileana] Sonnabend, André Emmerich, and others. At first there was only one watering hole, Fanelli's, on Prince Street, and no restaurants to speak of, only storefront *comidas criollas* with take-out food consisting mostly of chicken, rice, and beans. The lack of inspired dining led to the creation of Food, a community gathering place founded by artists with eclectic menus that sometimes surpassed the conventional notion of what real food might be. Gordon Matta-Clark, one of Food's artist founders along with Carol Goodden and Tina Girouard, famously produced a "Bones" menu that featured bones as a key ingredient of every dish.

Gordon Matta-Clark, *Splitting*, 1974.

Paradoxically, this burst of energy in Soho was taking place at one of the worst of times for New York City. The city was not in good shape, to put it mildly, either physically or financially. The streets were grimy and potholed, the benches on upper Broadway were filled with bundled-up homeless folk, their pilfered Gristedes shopping carts filled with their possessions, and trash blew into pedestrians' eyes whenever the wind came barreling across the Hudson from New Jersey.

The city was in the grip of a heroin epidemic, and crime was at an all-time high. Getting mugged was a commonplace occurrence; it happened to me on my way home in the West 70s one dark evening in 1976. We were all a bit naive about the dangers: I was certain that the gun shoved in my face was a starter pistol; it turned out to be a stolen police revolver used in a double homicide in Brooklyn a couple of weeks earlier. I was shaken but unhurt; much worse happened to other friends and acquaintances.

The economic downturn of the seventies was nationwide, but it was exacerbated in New York by years of political corruption; demoralizing labor disputes riling the police, fire, and sanitation departments; mob influence in the construction trades and unions; and a widespread sense across the country that inner cities were locked in a spiral of decay. It all came to a head when the New York City government under Mayor Abraham Beame faced bankruptcy and looked to the federal government for help. In October 1975 the *New York Daily News* published the now-legendary headline, "Ford to City: Drop Dead," after President Gerald Ford refused to consider a federal bailout.

When I studied nineteenth-century Russian literature it was suggested that the great novels of Fyodor Dostoevsky, Leo Tolstoy, and Ivan Turgenev could be attributed to the repressive czarist regime, from which these writers found solace in the world of the imagination even while reflecting on real social problems. The same theory might explain the great flowering of contemporary art in New York in the seventies: conditions in real life were so bad that artists banded together and sought imaginative ways to create a new order that would supersede the old, aesthetically and socially. This was true not only in the traditional visual arts but also in dance, theater, music, film, fiction, poetry—and photography. New York in the seventies turns out to have been a crucible in which all the arts were transformed.

I was fortunate to arrive just as Soho was taking shape, in large part because during my periods of unemployment I could get work as a day laborer helping to demolish the old interiors of prospective loft spaces. (*Loft* was Soho-speak for newly converted studio/living quarters, usually with open floor plans.) What kind of artists could afford to pay for such renovations I couldn't imagine; I only knew that at the end of the day someone would hand me a $20 bill, almost a tenth of the monthly rent for my one-bedroom apartment uptown. But I also benefited by being in on the ground floor as the market center of contemporary art shifted from 57th Street on either side of Fifth Avenue to West Broadway between Spring and Prince.

The friends I had made as an undergraduate at Cornell who had moved to New York after graduating were crucial to my introduction to the downtown art scene. They included Joan Simon, Sarah Bodine, Jeff Hannigan, Jabez Van Cleef, and the giant among us, Gordon Matta-Clark. Joan had founded Buffalo Press in Ithaca, and she hand-set the type, printed, and published my first book of poetry, *The Piedmont Manifest*. She had since settled down in an apartment overlooking Bleecker Street after getting married to Ted Greenwald, a young New York poet and poetry entrepreneur who took me under his wing. Joan worked in art publishing, first for a book publisher and then as the managing editor of *Art in America*, where she encouraged me to write my first reviews. Sarah, a potter and design scholar, had been Joan's roommate at Cornell and was now living in a loft in the financial district with Jeff, who had studied in the same architecture program as had Gordon. Jabez, a true polymath who had been in Cornell's six-year PhD program, worked with Gordon on film projects that took them underneath Manhattan to peer into subway and water tunnels.

Joan and Ted introduced me to 98 Greene Street Loft. The space offered art exhibitions, like its neighbor 112 Greene Street, but also performances and poetry readings; Ted was in charge of the poetry program. The Loft was the pet project of Holly and Horace Solomon, a glamorous couple who lived uptown in a posh art-filled apartment and who loved nourishing and being a part of the downtown creative scene. Horace's family was reputed to have made its fortune manufacturing the first rubber-tipped bobby pins, at a factory in New Jersey. Holly was an erstwhile actress and committed contemporary art collector who notably had had her portrait painted by Andy Warhol, an event she frequently mentioned. They parked their red Aston Martin sedan on Greene Street when they were downtown, which made the block seem quite chic.

Together the Solomons had the energy and drive to start a flourishing space for visual and performance art and poetry and the good sense to let artists lead the way. Until it closed in 1973, to be followed two years later by Holly Solomon Gallery on West Broadway, 98 Greene Street Loft was an incubator of new energy and new forms, including art fashion shows, art-inspired music and theater (notably, some of the first performances by Laurie Anderson), and shows of photography. Robert Mapplethorpe, Stephen Shore, and William Wegman are three now-prominent photographer/artists whose work Holly showed early in their careers.

By the time I had finished two years of graduate school and gotten

Gordon Matta-Clark, *Rope Bridge*, Six Mile Creek, Ithaca, New York, 1969.

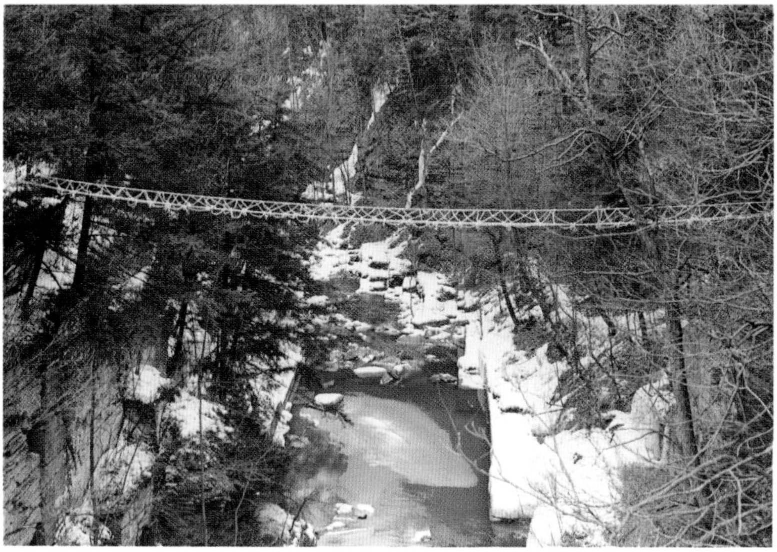

myself to New York Gordon, a son of the Chilean Surrealist artist Roberto Matta Echaurren and American artist Anne Clark, had established himself as a mercurial, inspiring figure embedded in the Soho scene. He had an entrepreneurial spirit that helped create 112 Greene Street as an important exhibition space for new art;[1] he designed 98 Greene Street Loft for the Solomons as a performance and art space; and he was the main impetus in the creation and success of the restaurant Food. At the same time he was making work that was widening the horizon of what art could be. Today, despite a career that was tragically cut short, he has been recognized as one of the most influential artists of the seventies.

Gordon and I had met in the late sixties while he was pursuing a degree in architecture at Cornell and I was an undergraduate English Lit major. Knowing I had a camera, he asked me in early 1969 to photograph his first public artwork, a rope bridge across the mouth of the Ithaca reservoir (aptly titled *Rope Bridge*). He was inspired by the Earth Art show put on a couple of months before at Cornell's Andrew Dickson White Museum of Art, which brought some of the most important vanguard artists of the day to campus. Gordon had assisted several of them—notably Dennis Oppenheim and Jan Dibbets—as they installed their work on and around campus (in most cases, they created their art in situ), including helping Oppenheim to chainsaw a channel in the ice of a campus lake. (More on this in Chapter 3, Down to Earth.) Judging from the direction his work would take later, this was a formative experience, a kind of multiplier to his eccentric architectural education.

Gordon hit the ground running when he moved back to New York from Ithaca after the spring finally arrived. He was invited by gallerist John Gib-

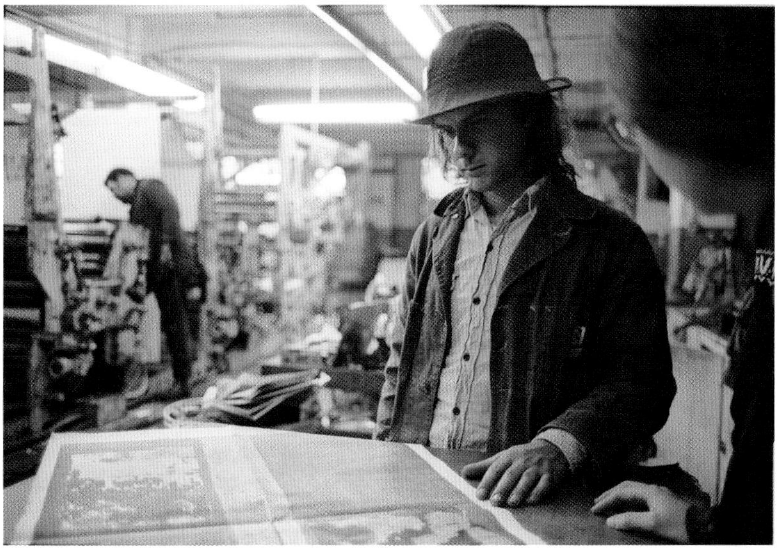

Press check for *Walls Paper*, with Gordon Matta-Clark, center, and Joan Simon, right, 1972.

son to participate in a summer group exhibition, and he put on a performance called *Photo Fry*, for which he dropped Polaroid photographs into a frying pan with hot oil, sprinkled them with gold leaf, and heated them until the emulsion and gold leaf melted. Not surprisingly, this created instant buzz about him in the art world. At the end of the year his installation of three spotlit trees marked the official opening of the 98 Greene Street Loft space, and he sent *Photo Fry* photographs of Christmas trees to friends as limited-edition cards to mark the occasion.

When I met up with Gordon again in New York he had his own camera and was busy photographing the walls of tenement buildings in the Bronx that were abandoned or slated for demolition. He decided for his fall 1972 show at 112 Greene Street to reproduce the images in newsprint and display the uncut sheets in floor-to-ceiling fashion, as works he called *Walls Paper*, together with pieces of the walls cut from the buildings. He consulted with Joan Simon, knowing that she was experienced in printing and publishing matters, and she decided to publish *Walls Paper* as an edition by her Buffalo Press. I had just gotten a job working at a start-up newspaper (the *Herald*) and had the responsibility for doing the press check, so Joan and Gordon asked me to come along when the printing took place, at a small offset newsprint plant.

After the three of us arrived I tried my best to get the printers to clean up the colors, which were coming off the press more than slightly muddied and out of register, but Gordon countermanded my suggestions. I now realize this must have been because he wanted the results to look as distressed as the homes themselves. He didn't hold my aesthetic ignorance against me, fortunately. While the *Walls Paper* was being shown inside 112 Greene

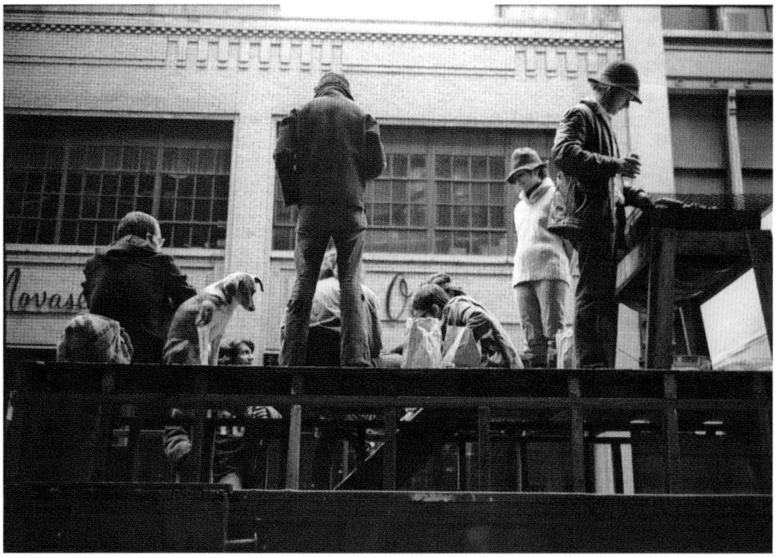

Gordon Matta-Clark barbecuing on the top floor of *Dumpster Duplex*, 112 Greene Street, October 1972.

Street, a dumpster (aka, drag-on) on the street featured another of Gordon's works, *Dumpster Duplex*, which was a reprise of a work he had made in the spring, *Open House*. Both the single-story *Open House* and the *Dumpster Duplex* were walk-in, quasi-domestic architectural spaces built of rough boards and discarded doors, and both served as performance sites. I was invited to the barbecue Gordon staged on the duplex's second story, cooking being another of his unusual artistic talents.

For a while afterward Joan and I made periodic pilgrimages to Gordon's studio on Wooster Street to see what he was up to. This included buying up inaccessible pieces of property at New York City public auctions and growing molds and bacteria in petri dishes, to the benefit of no one's health. (These apparently were remnants or recapitulations of earlier pieces made of agar, which he concocted himself and congealed in baking tins. When the agar sheet dried out and cracked Gordon gave the bits the title *Incendiary Wafers* because of their tendency to spontaneously combust.)

By far the biggest regret of my early years in New York is that I turned down Holly Solomon's invitation to join a field trip she organized to Englewood, New Jersey, to mark the official completion of Gordon's *Splitting*, one of his enduring (though vanished) masterpieces. *Splitting* (1974) was a brilliantly simple intervention performed on an abandoned wood-frame house with a stone block foundation. Using saws and a variety of demolition tools, Gordon and a few helpers bisected the building top to bottom after removing a row of foundation blocks from the back; gravity did the rest, creating an open slice that expanded to a gap of about a foot wide at the roof. He also cut off the four upper corners of the house, further compromising its integrity as a home while emphasizing its status as sculpture. Both an aes-

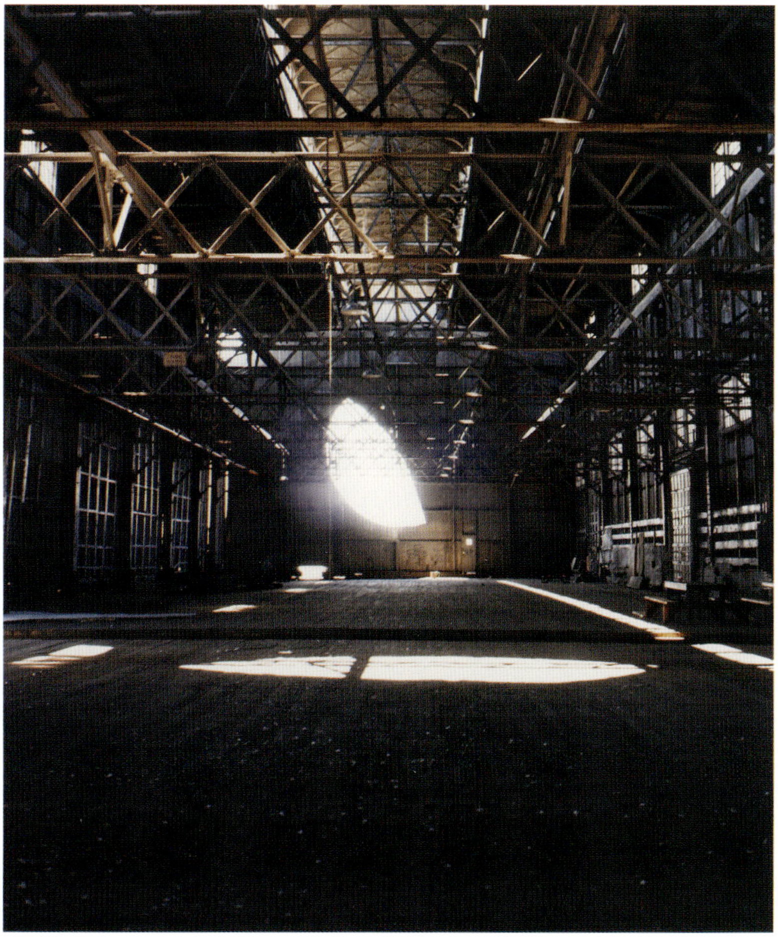

Gordon Matta-Clark, *Day's End (Pier 52)*, 1975.

thetic and engineering feat, *Splitting* put Gordon permanently on the map of hot young artists. He was interviewed in *Avalanche* and reviewed in *Art in America* and by Laurie Anderson in *Art-Rite*.[2]

Typically, though, he wasn't done until he had archived the project by taking photographs. He cut up several of his black-and-white prints of the house and created collages that he mounted on paper and assembled others into an artist's book that was published by the Solomons (*Splitting*, 98 Greene Street Loft Press, 1974). He also took color slides, which later on he would also turn into collages. His consciousness about the need for documentation of his activities, together with his impulse to alter the photographs to make them into something other than documentation, would stay with him for the rest of his career.

Gordon's archival impulse has turned out to be a good thing, especially since in the case of *Splitting* I and the rest of the world now have to content ourselves with the photographs and film that he took of it. These images do not fully compensate for my missed opportunity, but they register the having-been-there status that Roland Barthes identified as the fundamental truth of photographs. And, in Gordon's hands, they also are another register of his art.

I saw from a distance Gordon's next big architectural intervention in 1975, *Day's End,* for which he cut a rather bulbous, crescent-shaped slice out of the end of a covered Manhattan pier that extended over the Hudson River (his "rose window") and excised portions of the floor and sides. The pier cut had an advantage over the Englewood house because it was more convenient to the downtown art crowd, so many more people could see it, but it had the disadvantage of being illegal. To make it, Gordon had defeated a lock that was supposed to deter trespassers, and at the opening party for the finished work—with bus transport again supplied by the Solomons—city inspectors came to arrest the perpetrator. Shortly thereafter he left for Europe.

A few stout souls risked seeing *Day's End* from inside the pier, where the light entering from the west made the cut resemble a bright moon or a partial solar eclipse. Gordon again solved the problem of limited access by filming and photographing the pier inside and out. This may have been more than pure documentation, however; I suspect he also was learning more about what he had accomplished through the act of photographing and then studying the results.

In Europe Gordon completed another remarkable building cut, *Conical Intersect*, on the site of the construction of the Centre Pompidou, France's museum for contemporary art. Sanctioned to open up two adjoining, soon-to-be-demolished seventeenth-century townhouses, he chiseled through 8-inch-thick masonry walls to create a cone-shaped aperture that extended from exterior wall to exterior wall at a 45-degree angle to the street. Here again, as with his later building cuts *Office Baroque* in Brussels (1977) and *Circus* in Chicago (1978), he extensively photographed within and outside the structure in black-and-white and color, later creating collages that extend and alter the camera's single-point perspective. He also filmed the cuts—by this time he had graduated from a Super 8 to a 16mm camera—and invited filmmakers and videographers to make their own documentation of the process and the final result.

I was too preoccupied with my own fascination with photography to know it, but in the last years of his life Gordon became something of a photographer himself. There was a new process for color printing on the market, called Cibachrome, introduced in the United States in 1975, that allowed anyone with a darkroom to make color prints directly from their slides. And as a bonus, since color prints made with various Kodak processes were known to fade over time, Cibachrome colors were said to be nearly eternal—leaping a huge hurdle for those who had been chary of collecting

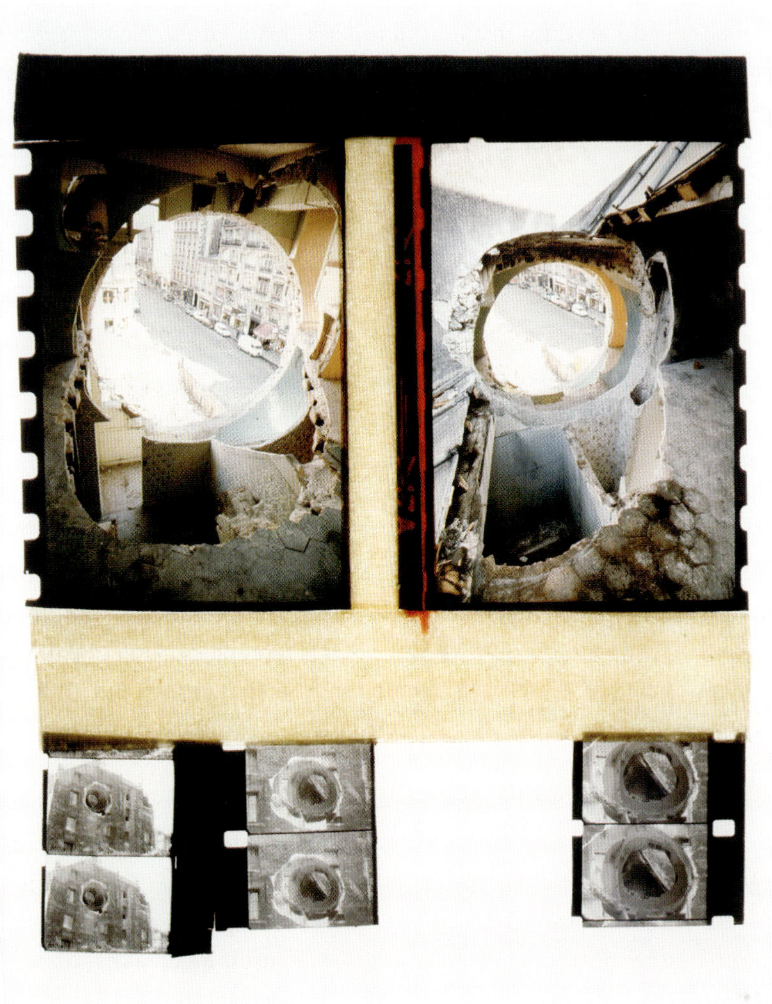

Gordon Matta-Clark, *Conical Intersect*, 1975 (printed 1977).

fugitive color photographs. Gordon cleaved to the process in 1977, building himself a darkroom in his new loft.

Cibachrome was a direct-positive process, meaning that a positive color transparency becomes a positive color print without an intervening negative. Gordon would cut and tape his 35mm slides into miniature collages and enlarge them to prints as long or wide as 40 inches. He used it to extensively document current projects like *Office Baroque* and *Circus*, and he even went back to old color slides from *Splitting* and *Conical Intersect* to make new pictures. Because these photographs are collages, often creating perspectives and points of view that a straightforward image could not achieve, they exceed mere documentation. Gordon claimed them as "a real part of my work."[3]

Finished Cibachromes have a unique look compared to other color prints. They are crisp, shiny, and colorific (highly saturated and "contrasty," in photo speak), giving them a commercial sheen. Some photographers spurned them as a result, but others loved their appearance and their aforementioned promise of longevity. I introduced Eve Sonneman to the process and she quickly became a convert. She had been an early part of the downtown scene by dint of her black-and-white photographs taken a second or two apart and paired as diptychs, some of which were shown at the pioneering Bykert Gallery in 1973, but her career really took off when she switched to color and began showing Cibachrome diptychs at Castelli Graphics. Ellen Brooks, Frank Majore, Laurie Simmons, Sandy Skoglund, and Neil Winokur also took advantage of the process at crucial points in their careers.

Unfortunately Gordon's exploration of this new process did not last long. Within the span of a year his twin brother committed suicide by jumping from the window of Gordon's loft and he was diagnosed with pancreatic cancer, leading to his death in August 1978 at age thirty-five.

Despite his short life Matta-Clark has proven to be enormously influential, a model for subsequent artists who felt no need to attach themselves to a specific medium or specific "ism" of art making. He was in essence a romantic materialist, casting himself in the role of laborer (cook, construction worker, cinematographer, photographer) to savor the material world physically as well as aesthetically. Cutting away at structures emptied of human life to bring light to their insides, digging holes beneath basements to liberate the soil compacted below, surveying the depths of the Paris catacombs and the New York City water and transit systems to show their hidden logic and magic, slicing and taping together celluloid negatives to exceed the physiological bounds of vision—all used physical energy to help us make emotional and intellectual connections among human beings, their constructions, and the natural world.

For me, Gordon represented an introduction to contemporary art's leading edge, prompting me to visit galleries and museum shows that had nothing to do with photography but offered insight into what artists of my and previous generations were thinking. His reliance on photographs and his fascination with the plastic qualities of camera images challenged the boundaries I had absorbed of what photography was supposed to look like and do to be art. What offered itself as a quandary turned out to be a blessing; I lost my interest in the old questions—Is photography art? What kind of art is it?—and started thinking about a new one: Would the art of our time exist without it?

I read my poetry at 98 Greene Street Loft in December 1972, thanks to Ted, and attended many events there, some of which I photographed but with mixed results. This could have been because I didn't have the right

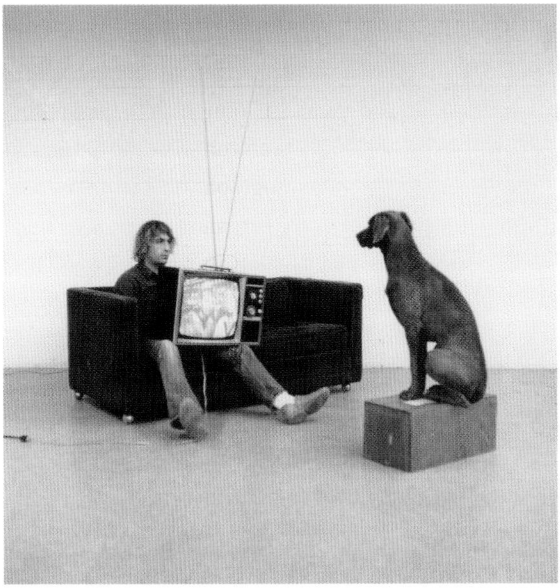

William Wegman, *What Is On*, 1973.

equipment, but more probably because I felt emotionally ambivalent. Besides imagining myself as a street photographer, à la Lee Friedlander, I was devoted to the classic Modernists such as André Kertész and Harry Callahan and edgy newcomers like Emmet Gowin and Duane Michals, all of whose work appeared dependent solely on their own sensibilities. In short, I wasn't really a documentarian, although in later years I got better at it. I also had the problem of not being prepared for what I was seeing; some of the performances were beyond my ken. Or anyone else's, for that matter; the new then felt truly new.

I was a bit taken aback one day in the early seventies when Holly Solomon offered to introduce me to an artist she was especially keen on, who she said had been making photographs of his dog. Pet photography was then worse than anathema in serious photography circles, so I initially found some excuse to put off any encounter. But when we met and I saw William Wegman's pictures, featuring his Weimaraner Man Ray in various set-up situations and guises, it was clear they were not examples of the genre I was expecting. He had an oddball sense of humor that was irresistible, and because of Holly we hung out a bit in Soho and once were guests for a weekend in Lake Placid, where the Solomons had rented a place for the summer.

Holly's endorsement and Wegman's obvious seriousness about making funny images made me want to learn more about how such pictures could count as art. I also knew by then that Gordon had been busy doing peculiar things with photographs, such as *Photo Fry*. So I started to look harder for photographs within the precincts of downtown art, and I would soon discover them virtually everywhere. In almost all cases, however, they weren't presented as photographs; they were simply the evidence of art.

Unfortunately, my attention to the great artistic ferment happening before my eyes was frequently diverted by the pressing necessity of surviving in the city. My wife was an illustrator and found work at a new magazine, *Ms.*, doing spot illustrations, but the pay wasn't enough to support even one of us. My early efforts to find work as an English teacher hadn't panned out, so I had arrived in New York jobless. Luckily I had worked, briefly, as a newspaper photographer while in graduate school, which seemed like a possible marketable alternative.

I took my slim résumé and little portfolio of newspaper clips up to the twenty-seventh floor of a new high-rise on Third Avenue in the 50s. Despite the corporate look of the offices, the place was the editorial home of a funky, fledgling weekly newspaper called the *Herald*, which had been launched by a trust-funded young guy who had the idea of challenging, or at least supplementing, the Sunday *New York Times*. The hubris of the enterprise was remarkable, but so was the fact that they hired me on the spot—not as a photographer, which is what I had been for six months at the *Reidsville (N.C.) Review*, but as the paper's copy editor.

The *Herald* is now legendary, at least among those of us who worked for it. It was designed by Massimo Vignelli, whose graphic sense was sophisticated, super clean, and Swiss. The national editor and my immediate boss, James R. Gaines, went on to become the top editor of *People*, *Time*, and *Life*, the cream of Time, Inc.'s magazine crop. The news copy boy was P. J. O'Rourke, who was funny then and got even funnier later as a full-time humorist and political satirist. George Delmerico, the art director, left to take the same job at the *Village Voice*, taking with him the original staff photographer, James Hamilton. Charles Churchward, who followed George, later became the head of design for *Mademoiselle*, *Vanity Fair*, and finally *Vogue* (he has a star turn in the 2009 movie *The September Issue*, a film about Anna Wintour as she puts out an especially mammoth issue of *Vogue*). The paper for a while had its own excellent interior design section, which was due mostly to Suzanne Slesin, who went on to have a long career at the *Times* as a design writer and editor.

Another news editor, Paul Violi, was a poet whose work I came to greatly admire; we also became good friends. Poetry, in fact, was practically a subtext of the *Herald*; a flamboyant woman named Shelley Lustig was in charge of selecting a "Poet of the Week," a responsibility she exercised with eclectic aplomb. I remember that Patti Smith was one of the chosen few, at a time when she was Robert Mapplethorpe's partner. I got to see her in person first when she visited the office to see Shelley and again when

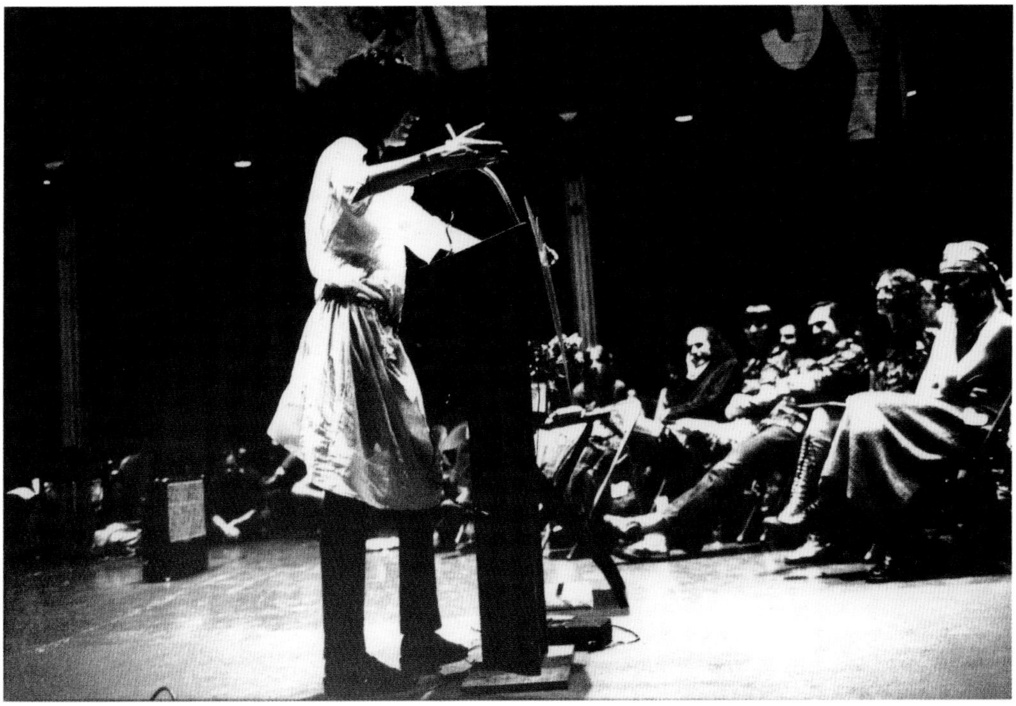

Patti Smith reading at St. Mark's Church in-the-Bowery, with, from right, Anne Waldman, Maureen Owen, and Ted Greenwald in the audience, c. 1971.

she read at St. Mark's Church in-the-Bowery one Wednesday night. I was more impressed by her green hair than by her poetry, which she presented in wild-woman declamatory style that seemed modeled on the manner of the Poetry Project's reigning queen, Anne Waldman. Soon, however, she solved that problem by putting her verses to music.

Unfortunately, the *Herald* never caught fire with readers, even when it switched gears to compete with the *Village Voice* instead of the Sunday *Times*. So after a long period of unemployment, I landed a job with a real paper, the *Record*, the daily of Bergen County. That lasted two years, during which time I became the resident expert on the Watergate scandal, first editing Bob Woodward and Carl Bernstein copy from the *Washington Post*'s syndication service and eventually running with the news of Nixon's resignation down the stairs to the composing room, where linotype operators turned sheets of wire-service copy into lines of lead. It was the last hurrah for Nixon, and also for the old "hot type" method of putting out newspapers.

While working as a copy editor with a reverse commute to Hackensack I took a semester-long photo workshop at the New School taught by Lisette Model. Model was a legend as a photographer, having started her photography career in France before arriving in the United States in the thirties and doing assignments for *Harper's Bazaar* and other magazines. Her specialty was portraits in which haughty, upper-class subjects or rowdy Bowery ones

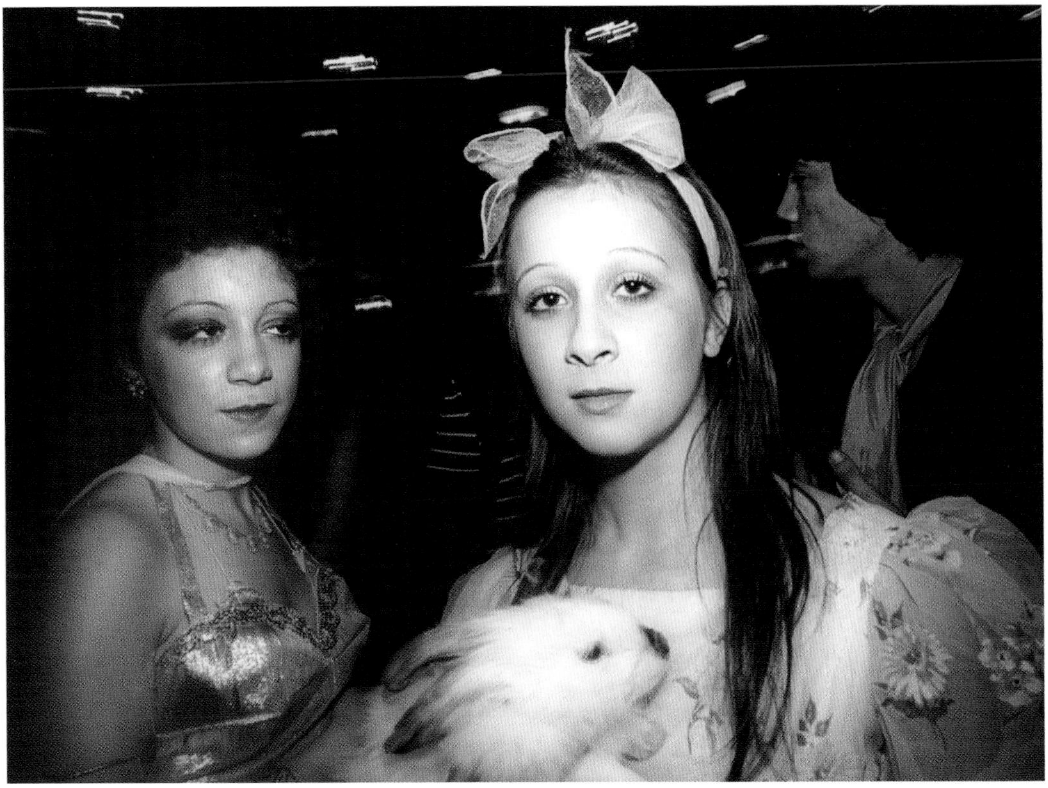

Andy Grundberg, *Halloween Revelers at the Waldorf Astoria, New York*, 1973.

loomed into the camera as if photographed from knee height—which, it turns out, was virtually the case. Model was barely five feet tall and used a camera that hung at her waist.

Model was even more of a legend as a teacher, based almost entirely, though unfairly, on one star student: Diane Arbus. Whether entirely true or a bit of afflatus, the word on the street was that Model had provided both the precedent (her own work) and the impetus (permission, even encouragement, to violate interpersonal norms) that allowed Arbus to become the great artist she briefly was. We all yearned to be Model's next discovery, the recipient of the fairy godmother touch. So popular was her class that it required a portfolio review to gain admission, administered not by Model but by Benedict Fernandez, a photographer who was running the New School's photo program.

I wasn't chosen for the class at first, but Fernandez convinced Model to teach a second section (sadly, she needed the money) and I got in along with a dozen others. Class was not a vastly encouraging experience: every week we would bring in our new pictures and tack them on a wall for her inspection, and every week she would walk around the room saying, "Not interesting. Not interesting." Rarely, she might say "Hmm, interesting," and the student whose work it was, and most of the class, would be struck dumb.

My work, sensitive and ickily romantic in retrospect, was "not interesting" in capital letters until I resolved to play her game. I went to a Halloween costume party at the Waldorf Astoria, presented by Howard Stein and featuring the band the New York Dolls, and photographed the freakiest folks I could find close-up with a wide-angle lens and flash. The next week, Model flattered me with my first "Interesting," and I was done with trying to be the next Diane Arbus. Now that I think back on it, I probably at that moment also was done with any ambition I harbored to be a famous art photographer. But I wasn't about to give up on photography.

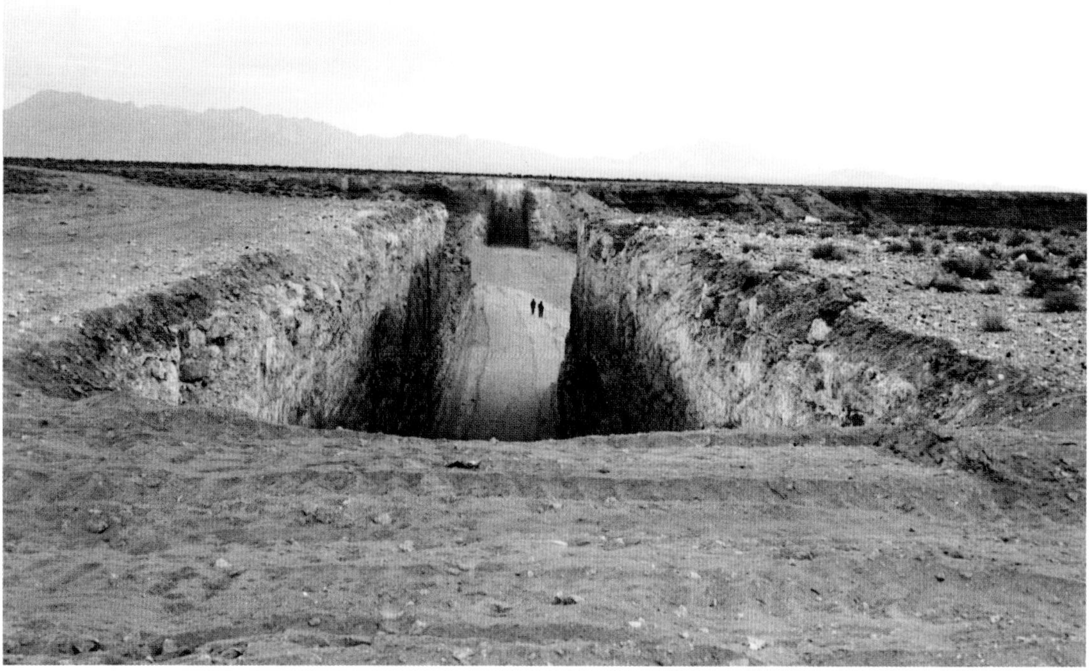

CHAPTER 3

Down to Earth

One day the photograph is going to become even more important than it is now—there'll be a heightened respect for photographers. Let's assume that art has moved away from its manual phase and that now it's concerned with the location of material and with speculation. So the work of art now has to be visited or abstracted from a photograph, rather than made. I don't think the photograph could have had the same richness of meaning in the past as it has now.

—Dennis Oppenheim, "Discussions with Heizer, Oppenheim, Smithson," *Avalanche*, fall 1970

One fading afternoon in the fall of 1972 I walked into the New York Cultural Center on Columbus Circle, originally the Huntington Hartford Gallery of Modern Art, celebrated as the most peculiar-looking modern building in Manhattan thanks to an orientalist design by architect Edward Durell Stone. There I saw an exhibition called *Making Megalopolis Matter*, a group show about the urban fabric of New York City. Why I chose to visit I can't remember—I was recently unemployed and looking for distractions, perhaps, or I had seen a review that noted the presence of photographs in the exhibition. Nor can I remember any art in the gallery save for one fixating exhibit, which since has become a legend within contemporary art: Hans Haacke's *Shapolsky et al. Manhattan Real Estate Holdings, a Real-Time Social System, as of May 1, 1971.*

Haacke, who grew up in Germany during the Nazi era and studied art there in the postwar years, had enough of a reputation in his adopted New York to have been selected as the subject of a one-person exhibition at the Guggenheim Museum that was planned for the spring of 1971. But weeks before the show was to open the Guggenheim administration preemptively canceled it and fired the curator who had organized it, ostensibly because the director and his trustees felt the work was not art—but more likely because its focus on Manhattan real-estate financial shenanigans hit too close to home.

Shapolsky et al. chronicles a shady network of property dealings of one of New York City's largest slumlords of the time, Harry J. Shapolsky, tracing

Michael Heizer, *Double Negative*, Mormon Mesa, Overton, Nevada, 1969.

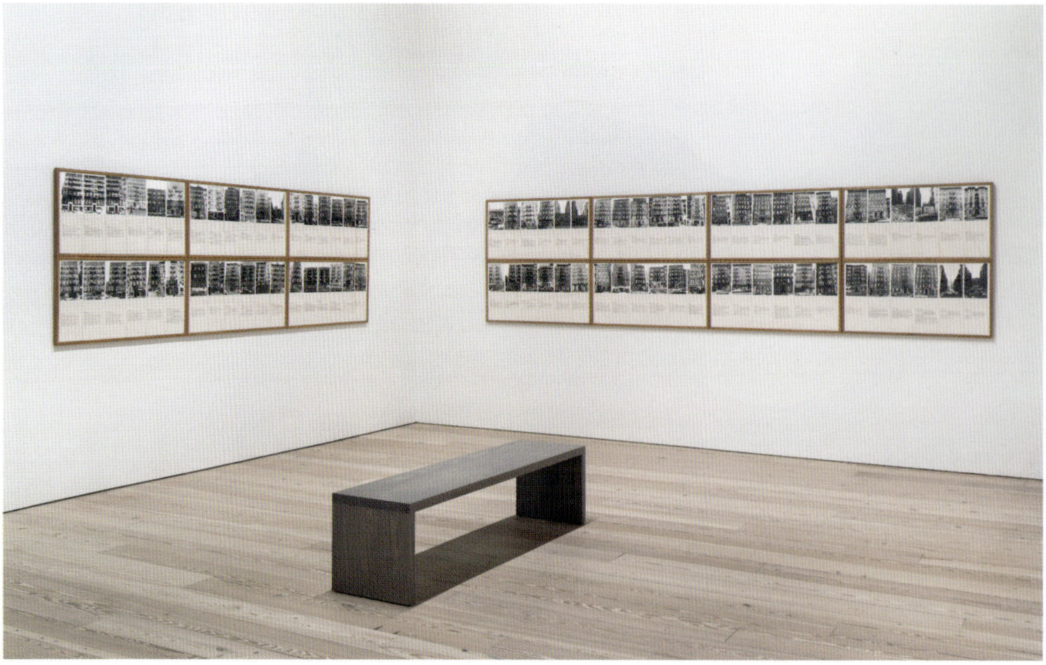

Hans Haacke, *Shapolsky et al. Manhattan Real Estate Holdings, a Real-Time Social System, as of May 1, 1971*, 1971. Installation view from *America Is Hard to See*, Whitney Museum of American Art, New York, 2015.

a web of shell corporations and their nominal corporate officers set up to disguise his ownership of more than one hundred Manhattan apartment buildings. The work on display consists of photographs of the buildings, most of them tenements, mounted on panels above typewritten texts with information about their location, ownership structure, and financial histories. (Location maps are included as well.) Haacke culled all of his data from public records, adapting a neutral presentational style that resembled a real-estate catalog as much as it resembled Conceptual Art.[1]

If the Guggenheim director and trustees couldn't see how this could be art, I could sympathize. The quality of the photographs was mediocre even by the standards of real-estate listings, and the texts underneath were typewritten as if by a detective filing a report on a crime. At the same time, the story they told was gripping and startling: a small-time investor had managed to assemble what amounted to a lock on the first few squares of a Manhattan version of Monopoly and, through guile and legal trickery, to disguise his ownership of more than 140 decaying rental buildings.

But what made it a work of art? After a little more than a year in New York of going to museums and hanging around with Gordon Matta-Clark and other artist friends in Soho, I knew enough to recognize its Conceptual origins, but this felt different. *Shapolsky et al.* was not an academic or aesthetic exercise, it was a pointedly political one. This was recognized at the time by the *Times*'s great architectural critic, Ada Louise Huxtable, whose review of the show I might have read before visiting. She concluded:

> The Shapolskys may be model realtors. But through these graphic devices, the artist defines the world of incestuous real estate relationships, transient and dummy companies, slumlords and sleazy property hide-and-seek against which planners and mere people are powerless. Presented as a succinct visual phenomenon, it may or may not be art, but it is superb social analysis and it's boffo.[2]

Boffo seems a bit theatrical for such a straightforward piece of documentation, but Huxtable recognized that the importance of Haacke's methodology lay in the accumulation of details, both textual and visual. And to answer her question: It *is* art, precisely because it extends the parameters of what art is supposed to look like, and be. It is art in the same universe as Marcel Duchamp's 1917 *Fountain* (a store-bought urinal turned upside down and signed) and Robert Rauschenberg's signature combine, *Monogram* (1955–59). And photographs, the most detailed and seemingly factual means of visual description available to Haacke, are a crucial part of the work's success. Because they appear to have no aesthetic pretensions, they deliver facts and only the facts—or at least are made to seem to.

Haacke, of course, was not the first artist of a conceptual bent to make use of photographs in this way—compare *Shapolsky et al.* to Edward Ruscha's 1963 classic *Twentysix Gasoline Stations* and his subsequent photographic artist's books, discussed earlier—but he was part of a new wave of artists following on the heels of Ruscha intent on expanding the parameters of art in ways that depended on photographs. Haacke's distinction is that he was among the first to harness the methodology and formal vocabulary of Conceptual Art for explicitly political ends; *Shapolsky et al.*'s photographs serve as documentary evidence of a pattern of dissembling and deceit while providing a structure to the presentation of that evidence. It was evidence that had enough social and political torque to cause the Guggenheim to bite its own tail.

Haacke had actually been one of the artists in the *Earth Art* show I'd seen as a student at Cornell University—although he was never really an Earth artist in the grandiose, bulldozer sense of the term. His piece then was called *Grass Grows*, and it consisted of a cone of dirt on the floor of a gallery that had been planted with grass seed. Over the course of the exhibition, the pile came to resemble a lawn.

I was starting my final semester at Cornell when the exhibition took place in the winter of 1969. I can remember on a cold, damp day walking past the old stone mansion that served as the university's museum and seeing earth-moving equipment and a couple of piles of fresh earth beside it, prominent on a hillside above the arts quad where I took most of my classes. I had no idea it was anything other than a construction project . . . which in

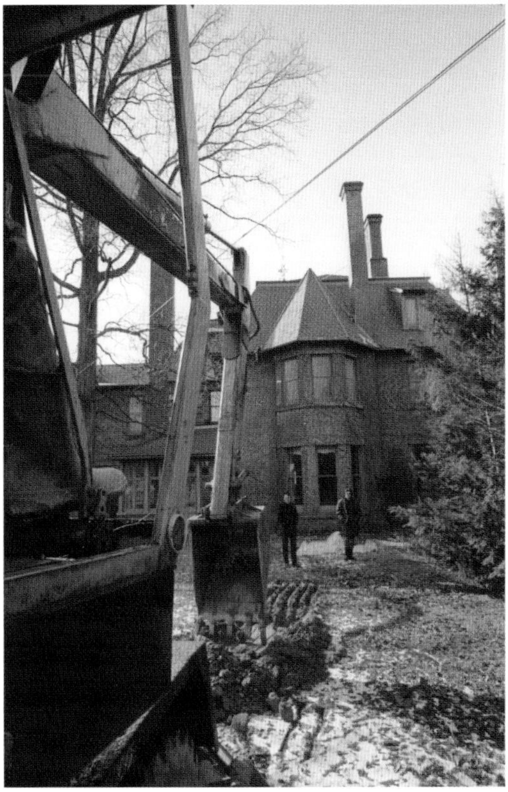

Earth Art installation view (in progress), with the Andrew Dickson White Museum of Art in background, Cornell University, Ithaca, New York, 1969. The earthwork seen under construction is possibly by David Medalla or an uncompleted Michael Heizer work not represented in the show's catalog.

a sense it was. Later, after the earth movers disappeared, I went back to see what the fuss was about.[3]

Inside the museum were Haacke's *Grass Grows* and several more piles of dirt, some holding mirrors, a flimsy construction of tacked-together 2 × 4s, and a few photographs recording activity elsewhere in Ithaca. I felt a bit nonplussed but, this being an era when conventions were being challenged in all areas of life, I was more curious than offended. And to be honest other events on campus seemed more important to me: a protest by African American students that led them to occupy the student union building in April, a takeover of the ROTC headquarters (also known as the college gym) by sympathetic white students led by Students for a Democratic Society (SDS), and a boycott of classes that essentially shut down the school for the rest of the semester. Plus the really important (and more frightening) event: my draft board had just requested that I appear in Philadelphia for a preinduction physical. From my perspective, the student revolution and the war in Vietnam seemed closer to the bone than an epochal artistic event.

Earth Art had been organized by Willoughby Sharp, a New York artist, critic, and founding editor (with Liza Béar) of the influential magazine *Avalanche*. He intended it to be the start of a series of elemental shows, with subsequent entries devoted to air, water, and fire—although those shows never took place. *Earth Art* itself barely happened, since by betting odds the tiny Cornell museum lacked the financial and logistical resources to pull it off. But the museum's fearless director, Thomas Leavitt, managed to bring an incredible group of artists to campus to execute their pieces in situ. Besides Haacke, the artists in the show were Jan Dibbets, Neil Jenney, Richard Long, David Medalla, Robert Morris, Dennis Oppenheim, Robert Smithson, and Günther Uecker. (In the late sixties, it seems, the idea that women artists should be included in the mix was a nonfactor.) Two other well-known male artists, Walter De Maria and Michael Heizer, also took part in the show's formative stages but were not credited in the catalog.[4]

Earth Art succeeded in becoming a landmark exhibition of the period, in part because it gave a catchy name to an aesthetic movement (heretofore, the terms *land art* or *earthworks* were used occasionally, and sometimes still are today)[5] and because of the high quality of the nine artists who ultimately participated. Curator Sharp proclaimed in the show's catalog that their work represented a watershed moment in both the practice and the aesthetics of contemporary art:

> It is understandable that earth art should throw open to question the exhibition system generally adopted throughout the world. The artist is traditionally expected to make a work in his [*sic*] studio; when the work is selected for an exhibit he rarely has further contact with it. Now it is possible for the artist to leave his studio and produce whatever he wants in the exhibition area itself, and this offers him a way of having greater control over his artistic output.[6]

Giving artists free rein of an exhibition space was not unprecedented, given the number of experimental galleries that flourished in New York City in the fifties and sixties,[7] but the idea that a museum could do the same would only come into widespread currency in the nineties. Often what resulted in the sixties took the form of interactive environments or free-form performances in galleries and storefronts, such as Jim Dine's 1960 *Car Crash*, Claes Oldenburg's *The Store* (1961), and Allan Kaprow's *Words* (1962). While still radical in 1969, when Sharp was writing, interactivity, installation, and performance have since become standard operating procedures in twenty-first-century art. Their perseverance has depended on the camera—whether still photography, film, or video—to record what otherwise would be only the stuff of legend.

The *Earth Art* show demonstrated that artists no longer required a gallery or museum space; they could achieve even greater control over their artistic output by working outside, often in distant or remote places. All they needed was a way to show people in the art world what they had done.

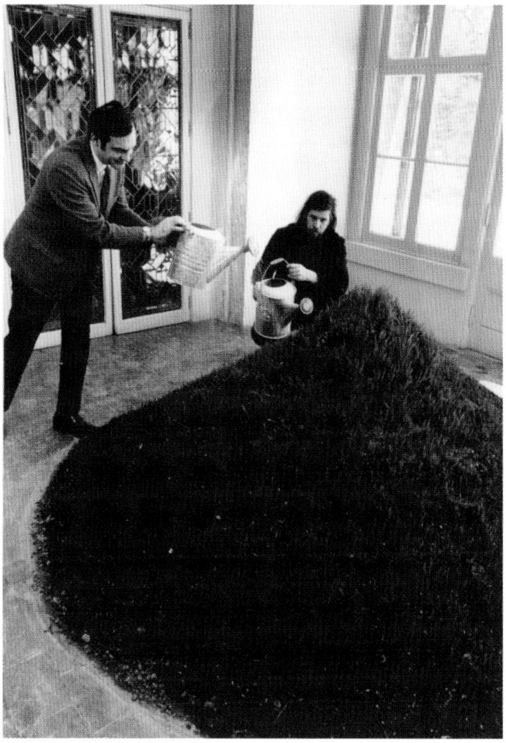

Hans Haacke's *Grass Grows* during the *Earth Art* exhibition, Andrew Dickson White Museum of Art, with grass being watered by the museum's director, Thomas Leavitt, and an unidentified person, 1969.

Sol LeWitt had alluded to this possibility a year before in a work he called *Buried Cube Containing an Object of Importance but Little Value*. Performed in the garden behind a Dutch collector's house, *Buried Cube* consisted of LeWitt digging a hole, putting a Minimalist-style cube into it, and shoveling dirt back into the hole. This, at least, is the story we are told, since there was no real audience for the performance. The work itself consists of a grid of nine black-and-white photographs showing the artist, the collector's family, the cube, the shovel, and the hole—first empty, then with the cube, and then refilled.[8]

Dennis Oppenheim's piece for the *Earth Art* show was also performed outside, but the audience for it was comparatively large, consisting of much of Cornell's faculty and students. Using a chain saw, and with the assistance of several students, including Matta-Clark, Oppenheim cut a sinuous, two-foot-wide, open canal in the ice of a campus lake. The task was perilous, not so much because of the thickness of the ice but because the cut ended at a dam, on the other side of which lay a steep and deep gorge. Today I can't imagine a school that would let its students participate in such a venture, or even allow an artist to execute such a plan, liability laws being what they are, but Oppenheim's *Accumulation Cut* was a feat that remains classic: audacious, open to interpretation, and ephemeral. Only a few photographs survive to confirm its existence.

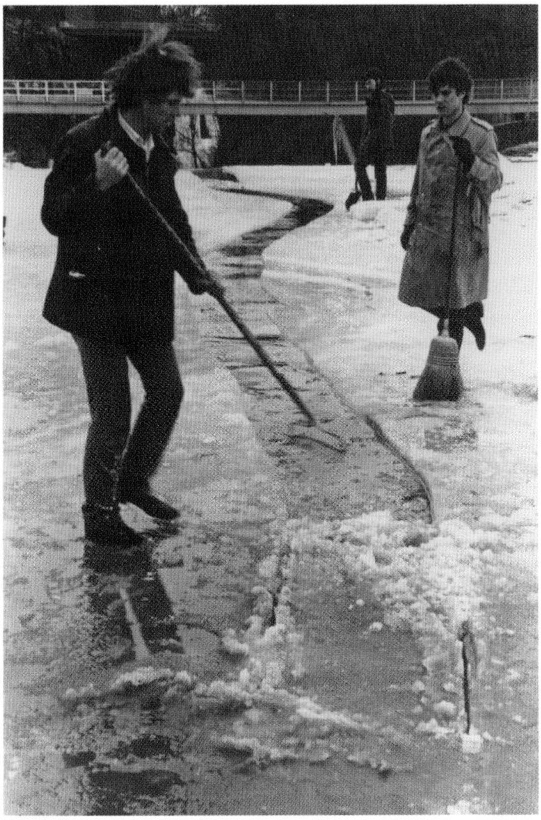

Dennis Oppenheim and Gordon Matta-Clark executing Oppenheim's work *Accumulation Cut* for the *Earth Art* exhibition, Andrew Dickson White Museum of Art, 1969.

Ephemerality became as much a hallmark of Oppenheim's work as earth, which made his art especially dependent on photography. Oppenheim seems to have been conscious of the medium's importance to his work; in *Reading Position for Second Degree Burn*, from 1970, he lies on a beach with the book *Tactics* across his chest in the top picture and with only its indexical trace visible in the picture below. The "joke," if one can call it that, is that the book's prior presence is marked by a case of sunburn, the result of lying motionless for five hours. Light, photography's sine qua non, is the developing agent and subject of the piece.

The artist who would become the biggest star of the Earth Art movement was Robert Smithson, justly famous for his masterwork *Spiral Jetty* (1970), built in the shallows at the northern end of the Great Salt Lake not far from the site where the transcontinental railroad was completed with a ceremonial "golden spike." Smithson's project for the *Earth Art* show, only a little more than a year earlier, involved the Cayuga Rock Salt Company mine, a 2,000-foot-deep warren of tunnels bordering Cayuga Lake from which rock salt, mostly used for deicing highways, was extracted. Smithson ventured into the mine and placed square mirrors within the chambers, which he then photographed in black and white. The mirrors functioned to

Robert Smithson, *Spiral Jetty*, Great Salt Lake, Utah, 1970.

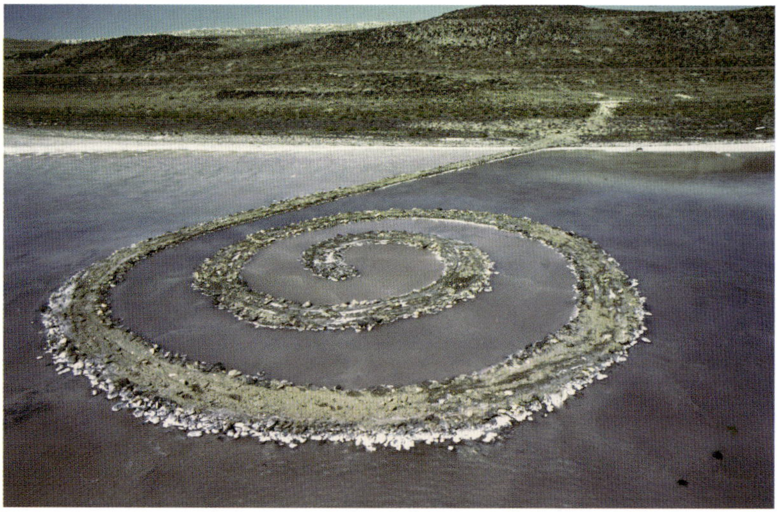

displace the normal spatial order of the scene, reflecting back piles of salt, for example, that otherwise would not be in the picture. The artist then moved a ton of the rock salt to the museum and made several piles out of it, into which he reinserted the mirrors. Nearby hung the photographs that he had taken in the mine.

The work's overall title, *Mirror Displacement*, refers to the action of the mirrors in displacing parts of the scene, both in the photographs and for real-time viewers in the museum, and their travel from what Smithson called "site" (the mine) to "non-site" (the museum).[9] After the show he went on to make similar pieces in the Yucatán and in England. Much later I learned that Smithson's interest in photography extended to quasi-documentary projects such as *The Monuments of Passaic* (1967), an apparently tongue-in-cheek homage to the New Jersey manufacturing city, which proposed decaying bridges and pipelines as its "found" monuments.[10]

Smithson's leading rival for critical attention at the time was Michael Heizer, whose earth-moving piece for the *Earth Art* show was omitted from the catalog without any explanation. (It may have remained unfinished—either because the ground froze or because he was excavating the garden next to the building, which the university administration found appalling.) Heizer went on that year to create his own masterwork: *Double Negative*, done in the Nevada desert, which rivaled *Spiral Jetty* in its scale and audacity and, like *Spiral Jetty*, became famous because of the photographs made of it.

Double Negative is a result of a huge earth-moving enterprise; Heizer used excavation equipment to cut a wide trench on the edges of two facing escarpments atop a mesa, with the cuts mirroring each other. As shown in photographs, which are how the vast majority of artists and critics have seen the piece, the paired cuts suggest a connecting space between them,

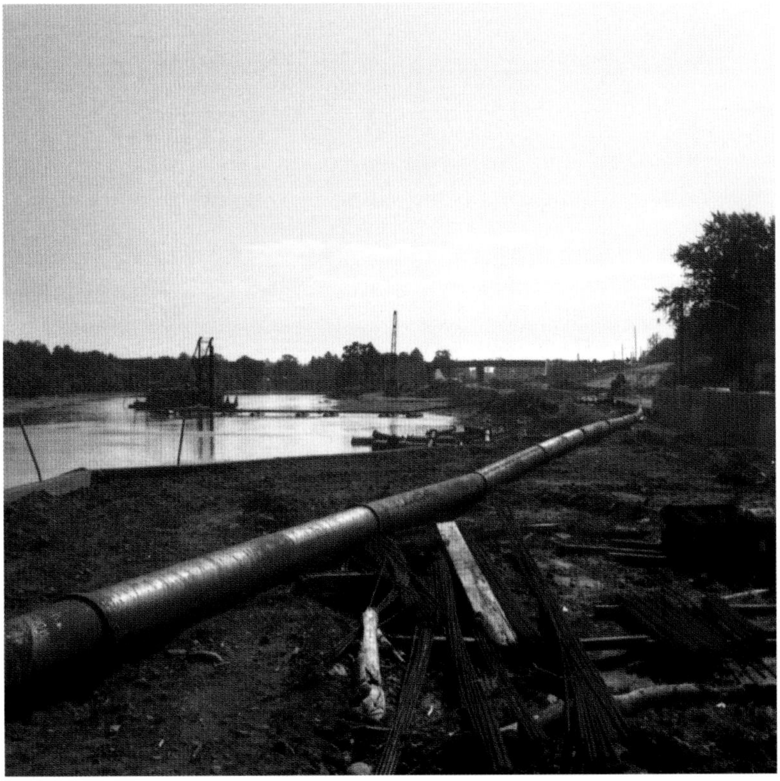

Robert Smithson, *The Great Pipes Monument*, 1967, from *The Monuments of Passaic*.

as if Heizer were drawing a fat rectilinear line through the air. Clearly visible from the air but difficult to discover at ground level, the piece required moving almost a quarter million ton of rock.

Double Negative and *Spiral Jetty*, as well as other earthworks constructed at the time and since (notably Christo and Jeanne-Claude's ongoing series of fabric and wrapping pieces, such as *Wrapped Coast* in 1969), depended on photography, either still or moving, to become known to their intended audiences. In a sense, the documentation was as much a spectacle as the piece itself, and the artists were savvy enough to develop their own photography skills or, more often, hire skilled photographers and filmmakers to make the pictures for them. Smithson, for example, arranged for the filming of *Spiral Jetty*, including a memorable segment in which he runs along the rocks of the jetty while a camera aboard a helicopter tracks his progress. He relied on the skilled assistance of his wife, Nancy Holt, and filmmakers Robert Fiore, Barbara Jarris, and Robert Logan.[11] Christo and Jeanne-Claude hired Harry Shunk and later Wolfgang Volz to photograph their installations.

This awareness of the importance of photography led some of the *Earth Art* artists—Oppenheim, as already mentioned, and also Dibbets, Haacke, and Heizer—to create work that highlighted the inherent fungibility of photographic documentation. Heizer, for example, commissioned Gianfranco

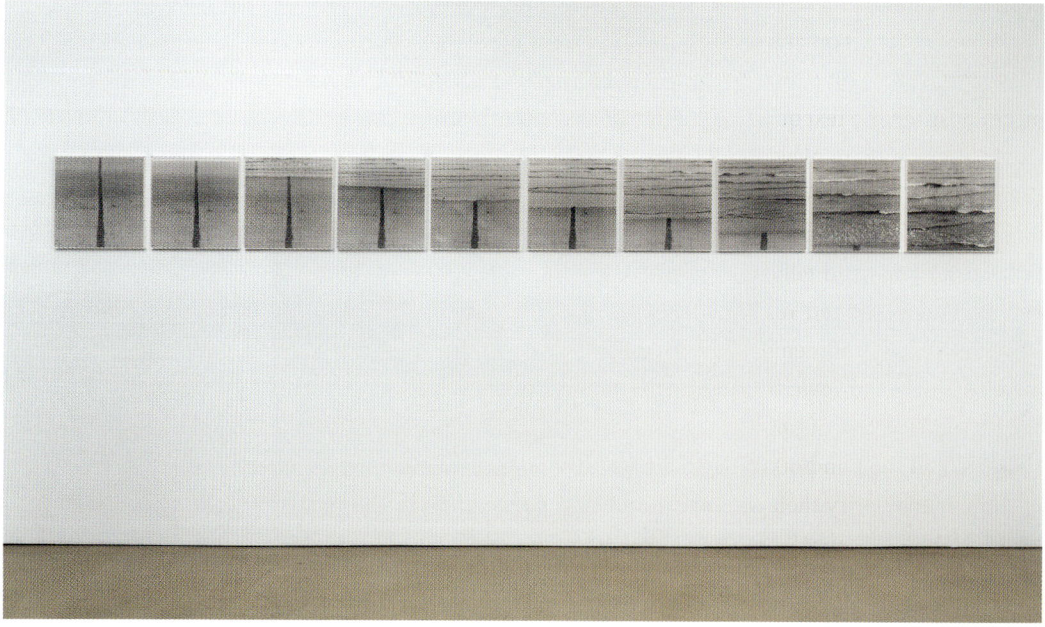

Installation view of Jan Dibbets's *Tide*, 1969.

Gorgoni to take bird's-eye photographs of tire tracks the artist had made by driving his motorcycle around in circles in a dry lake bed; he then assembled the prints in a circle for a piece he titled *Circular Surface Planar Displacement Drawing/90° Vertical Planar Rotary* (1970). Gorgoni, an Italian photographer who was in great demand in the Earth Art era, is best remembered for documenting Smithson's *Spiral Jetty* and later Christo and Jeanne-Claude's *Running Fence* (1976), among a number of other earthworks.

Dibbets's nearly concurrent work *Tide (Vloed)* is a set of ten black-and-white prints documenting the rise of the ocean as it overwhelms a beach, in the process erasing a vertical line that bifurcates each picture. Essentially, the work is a straightforward time lapse of the interval between low and high tides, about six hours, but by including the line he drew in the sand Dibbets shows how human activities, including earthworks, are subject to the greater forces of nature. In his *Dutch Mountain* series, begun in 1971, he went further and constructed an illusory horizon line that suggests hills where there are none. Consisting of multipart panoramas of the Dutch shoreline for which he tilted the camera from one picture to the next, the work demonstrates how even the most documentary of photographs can be contextualized to create a false report. These works were the focus of Dibbets's first gallery exhibition in New York, at the Castelli Gallery in Soho, in 1973.

As for Haacke, he went on to create confrontational pieces that challenged both the institutions in which they were shown and the ability of viewers to see them as art. His work for the group show *Information*, a landmark show that was organized by curator Kynaston McShine at the Museum of Modern Art in 1970, was site and context specific. Called *Poll*, Haacke's piece consisted of a text question painted on the wall asking museum visitors if the refusal of then–New York Governor Nelson Rockefeller to denounce President Richard Nixon's Vietnam policy would cause them not to vote for him. Ballots were collected in two Plexiglas boxes below—one for Yes and one for No—and tallied as the show went on. (Two thirds of respondents apparently voted Yes.) Rockefeller, of course, was not only governor but also a prominent member of the founding family of the museum, which made the piece particularly impertinent.

The appearance of photographs in work like Haacke's, Dibbets's, and Heizer's, and their and other Earth artists' dependence on photographs to document and verify their activity, would have been almost unimaginable ten years earlier. Indeed, they would have been unimaginable without the earlier appearance of an aesthetic known as Conceptual Art, which tossed aside Pablo Picasso as the exemplar of what a contemporary artist should be and instead adopted the example of Marcel Duchamp.

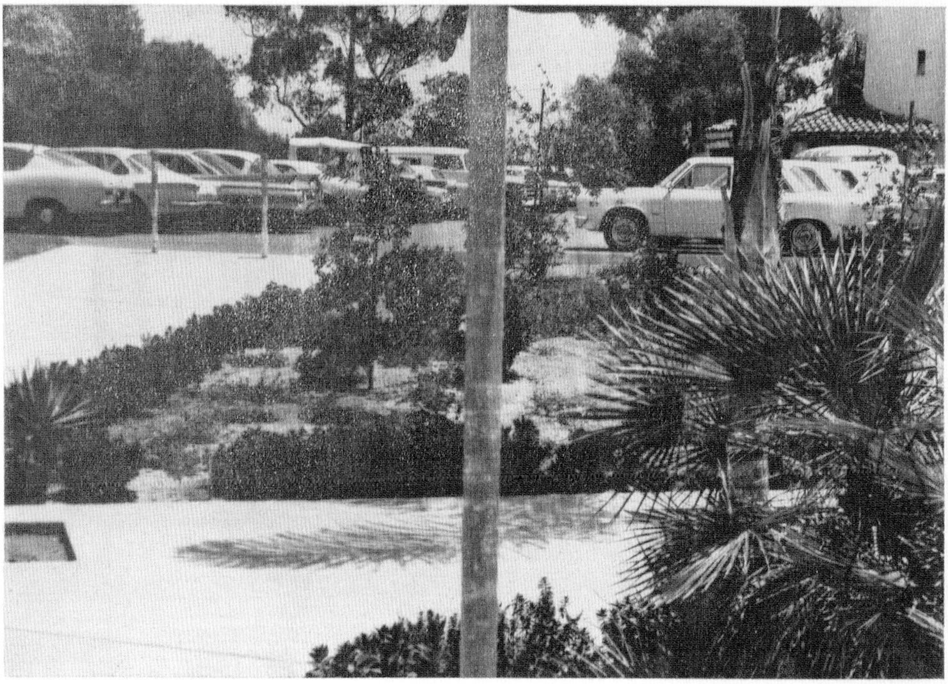

AN ARTIST IS NOT MERELY THE SLAVISH ANNOUNCER OF A SERIES OF FACTS, WHICH IN THIS CASE THE CAMERA HAS HAD TO ACCEPT AND MECHANICALLY RECORD.

CHAPTER 4

Getting the Concept

Because a great deal of postminimal art was inaccessible or ephemeral, artists photographed it to show what it looked like and to preserve its memory. The photodocumentation soon came to be thought of as integral to the work itself—a kind of trace of the real thing or event and a real work of art in its own right.

—Irving Sandler, *Art of the Postmodern Era,* 1996

Before closing his gallery at 291 Fifth Avenue in the spring of 1917, Alfred Stieglitz made one final, enduring, and perhaps unwitting contribution to the history of modern art, one that uncannily foreshadows the sudden appearance of photography within contemporary art some fifty years later.

Stieglitz's contribution took the form of a photograph he made of a urinal displayed on a pedestal at 291, in front of a Marsden Hartley painting. The signature on the urinal, "R. Mutt," identifies the object as what it actually was, Marcel Duchamp's *Fountain,* which Duchamp had surreptitiously submitted to the 1917 Society of Independent Artists' exhibition as the work of an unknown artist, Richard Mutt. The piece was summarily rejected, as Duchamp surely intended, and thus became the subject of some controversy, which again Duchamp intended. Other than Duchamp, Stieglitz, the jurors, and a few friends, no one ever saw the original *Fountain;* Stieglitz's photograph, reproduced in a broadside periodical Duchamp published called *The Blind Man,* is the only record of its existence.[1]

Fountain is a landmark of twentieth-century art because it marks a radically new approach to the task of making art. No artistic skill was involved to render it an artwork; Duchamp was not a ceramicist but an erstwhile painter, and all he did was add a bogus signature. The factory-made object exists because of its functionality, not its beauty. And yet by elevating it onto a pedestal and placing it in an art gallery, Duchamp gave it the status of art. His decision to do this—his concept, if you will—is the real work of art, and in that sense seeing a photograph of it is as good as seeing the real thing.[2]

Today it is hard to overestimate the influence Duchamp had on contemporary art, but until the sixties his work was largely unrecognized in the United States. That changed in 1963, when the curator Walter Hopps

John Baldessari, *An Artist is Not Merely the Slavish Announcer…,* 1966–68. Acrylic and photoemulsion on canvas.

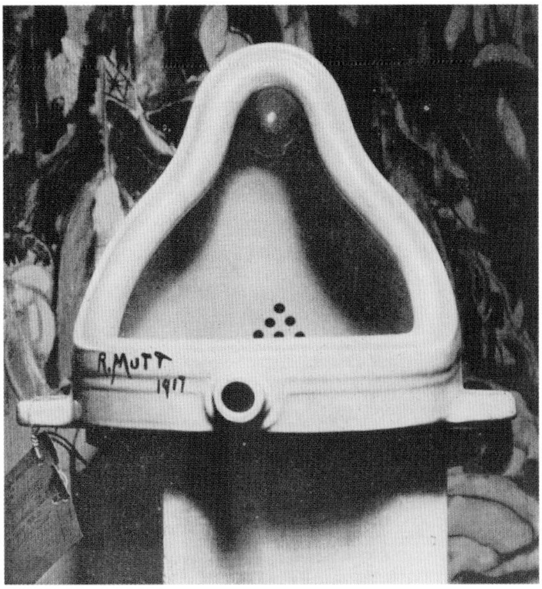

Alfred Stieglitz, *Fountain*, 1917.

presented a Duchamp retrospective at the Pasadena Art Museum—exactly a year after his *New Painting of Common Objects* show of Pop Art. Even though many of the works in the show were replicas or reproductions of Duchamp's "readymades"—including the urinal—its impact reverberated throughout California and all the way east. Seemingly every artist outside of Abstract Expressionism found inspiration in Duchamp's sly, unassuming, but profoundly subversive approach to making art. Or, as art historian Thierry de Duve has succinctly put it, "When a urinal is art, then anything and everything can be art, and chances are that anybody can be an artist."[3]

We now know the heritage of Duchamp's *Fountain* as Conceptual Art. Today's working notion of Conceptualism conceives of the movement broadly, encompassing any artist-designed activity that proceeds according to a preconceived idea or plan. As practiced in the sixties, however, Conceptual Art had a more narrow and rigorous definition, one that excluded performance and restricted its purview to work that focused on systems and structures; for example, Haacke's *Shapolsky et al. Manhattan Real Estate Holdings, a Real-Time Social System, as of May 1, 1971,* which exhaustively cataloged one family's entire real-estate holdings. Sol LeWitt was the central figure in promoting this brand of Conceptual Art, famously writing, "When an artist uses a conceptual form of art, it means that all of the planning and decisions are made beforehand and the execution is a perfunctory affair."[4]

Joseph Kosuth's *One and Three Chairs* (1965), shown in the 1970 *Information* show at the Museum of Modern Art, is a classic example. The work consists of a chair; an enlarged, almost-life-size photograph of the same chair; and the dictionary definition of *chair*, itself enlarged as a photograph.

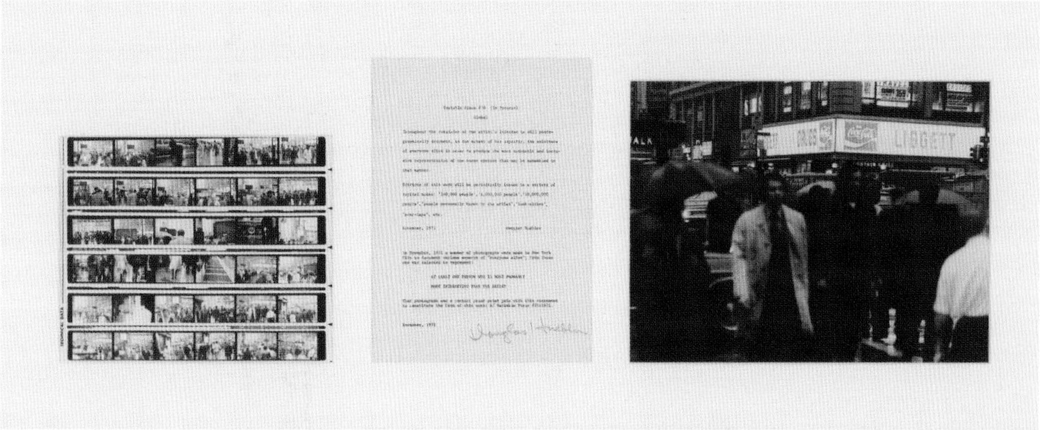

Douglas Huebler, *Variable Piece #70*, 1971. Photographs and typewriting on paper. The Museum of Modern Art, New York. Partial gift of the Daled Collection and partial purchase through the generosity of Maja Oeri and Hans Bodenmann, Sue and Edgar Wachenheim III, Agnes Gund, Marlene Hess and James D. Zirin, Marie-Josée and Henry R. Kravis, and Jerry I. Speyer and Katherine G. Farley.

The chair and the photograph of it are unremarkable, in the same sense as Edward Ruscha's gasoline stations, but they serve to represent the idea of chairness spelled out in the definition—there is, one could say, one idea of chair that is represented in three ways: object, image, and language, or in art terms sculptural object, visual object, and text object.[5] Kosuth seems to be saying that the physical chair is no more or less "chair" than its photograph or its definition; all are engaged in presenting the gestalt of chairness to the viewer, each in a distinct language.

The first Conceptual artist to grab my attention, and one whose work I vividly recall seeing in the early seventies at Castelli Gallery on West Broadway, was Douglas Huebler. What I saw at Castelli were panels from Huebler's *Variable Piece* series, and in particular the memorable *Variable Piece #70,* which consisted of a 35mm contact sheet, a typed piece of paper, and a black-and-white photograph from one of the frames of the contact sheet, arranged together in a single frame.

Huebler's typewritten (and signed) text for the piece begins, "Throughout the remainder of the artist's lifetime he will photographically document, to the extent of his capacity, the existence of everyone alive in order to produce the most authentic and inclusive representation of the human species that may be assembled in that manner."[6] He goes on to explain that the one image enlarged from the contact sheet is meant to represent "at least one person who is most probably more interesting than the artist." (The artist typed this last assertion in all capital letters.)

I found the hubris of the artist's ambition wildly funny—amusement was becoming my most frequent response to the art that I liked but didn't fully understand. Huebler's outsized ambition was undercut by an endearing modesty, in that the piece proposed that an out-of-focus stranger might be somehow more interesting than the artist, our usual focus of attention. I was confused, however, by the photographs themselves, which looked like half-baked versions of the kind of street photography that aspired to art in the hands of Robert Frank and Garry Winogrand (and that I aspired to make as a wannabe street photographer myself). The selected picture was badly printed, most of the negatives on the contact sheet were overexposed, and the moments recorded on film seemed random at best, without the "decisive moment" composition I had come to admire.

Conceptual artists as a whole were not concerned with the picturesque or craft qualities of the photographs that documented or abetted their work, which might explain why their use of the camera long escaped the attention of those who cared about photography as an art. Their amateurism in terms of craft was in most cases intentional; as photographer Jeff Wall has suggested, writing about Huebler's work, "The artistic, creative part of [the] work is obviously not the photography, the picture-making. This displays all the limited qualities identified with photoconceptualism's deskilled, amateurist sense of itself."[7] At the time most of my photographer friends dismissed Conceptual photography out of hand, naturally enough, but I remember being intrigued: why were these nominally "bad" pictures on display at Castelli, Sonnabend, and other top-tier galleries of contemporary art?

Knowing what a good photograph was supposed to look like was to my disadvantage in my attempts to fathom what Huebler was up to. While some may claim that he "wanted his art to negate the imperative that modernist photographers grasp condensed nuggets of reality," and that he "aimed directly at the center of American modernist photography" in such works,[8] artists and art audiences at the time were mostly unaware of American Modernist photography's ambitions. Their reference more likely would have been to Ruscha and his gas stations, to Kosuth and his chair, and to other practitioners of the "photoconceptualism" of the late sixties, including Huebler himself, the great majority of whom treated craft as an enemy of their art, which was, Conceptually speaking, about the notation of ideas and not the marketplace of objects. As Lucy Lippard famously put it in 1968, these artists sought to "dematerialize" the art object.[9]

Conceptual Art was not simply about negation or rebellion, however. As the *Information* show suggested, it actively addressed what today have become even more crucial issues: how we know what we know, how information is defined by the systems that deliver it, and what those systems are. Besides photographs, the most common items used by Conceptual artists to denote their activities were maps, the most prosaic and useful method for fixing one's location, and texts, a much more ambiguous sign system.

Huebler's *Variable Piece #70* (and the entire extended series) addresses an information issue that has gained even more currency today: the photographic archive. By including his contact sheet of thirty-six exposures along with a single, selected image, he alludes to the common practice of photographers and their editors of picking the "best" image from many. He also signals the arbitrariness of our encounters with camera images and the existence of scores of them—and thousands, millions, billions more—that we will never see. Since the introduction of the iPhone in 2007 and the development of apps like Instagram, the glut of images has become overwhelming, producing an information crisis of its own. Just imagine if Huebler had made good on his ambition to photograph everyone in the world: the archive of those pictures alone would number in the tens of billions.

In short, photography's unique "talents" (or peculiarities, some would say) were not simply useful to Conceptual artists and their kin; they were phenomenologically, ontologically, and epistemologically interesting. One could even make the case that photography helped lead to the creation of Conceptual Art in the first place, if we consider the career of LeWitt, a key figure in its development and theorization.

A first-generation American who grew up in Connecticut, studied art at Syracuse University, and arrived in New York in the midfifties, LeWitt by the midsixties had rejected conventional modes of art making. He started thinking about photography and in particular its ability to describe a series of actions sequentially. He was particularly fascinated with the work of the nineteenth-century photographer Eadweard Muybridge, which he discovered, legend has it, when he moved into an apartment where the previous occupant had left behind a copy of a book of Muybridge's motion-study photographs.[10]

Muybridge is best known for his stop-action sequences of humans and animals in motion, including photographs of horses that proved for the first time that all four legs of the animal are in the air simultaneously during its canter and gallop. To achieve these results he had to devise high-speed shutters and a means of tripping them in rapid order as a horse sped past a rank of as many as thirteen cameras.[11] Although the resulting sequences, first printed in 1881 as *The Attitudes of Animals in Motion,* are not as scientifically exact as they appear, they amazed his audiences by showing something impossible to see with the naked eye—and simultaneously by contradicting how painters for centuries had been depicting horses at a gallop.

That Muybridge's work would become the lodestone for LeWitt in particular and Conceptual artists in general—rather than the self-consciously artistic photographs of Stieglitz, say—is not surprising. LeWitt and the many Conceptualists who found in photography an essential tool for expressing their aesthetic concerns were distinctly not interested in the medium's artistic traditions and aspirations. If anything, they were anxious about keeping their distance from "art photography," as it was then known. Partly this was economic—photographs sold for a pittance compared to other forms of contemporary art—but mainly it was discursive: they wanted their work to be discussed by critics, curators, and collectors of vanguard art, not photography. Their artistic tradition stemmed from Duchamp, not Stieglitz.

LeWitt broke the rules of what an artist was supposed to be and do by making rules for his work ahead of its execution. Instead of producing objects that reflected the artist's manual skill or emotional state, he took an intellectual approach that valorized the thought process as much as the final product. He famously said of his work, "The idea becomes the machine that makes the art."[12] A gestalt of serial causality, of a quasi-scientific approach to visually demonstrating (and thereby exhausting) a set of possibilities, became the underpinning of all his subsequent work. After discovering Muybridge, LeWitt tried incorporating the photographer's figures directly into the paintings he was making at the time, as well as in elongated sculptural boxes in which photographs of a naked female model, seated or advancing toward the camera, are viewed sequentially through ten peepholes (*Muybridge I* and *Muybridge II,* both 1964).[13]

But his real breakthrough came when he began to reconsider Muybridge's seriality in a more conceptual mode. Photography was no longer front and center once LeWitt began to use the simple geometric forms that defined Minimalist sculpture, his signature one being the cube, as building blocks to present all the permutations of a given set.[14] A good example of this is his 1966 *Serial Project, 1 (ABCD),* in the collection of the Museum of Modern Art, a collection of open cube forms made of white enamel rods set on an aluminum grid. The different cube states reveal their logical connections only to viewers who actively engage with the forms as a series. Like his long-lived series of wall drawings, begun in 1969, the visual aspect of the work can be captivatingly beautiful but the full meaning is only revealed when we decipher the instructions or logical bases behind it.

LeWitt preferred to be known as a serial artist rather than a Conceptual or Minimalist artist, and he tellingly wrote, "The serial artist does not attempt to produce a beautiful or mysterious object but functions merely as a clerk cataloging the results of his premise."[15] (By this measure, Hans Haacke could count as a serial artist as well.) The "cataloging [of] the results of his premise" meant that, one, there was no hierarchy of materials involved, and two, photographs were useful tools for getting the artist's idea across. Not surprisingly, LeWitt often returned to photography throughout his later career, usually in book form. Examples include *Brick Wall* (Tanglewood Press, 1977), a thirty-two-image record of light changing over time; *PhotoGrids* (Multiples, 1977), with pictures of windows, panel doors, and other internally gridded objects; and *Autobiography* (Multiples, 1980),

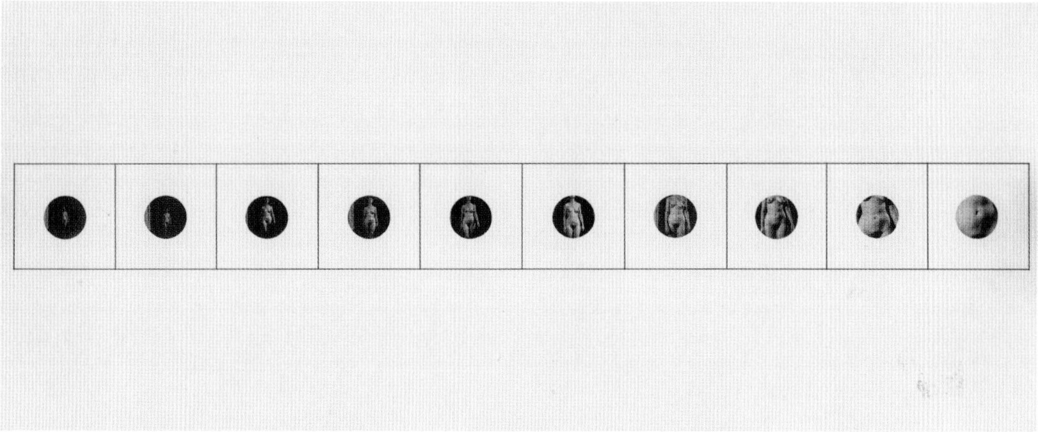

Sol LeWitt, *Schematic Drawings for Muybridge II, 1964*, 1970. Offset lithograph, edition of 1,200. Albright-Knox Art Gallery, Buffalo, New York. The Panza Collection and by exchange: George B. and Jenny R. Mathews Fund, Bequest of Arthur B. Michael, Albert H. Tracy Fund and Bequest of John Mortimer Schiff, 2015.

which exhaustively catalogs the contents of LeWitt's living and working spaces using grids of photographs, nine to a page, from the window grates to his ashtrays.

LeWitt passed along to other artists his fascination with seriality in general and Muybridge in particular. He wrote cogently and persuasively about the kind of art he practiced (most notably "Paragraphs on Conceptual Art," published in *Artforum* in 1967), and he distributed samples of Muybridge's work by buying individual plates from *Human and Animal Locomotion* and giving them as gifts to like-minded artists.[16] One was Jan Dibbets, the Dutch artist included in the *Earth Art* show.

Like LeWitt, the artist Dan Graham was captivated by the photographs of Eadweard Muybridge, so much so that he wrote an article about Muybridge that was published in *Arts Magazine* in 1967. While arguing that contemporary filmmaking was indebted to Muybridge's "series of static, unrelated moments," citing Andy Warhol and Jean-Luc Godard as examples, Graham also considered the implications for the still photograph: "What distinguishes one moment from another is a simple alternation in the positioning of things. Each object is re-arranged relative to every other object and to the frame. Things don't 'happen'; they merely re-place themselves in space."[17]

As he was thinking about Muybridge, Graham was also busy taking photographs for a project he called *Homes for America*. It was first shown as a slide projection in a group show at Finch College in the winter of 1966, and then reformatted for publication as an illustrated magazine article, "Homes for America." Graham's Instamatic color pictures of new, suburban-style houses on the outskirts of New York proper—Staten Island; Bayonne, Jersey City, and Westfield (his hometown), New Jersey—are mostly straightforward, documentary style views of similar or identical dwellings, often repeating themselves into the distance, but there are also images of people

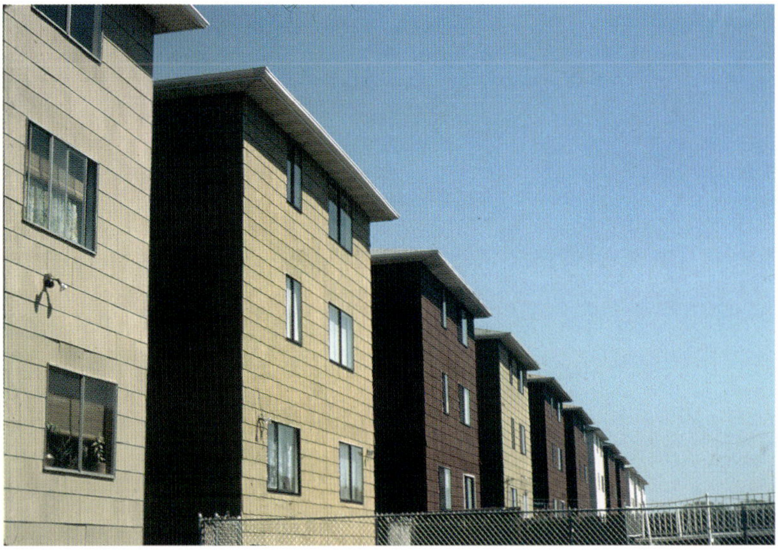

Dan Graham, *Homes for America*, 1966–67. One slide from twenty 35mm slides and Kodak Carousel projector.

at fast-food restaurants and in discount stores. In subject matter and in presentation, the idea of seriality, so essential to Muybridge's work, is made obvious, even concrete.

Graham's intentions for *Homes for America* also included the way photographs are used as illustrations in the media and how they are contextualized by captioning and layout. In a 2004 conversation with the artist Michael Smith he said: "When I did *Homes for America* it was a fake think piece about how a magazine like *Esquire* would often have a leading sociologist and a good photographer work together on a story. But my project actually wasn't about sociology. It was like Flaubert: It's a cliché. And it was supposed to be humorous, flat-footed humor." Confoundingly, when it did appear as an article, in *Arts Magazine,* the editors chose to strip off the photographs and present Graham's text as a piece of architectural criticism.[18]

Homes for America has cemented Graham's reputation as an early investigator of photography's possibilities for Conceptual Art, and served as a model for other artists' use of the camera in the built environment. (Lewis Baltz comes prominently to mind, as does early Jan Groover.) It also has an uncanny kinship with the contemporaneous photographs of a pair of German artists who worked throughout most of their lifetimes as a couple: Bernd and Hilla Becher. Of all the artists of the Conceptual era to have used photography to express their ideas, the Bechers have become arguably the most important and influential. (The argument, if there is one, would pit them against John Baldessari.) Born in the early thirties, the Bechers met at the state art school in Düsseldorf in the late fifties and began the project that would consume their joint career into the twenty-first century: photographing industrial structures such as water towers, blast furnaces, winding

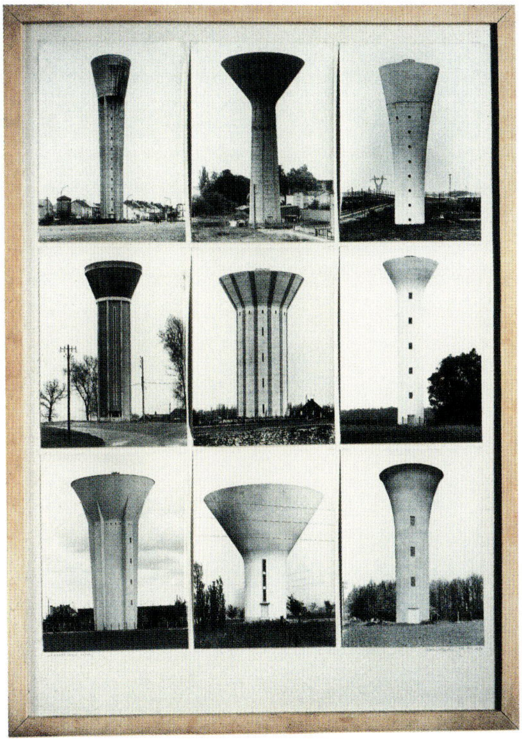

Bernd and Hilla Becher,
Water Towers, 1972.

towers, and coal tipples as well as facades of framework buildings and other aged structures.

Together the Bechers developed a style that seems declaratively objective: their subjects are seen head-on or in profile, in their entirety and centered in the frame; skies are blank and shadows absent; everything in the frame is in sharp focus and exquisitely detailed. In terms of photographic tradition, they were rejecting a contemporaneous European fad for "subjective" photography and returning to the Weimar period of the "Neue Sachlichkeit," or "New Objectivity," practiced by Werner Mantz, Albert Renger-Patzsch, and August Sander, among others.

But style alone does not account for the embrace of the Bechers' work by Conceptual artists and the art world as a whole. The Bechers' interest in comparing and contrasting different structures with identical functions—most notably in their series of water towers, of which they photographed hundreds if not thousands—led them to present their black-and-white pictures not individually but as grids. For MoMA's 1970 *Information* show, the Bechers presented forty photographs of cooling towers, along with a schematic drawing and a text panel. For their first appearances at Sonnabend Gallery in New York, starting in 1972, the prints were trimmed and mounted on large boards within single frames; later in the decade they framed the pictures individually but hung them together as a grid on the wall.

In a brief commentary written in response to the Sonnabend show in the December 1972 issue of *Artforum,* "A Note on Bernhard and Hilla Becher,"[19] the Minimalist sculptor Carl Andre noted how the couple's grids of industrial structures had internal structures of their own: similar function but different shapes and materials, similar function and similar shape but different materials, etc. He also referred to the work as "photographic typologies," noting that Bernd had instigated the project first with paintings and lithographs before the two collaborators turned to photography. In retrospect, this reference seems a strategic choice: to have seen the work as photographs pure and simple would have made Andre's claims for it more problematic.

Andre's article prompted a response, and another article, three months later. In the March 1973 issue of *Artforum,* on the cover of which appeared one of Muybridge's photographs, the critic and art historian Joseph Masheck argued that the Bechers' photographs are less "original" and contemporary than Andre had argued but nonetheless part of an artistic tradition:

> The art of the Bechers has levels of meaning and reference, but all of them are distinct and apparent. It is an art (photography) dealing with a subject matter that is itself an art (architecture), using a system of morphology and typology that is well-established in formalist art history, in terms of a recognizable artistic attitude (Romanticism).[20]

Despite their differences, both critics agreed that the Bechers were making art by using a camera. That they were even arguing the case suggests the changing status of photography in the art world at that precise moment.

In a few short years the conversation would change, not only in the art world but also in the world of photography. In the summer of 1972, Robert Sobieszek, a curator at the George Eastman House in Rochester—whose museum held the most comprehensive collection of the art of photography at the time—mounted a show of the Bechers' work, titled *Morphologies and Anonymous Sculptures.* Three years later their work reappeared at the same museum in William Jenkins's now-legendary show *New Topographics* (more about which later). Throughout the rest of the decade and the next, their photographs were frequently exhibited by photography museums or by photography departments within museums; they were, I would claim, the first Conceptual artists to be accepted within the precincts of photography-as-art.

They also were avatars of the art world's increasing attention to photography made by artists and by self-identified photographers. Sonnabend Gallery went on to show Gilbert and George's photomontage works; Christian

Boltanski's repurposed anonymous portraits; John Baldessari's *Blasted Allegories* and other series using found photographs; David Hockney's color snapshots and Polaroid SX-70 instant film collages; constructed photographs by Jan Groover, David Haxton, and Boyd Webb; and Hiroshi Sugimoto's movie palace pictures. After 1972 the gallery regularly featured the Bechers in solo shows, including in 1974, 1977, 1978, and throughout the eighties. The impetus for showing all this "photo-based art" was surely Ileana Sonnabend herself, in concert with Antonio Homem, her longtime gallery director and later her adopted son, but much of the credit also is due to Ealan Wingate, who managed the Soho gallery from its opening in 1971 until 1977, and who engaged with the curators from the George Eastman House and other institutions.[21]

Besides the Bechers', the most influential photo-based, Conceptual-based work of the seventies for American artists was that of Baldessari, a native Californian whose first show at Sonnabend Gallery in New York was the same year as the Bechers', 1972. His first New York show had taken place two years earlier at Richard Feigen gallery and was called, ironically enough, *John Baldessari: Recent Paintings*. Ironic, because 1970 was the year he executed a performance piece called *Cremation Project*, which involved incinerating all the paintings he had made between 1953 and 1966 at a crematorium in San Diego. By that time he had abandoned painting in the conventional sense in favor of transferring photographs onto canvas, adding hand-lettered texts (done by a professional sign painter), and documenting performances designed for the camera.

The works, described as photo-emulsion on canvas, hang on the wall like paintings, make self-conscious reference to received ideas about art and about photography, and are sardonic in effect—they have Graham's ideal of "flat-footed humor." In *Wrong* (1967), for example, he makes fun of the Kodak-inspired dictum that one should never compose a picture of a person with a tree behind his or her head. The picture, taken by the artist's wife of the artist himself, is typically boring, but the hand-painted word *wrong* gives it resonance. Is it really wrong? Does art have rules? Where does banality end and aesthetic pleasure begin? These were questions Baldessari asked himself:

> I thought, I'm not using paint, it's a photographic process, and so you can't claim that they're paintings. Rauschenberg had done overlaps of paint and screened photographic images, one over the other onto the canvas in a transfer method he had invented himself. But I wanted to be less artful than Rauschenberg and Warhol: this is a photograph, here's a text. That's it. And I thought, because they're done on canvas, they might be equated with art.[22]

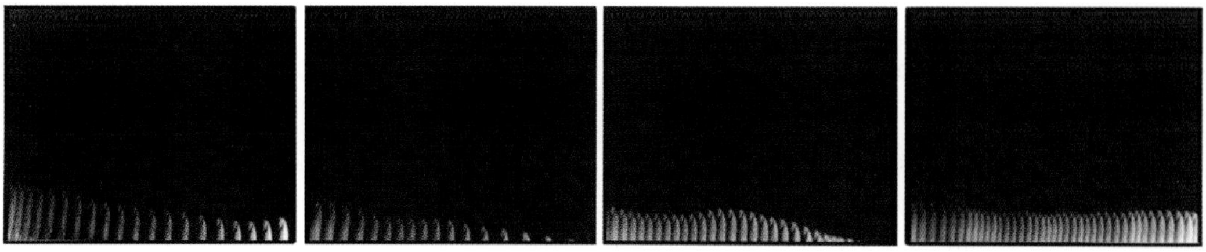

John Baldessari, *Strobe Series / Futurist: Trying To Get A Straight Line With A Finger*, 1975.

In questioning the "rules" of art, Baldessari came to also question the ways in which words and pictures convey meaning. "For most of us photography stands for the truth. But a good artist can make a harder truth by manipulating forms or pushing paint around."[23] Still, from *Wrong* on, Baldessari mainly dispensed with "pushing paint around," instead relying on context and juxtaposition, isolation and seriality, to make his photographs convey meanings they were never meant to have. When he did return to paint, in the eighties, it was in the form of circles that served to obscure the faces of people in found photographs he copied and enlarged.

In 1970 Baldessari left his native San Diego and began teaching at the California Institute of Art (aka CalArts) in Valencia, where he famously taught a course called "Post-Studio Art." There he mentored a surprising number of now-well-known artists, including Jack Goldstein, Matt Mullican, David Salle, and James Welling. All would become associated with the Pictures Generation of the eighties, which in essence replaced Conceptualism with Postmodernism. Baldessari himself bridges that divide in a way that makes him a central figure in anyone's history of contemporary art—and in the history of photography.

Along with the Bechers, Baldessari helped introduce the new forms of Conceptual Art to photography audiences. Unlike many of the "artists using photography" of the seventies, Baldessari was not defensive about his reliance on photographs or about any connection his work might have to photography as practiced by photographers aspiring to make art. In the winter of 1982 he and I participated on a panel convened for *California Photography*, a show at the RISD art museum organized by Deborah Johnson; I was the only non-Californian on the panel and he was the only nonphotographer, although he did not make that a point of distinction. He seemed curious about the photography world.

Baldessari's work also appeared in *California Photography: Remaking Make-Believe*, a 1989 show at the Museum of Modern Art organized by Susan Kismaric. Other artists in the show included Jo Ann Callis, Joe Deal, and Robert Heinecken, all of whom were well known to photography followers but not, like Baldessari, to the art world. By letting his work be seen as "California photography," Baldessari was crossing over from the art world in the same way that photographers like Lewis Baltz and Ralph Gibson—both of whom had shows at Castelli in the early seventies—were attempting to cross in the opposite direction. How this crisscross panned out is a long story, but first there is another tale to tell about an art practice that was as odd-seeming as Conceptual Art but much more in your face: performance.

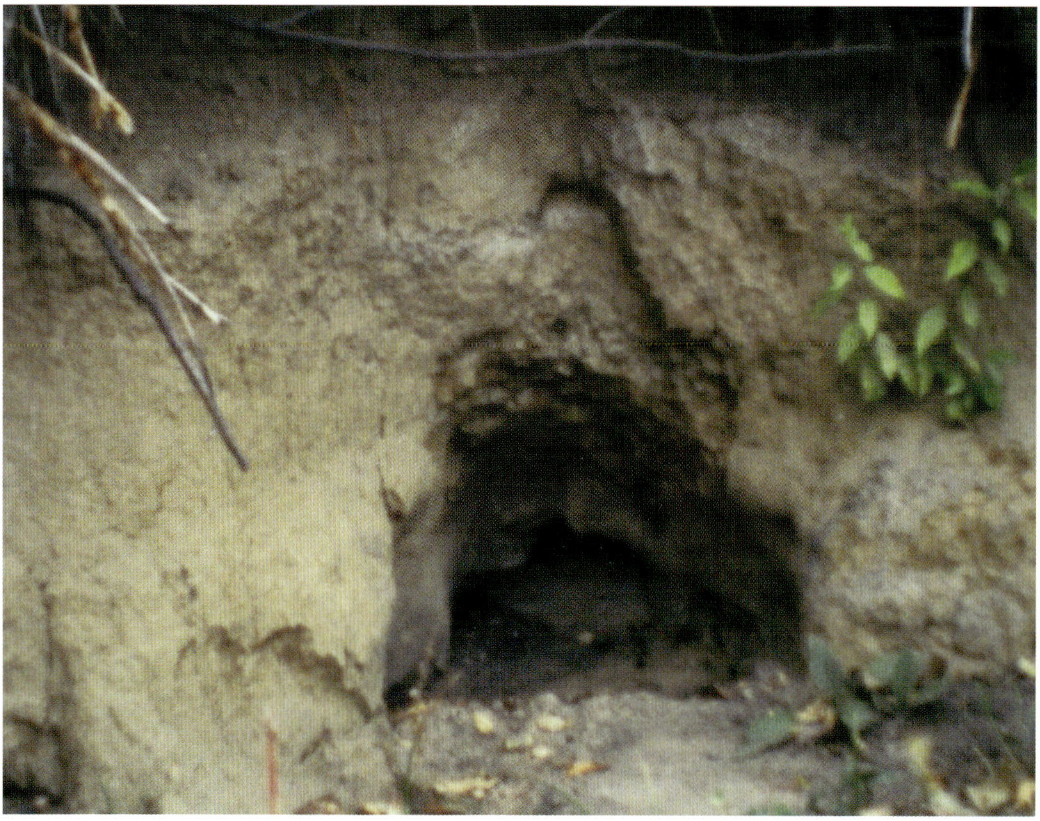

CHAPTER 5

Performers, Bodies, Cameras

One Saturday evening in the early seventies I went to a ground-floor space in Soho to see what was billed as a play, written by the poet Ted Greenwald. The audience was not large (there were only a couple dozen of us, friends of Ted's by all appearances), and we had to wait outside on the street until the appointed hour, when a door was opened. Once inside we found seats at one end of an open, loft-sized room, at which point the lights were turned off.

We waited in the dark for what seemed like fifteen minutes but might have only been five. After a short period of silence some nervous tittering started, as audience members offered wisecracks or opinions on whether something had gone awry with the production. Quiet again. Then someone with a flashlight appeared at the far end of the room—Ted, it turned out—and used it to scan the empty floor. A second figure with a flashlight appeared soon after, walking in front of us, and an attenuated conversation ensued: "Anything?" "Nope." "Okay." "Nothing here." "Yup, okay." The flashlights swept across us and then went off, and we were left in the dark again for another endless few minutes.

Finally the lights came back on, and we all looked at each other to judge what to do next. (Was this intermission? Would it be rude to put on our coats?) Mercifully Ted appeared by the door, signaling that it was over. The night watchmen had done their thing. I can distinctly remember being annoyed and confused on my way home afterward. Was Ted pulling our collective leg? I was, I realized, still in the dark long after the lights came back on. And I don't think I was alone: the audience members dispersed rather quickly, seemingly not eager to have a conversation about something they didn't fully comprehend.

I have since come to recognize this feeling of being at sea with my own experience as something not to be ignored. If anything, it is an infallible indicator that one may be experiencing real art . . . or at least real contemporary art. As a critic responsible for reviewing new exhibitions and books, I

Ana Mendieta, *Untitled*, 1979, from the series *Silueta*.

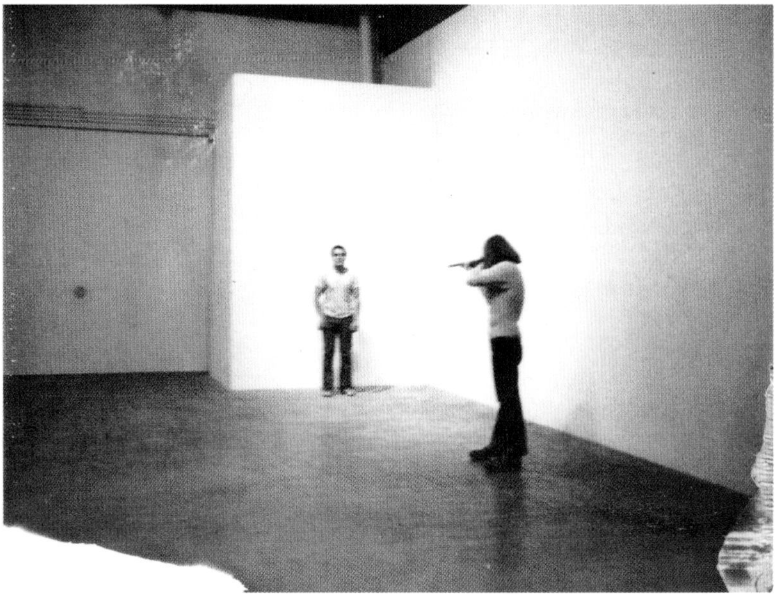

Chris Burden, *Shoot*, 1971.

learned to force myself to overcome the "fight or flight" defense mechanism in my psyche that seeks to protect me from the dangers of unknown territory—mostly, in my case, feelings of intellectual and cultural inadequacy. More times than I can count I've walked into a gallery, looked at what's on the wall, and done a 180 out the door. Halfway down the block I've made myself stop, wondered why the art made me do that, and gone back to have a closer look.

Often—or always, if the art is any good—there is a context for the mystery I am experiencing. In the case of Ted's performance, for example, it would help to have known about John Cage's famed composition *4′33″*, first performed in 1952, in which a pianist sits down at a piano and plays nothing for a little over four and a half minutes. Or about Bertolt Brecht's influential notion that theater needs to make the audience self-consciously aware of its own spectatorship. Or about Yoko Ono's 1964 *Cut Piece*, in which audience members were invited to use scissors to cut off her clothes, thereby making their responses an essential part of the performance.

Befuddling one's audience, making it squirm, or pissing it off were standard artistic practices in my early days in Soho. There was, for example, Vito Acconci's *Seedbed*, at the Sonnabend Gallery in 1972, during which the artist lay underneath a false floor and audibly masturbated as gallery goers walked above him. Or Joseph Beuys's 1974 performance at René Block Gallery on West Broadway, *I Like America and America Likes Me*; for three days the German artist shared a room with a coyote during the gallery's open hours. Unfortunately I missed both of these now-historic events, but I read about them later in articles that reproduced photographs of the scenes.

Photography, it was becoming clear, was essential to this new (at least to me) kind of art.

As was the case with Earth Art, photography meant that you didn't necessarily have to be there, an advantage when art was being made at a distance. Not long after I got to New York, Chris Burden, a recently graduated art student, did a performance in Los Angeles for an audience of twelve friends that consisted of a colleague shooting him through the arm with a .22-caliber rifle. The November 1971 event, called *Shoot*, was filmed and photographed. Several months later Burden arranged a live television interview during which he took the interviewer hostage with a knife. These performances, which quickly gave him a notorious national reputation, were documented in a 1974 limited-edition artist's book Burden titled *Deluxe Photo Book 1971–73*, with fifty-three photographs mounted in a loose-leaf binder. Burden's impulse to assemble his earliest works in a photo album suggests how much performance artists came to depend on the presence of a camera, in no small part because it gave them something tangible to sell.[1]

All of this superficially crazy, radical activity known as Performance Art could be laid at the feet of a generation of postwar artists, of which Ono is sometimes cited as a progenitor along with less-renown figures like Allan Kaprow, the founder of art "Happenings." Or one could date it to the fall of 1963, when the Pasadena Art Museum mounted its highly influential retrospective of Marcel Duchamp. Duchamp, whose career spanned Dada and Surrealism and more, was a performance artist *avant la lettre*. He produced the upside-down urinal signed by R. Mutt. He created a female alter ego, Rrose Sélavy, in whose guise he was photographed by Man Ray. In another identity-shifting, gender-bending stunt he affixed a mustache and beard to a postcard reproduction of the *Mona Lisa*. When he wasn't overtly making art, he was playing chess.

Unlike Earth Art and Conceptual Art, which were largely the province of male artists, Performance Art included many women among its major figures.[2] In one way this seems to mirror a cultural reality, that women are often (and often unhappily) in the position of performing for a male audience, but the appearance of Performance Art also coincided with a new wave of feminism that sought to extinguish the power of the male gaze and turn the presence of the female body into a sign and a source of female empowerment.

Early in 1963—before the Duchamp retrospective, and only a few months after Andy Warhol, Robert Rauschenberg, and Edward Ruscha started using photographs in their art—an abstract painter named Carolee Schneemann decided to literally put herself into her work. An admirer of Jackson Pollock, she proceeded to make her corporal presence the visible and visceral core of what soon mutated from a career in painting to one in

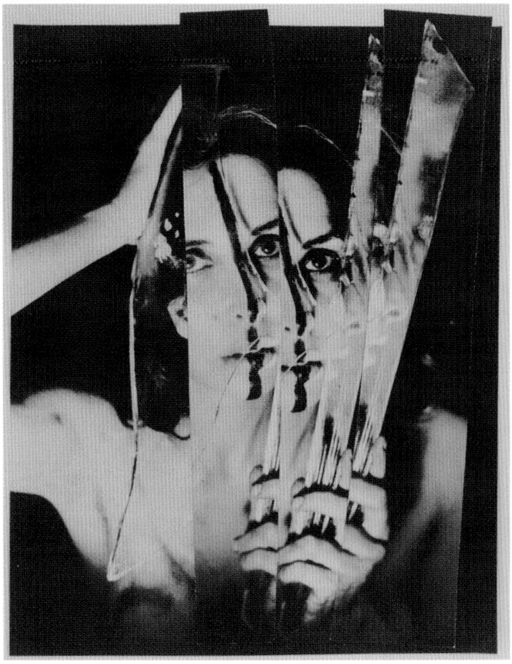

Carolee Schneemann, *Eye Body #11*, 1963, from the *Eye Body: 36 Transformative Actions for Camera* portfolio.

performance. In the process she became as wildly controversial as Warhol was among established artists of the period, if never quite as celebrated.

Schneemann admired Pollock for his "action paintings," which he made by walking on and around a canvas while slinging and dripping paint from an overloaded brush or paint can. The sheer physicality of Pollock's method, which became a part of the finished paintings' meaning, inspired Schneemann to try to integrate her body into her work. Her earliest effort, a portfolio of photographs taken in her studio by an artist friend and called *Eye Body: 36 Transformative Actions for Camera* (1963), shows her naked amid and beneath a semi-sculptural painting of hers, *Four Fur Cutting Boards*, her body covered with slashes of paint and other materials (fur, feathers, glass, snakes). Her intention: "I wanted my actual body to be combined with the work as an integral material—a further dimension of the construction."[3] As the title of the piece indicates, the performance was directed at a disembodied viewer, the camera lens, which functioned as her surrogate audience. Soon thereafter her urge to paint faded away. Associating with the Judson Dance Theater, a loose collective of choreographers, dancers, and visual artists that performed at the Judson Memorial Church in Greenwich Village starting in 1962, Schneemann created one of its most legendary performances, *Meat Joy*. *Meat Joy* (1964) consisted of eight dancers, half of them male and half female, interacting with each other and with an assemblage of chicken parts, sausages, fish, shredded paper, and paint. Dressed in their underwear, rolling on the floor with their legs and arms intertwined, they produced what Schneemann called "an erotic rite" that resembled an orgiastic fantasy.[4] Photographs and films made at the performance suggest that Schneemann's intention was achieved in spades.

I missed *Meat Joy,* since I was still in high school, and I wish I had seen Schneemann's most-admired and thoroughly documented later performance, *Interior Scroll,* which premiered in 1975. Famously, the then-thirty-six-year-old artist stood naked on a table in front of a small New York audience and slowly pulled a long scroll of paper from her vagina, reading from its previously prepared text as she went along. Like many others I only heard about this event later, when it became the talk downtown. Happily, the performance survives in photographs taken by Anthony McCall, a filmmaker and Schneemann's lover at the time.[5]

Done during a resurgence of energy within the feminist movement, *Interior Scroll* was considered by many a brave declaration of women's acceptance of their bodies, genitalia included. (*Our Bodies Our Selves,* a landmark book full of frank medical information on reproductive health for women, had been published commercially two years earlier.) But some feminists disagreed, viewing *Interior Scroll* as a retrograde maneuver that represented women as being defined by their sexuality—essentializing them, in short. This argument would animate the second-wave feminist movement through much of the seventies and eighties. Whether despite or because of its controversial status, Schneemann's example became an inspiration to younger generations of women artists who chose to use their own bodies as the primary focus of their art—from Ana Mendieta and Hannah Wilke to Cindy Sherman and Francesca Woodman. Not coincidentally, photography was their crucial instrument.

One male artist at the time who shared Schneemann's interest in sexuality and physicality, although in mostly mediated ways, was Vito Acconci, he of the notorious *Seedbed.* His work, like hers, would be especially influential with artists in the seventies and eighties. Like Schneemann, Acconci came to performance from another field of ideas, and, like her, he used his own bodily presence as both an object and the object of his art. Physically Acconci was no match—Schneemann's physique seemed descended from the ideals of Greek sculpture and World War II pinups, while Acconci was gangly and pasty faced, with long stringy hair that failed to disguise a bald spot—but his willingness to risk derision and incomprehension was at least equal to hers.

While Acconci originally aspired to be a poet, having earned an MFA from the prestigious University of Iowa writing program in 1964, at the end of the sixties he started doing performative "actions" such as *Following Piece* (1969), for which he followed strangers along New York City streets until they entered a car or building and disappeared from view. *Following*

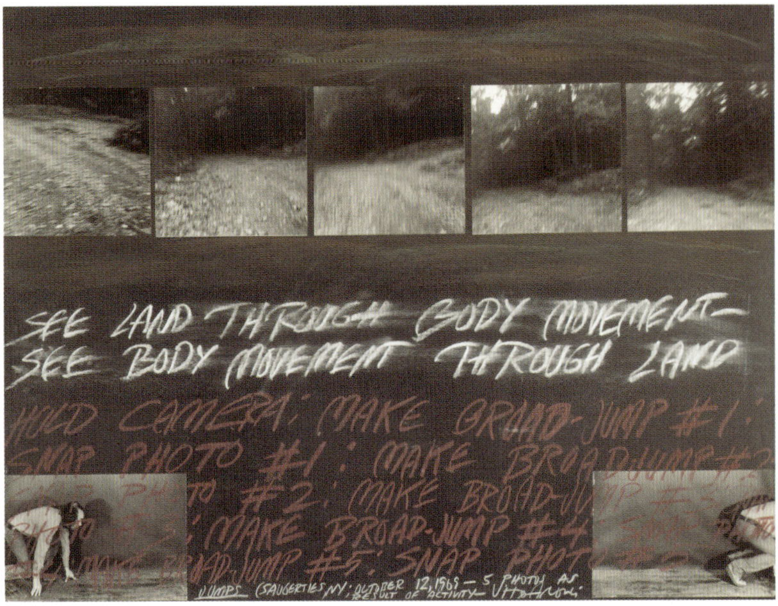

Vito Acconci, *Jumps*, 1969. Photographs and chalk on board.

Piece was documented, in part, with still photographs, which show both the person being followed and Acconci following. Clearly the artist was aware that he needed a photographer along to record the endeavor, although the conceit is that he was doing the "following" on his own.

Acconci gave the camera a leading role as the protagonist of his next work, a series of activities that highlight the artist's body, and the camera as an appurtenance of it, in relation to the natural world. Mostly occurring in upstate New York, these actions involve the artist taking photographs while performing various leaps or proscribed motions. *Jumps* (one of a series of similar works collectively called *Jumps*) is a typical photographic artifact of the enterprise: on the top of a blackboard the artist has mounted five photographs of a dirt path, each taken after the artist performed a crouching "broad jump." (The photographs in the bottom corners depict his jumping style.) The text, in white and red chalk, explains the Conceptual procedure and intention: "See land through body movement—See body movement through land."

While Conceptual in the sense of having a recipe for its execution, *Jumps* and its companion works are obvious examples of body art, in which the artist's physical being is a presence that determines the art's meaning. But just as important is the work's attention to the camera as a kind of prosthesis of the artist's vision. It is not just the artist's body position that determines the image we see but also the way in which the camera is held relative to the body. The camera is a performer, too, acting in effect as a third eye.

In the early seventies Acconci moved from still photography to video, a relatively new medium at the time, producing squirmingly intimate works in which he sometimes addresses the viewer directly and invites the viewer into his (virtual) space. Among the activities he performed were pulling the hairs from around his stomach (*Openings*, 1970), biting himself in all the places he could reach with his teeth (*Trademarks*, 1970), and burning the hairs on his chest to more resemble a woman (*Conversions*, 1971). In 1973's *Undertone* he invites us to share his fantasy that a woman is rubbing his legs while he sits at a table and talks to the camera. In these pieces the camera takes a new position: that of a voyeuristic viewer, not the artist. Acconci seems to be trying to make us the subjects of his attention, as our attention is mesmerized by his bizarre self-wounding and provocative come-ons.

While Acconci's art was beyond the ken of much of the art audience of the day—and probably beyond the pale for many—he was as inspiring to young artists as Schneemann. A new generation, mostly born in the forties and mostly women influenced by the rising tide of feminist consciousness, began to confront the viewer with their bodies. Sometimes this was an outgrowth of their more traditional involvement with painting and sculpture—many were classified as Postminimalist in revolt against an all-male Minimalism—and sometimes it was a reflection of the direct influence of public/private performances like Acconci's.

Adrian Piper seems to have developed a similar form of confrontational performance art independent of Acconci, using herself as the center of her work as an outcome of her roots in Conceptual Art. She also upped the ante of the critique of the power of representation by adding the issue of race: she is at once a woman artist and an African American one. In her 1968–70 *Hypothesis* series, Piper used photos, texts, and graphs to record her daily activities and spatial locations, using standard Conceptual tools presumably to confirm her identity in the physical world. For her contribution to the *Information* show at MoMA in 1970, she invited visitors to write down their thoughts and reactions in real time; the result was seven binders filled with comments ranging from reflective to profane.

The same year, for a groundbreaking piece called *Catalysis IV*, Piper rode buses and subways in New York with a white towel stuffed in her mouth; the photographs taken of her show most of her fellow passengers doing their best not to notice. One of her next pieces, *Food for the Spirit* (1971), was entirely photographic, consisting of fourteen black-and-white prints, printed so darkly that their subject, the artist in various stages of dress and undress, can barely be deciphered.

And in 1973 Piper put herself further into the public realm, albeit in disguise, in a series of performances called *Mythic Being*. The Mythic Being in Piper's case appears as a hyperstylized man, wearing an Afro wig, a mustache, and sunglasses, and acting out male behaviors. Photography and film were used to record the Mythic Being's encounters with her unsuspecting

Adrian Piper, *Catalysis IV*, 1970. Performance documentation. Detail: photograph #2 of 5. Collection of the Generali Foundation, Vienna. Permanent Loan to the Museum der Moderne Salzburg.

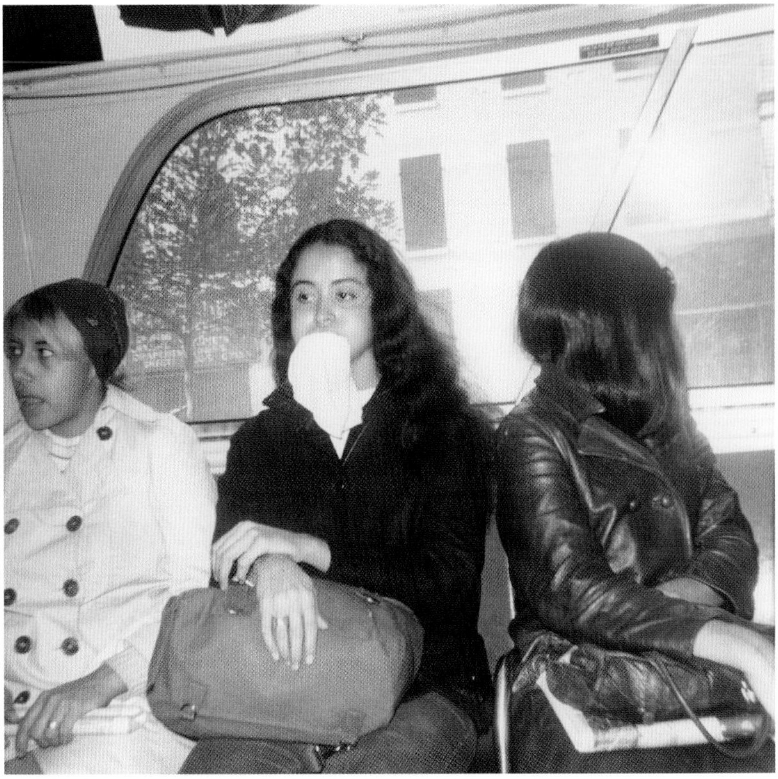

audience, which responds to the ambiguous signals being sent about the Being's gender and racial essence. (Piper, being of mixed race and light skinned, often seems to have situated herself in the middle of the black/white social divide.)[6]

A Conceptual contemporary of Acconci's and Piper's, Eleanor Antin performed more playfully transgressive actions. Antin was living in San Diego, where her husband was teaching at the state university, when she conceived the idea of *100 Boots*, a series of some fifty photo postcards purporting to show the boots of her title walking across the country and ending up in New York. Antin's conceit was part whimsy and part an effort to make art outside the gallery system, similar to what Performance and Earth artists had been doing; as the Museum of Modern Art's press release in 1973 put it, "Antin conceived of *100 Boots* as a means of circumventing some of the spatial and temporal limits imposed on an artist whose work is shown in a gallery situation."[7]

Antin did not disdain the museum situation, however, since MoMA was the ultimate destination of the boots, which appeared in the show *Projects: 100 Boots by Eleanor Antin*. The museum collected the postcards, which Antin had been mailing to its curators since 1971, and showed them together with an installation that featured the boots "resting" in a gallery

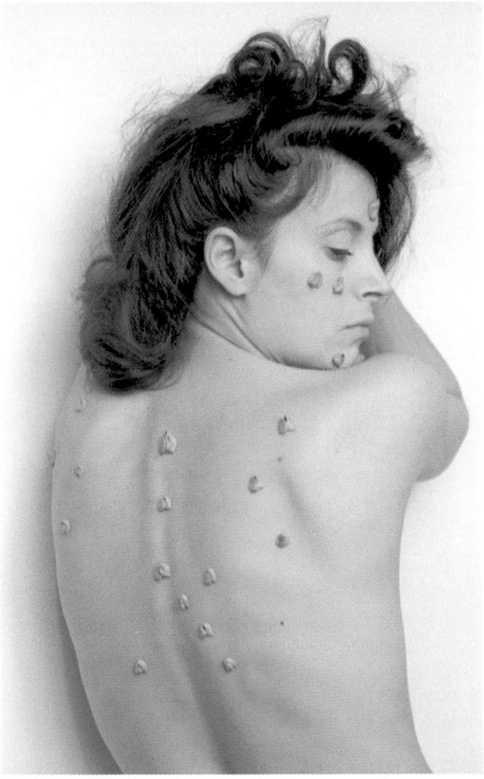

Hannah Wilke, *S.O.S. Starification Object Series* (Back), 1974.

outfitted with mattresses and sleeping bags. Unlike Ruscha and other artists who favored the "deskilled" photography look, Antin hired the photographer Phil Steinmetz to record the boots' traveling exploits.

Antin's subsequent performative career similarly depended on photography and video. When she started *100 Boots* she was also in the process of adopting the persona of a prima ballerina, whose awkward attempts to duplicate the moves of a real ballerina were videotaped and photographed for a 1973 piece called *Caught in the Act.* (The photographers helping her this time were Fred Lonidier and Allan Sekula, then students, who would go on to make their own reputations as left-leaning, labor-oriented art photographers and, in Sekula's case, a much wider reputation as a critic.) She later elaborated on her ballet-dancer persona to become Eleanora Antinova, a fictional African American figure who once danced with Sergei Diaghilev's Ballets Russes but had since fallen on hard times. Like Piper, if more problematically, Antin introduced race into her conversation about feminism.

Hannah Wilke was another powerful feminist artist of the seventies to follow in Schneemann's wake, making what she called "performalist self-portraits" to challenge how women were seen. A sculptor and ceramicist throughout her life, Wilke ventured into performance, photography, and film during her career. In her *S.O.S. Starification Object Series,* begun

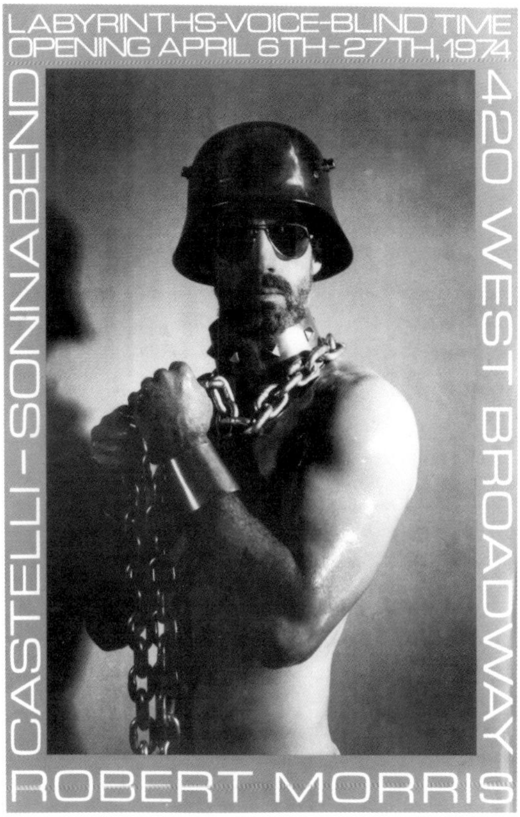

Advertisement in the April 1974 issue of *Artforum* for Robert Morris's concurrent exhibitions at Castelli and Sonnabend galleries.

in 1974, photographs show the young artist's nude body in conventionally glamorous poses, but any atavistic pleasure one might take from this is redirected by the presence of small chewing-gum sculptures stuck to her flesh, each fashioned in the shape of female labia. Again, feminists were divided over whether the display of flesh was encouraging a male gaze and objectifying the woman or conversely interrupting that reading by its "blemishes" of gum. Later, when Wilke was ill with cancer in the eighties and early nineties, she again photographed herself, this time as a resolute but clearly diminished figure, again complicating any conventional aesthetic enjoyment of her image.

Wilke's *S.O.S. Starification Object Series* coincided with a famous dust-up at *Artforum* magazine—then, as now, a leading journal for contemporary art in the United States—sparked by another feminist-inspired artist, Lynda Benglis. Benglis, a Postminimalist sculptor whose best-known works consist of poured latex, reacted to a poster and advertisement in the April 1974 issue of *Artforum* for a Robert Morris exhibition, in which an image of the much-admired but highly contentious artist was used in lieu of a more conventional picture of his artwork. Even more startling, Morris appeared dressed as an S&M figure, naked from the waist up, his skin oiled, wearing

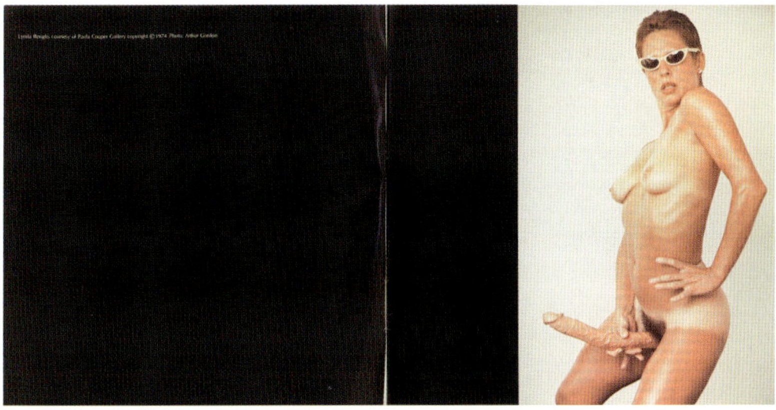

Lynda Benglis advertisement in the November 1974 issue of *Artforum*.

an army helmet and metal cuffs and a collar joined by a heavy chain. The photograph promoted his simultaneous April shows at Castelli and Sonnabend galleries in Soho.

Benglis's provocative response appeared several months later, in the November issue of the magazine, and featured a high-production photograph of the artist, naked above and below the waist and with her skin oiled and tanned, staring directly at the camera through a pair of sunglasses and holding a double-length dildo between her thighs. The photographer, Arthur Gordon, was credited on the black, left-hand side of the two-page ad.

I had recently subscribed to *Artforum*, and I remember wondering why such a seemingly pornographic image would appear in an art magazine and why any artist would want to expose herself in such a sexually frank fashion. Little did I know. My puzzlement was mild compared to the tsunami of indignation that followed in the art press, most prominently from *Artforum*'s own editors and critics, who set upon the magazine's editor-in-chief, John Coplans, for allowing such an ad to run. No complaint was ever uttered, apparently, when the Morris photograph appeared; the person who took that uncredited photograph, the critic Rosalind Krauss, was one of the writers who left the magazine in protest over the Benglis image.[8]

The incident had several unintended consequences. Krauss, along with the film critic and fellow *Artforum* contributor Annette Michelson, then founded the quarterly critical journal *October*, which became an important and influential theoretical sounding board for Postmodernist art in the early eighties. Coplans, who had been instrumental in founding *Artforum* on the West Coast in 1962, left it for good in 1978 and became a photographer himself, ironically enough specializing in nude self-portraits that examine his aging body (although none resemble the Benglis-style glamour photography in the slightest). And I, already a magazine junkie, had the realization that art, photography, and magazine reproductions were territories that overlapped in more ways than I could previously have imagined. I would find myself thinking and writing about this conjunction often in the eighties.

The influence of feminism on contemporary art, and of women artists who positioned their work against the prevailing, mostly male canon of what contemporary art was, remained in play throughout the seventies. Feminist artists in 1972 established their own cooperative gallery, A.I.R. Gallery, a space on Wooster Street in Soho that was somewhat off the beaten path literally and figuratively. Shorthand for "Artist in Residence," a Soho loft denomination, A.I.R. was founded by Dotty Attie, Agnes Denes, Howardena Pindell, Nancy Spero, and sixteen other women artists. It supported and promoted the careers of its original members and of many other women who joined later, none more important or influential than Ana Mendieta.

Mendieta joined A.I.R. in 1978, the year she arrived in New York. She was by then an already recognized figure in the growing feminist art movement; her work had been reproduced in early issues of *Heresies*, a well-regarded journal of women's art and feminist issues, and she had screened her films at 112 Greene Street in 1976. Even though she had been living in Iowa since her teenage years, her artwork was much discussed because of its centrality in arguments about representing the female body—and, in the case of Mendieta, who was born and partly raised in Cuba, its added cultural implications.

Like Gordon Matta-Clark, Mendieta was a catalyzing figure in the new phase of contemporary art that was emerging in the seventies. She made the first of her influential art early in the decade while she was a student at the University of Iowa, at a time when Matta-Clark was front and center in Soho.[9] Most of that art took the form of photographs and films, but whether these constitute the work or merely preserve its ephemeral, performative existence—or both—is an open question. As Judith Wilson neatly observed in a profile of Mendieta in the *Village Voice* in 1980, "For me, the confusion of documentation, art object, and art act that Mendieta's work provokes is one of its most compelling features."[10] Wilson goes on to say that Mendieta's work addresses "both the problems of art's definition and the problems of sexual, cultural, and ecological identity."

At Iowa Mendieta was the star student of Hans Breder, a German artist with New York connections who had started an MFA program in "intermedia." The two became lovers and partners, and along with others Breder helped make the photographs that document her graduate-student and postgrad actions and performances. Breder's frame of reference included Vito Acconci, Chris Burden, Bruce Nauman, and Carolee Schneemann, whose performative work emphasized their physical presence as essential to its meaning. Art and the artist were inextricably interconnected in Breder's aesthetic, even if the audience saw only an artifact of the performance itself.

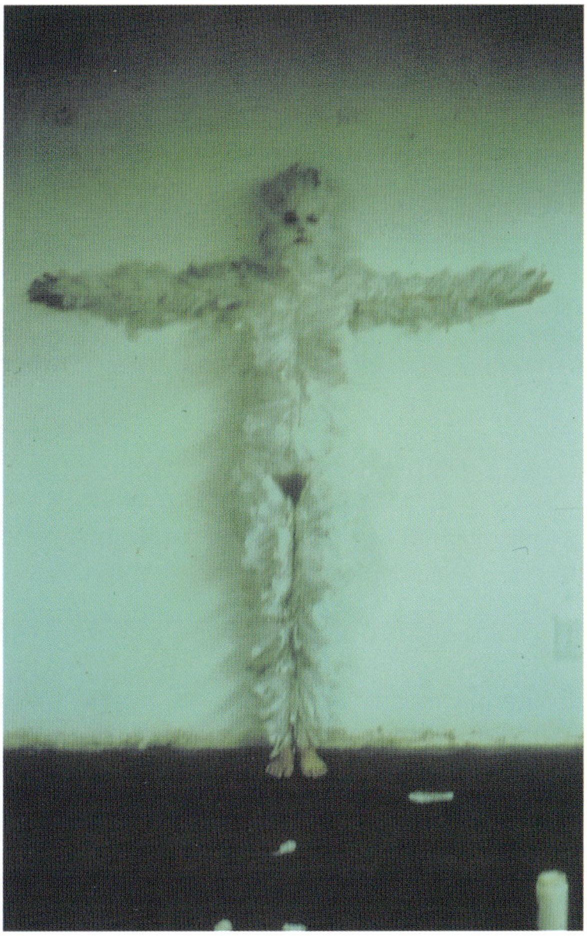

Ana Mendieta, *Bird Transformation*, 1972.

Acconci was perhaps an equally defining influence, coming to Iowa as a visiting artist twice during Mendieta's years there, which also included visits by Hans Haacke, Willoughby Sharp, and Robert Wilson. So was Robert Smithson and Earth Art as a whole, although Smithson's untimely death in a plane crash in 1973 meant that his influence was indirect. And while Mendieta adopted much of Acconci's performative approach, if less confrontationally, Earth Art was more of a foil; Mendieta saw it as a movement in which male artists asserted their dominion over nature. She saw herself as intimately a part of nature.

Mendieta's earliest work at Iowa consisted of performances done for the camera, both 35mm stills and Super 8 films, in which she usually appears nude and in natural settings. But her real breakthrough came in 1973, when her performances acquired an emotional urgency. A rape and murder on campus led Mendieta to invite her class to her apartment, where they found her stretched out on a table, bound and naked from the waist down, with blood running down her legs. A color photograph became the memento mori of this action (*Rape Scene*), joined shortly thereafter by a photograph taken at a similar staged event of the artist's prone and half-naked body in a woods (*Rape*). Blood—conventionally a symbol of essential femaleness and fertility, as well as of violence directed against women—reappears in her subsequent work, and figures in early examples of her extended *Silueta* series, photographs in which the artist's physical presence is marked by an imprint—real or "drawn" in the earth—of her body. In addition to blood, Mendieta's materials included feathers, fireworks, smoke, water, stones, earth, and trees. The *Silueta* series of photographs was shown in nascent form at a university gallery in Iowa in 1977 and again in 1979 at A.I.R. in New York, where the show was favorably reviewed in *Arts Magazine* and *Art in America*. In the fall of 1980 Mendieta gained still more critical attention for being an organizer of a group show at A.I.R. titled *Dialectics of Isolation: An Exhibition of Third World Women Artists of the United States*, and a year later she had another one-person show at the gallery, of black-and-white photographs made during her first return to Cuba a year earlier, showing carvings she made in sandstone that she called *Esculturas Rupestres*, or *Rupestrian Sculptures*. (*Rupestrian* means "carved from stone.")

Both *Dialectics of Isolation* and the *Rupestrian Sculptures* signaled Mendieta's growing consciousness of her cultural inheritance and consequently of her cultural difference from the mainstream of feminism. In her statement for the *Dialectics* catalog she wrote:

> During the mid to late sixties as women in the United States politicized themselves and came together in the Feminist Movement with the purpose to end the domination and exploitation by the white male culture, they failed to remember us. American Feminism as it stands is basically a white middle class movement.[11]

Mendieta, recognizing herself as a "woman of color" within the feminist movement, used her fascination with magic and talismanic symbolism in ways that over time became more culturally specific and less "essentialist." A 1978 issue of *Heresies* that included her work had been organized around the theme of "The Great Goddess," prompting Mendieta to point out that she was referencing specific goddesses in her work, not any overriding "Great" one. The *Rupestrian Sculptures* were titled with the names of "goddesses from the Taino Culture indigenous to the Caribbean," according to the gallery notes for the show.[12] In 1982 the artist resigned from A.I.R., feeling increasingly estranged from its mainstream feminist outlook. She may also have felt that her career had reached a point where it was time to move on. In the next two years she traveled again to Cuba and received a

Prix de Rome from the American Academy in Rome, where she spent a year in a studio residency.

Mendieta's status changed from influential to mythic with her tragic death in 1985, not long after she had married the Minimalist sculptor Carl Andre. The circumstances of how she fell from the high-floor apartment she shared with Andre remain contested in the art world—Andre was tried for her murder, and acquitted—but her bravery in centering her art on her own body and her own cultural origins is not. Even before her death, a generation of women artists raised with a consciousness of feminism, cultural identity, and sex and gender dynamics began to extend Mendieta's example in their own art, often using themselves as stand-ins to represent these issues and also using the camera as a medium for their transmission.

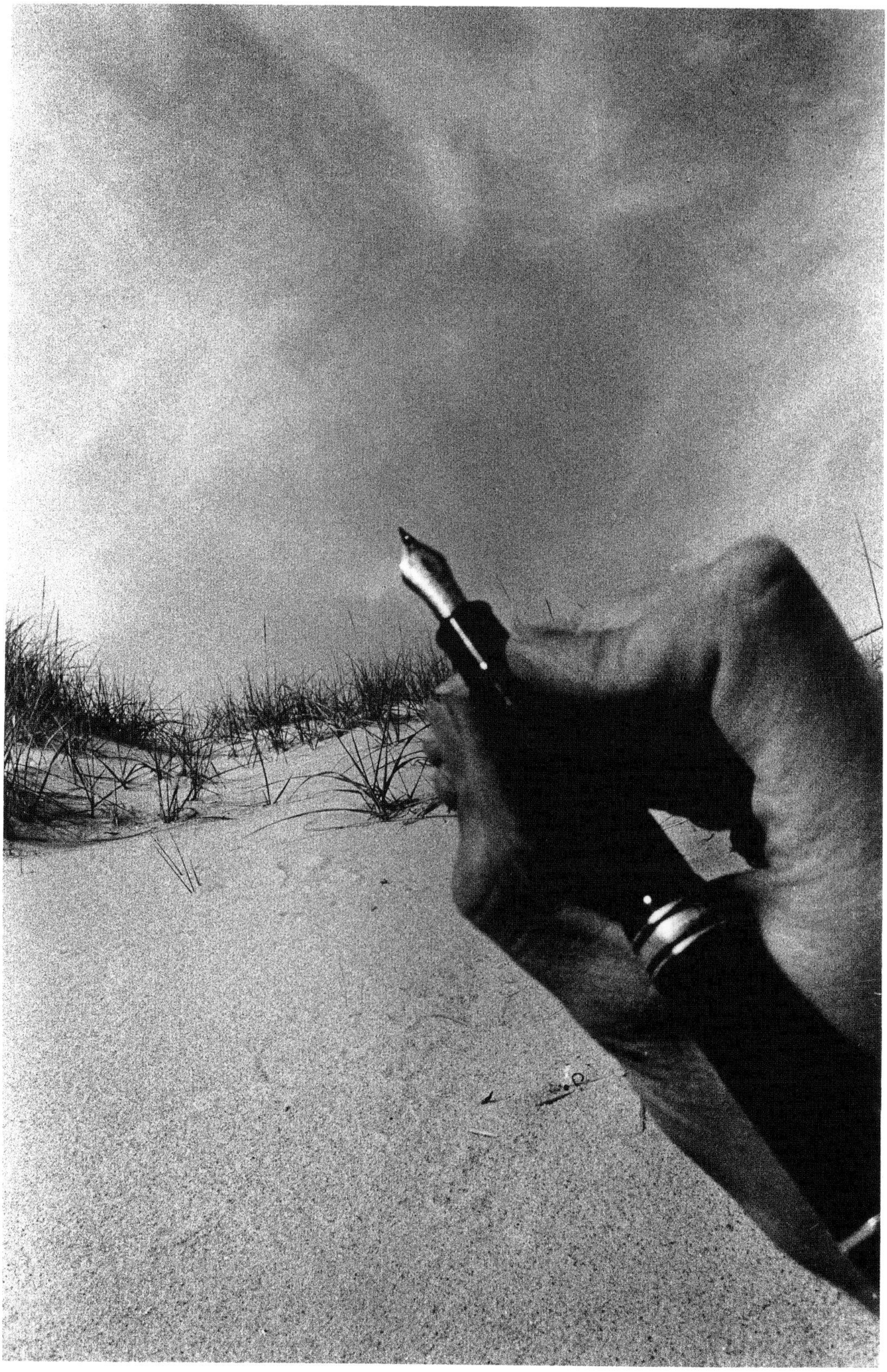

CHAPTER 6

Boom Years

By the midseventies it had become clear that the contemporary art world had given up on the idea that any singular movement or "ism" could embody vanguard art, as Abstract Expressionism and Minimalism seemed to have done in earlier decades. With Conceptual Art having crested, the seventies were pronounced the decade of pluralism, a low-grade "ism" not even warranting a capital letter, that permitted all manner of art to be made and shown, but that didn't really qualify as an aesthetic.[1] In such a world one had to be prepared to experience new and unanticipated forms of art, but no longer with the obligation to trim one's reactions to fit an existing corpus of critical thought. There was a certain kind of freedom in this: aesthetic opinions could flourish in an open marketplace of ideas. A new generation of critics took advantage of the opportunity to launch their careers. And a new generation of artists found new ways to make art.

In 1974 I left my newspaper job in New Jersey to become an editor at *Modern Photography*, a monthly magazine that mostly appealed to the kind of photographers who lusted after the latest professional-grade cameras and sought bragging rights for using the sharpest lenses—so-called serious amateurs. My title was picture editor, and along with the editor, Julia Scully, who hired me, I served another cohort, those who sought to understand what made a photograph good enough to warrant publication or exhibition.

Few magazines at the time were devoted to this task of showing photography as an artistic endeavor. At the high end of the spectrum were *Aperture*, a quarterly edited by Minor White and founded by the likes of Ansel Adams and Beaumont and Nancy Newhall, and my personal favorite, *Camera*. *Camera* was a Swiss magazine edited by an American, Allan Porter, which reproduced photographs using the deluxe gravure printing process. I saw Lee Friedlander's photographs for the first time in a 1968 issue of *Camera*, which moved me to pay for a subscription. Lower down on the ladder were *Modern Photography*, our close competitor and near twin *Popular Photography*, and *Camera 35*, all aimed at the mass market.

A consequential new publication arrived in 1973: Time-Life's *Photography Year* annual. A silver-covered, finely printed hardcover volume,

Ralph Gibson, *Untitled*, no date. From the book *The Somnambulist*, 1970.

it professed to cover the "technological and esthetic accomplishments in photography" of the prior year. On the technological side in 1972 were the introductions of the Polaroid SX-70 and the Kodak Pocket Instamatic. Aesthetically, the news included "Prints for Sale," marked by prices for prints by Alfred Stieglitz and other masters going for "as much as $1,000." Also, places where you could buy them: "Photographic galleries have sprung up everywhere, not only in the art centers of New York, London and Rome, but in scores of other places as well, from Vancouver to Sao Paulo, from Albuquerque to Tokyo."[2]

The *Photography Year: 1973 Edition* editors put the total number of photography galleries at more than eighty, and climbing, although they took pains to point out that the economics of the enterprise remained marginal for most—"The boom in the print market notwithstanding, the gallery business remains risky." Only Lee Witkin, who started his gallery in 1969, was deemed a success at tapping the new photo market, which now also included sales at auction houses. Sotheby's London held the first sale "devoted exclusively to photography" in December 1971; its second, in August 1972, grossed $35,000—"a formidable sum," according to the annual, but a pathetically miniscule one now.[3]

Conspicuously, *Photography Year: 1973 Edition* failed to note a seismic event of 1972: Time-Life's own centerpiece for great photographs, *Life*, ceased publication. A weekly picture magazine born in 1936, *Life*, in its heyday, was a home to both world news and the best in photojournalism, and it usually could be found in small-town barbershops and doctors' offices across the country. For a huge general audience *Life* represented the aspirations of photography to be a force for social good in the world as well as the photograph's ability to rise to the level of art. *Life* perfected a hybrid photo/text form known as the photo essay, and it featured such masters of the method as Margaret Bourke-White, Henri Cartier-Bresson, Alfred Eisenstaedt, and W. Eugene Smith.[4]

But as photojournalists were seeing their market for publication shrink in the seventies, those on the artistic side of the coin were experiencing what came to be called "the photo boom." The medium seemed suddenly to have sprouted anew from roots almost a century and a half old. Certainly this was true aesthetically, in terms of photography's practice, but the sense of renewal also was reflected in the widespread growth of institutions, media interest, and financial support. Besides the rapid rise of commercial galleries devoted to photography—from four to fifteen in New York alone between 1970 and 1974, according to Douglas Davis, who wrote a cover article about the "boom" for *Newsweek* in October 1974[5]—there was the decision of the National Endowment for the Arts (NEA), in 1971, to establish a separate granting division for photography, which allowed photographers to receive fellowships by competing against each other instead of against painters, sculptors, and all other artists applying in the "visual arts" category.

The NEA also treated photography as a special-needs case, much as it did with crafts and jazz. Programs were designed to provide financial support to photography exhibitions undertaken by museums and to promote curatorial and other scholarship and writing about the medium. A separate category of grants, without a counterpart in the other granting areas, funded what were called survey projects, for which groups of photographers undertook to document specific areas of the country, such as Long Island and Los Angeles. (The survey grants were aimed to reflect the nation at the time of the Bicentennial, in 1976.) The NEA's support and imprimatur arguably helped build photography's profile in the art marketplace and in public consciousness at a crucial time, but the agency also held it out as distinct from the rest of the visual arts.

To the existing strong programs in collecting and exhibiting photographs at the Museum of Modern Art in New York, the Art Institute of Chicago, and the San Francisco Museum of Modern Art, the early seventies saw more museums join in with commitments of funds, curatorial positions, and separate photography departments. The Amon Carter Museum of American Art in Fort Worth; the Museum of Fine Arts, Boston; the Corcoran Gallery of Art in Washington, D.C.; the Museum of Fine Arts, Houston; the Philadelphia Museum of Art; and many smaller museums began to make waves with photography, increasing their admissions numbers and their donor bases. A new breed of photography-focused collectors helped support these efforts, as did the widespread popularity of photography exhibitions among the general public. By 1978, Christie's, Sotheby's, and other auction houses were scheduling twice-yearly auctions of photographic prints.[6]

My nascent library of photography literature began to swell at the same time. Book publishers weren't yet plunging into the deep end of photography publishing or competing directly with Aperture, but publishers like McGraw-Hill; Viking; and Holt, Rinehart and Winston did dip toes in the water when they saw a chance for a bigger audience than just photographers. (Celebrity portraiture and photojournalism, as seen in *Life* magazine, often fit that bill.) Small publishers, some newly established, took on more serious and risky titles: Straight Arrow Books (Bill Owens's *Suburbia*, 1973), Morgan and Morgan (Jerry Uelsmann's *Silver Meditations*, 1975), David R. Godine, and Addison House among them. A framing start-up in Rochester, New York, Light Impressions, expanded its business and for a time became a mail-order book distributor of many of the photography titles of smaller, often marginal publishers.

All this was happening during my first years at *Modern Photography*. There I solicited photographs (and reproduction rights) from professional photographers in New York and elsewhere for articles about "creative" uses of depth of field, motion blur, framing, and other aspects of what might be considered the formal elements of photography. I also helped the editor on articles that reproduced portfolios of a single photographer's work. In this capacity I interviewed Ansel Adams and Brett Weston in their homes in California and visited the commercial studios of Ernst Haas and Pete Turner in New York; I also got to know André Kertész, Helen Levitt, W. Eugene Smith, and many other photography "masters" during the course of my job. In retrospect it seems highly glamorous, but at the time I was mainly happy that I was finally earning a stable salary and working in a place with a well-equipped, well-ventilated darkroom I could use after work.

Some of the stories I did were focused on what we considered trends in picture taking. One such feature was going to be about street photography. The quintessential street photographer of the time was Garry Winogrand, famous for his tilted horizons and randomized compositions with multiple centers of interest. (These compositions made him arguably the most outré artist of the influential 1967 MoMA exhibition *New Documents*, which also featured Diane Arbus and Lee Friedlander.) I called Winogrand directly (those were the days) to get permission to reproduce two of his pictures in the story, and he said, gruffly and in no uncertain terms, "That's a dumb idea. I don't photograph streets." "But there *are* streets in your pictures," I insisted, "and in any case everyone thinks you are the genius of the genre. And everyone calls it 'street photography.'" "Why would anyone photograph streets?" he persisted. "There are plenty of sidewalks in my pictures, too, would you call me a 'sidewalk photographer'?"

I didn't win that argument, which in Winogrand's case put me in good company. Nor did I prevail the time I called Richard Avedon's studio to ask if we could reproduce *Dovima with Elephants*, his classic Paris fashion photograph, in an article about fashion photography as an art form. (My fascination with Guy Bourdin, Helmut Newton, and Deborah Turbeville was the spark behind this idea.) His studio manager said she'd get back to me, and when she did, she said he would agree to participate only if he had a double-page spread to himself, and if two of his pictures were used, neither of them *Dovima*. He got his wish, needless to say.

Over the years I had taught myself to be an average darkroom technician using makeshift quarters in various closets and kitchens, but having a dedicated space with the very best equipment helped me improve my film developing and printing skills. I especially benefitted from the presence of Peter Moore, an editor whose knowledge of darkroom techniques was encyclopedic. He was sympathetic and mentoring toward me, teaching me how to selectively bleach areas of a black-and-white print while telling stories about what the art world was like before I got to town.

Peter arrived at *Modern Photography* four years after I started and had the title of Senior Technical Editor, which belied the fact that he was more interested in pictures than cameras. Or clothes. Always slightly rumpled and sometimes accused of wearing pajama tops instead of dress shirts to the office, Peter had been a professional photographer, starting his career as an assistant to O. Winston Link. Link became famous for photographing steam trains, but Peter's main interest was documenting the downtown art scene in the sixties, when performances were radically new.

It turned out that he had seen and photographed dozens of Fluxus events in the sixties, featuring the likes of Yoko Ono, Nam June Paik, and Charlotte ("The Topless Cellist") Moorman. He also documented most of the performances of avant-garde dance at the Judson Dance Theater, including Trisha Brown's troupe dancing down the side of a building while suspended by ropes. These were all new to me at the time. He also attended and photographed some of the key performances of Carolee Schneemann. His work and his archive are invaluable, since in many cases his pictures are the only record of these important events; only recently has this realization garnered Moore a posthumous reputation.[7]

Modern Photography, which was owned by Billboard Publications when I started but soon thereafter was bought by ABC, apparently was making a ton of money and was fairly permissive about how editors spent it. Working hours were somewhat discretionary. This meant martini lunches for some, but for me it was an opportunity to travel around town to meet photographers and, best of all, to go see shows that seemed important. Some were close at hand. Witkin would show overlooked but important photographers and often brought them to the gallery for its opening parties, which is how I first met (or at least laid eyes on) Berenice Abbott, Manuel Álvarez Bravo, Margaret Bourke-White, Brassaï, Imogen Cunningham, Judy Dater and Jack Welpott, Roy DeCarava, Russell Lee, Joel Meyerowitz, George Tice, Roman Vishniac, and other stars of the then-firmament of art photography.

When Lee Witkin first opened his gallery in 1969 it was on East 60th Street off Second Avenue, near the entrances to the Queensboro Bridge (and the future passenger tramway to Roosevelt Island), a two-room walk-up that looked more like an antiquarian bookstore than the typical white-cube gallery of today.[8] For a while in the midseventies the *Modern Photography* offices were only a few blocks away, so I could walk over at lunchtime or, when there was an opening, after work. I was a fly on the wall most of the time, but I vividly remember a Les Krims opening in the spring of 1972 at which I saw Les and his celebrated mother, who were there for the release of Krims's *Making Chicken Soup*, a visual book that depicted Mrs. Krims, wearing panties but otherwise nude, in her kitchen preparing the title dish—a perverse, avowedly Jewish version of Julia Child. If I remember correctly,

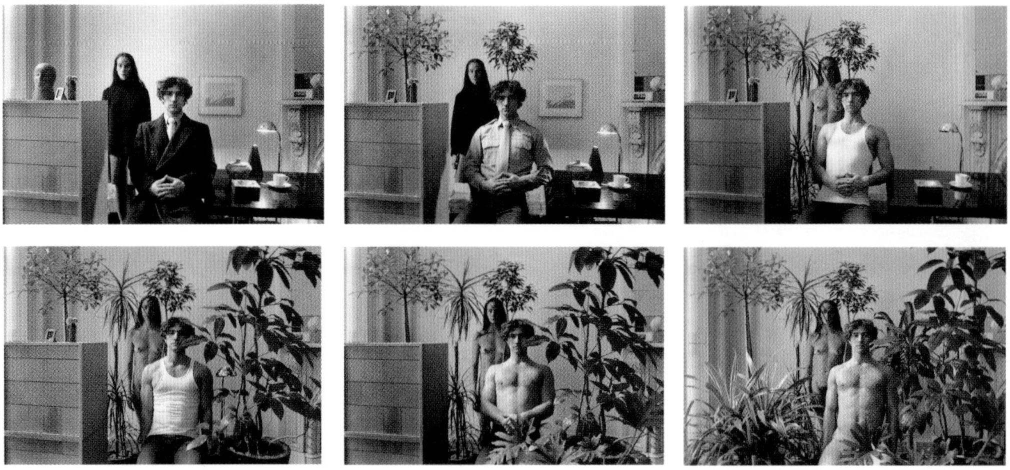

Duane Michals, *Paradise Regained*, 1968.

she had all her clothes on for the opening, although chicken soup she had made was being served.

Krims was a superstar of new photography at the time, producing comic, improbable tableaux that seemed surrealist in spirit and irreverent toward the high aspirations of serious art photography as represented at Witkin by Adams, Cunningham, and Weston, from an earlier generation, and Dater, Meyerowitz, and Tice, from Krims's own. His taste in subject matter tended toward dwarfs and naked young women, and he added further salt to the wounds of serious photography by assembling his pictures into boxed sets of postcards, which he sold under the imprint of Humpy Press.

Krims became associated with two other artists who were violating the medium's standard documentary codes: Duane Michals, whose multi-image narratives, which he called "sequences," were sly and humorous send-ups of photographic veracity, and Ralph Gibson, whose books *The Somnambulist* (1970) and *Deja-Vu* (1973) created a similarly nonliteral, imaginative space for the viewer by sequencing mysterious photographs that were, on the face of it, unrelated. Michals, who was one of the five photographers in Witkin's first show, began showing his sequences at Light Gallery soon after it opened in 1971, and Gibson became part of the prestigious stable of artists at Castelli Graphics, which added photography to its print sales in the early seventies.

All three were indebted, consciously or not, to the recent example of Jerry Uelsmann, who had been trained in the tradition of Stieglitz and Minor White but rebelled by perfecting a way of printing from several negatives to produce one seamless, seemingly "straight" black-and-white image. Uelsmann's *Equivalent* (1964) is typical, showing a man's clenched fist in the foreground with a similarly lit and posed female nude figure in the back-

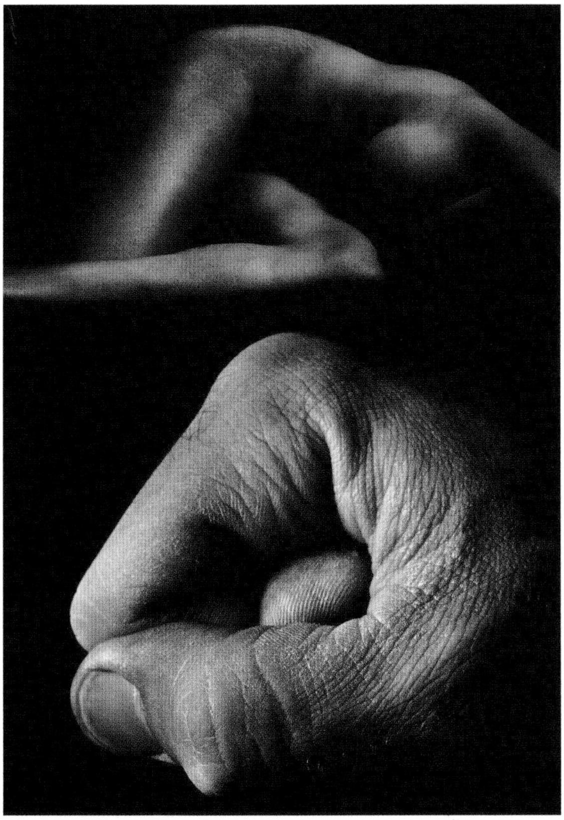

Jerry Uelsmann, *Equivalent*, 1964.

ground—a bald joke on Stieglitz's and White's belief that an artistic photograph represents not just its putative subject but also a kind of allegorical or emotional counterpart. Other Uelsmann images from the sixties are landscapes, often modeled on René Magritte paintings, in which rocks float in the sky or trees grow upside down. Uelsmann had the next exhibition at Witkin after Krims's chicken-soup show.

Light Gallery, started in 1971 by Tennyson Schad, an intellectual-property lawyer, in concert with his wife, Fern, who had been a picture editor for *Life*, was another beacon of the new interest in photography and one that was formative in my experience. I can't remember exactly when I first visited its space at 1018 Madison Avenue in the upper 70s; possibly it was during Stephen Shore's now-legendary 1972 show of Americana-themed snapshots he had taken, *American Surfaces*, a precursor to his more famous *Uncommon Places* series of color 8 × 10-inch view-camera pictures.[9] But I can vividly recall seeing other shows there during the midseventies, including Mark Cohen's idiosyncratic pictures of Wilkes-Barre, Pennsylvania, in a 1974 show (during which the gallery also displayed a selection of Man Ray prints), and Garry Winogrand's show in March 1975, for which his prints were hung in tight rows that went from the ceiling practically to the floor.

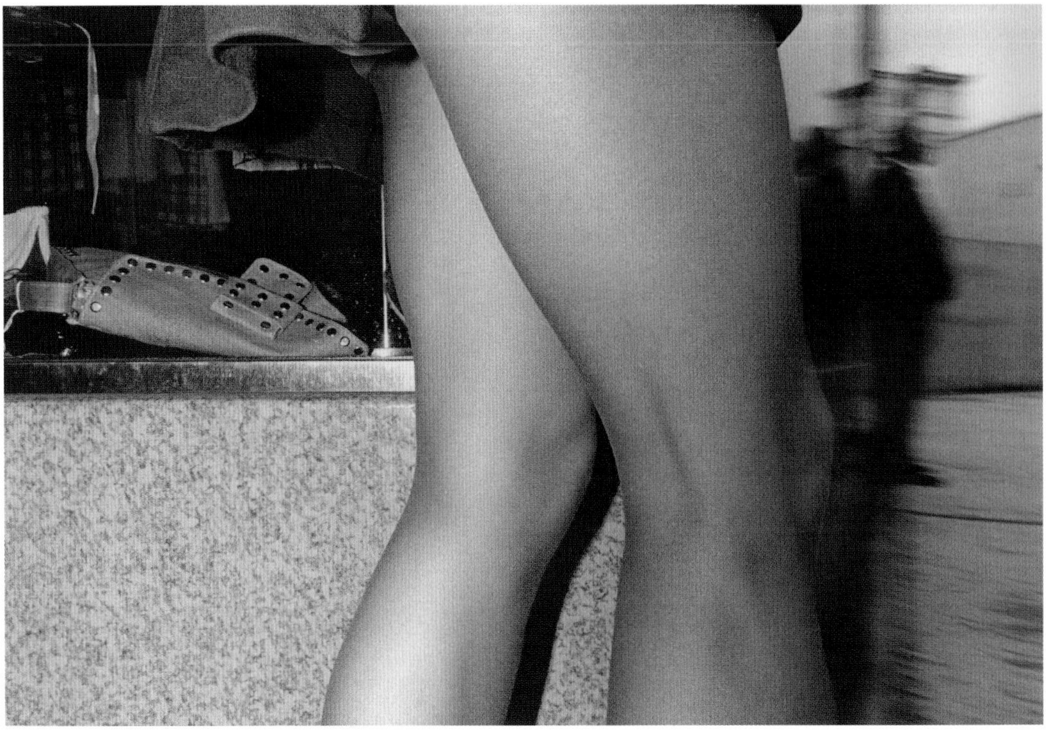

Mark Cohen, *Bare Legs by Store*, 1974.

Light's director then, and the genius behind its breakthrough success, was Harold Jones. Jones was a graduate of Van Deren Coke's influential graduate program in photography and art history at the University of New Mexico and had been working as a curator at the George Eastman House when Schad selected him to run his new gallery.[10] The young and unexperienced gallery director hired an estimable crew of assistants to deal with inquisitive and puzzled folks like me; in the early seventies these included Marvin Heiferman, Sally Stein, Diana Edkins, and Irene Borger.[11] Peter MacGill, who would later direct the gallery, was a summer intern there in 1973, while he was a photography grad student at the University of Arizona.

The contemporary photo world was small enough then that those of us who evinced enthusiasm for new and challenging work developed long-lasting bonds. It was also largely uncredentialed: no one particularly needed a degree in art history or even in photography to take part. Harold Jones thought of himself mainly as a photographer. Irene Borger had studied dance. Jones hired Heiferman, who had dropped out of Columbia's film school to become a painter, after observing him spending hours in the gallery over the course of several days, looking hard at the pictures on view.[12]

MacGill, along with Light employees Laurence Miller and Robert Mann, would later flourish as photography dealers with their own galleries. Edkins went on to MoMA and later the photo archives of Condé Nast. Stein became a photography art historian at the University of California, Irvine. Heiferman ran the photography department of Castelli Graphics, helped put Nan Goldin on the map, and edited and produced innovative photo books in partnership with Carole Kismaric. Jones was not at Light that long—he left in 1975 to become the founding director of the Center for Creative Photography at the University of Arizona in Tucson, and later a professor in the university's art department—but his few years in New York had an amazing resonance.

Light's roster of photographers was impressive from the start, including some established older figures such as Kertész, Arnold Newman, Paul Strand, Frederick Sommer, and most significantly Harry Callahan and Aaron Siskind.[13] Callahan and Siskind became the mainstays of the Light stable just as they were ending their long teaching careers, which started at the Institute of Design in Chicago and, after some years apart, ended back together at the Rhode Island School of Design. Many of their former students came to show at Light as well: Thomas Barrow, Linda Connor, Eileen Cowin, Emmet Gowin, William Larson, Ray Metzker, and Keith Smith. I soon came to realize that they were part of a generation of former Callahan/Siskind photography students who had gone on to careers not only as photographers but also as photography teachers, filling scores of recently created faculty positions at colleges and universities around the country.

All of this nontraditional, sometimes out-there activity was not what Schad, the owner, had expected Light Gallery to promote, but to his credit he let Jones run with the ball he had been handed. According to Heiferman, what fueled the gallery was enthusiasm more than money; sales were few and far between for long stretches. One saving grace was the National Endowment for the Arts' program of support for museum photo programs, which accounted for many of the purchases. And there was serendipity: Alger Hiss came in one day, Heiferman remembers, and bought an entire Stephen Shore color show, presumably because Hiss's son, Tony, was a childhood friend of Shore's.

I bought a work of art for one of the first times in my life from Laurence Miller, who started working at Light in 1974. The image was Kertész's well-known image *Satiric Dancer* (1926), for which I paid the then-princely sum of $300. Kertész relied on a custom printer to make all his prints, as did Henri Cartier-Bresson and many other photographers of that era, but the results were not always uniform. Miller showed me three newly minted copies of the image, each slightly darker or lighter than the other, and let me pick my favorite—this seemed odd even at the time. I became more sophisticated about print values and artistic intention later, as did Miller and Light, but I didn't become a collector. For financial reasons I mostly was content to look at work on the walls. Later, when I became a reviewer, I decided that collecting would be a conflict of interest.

At the same time that I was making monthly visits uptown to Light, Witkin, and a handful of other first-wave photo galleries—Neikrug, in the parlor of Marjorie Neikrug's Upper East Side brownstone; Prakapas and Robert Schoelkopf, in commercial space on or near Madison Avenue not far from Light—I was also frequently heading downtown to keep tabs on the contemporary art and poetry scene. Other than the Wednesday night readings at St. Mark's Church in-the-Bowery, downtown for me meant Soho. Mostly I trolled for shows that included photographs, since that would put them in the category of research for my job, but in the process I was exposed to plenty of activity in other media and in aesthetic realms beyond the purely visual.

Castelli and Sonnabend were the big-gun galleries at 420 West Broadway; both opened in 1971 with vast, full-floor spaces to house the era's increasingly large art, Sonnabend's floor being just above Castelli's. (Leo Castelli and Ileana Sonnabend had been married but were divorced in 1959, so their proximity was a tangible sign of their reconciliation.) The original plan for the building was for four galleries, with André Emmerich and Virginia Dwan filling out the roster, but when Dwan bailed, her New York gallery director leased the ground floor and started the John Weber Gallery.[14] Weber later moved, and Emmerich left Soho and consolidated back to 57th Street; I remember the top floor of "420" as housing 49th Parallel, a gallery sponsored by the Canadian government, and the ground floor as a succession of mostly undistinguished painting galleries.

Just a block further south, at 392 West Broadway, was a building with Holly Solomon Gallery on the ground floor (it opened in 1975); an elevator in the same building took me up to the John Gibson Gallery, which was known as the headquarters of "story art," a kind of narrative impulse that used plenty of pictures and words. Gibson's shows featured artists like Mac Adams, Bill Beckley, Peter Hutchinson, and Jean Le Gac, all of whom made photographs the centerpiece of their work. One of the artists I had befriended at 98 Greene Street Loft, Roger Welch, showed at John Gibson as well; he did a memorable piece about a seven-year-old boy who survived an accidental trip over Niagara Falls, using photographs and videos from his interview with the lucky guy (*Roger Woodward—Niagara Falls Project*, 1975).

Across West Broadway from Solomon and Gibson was OK Harris, another one of the pioneering galleries in the neighborhood. It was run by Ivan Karp, who had been part of the scene in Los Angeles and then worked for Leo Castelli when his gallery was uptown on East 77th Street. On his own, Karp promoted Photorealist painters and also made a point to encourage up-and-coming artists of all stripes, and he fashioned one of the massive gallery's several rooms into a place for photographs. Unfortunately, with few exceptions, the talents he identified this way did not strike me as particularly distinguished or groundbreaking, although some went on to make their reputations elsewhere. I forced myself to go into the gallery for most of the seventies, hoping for a discovery, but eventually gave up.

Of all the early Soho galleries, Leo Castelli's was the most talked about and became the most legendary, as his stable of artists achieved blue-chip status. Leo had started uptown in the late fifties with Jasper Johns, Robert Rauschenberg, Frank Stella, and Cy Twombly, and in the sixties he added important Pop artists, including Roy Lichtenstein, James Rosenquist, and Andy Warhol. Downtown his focus shifted to Conceptual artists, including Joseph Kosuth and Lawrence Weiner; Minimalists such as Dan Flavin and Donald Judd; and Postminimalists like Robert Morris. In terms of artists whose work included photographs, he showed Jan Dibbets, Douglas Huebler, Bruce Nauman, and Edward Ruscha.[15] He was also a supporter of the photographer Lewis Baltz, showing his early pictures at the uptown gallery in December 1971 and the *New Industrial Parks near Irvine, California* series in Soho at the end of 1975.

Castelli also plunged headfirst into video art, starting with group video exhibitions in 1973 and 1974 and following that with an influential sequence of two-artist video shows in 1975 with Peter Campus/Paul Kos, Joan Jonas/Charlemagne Palestine, and Frank Gillette/William Wegman.[16] At the same time he, together with his ex-wife, established Castelli-Sonnabend Videotapes and Films, a separate entity dedicated to distributing artists' films and videos—probably the world's first video rental business, long before Blockbuster—and serving mostly universities and art schools.

In terms of impact on photography's artistic status, however, the gallery that most made its mark is Sonnabend. Ileana had started her gallery business in 1960 in Paris, partnering with her second husband, Michael Sonnabend, and mostly showed American Pop artists who were represented by Castelli. The move to Soho meant that she had to develop her own stable of artists, and consequently her own taste. That taste increasingly favored artists who used photographs and photography itself. This may have confused the collectors she had nurtured to love Pop Art, but it opened the door for a new generation of artists that enlarged the possibilities for both art and photography.[17]

Sonnabend's ventures into the photo-based Conceptual and Postminimalist Art of the early seventies were her own idea, but she had a savvy assistant and collaborator in Ealan Wingate, her gallery director. Wingate had been a college student at Case Western Reserve University in Cleveland when he stumbled into a job nearby at a gallery started by Nina Sundell, Leo and Ileana's daughter. This led to his meeting Ileana, not long returned from Paris, and after that her invitation for him to come to New York to help open her planned Soho space. (Antonio Homem, who later directed the gallery, and who became the adopted son of the Sonnabends in the eighties, was running the Paris gallery at the time.) From 1970 to 1977 the Sonnabends and Wingate embarked on an agenda of supporting the most radical figures of the radical avant-garde.

The gallery at 420 West Broadway opened in September 1971 with a show of Gilbert and George, British artists (sculptors, nominally) whose work on the walls consisted of a series of twenty-three large drawings titled *The General Jungle or Carrying on Sculpting*. But the centerpiece created a sensation: the two artists, dressed as English gentlemen, stood on a platform in the center of the room and sang along with a recording of a prototypically British music-hall tune. This performance, *Singing Sculpture*, was the first of many that Sonnabend hosted, the most notorious of which, Vito Acconci's *Seedbed*, took place less than six months later.[18]

These historic events live on because of the photographs taken of them, of course, but Sonnabend understood photography to be something more than documentation. Primarily this came about because of Bernd and Hilla Becher, whose photographs of water towers, mill buildings, and workers' housing Sonnabend began showing in 1972. According to Wingate, the Bechers introduced Sonnabend and him to the work of August Sander and other Neue Sachlichkeit German photographers of the twenties and thirties, presumably with the intention of providing an art-historical frame of reference for their work outside the discourse of present-day Conceptualism. Soon enough Sonnabend began collecting this work and expanding to early twentieth-century American photography as well. Wingate remembers them spending time together going through the bins of photographs displayed at Witkin, occasionally finding gems she would buy.

It may also have helped that Ileana Sonnabend was a lifelong friend of Robert Rauschenberg, who as a student had planned to be a photographer and who had been using photographs as material for his work ever since. In any case, many of the artists the gallery showed included photographs in their work or as their work; John Baldessari, Christian Boltanski, and Dennis Oppenheim, along with the Bechers, were prominent in the gallery's first few years. By the end of the seventies Jan Groover and Boyd Webb had been added to the roster, and Hiroshi Sugimoto had the first of several shows there in 1981. There were also a number of exhibitions devoted to video, with Acconci and Wegman shown regularly. I became a frequent visitor, often trekking up and down 420's side stairs because the elevator was so slow, and I saw my first Bechers' water towers when Sonnabend still showed them in grids within a single frame.

A discovery of lasting significance for me happened around the corner from West Broadway, further down on Spring Street, in the form of a bookstore named Jaap Rietman. Rietman, a mustachioed Dutchman, was a veteran of George Wittenborn's venerated uptown art bookstore and blessed with exquisite taste in books and an historian's sense of what was important in art, architecture, and design. My wife and I would browse the shelves and tables, discovering illustrated books about figures of the twentieth century who were legendary but little known, like Alexandra Exter and Alexey Brodovitch. Exter, a Russian Constructivist, designed amazing costumes for theater and opera; Brodovitch, a Russian ex-pat, designed posters and publicity in Paris before becoming the art director of *Harper's Bazaar* in the United States. We also doted on books about the German Bauhaus, and I discovered for the first time László Moholy-Nagy's Bauhaus chapbook *Painting, Photography, Film*, a manifesto of sorts for the radical importance of photography within all the arts and design.[19]

Moholy-Nagy, I learned, had come to the United States in the late thirties and started a Bauhaus-style school in Chicago, originally called the New Bauhaus School of Design but soon rechristened the Institute of Design. In 1946, shortly before his death, he hired a young Detroit photographer, Harry Callahan, to teach at the school. Callahan later hired Aaron Siskind, who spent twenty years teaching there, until 1971 when he left to join Callahan at the Rhode Island School of Design. I found this linkage between a Bauhaus-era advocate for photography and two of the mainstays of Light Gallery irresistible, and I started research on what would become my second major article for *Art in America*, "Photography: Chicago, Moholy and After," published in the magazine's September/October 1976 issue. (My first article, "Edward Weston Rethought," occasioned by a Weston retrospective at the Museum of Modern Art, appeared in the July/August 1975 issue.) The project took me to Providence, Rhode Island, to interview Callahan and Siskind, and to Philadelphia, where I talked to Ray Metzker, one of their earliest and most illustrious students, who was teaching at the Philadelphia College of Art (now the University of the Arts).

Metzker's work had started out in Callahan's mode, focusing on light and shadow arrayed on pedestrians in urban locales, but his urge to follow his own path led to a series of paired frames of bathers (*Sand Creatures*, 1969), images in which the putative subject is obscured by objects held in front of the lens by the photographer (*Pictus Interruptus*, late seventies), and most radically large gridded images consisting of scores of small details of buildings or nudes (*Composites*, begun in the early sixties). Metzker's constant in

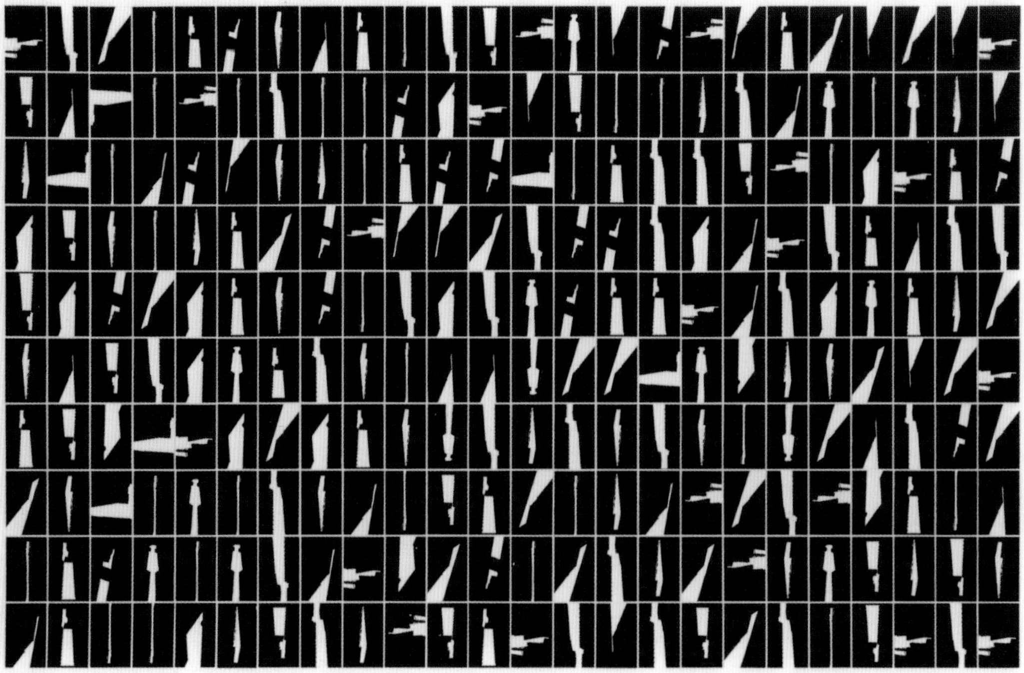

Ray Metzker, *Apertures*, 1965. Two hundred and forty black-and-white prints mounted on board.

all the diverse forms of his series and single pictures is an insistent graphic sensibility, which organizes the scene before the camera into a coherent puzzle of shapes.

Studying at the same time as Metzker at the Institute of Design were two other experimentally inclined photographers, Joseph Jachna and Kenneth Josephson. Jachna's *Door County* series, taken in Wisconsin in 1969 and 1970, consists of scenes reconfigured by a mirror he held in front of the camera, a variation of what Metzker would do later. Josephson's work reflects on photography's own history and practice, creating what could be called ontological puzzles. *Stockholm* (1967) is as simple as an enigma can get: a dark bubble-back Volvo parked on the roadside seems to cast a negative shadow of itself, inverting photography's venerable positive/negative system. The bald fact that the mirror image of the car is not a shadow but the outline of hoarfrost unmelted by the morning sun does little to dissipate its enigmatic aura.

I was, through my research into the legacy of Moholy-Nagy, Callahan, and Siskind, beginning to connect the dots between the sometimes strange and surprising appearance of what Light Gallery was showing and an earlier era when experimental images made with the camera were in vogue, primarily in Europe. This tradition did not quite explain the camera images that were appearing contemporaneously in Conceptual Art and its allied genres, but it demonstrated an historical linkage between the camera and

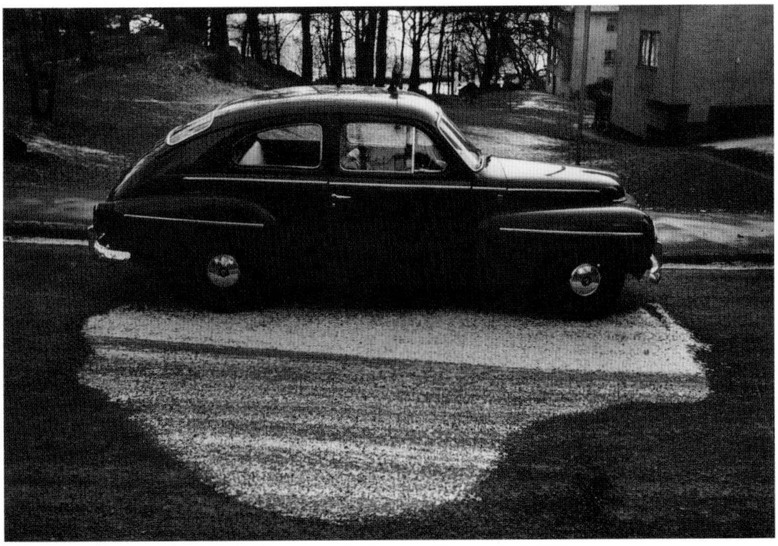

Kenneth Josephson, *Stockholm*, 1967.

the ambitions of a larger art world that seemed to have been erased by a postwar emphasis on abstract painting and sculpture, in the art world, and reportage, in photography. I sensed that photography was again becoming a part of the ambitions of the larger art world, and that my generation was poised to carry this to its completion.

One of the most underappreciated artists to bridge the gap between photography and the other, more traditional mediums of art was Robert Heinecken, an ex-Marine who studied printmaking at UCLA in the fifties, gravitated to photography, and in the early sixties started a photography program at his alma mater. While unconnected to the influence of Moholy-Nagy, his approach to photography was wildly unconventional, ranging from vacuum-formed plastic photograms of TV dinners to collages on canvas of pornographic images purchased through the mail as undeveloped negatives. He proudly maintained that he spent his entire career in photography without owning a camera.

Heinecken's *Are You Rea* series of offset lithographs, published in 1968, is in many ways his most important work, and a harbinger of concerns with mass media that would dominate the discussion of photography in the early eighties. The black-and-white prints consist of magazine-page images in negative that are superimposed to create a visual experience that is both graphic and political; images of idealized women's bodies coexist with advertising products and incongruous text headlines, such as "The Fortunate, Fashionable Rescue" or "The Considerate Console." (The title piece has the fragment "Are You Rea" atop what appears to be a bra advertisement.) Heinecken recontextualizes mass-magazine reproductions in a way that complicates their intended messages.

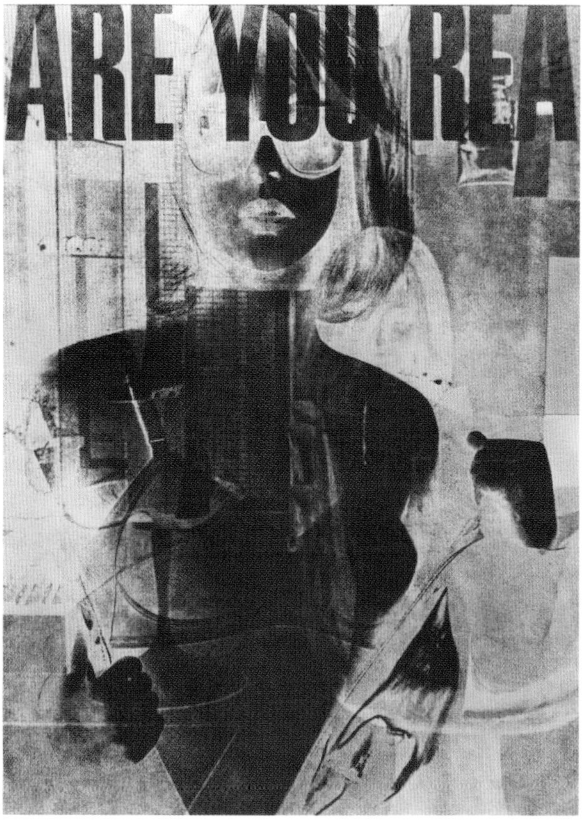

Robert Heinecken, *Are You Rea*, 1964–68. Offset lithograph.

From the midseventies into the eighties Heinecken was central to an efflorescence of nontraditional photography using both arcane, outmoded processes left behind by art photography a half century earlier (gum bichromate, cyanotype, platinum-palladium) and newfangled, freshly minted technologies (fax machines, photocopiers, Polaroid "instant" films). Robert Fichter, Betty Hahn, and Todd Walker exemplified practitioners of the former sort, producing pictures that usually looked more like prints than photographs. Their work, and that of others dissatisfied with the conventional silver gelatin print, gave rise to the term *alternative processes*, which found more traction in academic curricula than in the marketplace. More progressive were artists like William Larson, who used an early version of a fax machine to create collage-like renderings that combined photographs, texts, crumpled paper, and even visual traces of sound on one sheet of paper.

Similarly Thomas Barrow, who, like Larson, had studied at the Institute of Design with Siskind, experimented in the early seventies with a prototype version of a copy machine, called a Verifax, to produce a series of collages under the title *Trivia*.[20] A later Barrow series, *Cancellations*, which I saw at Light Gallery in the midseventies, was more aesthetically disruptive even though it was printed conventionally. Each picture showed a mundane land-

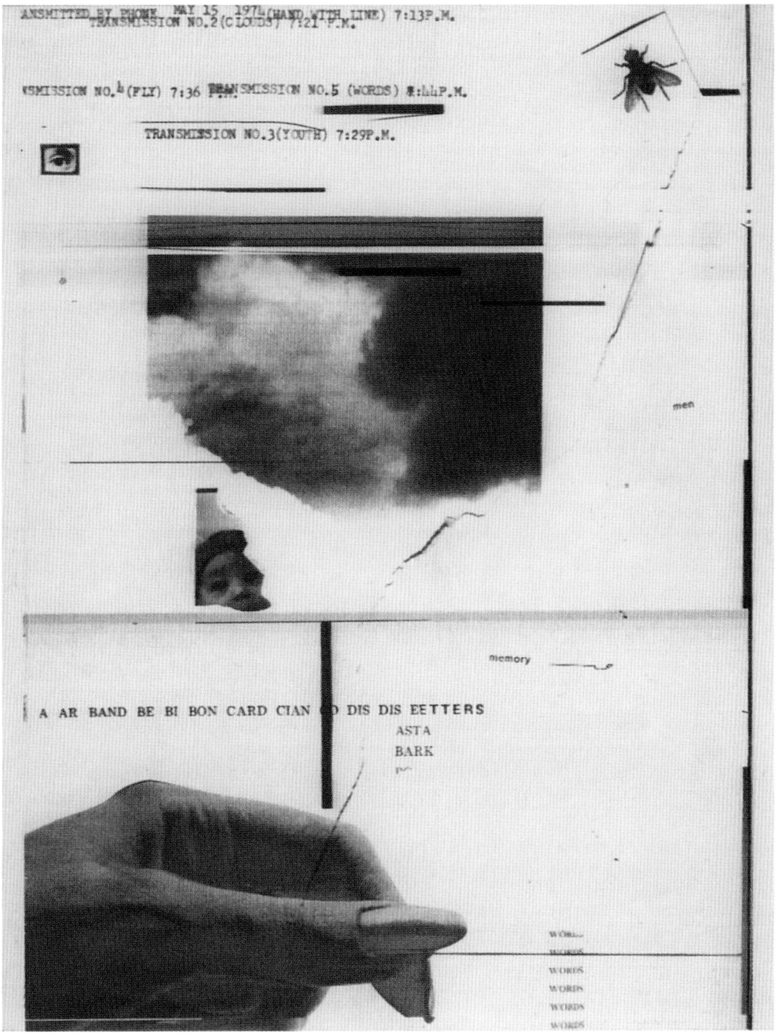

William Larson, *Untitled,* May 15, 1974, from the series *Fireflies*. Electro-carbon print.

scape scene, interrupted by a vivid "X" mark across the entire image surface. Barrow had "canceled" the negatives before printing them by scratching out the silver emulsion, a perverse variation of the printmaking practice of canceling a plate after an edition has been printed. By canceling the image *before* printing it, Barrow suggested a negation of conventional artistic understandings—presumably privileging photography in the process. But he also inverted the conventional photographic practice of ignoring the "outtakes" on a contact sheet in favor of the chosen few that get printed; in *Cancellations,* the losers are defaced but are also the winners.

The enthusiasm for melding photography with copy machine technology increased as the capabilities of copiers advanced. The apogee of the machinery of the day was 3M's Color-in-Color device, which was the first easily available color copier and one that attracted the attention of several

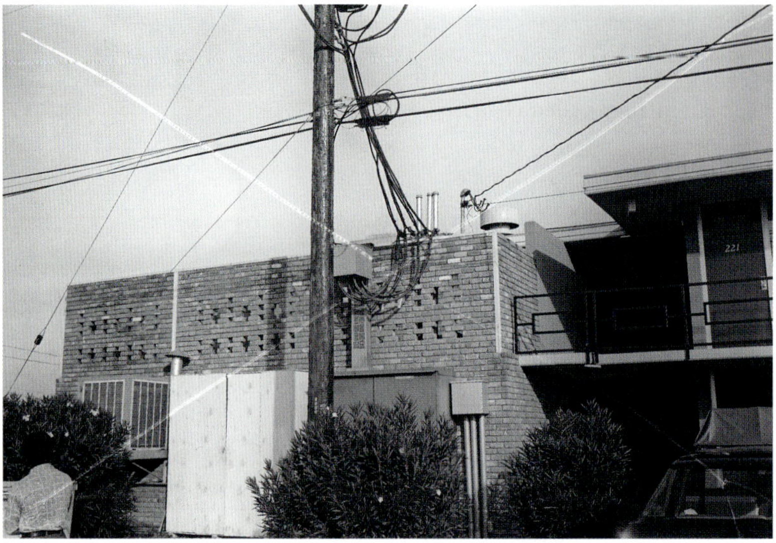

Thomas Barrow, *Kingman Holiday*, 1974, from the series *Cancellations*.

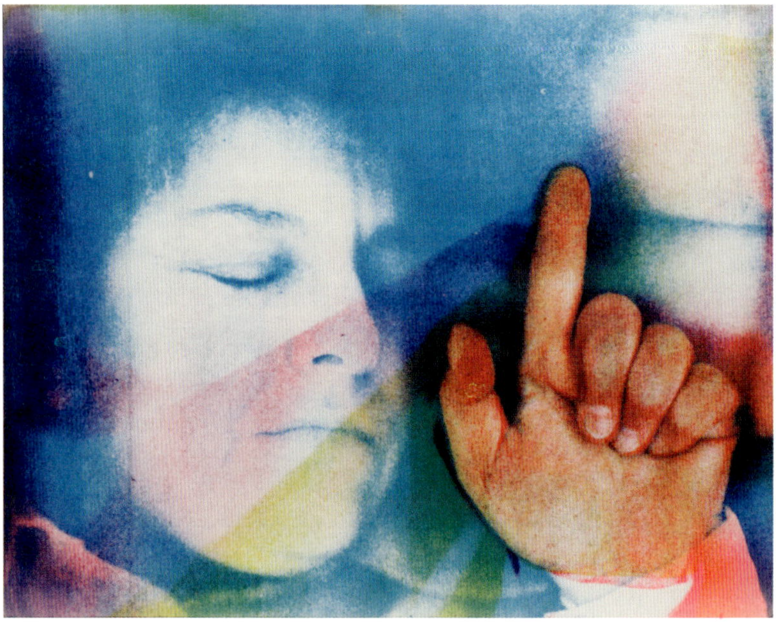

Sonia Landy Sheridan, *The Magic Finger (Self-Portrait with Pointing Finger)*, 1970. 3M Color-in-Color I on paper. Hood Museum of Art, Dartmouth College. Gift of the artist.

artists, notably Sonia Landy Sheridan, who made it the centerpiece of her art and of a program she established at the School of the Art Institute of Chicago in 1970 called Generative Systems. (She preferred *generative systems* to the much more widely used term *copier art.*) Using the same color machine, Ellen Land-Weber produced a widely seen series of floral still lifes that seemed out of an earlier century. But following a huge 250-print, traveling exhibition organized by the George Eastman House, *Electroworks*, which I traveled to Rochester to see in 1979, and the closing of Sheridan's Generative Systems program in 1980, it became clear that copy machines had a limited run as artistic tools.

These experiments are worth remembering not so much because of the beauty of the work but because they gave photographers permission to take the medium into untrodden territory. And the influence of the Bauhaus-derived Institute of Design continues even today, although disguised in the form of the curriculum at almost all photography programs in colleges and art schools—and increasingly in high schools. The kind of "first principles" approach toward the medium pioneered by Moholy-Nagy, which encourages students to experiment with light, camera controls like apertures and shutter speeds, and darkroom interventions, remains foundational not only to most "Photo 101" courses but also to contemporary practice. Artists like Adam Fuss and Abelardo Morell remind us that creative attention to the mechanisms of light and lens can still produce work of incredible originality and beauty.

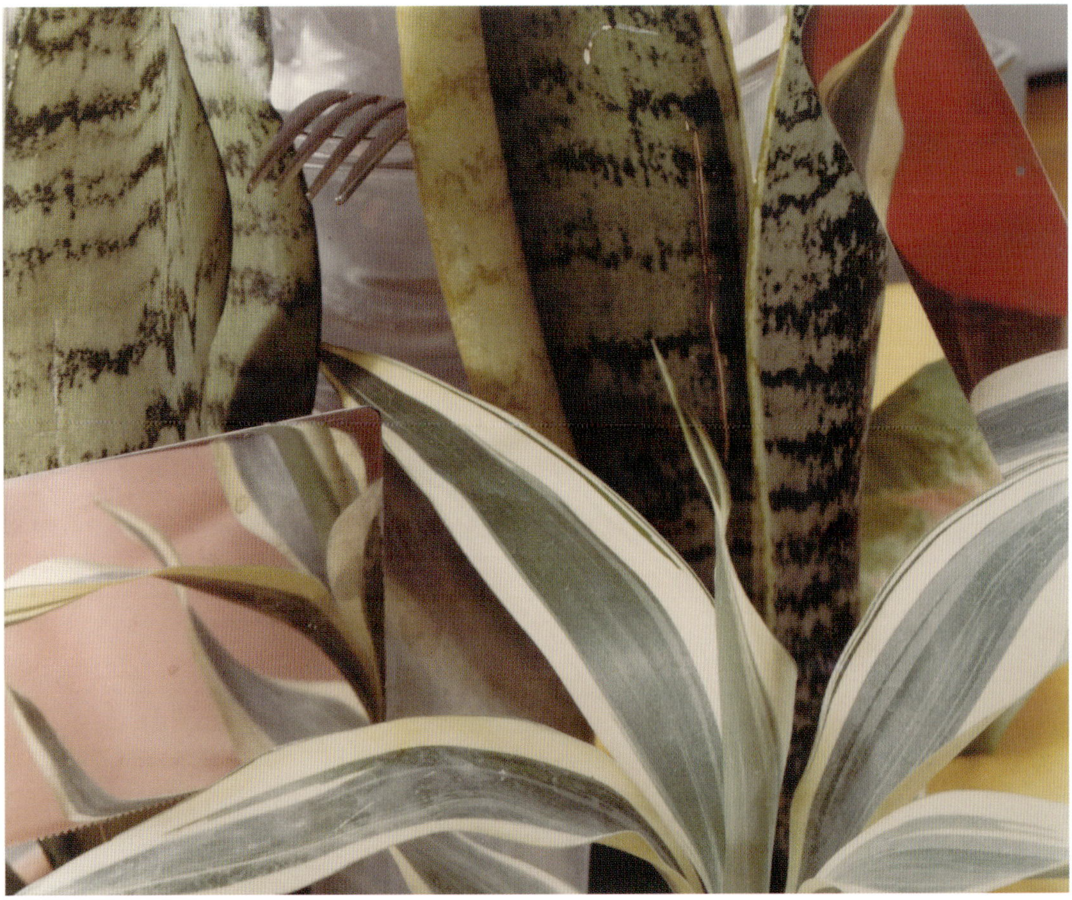

CHAPTER 7

Crossing Over

My career as a critic stemmed in part from my connections to the downtown art world—and in particular to my friendship with Joan Simon, who opened the door for my writing to appear on the pages of *Art in America* in the midseventies. It also helped that I had something of a catbird seat at *Modern Photography*, where my editor, Julia Scully, gave me the opportunity to follow my own nose when it came to scouting out new contemporary work.

I also had the luxury of being paid (or at least reimbursed) to go see shows that were being mounted by museums outside of New York. One of the most important of these for photography was the George Eastman House in Rochester. Eastman House, as it was familiarly known,[1] had been the residence of George Eastman, the inventor of the process for manufacturing flexible film as well as of the Kodak snapshot camera. Eastman Kodak, his company, became the dominant player in photography and, via its marketing campaigns, helped make picture taking a widespread, democratically arrayed practice. His house was rumored to be haunted—Eastman had chosen to commit suicide upstairs in 1932, at the age of seventy-seven—but nonetheless it was converted into a museum in 1949 with the major support of Kodak.

My first trip to the Rochester museum may have simply been to see it and its unparalleled collection. Remarkably, I was given free access to the boxes in which the original prints were stored and left alone at a table to sift through them. This would never happen today: now you have to ask to see specific work, and prints are handled judiciously one at a time by staff wearing white gloves.

A more memorable trip was occasioned by an exhibition that opened February 1, 1975: *The Extended Document: An Investigation of Information and Evidence in Photographs*, which was organized by a curator not much older than myself, William Jenkins. Jenkins has since become legendary for the exhibition he would organize for the fall of that year, *New Topographics*. Being on *Modern Photography*'s dime, I was one of the few people outside of Rochester fortunate to see both of these prescient shows.

Jan Groover, *Untitled*, 1978.

The Extended Document, the lesser known of the two, was a Postmodern riposte to John Szarkowski's *New Documents* exhibition eight years earlier. Where *New Documents* emphasized subjectivity within the confines of "straight," unaltered photography, using Diane Arbus, Lee Friedlander, and Garry Winogrand as its examples, *The Extended Document* suggested that the veracity of photographs was a fiction. The photographs on view showed that they could be manipulated or altered to give meanings unconnected to visual reality—and by implication that ultimately all photographs are constructs fashioned implicitly or explicitly by their makers.

The artists in *The Extended Document* were John Baldessari, Thomas Barrow, Michael Bishop, Marcia Resnick, Richard W. Schaeffer, and William Wegman. All the work shown had been made in the seventies, with the vast majority dating from the year prior to the exhibition. Barrow's and Bishop's images came "courtesy Light Gallery," where they had recently been shown, and Baldessari's and Wegman's were "courtesy Sonnabend Gallery." This was unusual for the time: photography curators usually confined themselves to looking at galleries devoted solely to photographs, or they dealt with photographers directly (which seems to have been the case with Resnick and Schaeffer). But Jenkins crossed the divide to produce a provocative and, for the time, highly contentious exhibition.

In his brief essay for the show's compact catalog, Jenkins focuses on the paradoxical relationship of modern subjectivity to the supposed objectivity of "the document," citing Winogrand's and Friedlander's "highly personal and often distorted pictures"—an overt reference to the *New Documents* show. But, he argues, the meaning of their pictures "is still totally dependent on the implied relationship between the photograph and the photographed," whereas with the artists in his show, "the meaning of photographs is, at least in part, the subject of their photographs."[2]

This was an essential realization, for it pinpoints exactly why Jenkins could mix together photographers working in the territory of contemporary photography with artists working in the territory of contemporary art. The idea that photographic meaning was both complex and important enough to be a subject of investigation unites Barrow, Bishop, and such precursors as Kenneth Josephson and Robert Heinecken, with Baldessari, Wegman, and their precursors Sol LeWitt, Douglas Huebler, and Bruce Nauman. It was this idea—that what a photograph delivers is not self-evident and can be toyed with or slyly manipulated—more than market conditions, government support, and acceptance into academe, that propelled photography into a central place in the contemporary art of the seventies.

Although based in Southern California, Baldessari had already been shown at Sonnabend in New York, as had Wegman, who left Southern California for Manhattan in 1972, so both were established figures in the

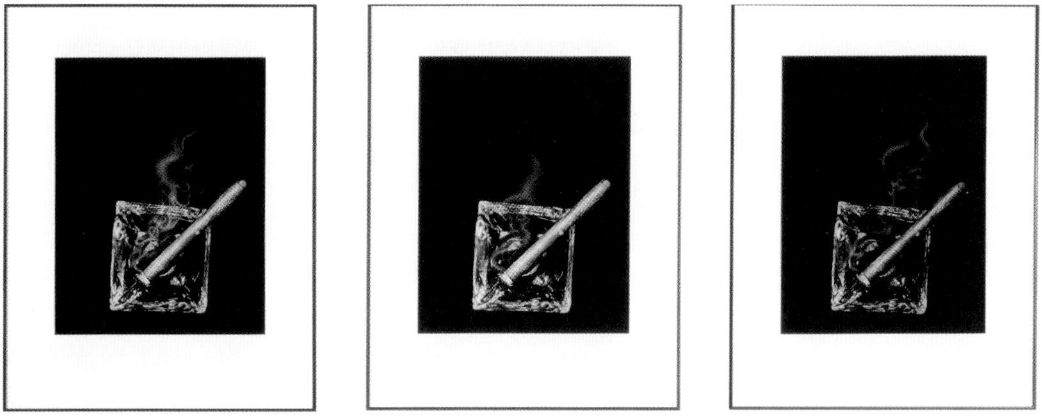

John Baldessari, *Embed Series: Cigar Dreams (Seeing is Believing)*, 1974. Three retouched black-and-white photographs.

Soho scene. Together they leavened the daunting diet of Conceptual Art to include humor. In Wegman's case, it took the form of photographs and short videos he made in the studio with his Weimaraner Man Ray and occasionally another dog or two. Baldessari is equally esteemed for his questioning approach to photographs as evidence, using found photographs and his own to create puzzles of meaning, most notably in his *Blasted Allegories* series of 1978.

In *The Extended Document* Baldessari showed work from his *Embed Series*, for which he enlisted photo retouchers (this was long before Photoshop) to alter the camera's rendition of various scenes. In a diptych titled *Embed Series: Rose; Orange (Death)*, the word *death* has been added to close-up pictures of a rose and an orange in a way that makes it indiscernible unless one knows to look for it. *Embed Series: Cigar Dreams (Seeing is Believing)*, a triptych that the Eastman Museum wisely acquired from the show, is only slightly more obvious: a lit cigar perched on a glass ashtray miraculously produces the words of the title in the plumes of smoke that rise above it.

Baldessari's method of making fun of our conventional beliefs about photographic representation is part of a more serious enterprise of questioning ideas about art itself. He, like the Conceptual artists whose concerns he shared, was influenced by Muybridge's motion studies and how they sliced time into quasi-scientific slices (see, for example, *Strobe Series/Futurist: Trying To Get A Straight Line With A Finger*, done in the same year as the show [page 64], and *Throwing Four Balls in the Air to Get a Square [Best of 36 Tries]*, from 1974).

Wegman's work in *The Extended Document* was part-dog, part-portraits. In *Folly, Suicy, Man Ray*, a six-print piece, the front and back halves of two dogs occupy the edges of each frame in various combinations; figuring out which is which is complicated because Folly and Suicy are nearly identical. In *Blondes/Brunettes*, two sixteen-print grids of women's faces, the

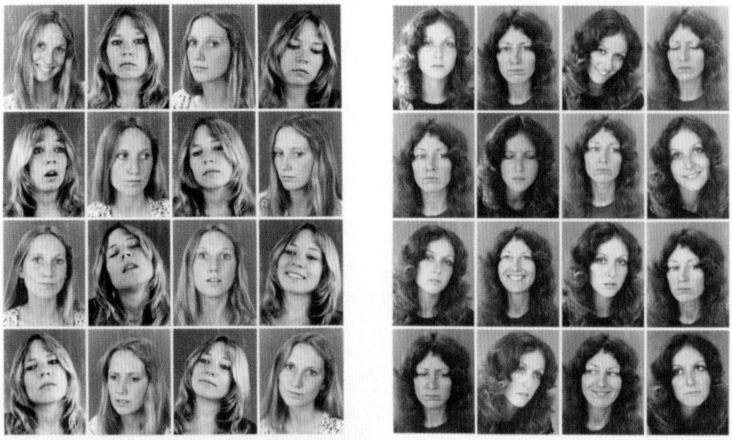

William Wegman, *Blondes/Brunettes*, 1974. Thirty-two black-and-white prints on two panels.

individual identities are also hard to discern. Only careful examination (or curatorial explanation) reveals that there are only two blondes and two brunettes, and that their portraits alternate within each grid. While reasonably well-crafted as photographs, the pictures are not individually distinguished; like their subjects, they represent a broader categorical idea: blondes and brunettes, for the women, and, in the large scheme of things, identification and misidentification, classification and stereotyping.

The pure photographers in the show made similar attempts to interrogate photography as a cultural presence. Bishop's pictures seem to distort standard camera perspectives, with the added complication of irregular dark edges similar to vignetting, which he produced by pushing a flexible lens hood into the path of the camera lens. Barrow's *Cancellations* series takes a dig at the marketplace analogies between fine-art photography and printmaking, which were commonplace at the time, but also confounds our expectations that the art of photography lies in the selection of one "best" image over all others.

Marcia Resnick's two series in the show, *See* and *See Changes*, present the back of a human spectator looking out at a natural scene. In *See* the spectators and scenes vary; the only constant is their relationship. In *See Changes* a man looking at the Grand Canyon is replicated twelve times, but each print has been altered; instead of a definitive version of the situation, we see variations, some of which have been worked on by hand and some cleverly reconfigured in the darkroom. Richard W. Schaeffer's images were similarly dissembling, depicting seemingly real material that slowly reveals itself to be only an image or model of the real thing—a Manhattan skyscraper, for example, apparently erected within a hotel conference room.

For me, seeing *The Extended Document* not only reconciled, at least in part, my previously separate experiences of contemporary art and con-

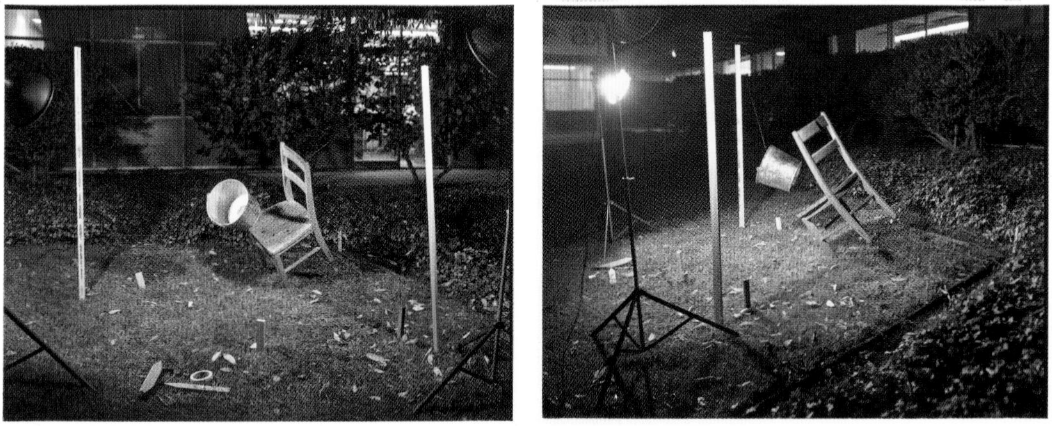

Robert Cumming, *Two Views of One Mishap of Minor Consequence*, 1973.

temporary photography-as-art, but it also suggested a new way of thinking about photography. By poking holes in the medium's documentary veracity and showing how susceptible we are to taking that veracity at face value, the work in the show anticipated a major direction artists and photographers would take later in the decade and well into the eighties. Instead of using the camera to investigate the world, they would use it to investigate photography itself.

Looking back, the one thing I would change about the exhibition would be to add Robert Cumming, a friend and grad-school classmate of Wegman's whose work also encompasses a range of mediums and who became almost as well known for challenging our notions about the truth of photographs. Cumming trained as a sculptor and painter but had taken a photography course in grad school at the University of Illinois, and after moving to Southern California he made several series of pictures addressing how photographs are apprehended or "read"—or misapprehended and misread. In one of the best known, *Two Views of One Mishap of Minor Consequence* (1973), a diptych shows a side and front view of what appears to be a bucket and chair toppling over together. But the surround for this "event," which includes visible evidence of a photo light, two poles, and wires that connect the bucket and chair to the poles, belies the implied instantaneity of the scene—a kind of anti-Muybridge image, if you will.

Another Cumming image from about the same time, *8 Year Old Girl, 6 Month Old Weed* (1974), simply "documents" in deadpan fashion that the weed is taller than the girl. And *Watermelon/Bread* (1970) focuses on a watermelon with a slice of bread neatly inserted in its side—an absurd object rendered with great seriousness. The artist incorporated many of these works in a series of narrative artist's books he self-published, notably *A Discourse on Domestic Disorder* (1975).

Because Cumming's pictures were so technically polished, which distinguished his work from the Conceptualist trope of downplaying photographic craft, they appealed to a traditional art-photography audience. In 1975 his work was included in *14 American Photographers*, a show organized by Renato Danese and John Gossage for the Baltimore Museum of Art. In 1979, The Friends of Photography, a mainstream photography support organization founded in the sixties by Ansel Adams, devoted an entire volume of its *Untitled* book series to Cumming. At the same time, he was recognized by an art audience as a "story artist" alongside Bill Beckley, Peter Hutchinson, and Jean Le Gac; like them he was part of the Soho stable of John Gibson Gallery. Like Baldessari and Wegman, he could legitimately claim to have crossed over the photo-art divide, having secured an audience in both territories.[3]

After seeing *The Extended Document* I went back to New York and wrote a brief notice about it for *Modern Photography* (I was then editing a news-and-notes section called "What's What"). The exhibition also received some press attention in Rochester, but seemingly its broad significance escaped the rest of the world. Not so Jenkins's next show, which opened that fall and proved to have extraordinarily long legs: *New Topographics: Photographs of a Man-Altered Landscape.*

Called no less than "a turning point in photographic history" when it was reconstituted in 2009,[4] *New Topographics* marked a rejection of the theatrical, heroic model of landscape photography represented by Ansel Adams and other West Coast Modernists by a cohort of photographers of my generation. I was ready to vote with my peers, having already decided that Adams was a second-generation echo of Edward Weston's real genius. Once again *Modern Photography* paid the bill for me to go to Rochester, and I got to spend time with the curator (martini-fueled lunch included) after looking closely at the work.

The show was life altering, at least for me. I had seen some of the ten photographers' work before—Stephen Shore and Frank Gohlke shared the walls at the beginning of the year at Light Gallery, Robert Adams and Henry Wessel Jr. were favorites of John Szarkowski's at MoMA, and Bernd and Hilla Becher had been shown there and at Sonnabend—but having their work together in one large gallery made their similarities strikingly apparent. The word *trend* is perhaps too debased to use, but the exhibition definitely altered the way photographers thought about their mission.

Beyond the exquisite clarity and descriptiveness of the prints, the most remarked-on quality of the work in the show was its apparent strident objectivity, or seeming emotional neutrality, a result of using the camera straightforwardly at a middle or far distance from the subject. This of course was an illusion; some photographers felt strongly about the intrusions of human

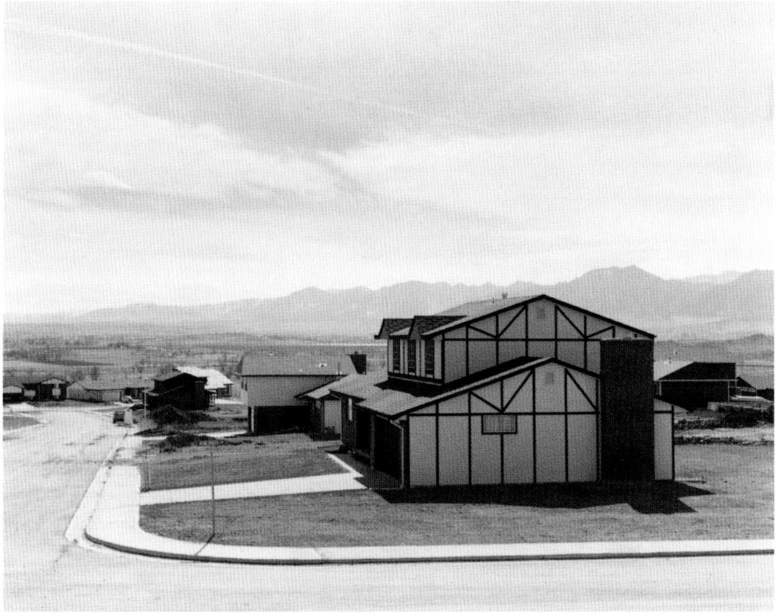

Robert Adams, *Colorado*, c. 1973.

occupation and others cared deeply about preserving evidence of an earlier era. Nicholas Nixon's statement, quoted by Jenkins in the show's slim catalog, is often invoked to characterize what *new topographics* meant as a style: "The world is infinitely more interesting than any of my opinions of it."[5]

Robert Adams was arguably the exemplar of the new genre and much looked up to by most of the photographers in the show. His early work had been shown at MoMA in 1971–72, alongside that of Emmet Gowin, and Lewis Baltz had recently reviewed his book *The New West* in *Art in America* (March–April, 1975). I'm fairly certain I saw the MoMA show, although my memory of Gowin's work is stronger than that of Adams's, and I definitely read Baltz's review (with a bit of envy, I have to say, since by then I had embarked on writing photography-related reviews for the magazine myself). In any case, Adams's pictures of tract houses and mobile homes set against unspoiled distant mountains required a new approach to the definition of beauty in photography. The prints are impeccably made, filled with bright crisp light, and thus beautiful in themselves, but what they depict is more interesting in an archaeological sense than outright beautiful—as opposed to, say, Ansel Adams, whose achievement consists of beautiful scenes beautifully described.

Other work in the show followed the same script: beautiful pictures of less than beautiful (or, in conventional terms, ugly and kitsch) subjects. Baltz's work, from his best-known series *The New Industrial Parks near Irvine, California* (published by Castelli Graphics as a fifty-one-print portfolio and book in 1974 and exhibited at Castelli downtown at the end of 1975),

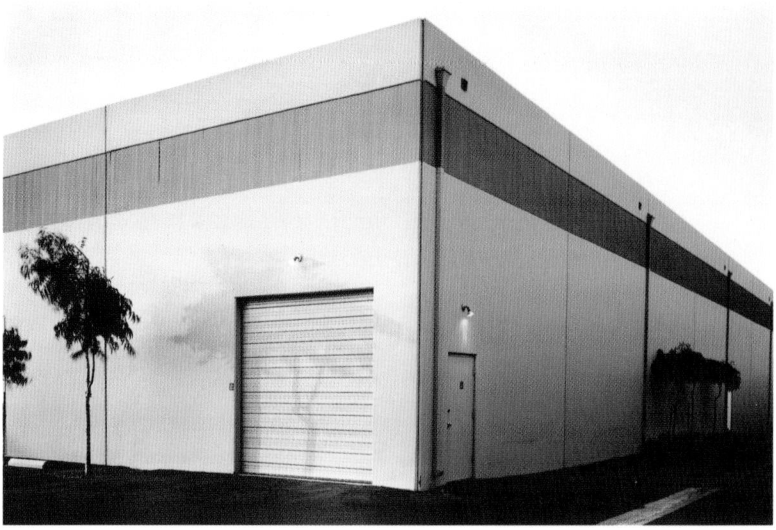

Lewis Baltz, *Southeast Corner, Semicoa, 333 McCormick, Costa Mesa,* 1974, #50 from the series *The New Industrial Parks near Irvine, California.*

seemed to take the lessons of Minimalism and apply them to the interchangeable concrete structures of single-story manufacturing and office buildings. Their distinctive appearance, a result of using a 35mm recording film designed for photographing documents and developing it to produce a full range of tones, gave the pictures a resemblance to NASA photographs made on the moon—an impression reinforced by the seemingly alien territory of the pictures' locale.

The oddness of the American landscape was a theme for several of the other photographers: Route 66 motels (John Schott), suburbs on the verge of the desert (Joe Deal), California cottages and bungalows (Henry Wessel Jr.). Nicholas Nixon surveyed cityscapes of Boston with his 8 × 10 view camera, using an elevated vantage point to meet skyscrapers head-on, and the Bechers weighed in with their trademark typological grids showing coal-mining structures photographed in Pennsylvania the year before. Their pictures were the largest in the show (about 12 × 16 inches individually, but shown in groups of from two to sixteen prints); the rest were 8 × 10-inch prints or close to it.[6]

Only one photographer showed work in color: Stephen Shore. Shore, who grew up in Manhattan, was a prodigy photographer. At the age of fourteen several of his prints were purchased by Edward Steichen for the Museum of Modern Art. As an older teenager he documented the goings on at Andy Warhol's free-form studio, called the Factory. In 1971, at the age of twenty-three, his black-and-white pictures were shown at the Met; from descriptions of them in *New York Times* reviews, they took the form of several conceptually inspired series in which the photographer walked a predetermined path or took in a 360-degree view one frame at a time.[7]

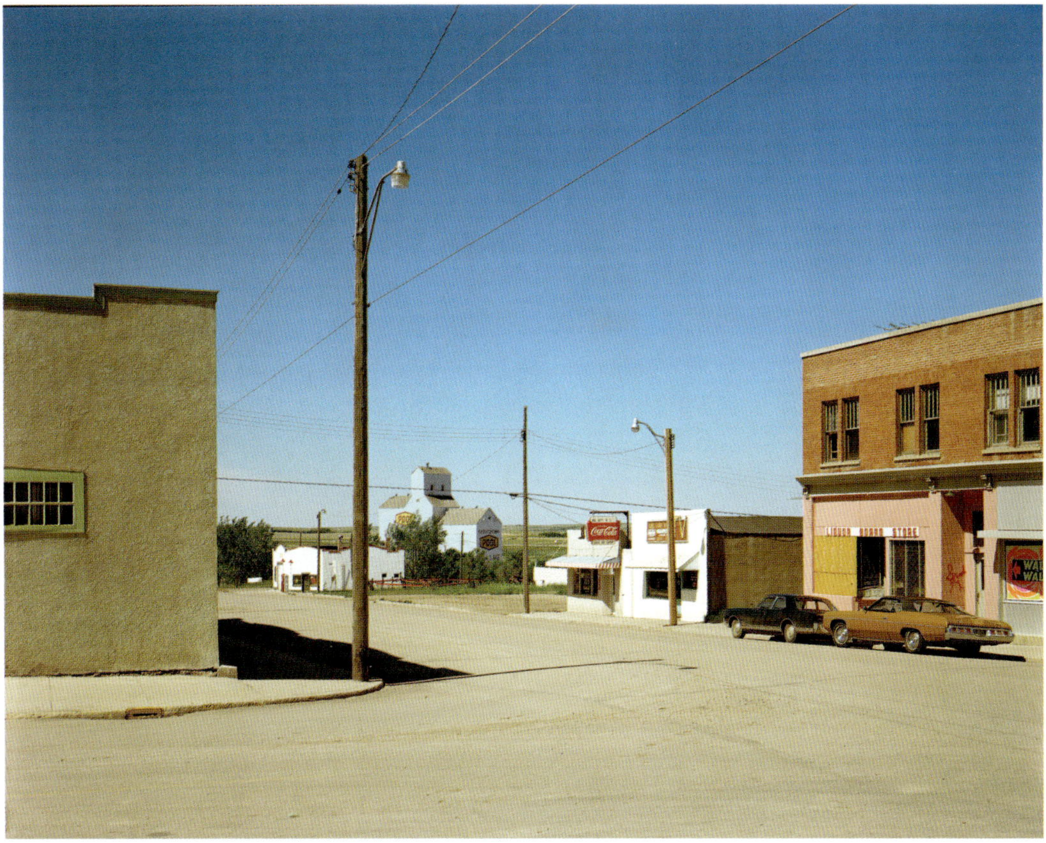

Stephen Shore, *Main Street, Gull Lake, Saskatchewan, August 18, 1974*, 1974.

Shore began using color the same year, with a 35mm camera, and traveled to the West Coast photographing along the way. Light Gallery exhibited some of this work in fall 1972.[8] But he made a much bigger splash when he adopted an 8 × 10 view camera and, traveling again around the United States, starting in 1973, made the color photographs for which he is most famous, known as the *Uncommon Places* series. These views constituted his contribution to *New Topographics*: small-town New England buildings, straight-on studies of Midwestern Main Streets, corner perspectives on cities like Little Rock and Philadelphia. Light Gallery showed similar pictures the same year, which happened to be a year before John Szarkowski made color photography the center of attention with his exhibition of the work of William Eggleston.

New Topographics has been credited with marking a paradigm shift from photography's isolated practice to an engagement with the wider art world.[9] How it became a fabled game-changer may be partly a function of its catchy title, partly the smart combination of the Bechers with Adams, Baltz, Nixon, and Shore, all of whom became art stars in their own right, and partly its timing: it caught the wave of a generational transition in which the studied, observational "documentary style" of Walker Evans took center stage after years in which on-the-fly, fly-on-the-wall street photography seemed the hip thing to do. And unlike *The Extended Document*, *New Topographics* toured outside of Rochester, traveling to the West Coast to appear at the Otis Art Institute, where it was reviewed in *Artweek*, a widely read California art journal, and finally to the Princeton University Art Museum.[10] It was reviewed by Carter Ratcliff in *Art and America* and by Charles Desmarais in *Afterimage*.

The retrospective claims for the exhibition more than forty years later now seem overblown to some—including its curator, who intended it as a provisional exploration of a new tendency in photography rather than as a definitive codification of a new style.[11] But if anything its reputation has grown over time, influencing not only contemporary photographic practice well into the current century but also the art world's understanding of what makes photography an art.

New Topographics might be considered the high-water mark of Eastman House's influence on contemporary photography as it connects to the art world, but during a period from that show until Jenkins's departure at the end of the seventies the museum continued to mount exhibitions that identified significant new developments in that arena. A year after *New Topographics* the museum showed color triptychs by Jan Groover, who used a stationary camera mounted on a tripod to record passing cars and trucks on city streets. David Hockney's snapshot-like forays into photography were shown in 1977, and David Levinthal's series of make-believe war photojournalism, *Hitler Moves East*, in 1978.

At Eastman House I met Janet Borden and Roger Bruce, who became lifelong friends. They were attracted to the place by a master's program in photographic museum practices offered by the Rochester Institute of Technology, which required an internship at the museum. Borden, fresh from an undergraduate degree at Smith College, was assigned to Jenkins ("the smart guy" there, she recalls), starting in 1975, and among other duties went with him to New York to pick up the Bechers' work for *New Topographics* from Sonnabend. Two years later she moved to New York, helped Robert Freidus open the Freidus Gallery on Lafayette Street, worked as a private dealer representing Tina Barney, Jan Groover, and Neil Winokur, and in 1987 opened her own gallery, Janet Borden.[12]

Bruce's career was different but no less influential. Facing military service in Vietnam, he managed to receive conscientious objector status and was assigned to the Eastman House (the same was true of Joe Deal, Bruce recalls). In his free time he hung out at the Visual Studies Workshop, drinking in the atmosphere of aesthetic and critical discussion about photography's nature led by Nathan Lyons. In 1972 he managed to complete his

MFA degree in RIT's museum program and was hired by Eastman House's then-director Robert Doherty to be the museum's director of education; later he was named the museum's assistant director. In 1980 he left Rochester to become the photography program specialist at the National Endowment for the Arts in Washington, D.C., replacing the first occupant of the position, Kathleen McCarthy Gauss. Later he worked for the New York State Council on the Arts and eventually returned to Rochester to work at the Eastman House again.[13]

Either Janet or Bruce, or both, took me on my first tour of the Visual Studies Workshop, soon after it had moved into its permanent location at 31 Prince Street. There I found the same stimulating and serious commitment to photography that I had found at Eastman House. In many ways, it was even more intense.

"The Workshop," as the insiders call it, was the creation of Nathan Lyons, photographer, entrepreneur, and guru to much of my generation. Nathan (everyone referred to him as Nathan) had been a curator and associate director at Eastman House when, in 1969, he had a job-ending falling-out with management—management being in this case the museum's trustees and its director, the historian Beaumont Newhall. Feeling disrespected and no longer constrained by museum conventions, he began the Workshop on a shoestring and centered it on critical practice, pedagogy, and community—with *critical* being the key word.

Within a few years Lyons had attracted some brilliant students and inspiring teachers, all more or less unconventional. Aspiring photographer Charles Hagen, newly graduated from Harvard, came to study in 1971 and became the founding editor of *Afterimage*, the Workshop's influential journal, two months later. Anne Tucker, who would have a distinguished career as the curator of photography at the Museum of Fine Arts, Houston, was there; she was joined by Brent Sikkema, now a Chelsea gallerist; Charles Desmarais, later a museum director and critic; and William Jenkins, who later went to Eastman House. All arrived via an informal referral network that included the Workshop's nearest equivalent, Cherie Hiser's Center of the Eye in Aspen, Colorado.

By the midseventies the cast had grown larger: students included Martha Chahroudi, Willis "Buzz" Hartshorn, Catherine Lord, Don Russell, Charles Stainback, David Trend, and Adam Weinberg. The number of museum directors to emerge from this group (Desmarais, Hartshorn, Stainback, Weinberg) as well as writers (Hagen, Lord, Martha Gever, Michael Starenko, Marita Sturken, and others) is testament, in part, to the influence Lyons came to command as an intellectual voice for the field.

Teachers at the Workshop included Joan Lyons and Keith Smith, who were interested in book making; resident photographer Michael Bishop;

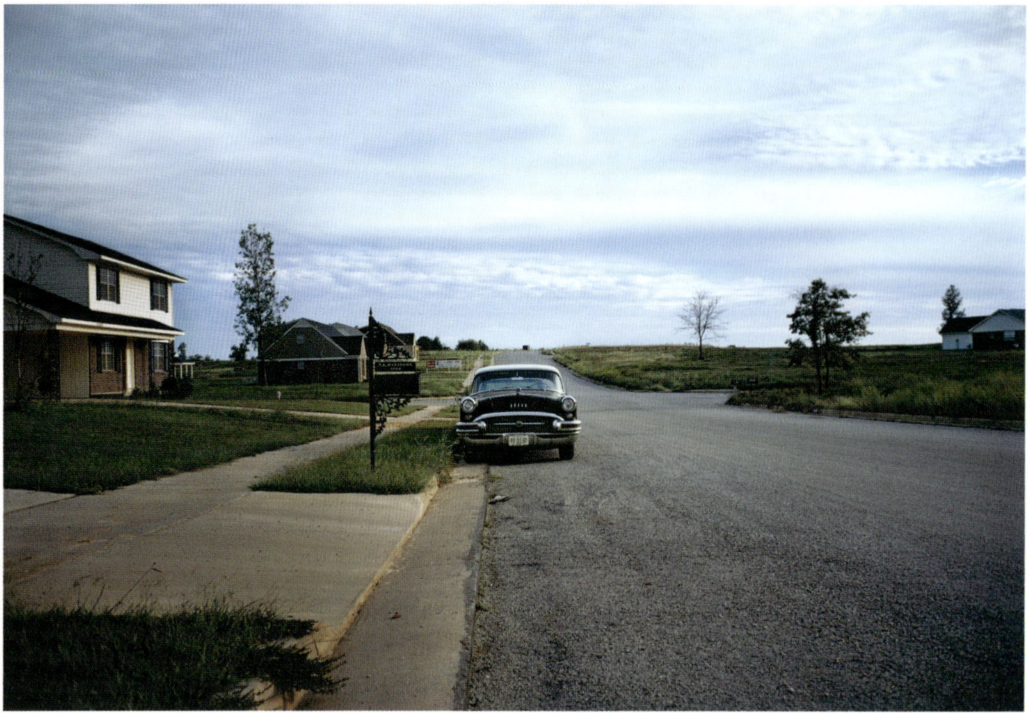

William Eggleston, *Untitled*, c. 1969–71.

and a rotating cast of regular visitors, including Michael Lesy, whose 1973 book *Wisconsin Death Trip* was widely admired for its recontextualized narrative of a small-town photographer's archive. Guest speakers included Aaron Siskind, Henry Holmes Smith, Jacques-Henri Lartigue, Light Gallery director Harold Jones, and a long list of curators and critics, eventually including me.

Though unaccredited itself, the Workshop offered master's degrees through an association with the State University of New York at Buffalo. Thus credentialed, Visual Studies Workshop alumni soon were salted throughout the country, mostly in academic and museum positions. But the biggest engine of the Workshop's national reputation was *Afterimage*, the critical journal first edited by Hagen but dreamed up by Lyons. Lyons was responsible for the title, which was a sly reference to Eastman House's quarterly, *Image*. Produced on a shoestring, *Afterimage* established itself as a place for serious commentary about new photography and new media. It was a pioneer in covering independent film and video, influenced in part by a strong group of filmmakers teaching at Buffalo, most prominently Hollis Frampton.[14]

As important as Rochester and Buffalo would briefly become, the center of attention in America for photography as an art remained in New York City, home to the art world, media world, and a world of wealth that could sustain artists, galleries, and museums. MoMA was the center of the center.

This was demonstrated in 1976, the nation's Bicentennial year, when John Szarkowski decided to forego any patriotic-themed celebration of photography in America in favor of a major show devoted to a practically unknown contemporary photographer from Memphis, Tennessee: William Eggleston.

Eggleston was a bit of a mystery to those of us enmeshed in the New York photo scene, which by then featured more than a half dozen galleries devoted to showing photographs and even more that occasionally put photographs on view. None had yet shown Eggleston's work. Szarkowski surely relished this element of discovery, although if I had been paying closer attention to the bigger picture, I might have known that Eggleston's work already had a following. Harry Lunn Jr., the influential prints and photographs dealer in Washington, D.C., had published an Eggleston portfolio of expensive color dye-transfer prints, *14 Pictures*, in 1974, the same year that the photographer had received a Guggenheim Fellowship and taught a class at Harvard.

Eggleston had first met Szarkowski at MoMA in 1967, the same year as the *New Documents* show, and while in New York he pursued meetings with Arbus, Friedlander, and Winogrand. Through his friend William Christenberry, who in 1968 had moved from Memphis to Washington, D.C., to teach at the Corcoran School of Art, Eggleston met Walter Hopps, who had left Pasadena to work at the Corcoran Gallery of Art. Christenberry's early interest in color photography helped Eggleston decide to switch from black-and-white to color in the midsixties, and Hopps became a good friend, traveling companion, and supporter.[15]

Even knowing about these out-of-town bona fides, New Yorkers had a hard time digesting the seventy-five-print show and its accompanying monograph, *William Eggleston's Guide*.[16] The prints themselves were gorgeous, as dye transfers made from transparencies tend to be; the problem was what they depicted, how they depicted it, and what Szarkowski said about them.

On first glance, what they depicted appeared to be everyday, undramatic subject matter, rendered with a seemingly haphazard pictorial structure and commonplace color. The effect suggested nothing so much as family snapshots—albeit taken by a rather peculiar family member. This, in Szarkowski's universe, was a source of their brilliance, because they adopted a large slice of the medium's vernacular practice as the arena for making art. In a sense Eggleston's show was a color update of *New Documents*, something that Hilton Kramer, the *New York Times*'s chief art critic who occasionally ventured to write about photography, sagely noticed:

> The truth is, these pictures belong to the world of snapshot chic—to the post–Diane Arbus, antiformalist esthetic that is now all the rage

> among many younger photographers and that has all but derailed Mr. Szarkowski's taste so far as contemporary photography is concerned.
>
> To this snapshot style, Mr. Eggleston has added some effects borrowed from recent developments in, of all things, photorealist painting—a case, if not of the blind leading the blind, at least of the banal leading the banal.[17]

Banal seemed to summarize Kramer's response, since he used the word earlier in the most-remembered line from the review: "Mr. Szarkowski throws all caution to the winds and speaks of Mr. Eggleston's pictures as 'perfect.' Perfect? Perfectly banal, perhaps. Perfectly boring, certainly."[18]

Szarkowski's use of *perfect* was more nuanced than Kramer made it out to be, but at the same time the curator seemed to go overboard to convince nonbelievers of Eggleston's talent. First, while he mentioned photographers who had done worthy color work prior to Eggleston, including Helen Levitt, Irving Penn, and Eliot Porter, or were the photographer's peers, namely Joel Meyerowitz and Stephen Shore, he gave them only passing attention. Ernst Haas, whose abstractionist color reflections had been the subject of Szarkowski's first show at MoMA, in 1962, went unnamed.[19] The curator left the impression that if Eggleston had not invented color photography, he at least had been the first to fully master it—perhaps this is really what he felt. Second, he attempted a formal analysis, tying the pictorial structure of the images to their color and arguing that they were functionally synonymous. ("One can say that in these photographs form and content are indistinguishable.") He went on to note that Eggleston had compared their compositions to that of the Confederate battle flag, an ill-chosen analogy then and even worse now.

And then there was the problem of Eggleston himself. Instead of ingratiating himself into the photo community in New York, he presented as a distant, somewhat disagreeable alien. I, along with hundreds of others, was there the night of the exhibition opening, which took place after a more exclusive patrons' showing, and we eagerly looked forward to at least seeing the man who was creating such a stir among us. We waited, drank more mediocre wine than we should have, and still Eggleston did not appear. Finally, a rumor spread that he was unable to make it to his own opening because of a freak accident: he had cut his eye on the sharply creased edge of a pillowcase while resting back at his hotel. Whatever really happened, that night soon added to his mystique as the eccentric wizard of contemporary photography.

Photographers and writers I knew were quick to take sides on the issue, with the more traditional aligning with Kramer and Szarkowski's acolytes

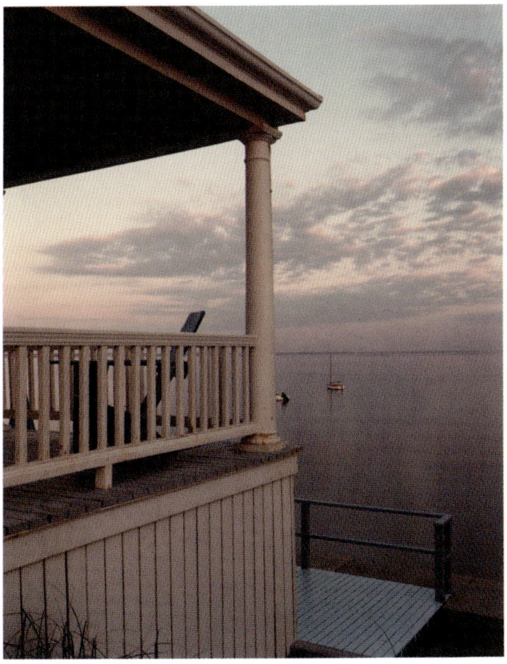

Joel Meyerowitz, *Porch, Provincetown, Massachusetts*, 1977.

naturally siding with him. It made for good barroom conversation for the rest of the year. But far more important than that was the impact that the exhibition had on photographers. Suddenly, it seemed, color was everywhere, as any review of books and exhibitions that appeared during the rest of the decade and into the eighties will attest.

Prominent among the newly celebrated color practitioners was Joel Meyerowitz, whose book *Cape Light* was published in 1978.[20] Meyerowitz had been a street photographer sharing the New York sidewalks with Garry Winogrand, but he used color as well as black-and-white film as early as 1962. In 1976 he began making color negatives on Cape Cod with a newly purchased 8 × 10 view camera, in technique much like the photographers in *New Topographics* but with gorgeous expanses of sand, sea, and sunsets. The tonal beauty of these pictures seemed to place him in an aesthetic tradition of the picturesque, harkening back to the Hudson River School in painting rather than the gritty school of street photography from whence he came. The work that followed, focused on the Gateway Arch in Saint Louis and the Empire State Building in New York, returned to city subjects but maintained much of the chromatic beauty of the beach pictures.

Also in 1976 Sonnabend Gallery exhibited David Hockney's photographs for the first time. Hockney had been taking color snapshots for several years, but the idea that this could constitute his "work" was radical—at least in the eyes of collectors of his paintings. Published by the gallery as a portfolio called *Twenty Photographic Pictures by David Hockney*, in an

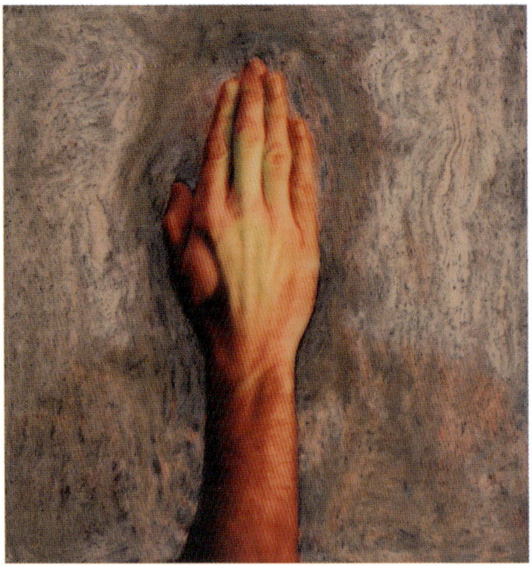

Lucas Samaras, *Photo-Transformation*, December 17, 1973.

edition of eighty, the pictures take their cues from vacation snaps, showing swimming pools, an easel set up *en plein air*, several lounging figures (including Met curator Henry Geldzahler), and the naked backsides of two young men. There is also a charming portrait of Hockney's parents, in which his father clasps a camera and points the lens at his son.

Photographers were puzzled by Hockney's photographic pictures, since they seemed so casual and inconsequential; artists were left to wonder if the photos were simply studies for paintings that would come later (and in some cases, they did). Still, the fact that one of the world's most popular living artists was taking photographs was news. And Hockney persisted, upping the ante in the early eighties by producing a series of photocollages—first using Polaroid SX-70 prints in a grid and then more freely overlapping garden-variety drugstore prints—that when assembled together yielded a quasi-coherent scene of many individual parts.

Surprisingly, the acceptance of color photography had happened earlier in the art world than in the so-called art photography world. Dan Graham's *Homes for America* series, for example, was shot in color in the sixties—albeit with publication in mind—and no one found it unusual; by that time every home in America probably housed a camera loaded with Kodak Ektacolor film. A significant alternative to Kodak film—Edwin Land's Polaroid "instant" process—attracted the attention of sculptor Lucas Samaras in 1969. The Greek-born Samaras had been a student of Allan Kaprow's at Rutgers and fell into the "Happenings" and performance scene in New York. His first Polaroid series, called "Auto-Polaroids" in part because the pictures were self-portraits, used a conventional Polaroid "peel-apart" print that he heavily altered using ink and paint mainly to highlight the figure.

In 1973 Samaras switched to the new Polaroid SX-70, which produced a square image that after being spit out of the camera developed in front of one's eyes over the course of several minutes. Finding that during this developing time the dyes in the image could be moved around, the artist proceeded to use his finger, various styli, and other implements to create one-of-a-kind, phantasmagoric miniatures. These "Photo-Transformations" were shown at Pace Gallery, which already represented him, and in a group show at Light Gallery devoted to SX-70 pictures. That was enough to cause a number of photographers to become addicted to the SX-70 and undertake poking away at their own pictures.

Polaroids in general, and the SX-70 in particular, were heavily promoted by the company's marketing division, which supplied both photographers and artists with free film. Some were big names at the time: Ansel Adams worked for years as Polaroid's technical consultant/artistic advisor, and Andy Warhol helped popularize its amateur Big Shot camera in the early seventies by using it to make the source images of celebrities that appeared on the covers of *Interview* magazine. Several Polaroid employees in different divisions of the company—Barbara Hitchcock, Eelco Wolf, and Sam Yanes among them—fostered individual relationships with lesser-known, emerging talents. Exhibitions were held, a corporate collection established, and an artist support program put in place to associate the brand with contemporary art.[21] Even Walker Evans, one of Eggleston's influences, went out with an SX-70 camera in 1973, at the age of seventy, and announced that for the first time in his career he was ready to take color seriously.

When Polaroid introduced the 20×24 Studio at the end of the seventies it attracted William Wegman, who up to that point had confined his photography and video to black-and-white. Since the camera (there were seven in all, based in New York, Boston, and cities around the globe) was huge and seldom traveled, Wegman came to the Polaroid studio with props: his first dog, Man Ray (and his successor, Fay Ray, and subsequent generations), and a variety of costumes. The pictures that resulted caused a sensation and transformed Wegman from a Postconceptual niche artist to a worldwide sensation. His humorous pictures soon appeared in calendars and his educational video shorts enlivened *Sesame Street*; few of his fans knew that the "dog photographer" was really a downtown artist with a history of making drawings, paintings, and short videos, all with a peculiar, dry sense of humor.

Wegman's enthusiasm for the Polaroid 20×24 Studio was shared by the portrait painter Chuck Close, who saw it as a new medium with which to make his art. Close, who gained recognition as a Photorealist painter in the sixties, had long used everyday Polaroids, in black and white, essentially as preliminary drawings for his work. He would take a head shot of himself or

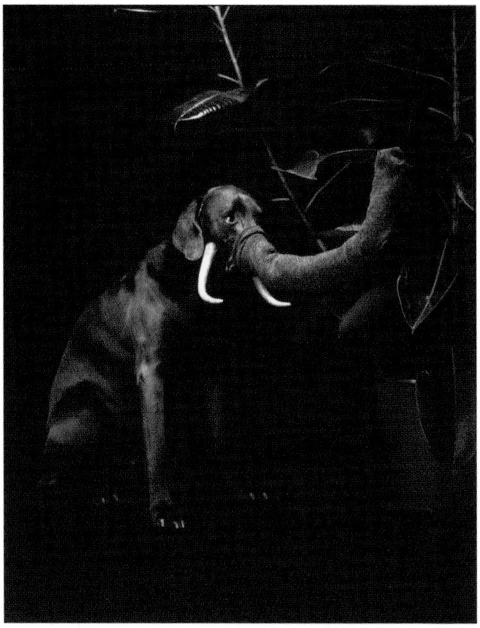

William Wegman,
Elephant, 1981.

a friend and then divide the print into a tight grid; he drew a corresponding grid onto his canvas and then painstakingly painted each cell one at a time—starting out using only a gray scale, since his first Polaroids were in black and white. But with the large-format Polaroids, Close for the most part let them exist as taken, finding in their seemingly infinite descriptive detail a pleasure that needed no elaboration.

In my early years in New York, Photorealism was a big deal, or at least a fresh one, simultaneously demonstrating the peculiarities of the camera lens and rebuking whatever remained of the aesthetic of Abstract Expressionism in painting. Its practitioners—besides Close, I remember seeing shows of Robert Bechtle, Richard Estes, and Audrey Flack, all at the Louis K. Meisel Gallery in Soho—painted faces, flowers, and street scenes with such great detail the everydayness of the subject came to seem uncanny. Estes in particular doted on shop windows and reflections, reproducing specular effects usually only noticed in photographs. But while I felt a responsibility to know what Photorealism was about, I was never particularly a fan.

My problem with Photorealist painting was that it seemed to be recapitulating what realist photography already could do. I say this not in the sense that Photorealist painters all started with a photograph as their source material, which happens to be the case, but because they seemed to claim that they had discovered the oddities of photographic representation and, by implication, that photographers hadn't. To my mind, Photorealist painting just seemed a way to talk about photography while still pleasing collectors who couldn't imagine buying a simple photograph as art.

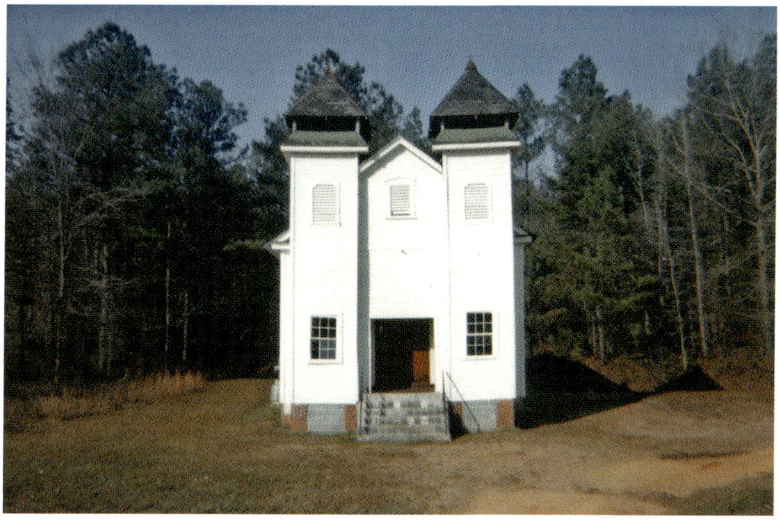

William Christenberry, *Church, Sprott, Alabama*, 1971.

Painting photorealistically in color perhaps made sense when most photographs hung on museum walls were in black-and-white, but that era ended with Eggleston. "The new color photography" became a catchphrase and, in 1981, the title of an exhibition and book by Sally Eauclaire, a Rochester art critic, which surveyed recent photographs in color by more than forty artists, leading off with Eggleston and Shore.[22] At *Modern Photography* Julia Scully and I had helped fan the flames somewhat earlier, producing an article at the end of 1976 called "100 Years of Color," which tried to make the point that photographers had been fascinated with color practically from the medium's beginnings, not just in the last five years.[23]

In 1978 Julia and I started a series of articles called "Currents in American Photography Today" in which we highlighted contemporary photographers and reproduced their work. In addition to features on the *New Topographics* photographers Robert Adams and Nicholas Nixon, who worked in black and white, many of the articles looked at the "new" color scene. We wrote about Joel Meyerowitz and his former students Mitch Epstein and Len Jenshel in June 1980, and about California color photographers, including Jo Ann Callis, John Divola, and Kenneth McGowan, in October 1980. In the next month's issue the magazine ran an article written by Charles Desmarais, "Local Color, Chicago Style," that highlighted a number of emerging color photographers there, including Patty Carroll, Lynn Sloan-Theodore, and Wayne Sorce.

The sudden attention to color photography also brought to light work by artists trained in other mediums who had strayed into color before the Eggleston show. Foremost among these was Eggleston's friend William Christenberry, who had started taking pictures of his native Hale County, Alabama, with a Brownie camera in the late fifties, graduated to a 35mm

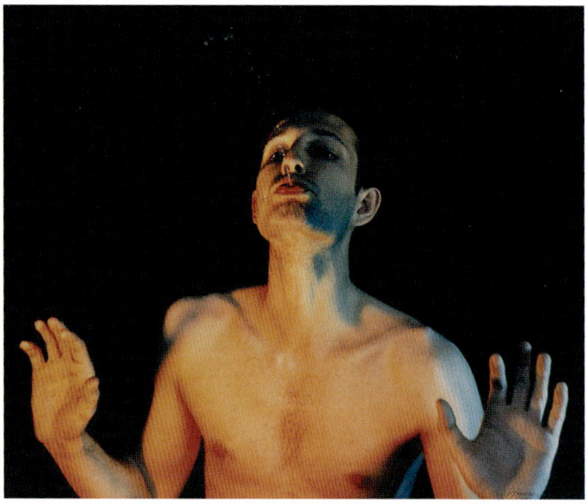

Bruce Nauman, *Self-Portrait as a Fountain*, 1966.

camera in the sixties, and evolved to an 8 × 10 view camera in the late seventies. Working across media, Christenberry used his miniature snapshots as source material for his semiabstract canvases before switching primarily to sculpture, for which the images also came in handy. Christenberry would create miniature buildings based loosely on those he photographed in rural Alabama, and in some cases he showed the sculptures and his photographs together. But starting in 1973 his color photographs came to be exhibited by themselves, initially at The Octagon in Washington, D.C., and the Baltimore Museum of Art.[24]

More off the beaten path, for photography audiences at least, was the 1970 portfolio *Eleven Color Photographs* by Bruce Nauman. Nauman made the pictures between 1966 and 1967, using himself as a subject and relying on the expertise of Jack Fulton for photographic technique, essentially as a way of extending his interest in performance and body art. The most famous image of the group, *Self-Portrait as a Fountain*, was hung in Nauman's debut show at Leo Castelli's uptown gallery in 1968, together with sculptural casts of the artist's body parts, neon lights, and a painting with the words "the true artist is an amazing luminous fountain." Clearly Nauman, then twenty-seven, wanted to locate the essence of art in the figure of the artist (in this case, himself), although the hyperbole of "amazing luminous fountain" and the ridiculous afflatus of his spit-fountain photograph suggests a skepticism toward conventional ideas about inspiration.

The contemporary art world's wholehearted adoption of color photography in its "pure," non-Conceptual form arguably can be dated with precision to January 1979, when *Artforum* featured one of Jan Groover's new "kitchen sink" still lifes on its cover, accompanied inside by an article by Jeff Perrone. Groover was trained as a painter but had adopted photography while teaching at the University of Hartford at the beginning of the seventies. In the middle of the decade, living in New York, she made triptychs of street scenes differentiated by the colors of passing cars and trucks that harked back to Conceptual artists like Dan Graham; however, she soon loosened the format to allow for purely visual connections between adjacent images. These pictures were exhibited at Max Protetch Gallery and other art galleries, and also found their way into photography galleries, Light Gallery being the first, making her another exemplary "crossover" artist of the period.

In 1978, now using a large-format camera, Groover divorced the outside world to deal solely with a visual arena she would create within the confines of her kitchen sink, using as materials plants and cooking utensils. These pictures, intensely colored and reflective almost in the manner of Photorealist painting, and relatively large for color prints at the time, were exhibited at Sonnabend Gallery in fall 1978 and caused a sensation among the Soho crowd akin to what Eggleston's work had ignited uptown. As Perrone put it in *Artforum*, "the color kicks you right over."[25]

"Before anything else, the photographs are about color as the surface of objects, about objects as reflected, colored light, about the content of color photography," he continued. It was as if, for Perrone and undoubtedly for others, Groover's color still lifes had usurped one of the most cherished and primary functions of painting by grounding the description of objects in their color and their form, much like the Postimpressionist Paul Cézanne. As Groover would say, "Formalism is everything." She meant it to be contentious.

Taking the long view, more than forty years later, it seems fair to say that at the beginning of the seventies photographers saw new opportunities to make and exhibit work intended for the sole purpose of being seen as art. Artists, meanwhile, seem to have sensed that photographs were more than mere records of artistic performances and interventions, that they were fascinating in and of themselves. Broadly put, photographers then were intent on probing their medium's metaphysics, its first principles; artists were more interested in its functionality, in how photographs convey information and how we interpret them.

By the end of the seventies, these threads had woven together, if not into a single garment, then into a mesh that no longer could pull apart. Artists were regularly seeing photographs in museum and galleries and reading responses to them in magazines and newspapers; photographers now saw their medium in terms of its broader relevance to contemporary art and hoped to hop on board. It was all a bit confounding on both sides, and plenty of naysayers hoped art would learn to leave photography alone, and vice versa. But there was no turning back; photography had come to contemporary art to stay, not to visit.

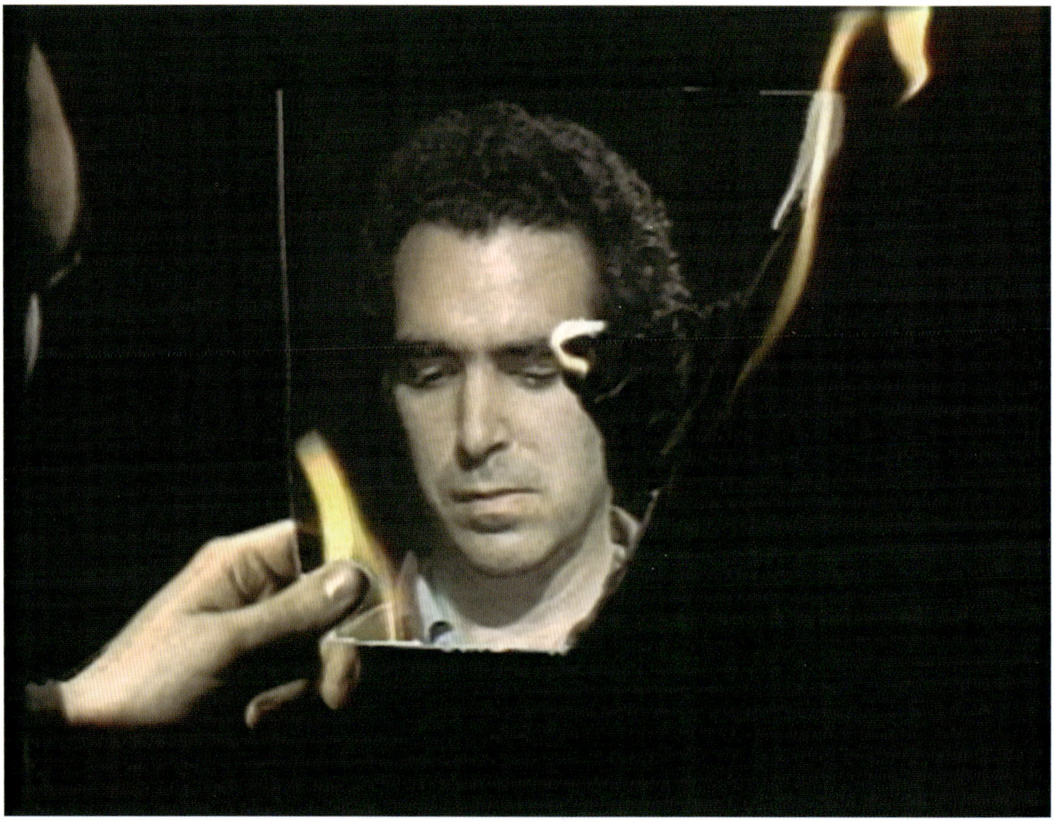

CHAPTER 8

Video, the Other Newcomer

I first had the urge to write for the *New York Times* one Sunday in 1980 when I was staying at the Chateau Marmont in Los Angeles, courtesy of an assignment from *Modern Photography,* where I continued to work while writing reviews for the *Soho Weekly News.* (This was before John Belushi's death made the hotel notorious and wildly popular.) I remember walking across Sunset Boulevard to Schwab's Pharmacy to buy the paper and opening up the Arts and Leisure section back in my room. The first thing I read was that week's review of a photography show, and it thoroughly annoyed me—probably because it seemed to be telling me only what I already knew. I could do better than that, I remember thinking, without a modicum of humility in sight. I suppose at that moment I recognized that what had been a pleasant sideline to my magazine job was becoming my career. But oddly enough, in retrospect, I didn't make a beeline to the *Times*'s offices when I got back.

So it was a surprise some weeks later when I got a call out of the blue from Hilton Kramer, the *Times*'s chief art critic, who asked if I would be interested in writing reviews for the paper. He explained that he was trying to add to its photography coverage and asked me to send clips of my work for *Art in America, Modern Photography,* and the *Soho Weekly News.* Apparently he had been following my writing, unbeknownst to me. Thus began a courtship that lasted several months, during which he called me multiple times to see if there were a show that I could write about for the next week's paper, only to call back the next day to say it wouldn't work out. I imagined that he was having a difficult time convincing the higher-ups that photography needed another writer, since Gene Thornton's reviews appeared regularly. Arthur Gelb, known as the paper's "culture czar," was not an easy man to convince of anything he did not already agree with.

When at last all parties agreed and I started writing for the *Times* in the spring of 1981 I joined a regular cast of bylines to be found on the Arts page of the Arts and Leisure section. Kramer usually wrote the lead review,

Still from Peter Campus's *Three Transitions*, 1973. Videotape (sound, color, 4:53 minutes).

although sometimes the honor went to John Russell, second in the critical pecking order. In either case, they appeared on the same page with two more critical contributions, one for architecture and one for photography. Paul Goldberger had just replaced the Pulitzer Prize–winning Ada Louise Huxtable on the architecture beat, and Thornton and I shared the photography spot. When I started we alternated weeks, but he moved on in 1987.[1]

Russell, a Briton by birth and a gentleman by nature, joined the *Times* in 1974, shortly after Kramer, who had begun working at the paper in 1965, was named the chief art critic. When a year after I came on board Kramer announced that he was leaving the paper to start a conservative cultural review, *The New Criterion,* Russell became the chief art critic and my de facto boss. Unlike Kramer, who let me know I should call him to get his agreement on what I thought worthy of reviewing, Russell was laissez-faire. He told me that since he knew nothing much about photography, I should consider myself the expert and review what I thought was important. It was an open invitation I much appreciated and promptly took advantage of.

Besides my column for the Sunday paper, I also contributed "Critics Choices" to the now-discontinued Guide section, obituaries, book reviews, and still more reviews when the paper started running a weekend visual-arts section in the Friday edition in the mid-eighties. I was assigned a couple of Sunday magazine articles involving Robert Rauschenberg and Robert Frank, and after a few years I inherited the weekly Camera View column, for which I wrote about new camera introductions and gave tips on how to take better pictures. But the Arts page on Sunday remained the biggest deal, in terms of both readership (I was told then it was more than a million) and influence.

The Arts page's layout changed over the ten years I wrote regularly for the *Times,* but some things remained consistent, including the writers serving as critics, with arts reporter Grace Glueck stepping in for a time, and the addition of Roberta Smith in 1985 and Michael Kimmelman in 1987. Another constant was the use of "slugs" to identify the genre of criticism: "Art View" and "Gallery View" for reviews by Kramer, Russell, and later Smith and Kimmelman, "Architecture View" for Goldberger, and "Photography View" for most of what I wrote.

I frequently chafed at this distinction. It probably didn't mean much to informed readers, who I imagine looked first at what the article was about and then at who wrote it, but the editors believed the slug helped the great unwashed locate what interested them. The problem was, what made sense in the seventies was seeming increasingly peculiar in the eighties—especially since artists like David Hockney had started showing photographs, and photographers like Cindy Sherman had started appearing in art galleries. An artist like Richard Prince would switch from photographing photographs to making fiberglass replicas of muscle-car hoods. This wasn't even all that new: Bruce Nauman had been traveling in and out of photography, film, video, neon, fiberglass, and wallboard since the sixties.

My issue with the "Photography View" slug came to a head when I wrote an appraisal of a video exhibition at the Museum of Modern Art ("Is Video at Odds with Photography?," Feb. 5, 1984). I argued to my editors that since it was really about video it shouldn't be slugged "Photography View" but maybe "Video View" or—better in my opinion—the generic "Art View." But they argued back that readers (always the disembodied court of last resort in any newsroom dispute) associated my writing with Photography View, so they would locate it more easily that way. So Photography View it stayed.

Now that I've looked at the article again, the editors' decision makes some sense, since I spent most of my review comparing video's place in the art world to photography's:

> Both were initially received in the world with all the enthusiasm due a pariah. . . . Based on the optics of Renaissance perspective, [photography] was seen as a degraded form of painting, yet threatening because of its purported "closeness to nature." Video, which uses photography's optics but electronic rather than chemical recording mechanisms, was born as commercial television. Commercial television quickly distinguished itself as Newton Minow's "vast wasteland;" when the first artists began to explore non-broadcast electronic imagery (strictly "video," that is, as opposed to "TV"), they stepped into waters already considered polluted.

I went on to note how the aesthetic practices of the two mediums were similarly split in two: "In the realm of art—or at least that which aspires to art—one finds photography and video sharing yet another division, this between documentary and formalist modes." I cited the documentary video maker Skip Blumberg as an example of the former; his *Pick Up Your Feet: The Double Dutch Show* was sufficiently conventional to be shown on public television. Nam June Paik, Bill Viola, and Steina and Woody Vasulka represented the experimental camp with their concentration on image manipulation and perceptual issues. I added that what seemed to me the best video work of the moment—by Juan Downey and Dara Birnbaum—lay between these two poles.

I was not alone in latching on to video as the new critical challenge of the moment. My colleague Grace Glueck had written an Arts and Leisure piece the previous spring about video's major presence in the Whitney Museum of American Art's 1983 Biennial—that ongoing litmus of what's contemporary and hip in the art world. What she had to say ("Video Comes into Its Own at the Whitney Biennial," April 24, 1983) could have been written about photography ten years earlier:

> We'd do better if we stopped trying to relate video to fine art, film, or even commercial television, and began to regard it as a developing medium in its own right, whose expressive capabilities are challenging some very innovative artists. What's good about the program at the Whitney—though not all of it is video at its best—is that it gives us an excellent idea of the strength and awesome flexibility of this sprawly medium, in offerings that range from narrative-documentary to essays in pure form.

In other words: Video, seen "as a developing medium in its own right," looked a lot like photography, another "sprawly medium" construed as ontologically unique under the banner of late Modernism. And both mediums seemed particularly suited to the historical moment.

My generation was the first to grow up with video—television, we called it—so it's no accident that people roughly my age were the pioneers of video art. I actually can remember life before a TV came into our house, when my family would gather around the radio on a weekday evening to listen to western serials and comedy shows performed in New York. Oddly, our first TV set, acquired in the fifties, didn't significantly change that ritual, since the fare—westerns, comedy—was pretty much the same, and the screen was so small and the black-and-white reception so poor that we all huddled together and pretty much listened.

Things got better by the sixties. Screens grew larger and color became the norm. The TV set became a piece of furniture positioned across from the couch. But there still were annoyances like horizontal drift, where the picture tipped over on its side, and vertical roll, where the picture scrolled up or down a frame at a time like an angry window shade. (This last defect is now immortalized in a classic artist's video by Joan Jonas, discussed later.) Then there were ghosts, shadow images caused by the broadcast signal reflecting off intervening obstructions. In my early years in New York, I greatly resented the World Trade Center far downtown because it had ruined my TV-watching ability, producing two dark tower-shaped shadows on my screen. Cable, which would have solved my problem, was just making its way into Manhattan and was widely marketed, but I couldn't afford it.

Considering the ubiquity and spectacular nature of video displays today, it bears remembering that early television, and hence early video art, was limited by the size of cathode-ray screens, which were encased in cabinets that more often than not resembled dressers. And it was television's sculp-

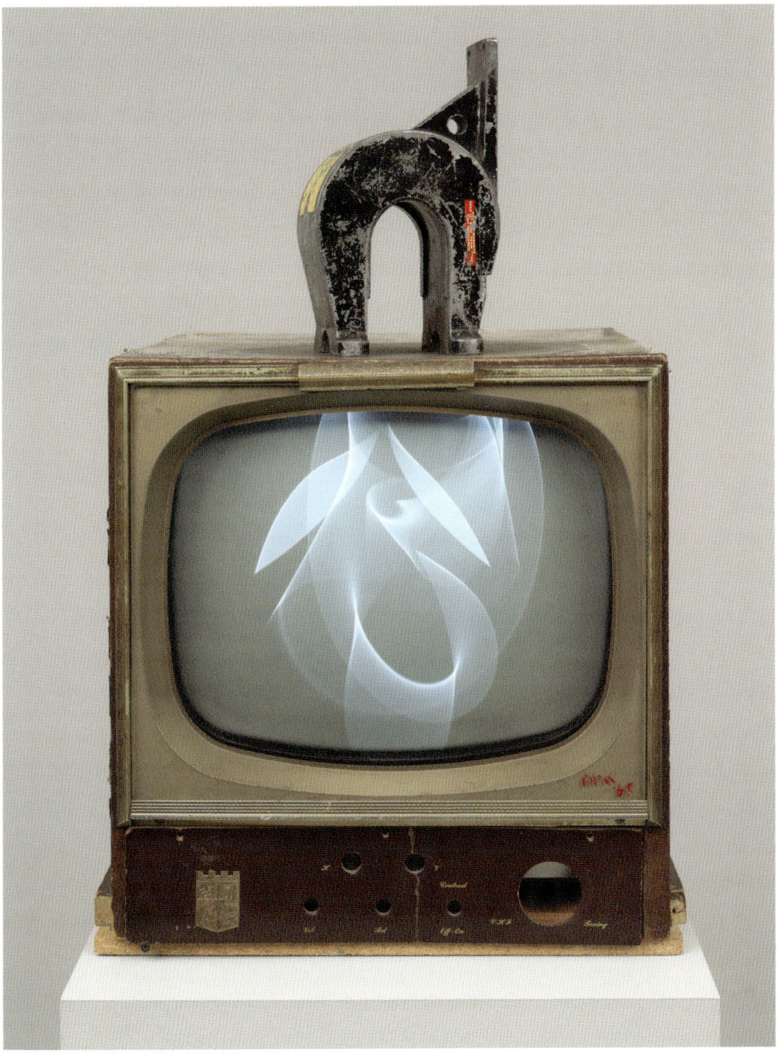

Nam June Paik, *Magnet TV*, 1965. Modified black-and-white television set and magnet. Whitney Museum of American Art, New York. Purchase, with funds from Dieter Rosenkranz.

tural presence, as a familiar everyday object, that led to what I think of as the beta version of video art. The Korean-born artist Nam June Paik, who while studying to be a composer in Europe fell under the influence of John Cage and the Fluxus art movement, showed what he called "prepared" television sets in a landmark exhibition at a gallery in Wuppertal, Germany, in 1963.

Each of the thirteen TV sets in the show had been manipulated so that its display of the broadcast signal it received was unconventional, if not bizarre. One of the pieces, *Zen for TV*, for example, reduced the broadcast image to a single vertical line in the middle of the screen. Paik also embellished the sets with sculptural appurtenances and included in the show three prepared pianos, a direct homage to Cage. Shortly after moving to New York City in 1964 he showed *Magnet TV* (1965), a television set with a powerful magnet on top that distorted the electron beam produced by the cathode-ray tube, making the broadcast image unreadable. Visitors to the gallery were invited to move the magnet around, creating new forms of distortions.

For many historians of video, Paik's prepared and magnet TV sets mark the birth of video art, but his work of the seventies is more foundational to what video art has become. That's because he went past his early focus on the television, with its broadcast-TV signal, to devise video experiences that make use of his own camera images or recycle and collage fragments snatched from commercial TV. *TV Buddha* of 1974 is exemplary: Paik placed a small statue of Buddha in front of a monitor and pointed a closed-circuit camera at the statue; the result was that the figure of Buddha appeared to be endlessly watching himself on screen in real time (although nothing really moved). The development of consumer-friendly video equipment in the midsixties helped Paik make this transition from altered set to intentional signal, as did his collaboration with an engineer to create one of the first video synthesizers, the Paik/Abe, which allowed him to mix video signals much like a twenty-first-century music DJ samples songs.

Sony's 1965 introduction of the Portapak system into the United States was a game changer that unleashed a wave of video experimentation by many of the artists who were already on a hunt for new means of art making. Paik was one of the first to acquire one in New York. The Portapak had several advantages for artists as well as for social activists interested in media. It was, first of all, and as the name implies, portable. The camera and its tethered recording deck could be carried by one person, or more comfortably by two, and it ran on batteries, so it could be used outside the studio. It recorded what the camera saw onto ½-inch videotape, which allowed for later editing (albeit primitive compared to the digital editing tools of today) and, most importantly, later presentation and duplication. And the price, while expensive for most of us at about $1,500, was low enough to allow successful and/or ambitious artists (or their dealers) to buy one.

In some cases, video simply served as a convenient replacement for film. But just as there were filmmakers who were fascinated by the unique qualities of film, there were artists like Paik who decided to investigate the experimental potentials of video. To a degree these artists took their cues from what was known as structuralist filmmaking, as practiced by the likes of Stan Brakhage, Hollis Frampton, Ken Jacobs, and Michael Snow, which largely jettisoned the plot-based, narrative structure of Hollywood films for structures based on formal cinematic elements. Snow's *Wavelength* (1967), for example, is one 45-minute long zoom that takes the audience from a wide view of his loft to a close-up of a seascape hanging on the far wall. Jacobs's *Tom, Tom, the Piper's Son* (1969) takes footage from an old silent film and recasts it by playing parts of it backward, zooming in on parts of the frame, and otherwise distorting its original conception.

The video artists Steina and Woody Vasulka took a similar approach in investigating the given formal elements of video and its distinct differences from film. Primarily this involved intervening in the electronic signal, à la Paik, producing abstract and painterly effects with arbitrary colors and shapes—effectively "violating" the standard television signal, in the Vasulkas' understanding. This was, in essence, the beginning of computer art, since the artists relied on custom-made signal generators and processors that in some cases were cobbled together by electronics engineers and self-styled video "freaks" (or, in the parlance of a pioneering video collective, "Videofreex") using primitive computerized devices. The Vasulkas played a central role in these early developments via the Kitchen, an artists' space in downtown Manhattan largely dedicated to showing video, which they founded in 1971.[2]

Other artists of the period investigated the formal possibilities of using video in unconventional ways without disrupting the signal itself. Richard Serra, known now for his large steel-plate sculptures like the controversial *Tilted Arc*, produced a pair of influential tapes, *Television Delivers People* (1973) and *Boomerang* (1974). The former consists of a rolling text didactically describing how commercial interests manipulate us ("the audience") via entertainment; *Boomerang*, cocredited to Nancy Holt, Robert Smithson's widow and an environmental sculptor herself, shows Holt trying to keep in sync with a voice-delay system that echoes her words back to her. Both videotapes try to create a critical awareness of how television works (and works on us).

In similar fashion, but with a much more perceptual focus and psychological impact, Peter Campus mixed the signals of two video cameras so they would display on a single monitor and proceeded to perform various actions bringing the cameras in and out of sync. In the different sections of this work, *Double Vision* (1971), the cameras are set to different focal lengths, show slightly different views of a room, and create a parallax effect, suggesting eyes that are too tired to focus.

Campus's *Three Transitions*, made in color in 1973 with the support of the New Television Workshop at WGBH, a public television station in Boston, is even more body-centric; each of the three sections shows the artist himself—as an image that disappears as it burns, as a figure that emerges from the backdrop even as it disappears from the foreground, and as a face that vanishes as cream is applied to its features. (Chroma-key, the technique of replacing one hue with a separate image, as is done with weather maps behind the weather person on the news, was used to create the uncanny effects in *Three Transitions*.) Campus also, as did Vito Acconci and Bruce Nauman, produced interactive "live" video works using close-circuit cameras in gallery spaces.

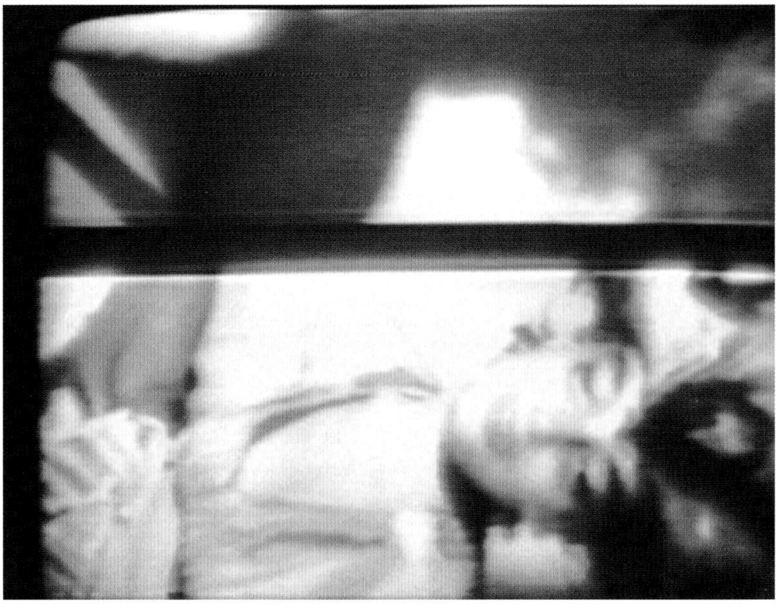

Still from Joan Jonas's *Vertical Roll*, 1972. Videotape (sound, black and white, 19:38 minutes).

Campus's *Three Transitions* has justly been called one of the seminal works in early video art,[3] but perhaps the ultimate honor should go to Joan Jonas's *Vertical Roll* (1972), which combines structuralist rigor, psychological intensity, corporeal presence, and feminist conviction in one 20-minute, black-and-white videotape. It is excruciating to watch, in large part because the picture frame rhythmically scrolls from top to bottom accompanied by the sharp thwack of what sounds like a blacksmith's hammer (actually, only a spoon[4]). Beyond these "surface" effects, one slowly perceives a female figure who presents herself to the camera in various forms, masked, costumed, or naked, including in the guise of a belly dancer. The camera slowly scans the body as the screen flickers, producing a queasy sense of unease and, in theoretical terms, disrupting the male gaze, until at the end the artist's face turns to the camera and stares directly at the viewer. But *Vertical Roll,* which was first shown at Castelli Gallery in 1973,[5] is also mesmerizing, hooking the viewer for its duration without delivering even the most remote hint of a plot.

Vertical Roll and its experimental ilk were never intended to be broadcast on television, even though many of the efforts of early video artists were assisted by WGBH in Boston, WNET in New York, and a few other public stations around the country. Instead, video art found a home, only slightly uneasily, in contemporary art galleries like Castelli and Sonnabend. Leo Castelli's Soho gallery presented shows of artists' films starting in 1971 and added video to the list in 1972, with a group show that included Jonas, Nauman, and Serra. Still, the market for video work was miniscule. So in 1974 Castelli joined forces with Sonnabend and formed Castelli-Sonnabend

Videotapes and Films in an effort to distribute, if not profit from, their gallery artists' work. (As it turned out, most of the distribution was to art schools and artists' spaces, which received a reduced rental rate, so the venture was in effect a loss leader.)[6]

The confrontational, even aggressive aspect of Campus's and Jonas's video experiments have much in common with the video works of Acconci and Nauman, which were not so much about the formal possibilities of the medium as about the relationship of the artist/maker to the audience. Acconci's *Claim* (1971) is probably the most dramatic: Blindfolded, and wielding a metal pipe, the artist stood at the bottom of the basement stairs of a loft building at 93 Grand Street with a video camera trained on him, repeatedly asserting that the space around him was his. Visitors confronted by a closed door at the top of the stairs could see and hear him on a closed-circuit monitor placed nearby. Some chose to open the door, thereby viewing Acconci directly; a very few chose to descend and ended up scuffling with him briefly before they were forced to retreat. As in *Seedbed*, the artist's presence in real time (or "live," in TV lingo) forced his audience into an ambiguous, discomfiting position. But the experience of *Claim* also was mediated by the closed circuit of the video.

Nauman, whose work has had a profound influence on the artists of his and my generation, started creating performances for the camera in his studio in San Francisco's Mission District soon after moving there in 1966, after finishing grad studies at the University of California, Davis. At first his activities were recorded with still photographs and short 16mm films. Two years later he switched to video, a move no doubt helped along by his being newly represented by Leo Castelli, who was encouraging several of his artists to try making art with the Portapak system he had recently purchased.

Nauman has been called a Postminimalist (by Irving Sandler, for one) because his early work took the form of sculpture. In reality, Nauman is sui generis: sometimes a sculptor, sometimes a Conceptual artist, sometimes a performance artist, always an artist exploring the boundaries between his own body and the physical world and between his private existence and his public audience. In San Francisco, Nauman produced two distinct kinds of objects: casts of various parts of his body (e.g., *From Hand to Mouth*, 1967, made of wax) and neon signs that he commissioned from commercial makers (most famously, *The True Artist Helps the World by Revealing Mystic Truths*, 1967). Sometimes the two modes merged, as in *Neon Templates of the Left Half of My Body Taken at Ten-Inch Intervals* (1966), a series of glowing green arcs that together suggest the artist's body standing in profile.

At the same time he ventured into less-tangible materials: photography, film, and video. One of Nauman's earliest video efforts, *Stamping in the Studio* (1968), also became one of the most enduring. In *Stamping*, Nauman

Still from Bruce Nauman's *Stamping in the Studio*, 1968. Videotape (sound, black and white, 62:00 minutes).

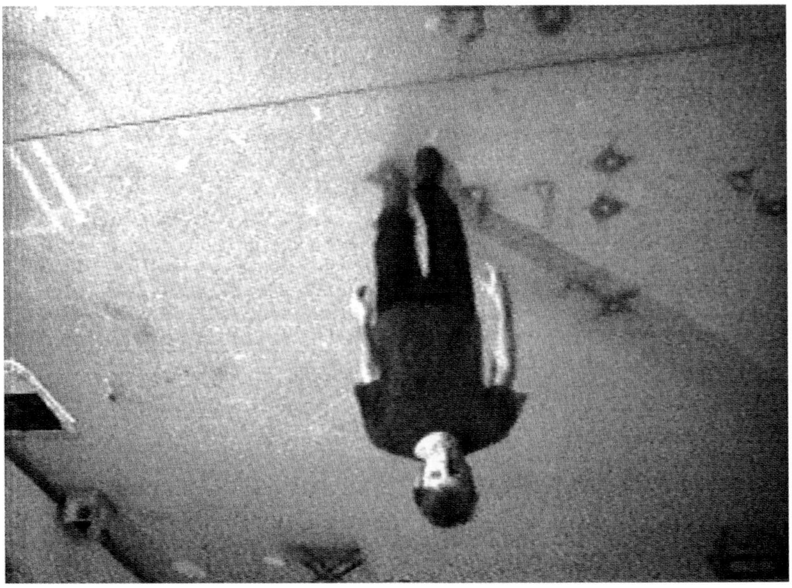

trudges around the edges of a bare studio space (at a rented house on Long Island) for what seems an eternity, although it is really "only" 60 minutes, the length of the video reel he used.[7] Disconcertingly, the action is shown upside down, as if the artist were stamping on the ceiling.

Nauman was drawn to lens-based media for a reason: "Films are about seeing. I wanted to find out what I would look at in a strange situation, and I decided that with a film and camera I could do that." And like the Earth and Conceptual artists working at the same time (Robert Smithson, John Baldessari, et al.), he liked the inherent veracity of the camera image: "You tend to believe that what is shown on a film is really true—you believe a film, or a photograph, more than a painting."[8] Some of his short, 16mm films seem to be about this idea and nothing more: a door closing, or a window shade rolling up, both apparently on their own.[9]

The videotapes, however, seem to be less about the veracity of the camera image and more about the endurance and patience of the viewer. Most last an hour, which is a fairly comfortable interval if we are sitting on a couch in our living rooms watching network programming but interminable for anyone standing in a gallery or museum. And the actions they depict—Nauman's repetitive motions with little to no external significance—numb the mind long before the tape reaches its end. (A more recent Nauman work, *Mapping the Studio I [Fat Chance John Cage]*, from 2001, takes this to a radical extreme, charting some forty hours of his studio during the night. The occasional entrance of a few mice and a cat provide the sole action.)[10]

I was introduced to the world of video art soon after landing in New York through my acquaintance with William Wegman, whose work Holly

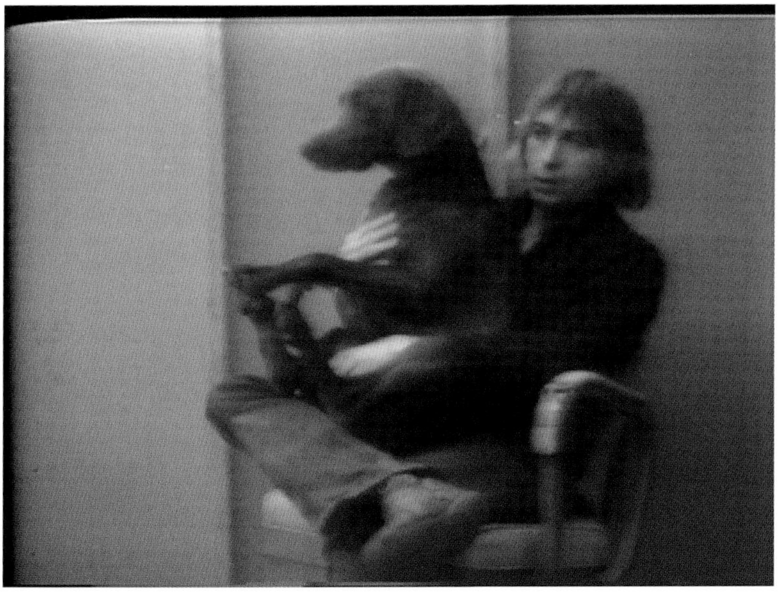

Still from William Wegman's *New and Used Car Salesman*, 1973. Videotape (sound, black and white, 1:31 minutes).

Solomon supported even when he linked up with Castelli Gallery, which distributed his short videotapes and gave him a show, together with another video artist, Frank Gillette, in 1975. Solomon had first turned me on to Wegman's photography, but I ended up enjoying his videos even more because they tended to be send-ups of what we had come to expect from television—earnest car salesmen imploring us to visit their lots (*New and Used Car Salesman*, 1973)—or absurd demonstrations of dog behaviors (*Dog Duet* and *Dog Biscuit in Glass Jar*, both 1972). And unlike other videos I had happened upon up to that point, they were mercifully short: a minute or two on average. In this sense Wegman and Nauman were making video art on opposite ends of the fourth dimension.

In terms of sheer amusement, or deadpan humor, the artist whose videos come closest to Wegman is John Baldessari—coincidentally, their still photography appeared adjacent to each other in the Eastman House's *The Extended Document* photography show. In a now-classic 1972 video, *Baldessari Sings LeWitt*, the California artist "covers" the complete text of Sol LeWitt's famous *Sentences on Conceptual Art* using a sing-song voice that is at once nerve-grating and deconstructive. Baldessari's *Teaching a Plant the Alphabet*, done the same year, is similar in its human presumption to Wegman's *Spelling Lesson*, a brief vignette in which Wegman grades the results of a spelling test supposedly completed by his dog Man Ray. Like Wegman's, Baldessari's videos were distributed through the partnership of Castelli and Sonnabend galleries.[11]

Video and photography shared more than being the new kids on the block in the art world of the seventies. Unlike painting and sculpture, and

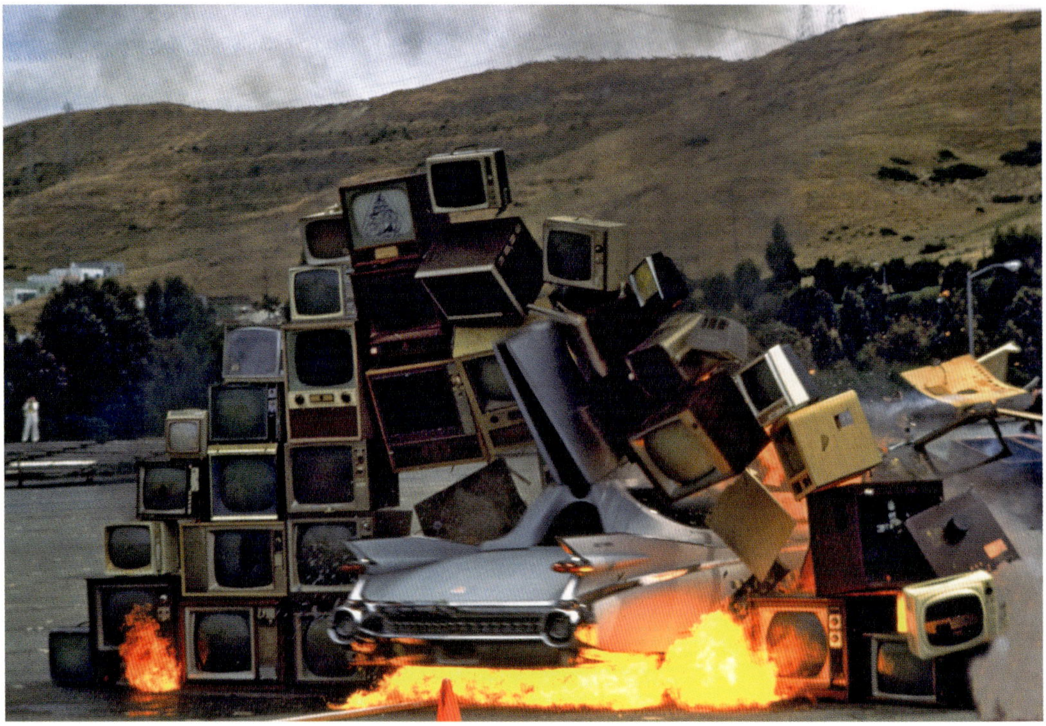

Still from Ant Farm's *Media Burn*, 1975. Videotape (sound, color, 23:02 minutes).

even installation and performance art, their practices extended well beyond the aesthetic. A version of the two mediums was visible on a daily basis in the mass media, in print and broadcast on the air, and like film they were widely used to deliver verifiable information in a way that could be believed as true. The lenses of their cameras, after all, were known as "objectives." Their audiences were huge, and presumed by theorists to be blissfully unaware of how mass media were influencing their lives.

Some artists in video's early days were attracted to the more traditional documentary function of the camera, producing broadcast-style tapes filled with interviews and on-the-scene news clips. Top Value Television (TVTV), for example, gained a modicum of fame for its cinema-verité-style documentaries on the 1972 presidential nominating conventions, which were originally aired on cable television. TVTV's founder, Michael Shamberg, was the author of *Guerrilla Television* (Holt, Reinhart and Winston, 1971) and an early believer in documentary video as a radical social instrument, despite its reliance on a commercial-television model. Paper Tiger Television, in New York, produced a long series of cable TV shows that critiqued mass media, most notably six half-hour segments of *Herb Schiller Reads the New York Times*, during which the University of California, San Diego professor provided an anticapitalist textual analysis of the American newspaper of record.

This urge to critique the dominant forms of mass media, and in particular television itself, extended to video artists who riffed on the documentary mode. A West Coast collective called Ant Farm, whose members included Chip Lord and Skip Blumberg, created *Media Burn* (1975) in an empty parking lot in San Francisco; the "plot" consisted of driving a customized Cadillac convertible into a pyramidical wall of burning TV sets, but the action also includes clips of local TV news coverage of the event and an artist, Doug Hall, who makes an appearance impersonating President John F. Kennedy.

Hall reprises his Kennedy role in another madcap/perverse video made the same year by Ant Farm and a second San Francisco–based collective, T. R. Uthco, *The Eternal Frame*. *Frame* restages the Kennedy assassination in Dallas complete with a Dealey Plaza drive-through based on the famous Zapruder film, and, like *Media Burn*, features real news coverage of the patently fake "event." Needless to say, these tapes were not destined to appear on broadcast television, nor did they feature much in the domain of the Soho galleries; mainly they were seen on cable channels designated for "public access," which were available for everything from satiric documentaries to a topless talk show.[12]

The rest of the art video activity of the time took place in galleries, artists' spaces, lofts, and museums, where it was distinct from the standard fare of audiences for the visual arts, whose attention span for looking at a work of art averages around 15 seconds. This, and the fact that the screen was relatively small and embedded in a box, put video art at a real disadvantage. A few foresighted museum curators established credible video departments and programs in the seventies—John Hanhardt at the Whitney Museum of American Art, Barbara London at MoMA, David Ross at Boston's Institute of Contemporary Art, Kathy Rae Huffman at Long Beach Museum of Art—and were supported by a handful of early video critics (notably Lucinda Furlong) and some sympathetic journals, such as the Visual Studies Workshop's *Afterimage*.

Hanhardt came to the Whitney as a curator of film in 1974 but soon added video to his domain, securing a Rockefeller Foundation grant to enable videos to be projected within the museum's existing theater built for exhibiting artist-made films. Projecting video then was unusual and difficult, requiring an expensive device and a darkened room; nonetheless, Hanhardt mounted a group video show in 1975 that was all projected. The same year, video was officially recognized as a part of the Whitney Biennial for the first time. The "single channel" works projected in the theater were complemented by videos shown as parts of installations in the galleries, where they had to appear on conventional monitors.[13] Important video makers like Juan Downey, a Chilean-born artist who had moved to

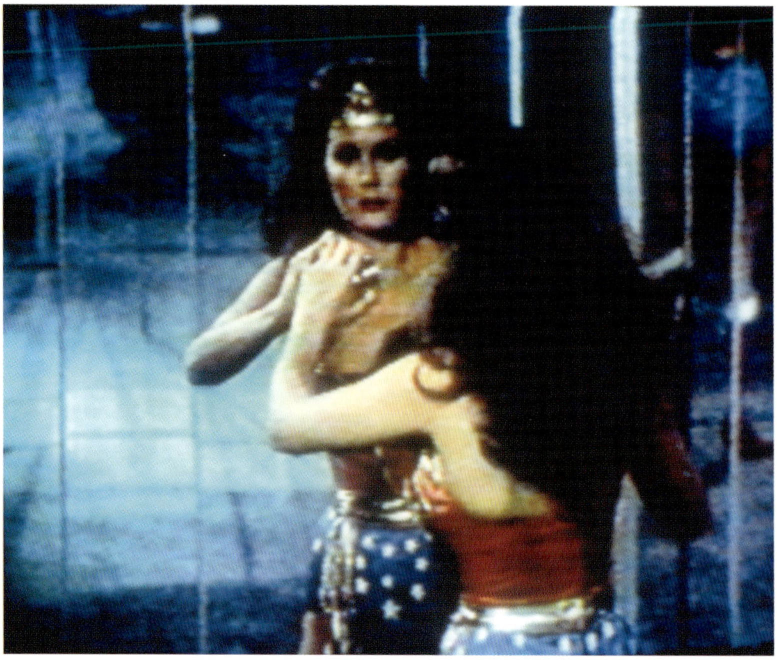

Still from Dara Birnbaum's *Technology/Transformation: Wonder Woman*, 1978–79. Videotape (sound, color, 5:50 minutes).

New York in 1969, were included in the 1975 Biennial; with Hanhardt's backing, Downey's work was part of eight Biennials prior to the artist's death in 1993.

According to records at MoMA, in 1976 a *Projects* show featuring Peter Campus included a video projector as well as a camera, two "closed-circuit video machines," four videotapes, and six Polaroid photographs. The projection, in a room with dark-painted walls, showed Campus's face as an outsized, upside-down mask. The exhibition was organized by Barbara London, then a young assistant curator in the Department of Prints and Illustrated Books; shortly thereafter she was named the museum's first curator of video, within its existing Department of Film.

By 1980 video art had enough institutional support to attract artists just starting their careers, like Dara Birnbaum, who came to video with degrees in architecture and painting. Her six-minute masterpiece *Technology/Transformation: Wonder Woman* (1978–79) and a nearly concurrent work, *Kiss the Girls: Make Them Cry* (1979), both appropriate standard broadcast television shows of the time (*Wonder Woman* and *Hollywood Squares*, respectively) and through editing and sound refashion them into critiques of television's depiction of women. In the *Wonder Woman* piece, for example, the eponymous heroine repeatedly transforms herself into character (and costume) while surrounded by dressing-room mirrors, which reflect her in near-infinite regress. The soundtrack at the end of the piece is a contemporaneous and apt disco song, "Wonder Woman Disco" by The Wonderland

Disco Band, the lyrics of which scroll down the screen, urging listeners to "shake your Wonder Woman." Feminist and Postmodern in equal measure, Birnbaum's work was one of the first to directly quote from video's most public face, at the same time that artists like Barbara Kruger and Richard Prince were starting to use commercial photographs to reflect the medium back on itself.

In part because of artists like Birnbaum, video art began to attract the attention of serious art historians and critical theorists just as photography was getting the same kind of scrutiny. In 1980 the Kitchen organized a symposium called "Television/Society/Art"; among the speakers and panelists were Benjamin Buchloh, Fredric Jameson, Rosalind Krauss, Martha Rosler, and Allan Sekula, all of whom were associated directly with the journal *October* or affiliated with its theoretical bent.[14] And like photography, video art was fast becoming a "field" of its own, with an attendant rise of self-consciousness about its own (brief) history and traditions. The American Film Institute organized the National Video Festival in Washington, D.C., starting in 1981; the Walker Art Center cosponsored "The Media Arts in Transition," a conference in Minneapolis in 1983; and in 1984 both the Long Beach Museum of Art in California and the Museum of Modern Art in New York mounted two-part histories of video art (*Video: A Retrospective* and *Video Art: A History*, respectively).[15]

In terms of the mainstream of contemporary art and its audiences, however, video remained a small tributary until the 1983 Whitney Biennial, when critical attention garnered by Mary Lucier's *Ohio at Giverny* launched a much broader appreciation of video's potentials. Her piece was—in a word previously unheard in video criticism—beautiful. My colleague John Russell put it on the map with a gushing review in the *Times*, despite what he admitted was "a lifelong allergy to video in most of its forms." Lucier's work, which interplayed two 20-minute videotapes on seven screens, mostly portrays Monet's famous small-town home and garden, using luscious colors and ambient sounds. For Russell,

> What may sound like a travelogue, seemed to this visitor to have a poetry without precedent. It is hard to know which to admire most—the shifting movement of the sevenfold image, the implications of memory, renewal and loss, the sudden stab of sound or the blessed freedom from banality.[16]

What made Lucier's piece distinct, in my memory of seeing the show, was its location in the main galleries of the Biennial, together with painting, sculpture, and photography, and the fact that it seemed to have no beginning or end (although, of course, it did loop back on itself). I could, that is

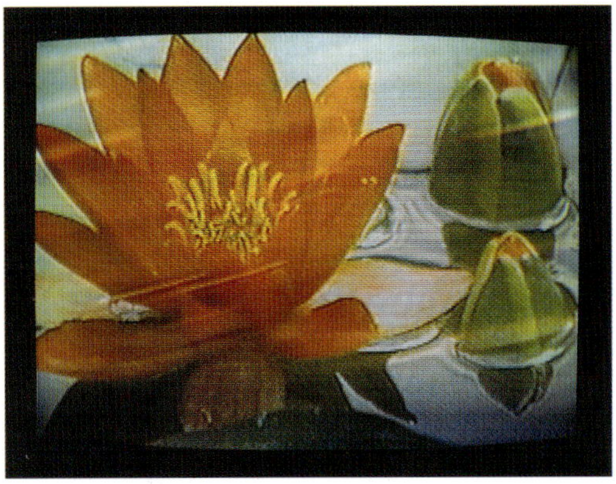

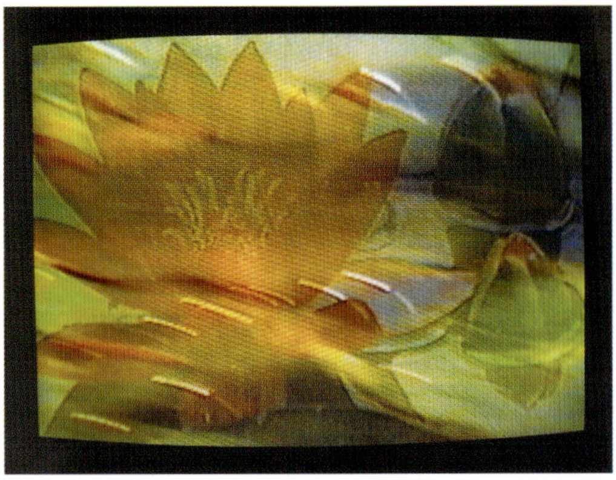

Four stills from Mary Lucier's *Ohio at Giverny*, 1983 (excerpt of *Water Lily Dissolve*). Videotape (sound, color, 19:00 minutes).

to say, walk up to the piece—its seven monitors were embedded in a wall, and the images shifted from one screen to the next in a slow glide—and not worry that I had not seen the start. Nor did I feel compelled by any narrative to stand there for 20 minutes, shifting from foot to foot. Instead, I stood there because the progress of the images was so captivating that I didn't want to leave.

Critics of the Biennial also singled out for praise Bill Viola's *Hatsu-Yume (First Dream)*, a 56-minute lyric that surveys the Japanese landscape from ocean's edge to a bamboo garden and back to the sea, verging from day to night. Equally beautiful (and haunting) as *Ohio at Giverny*, it was screened in the museum's film and video theater according to a set schedule. This enforced the idea that you were meant to see it from start to finish, a nearly one-hour commitment that few casual museum-goers would be willing to make. *Hatsu-Yume* is a form of cinema, in short, providing one model of what the art of video could become. Viola had made several equally meditative and beautiful studies like his 1979 *Chott el-Djerid (A Portrait in Light and Heat)*, in the same cinematic vein, before verging into installation pieces that, like Lucier's, command the gallery space. His *Room for St. John of the Cross*, created in 1983, includes a wall-sized video projection of mountains set behind a small box in the center of the room that contains a table, chair, and tiny monitor. Viola has gone on to create magical theatrical effects with rear-projection, double-sided freestanding screens, and other cutting-edge projection techniques.

Advances in video projection, including an eventual convergence with computer-based projectors that use a digital signal, helped liberate video art from what media scholar Margaret Morse has called "the apparatus of television," but for much of the eighties artists were still pressing against the limitations of the medium as defined by the cathode-ray tube and the TV

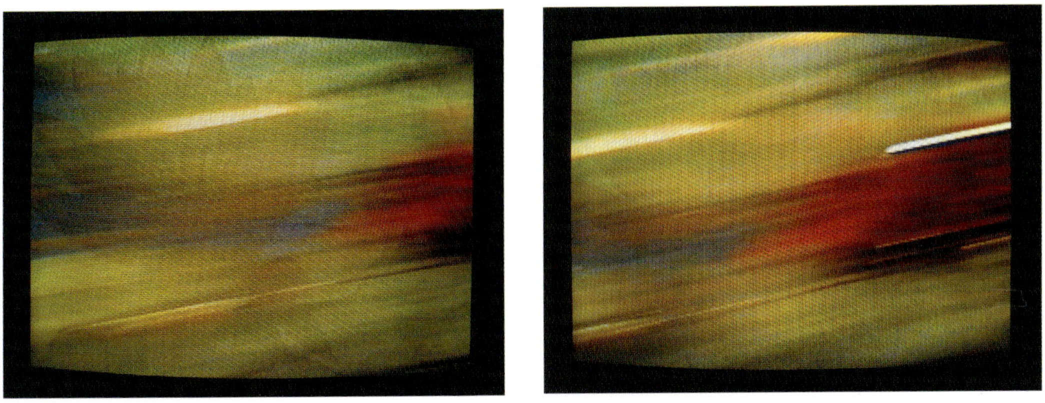

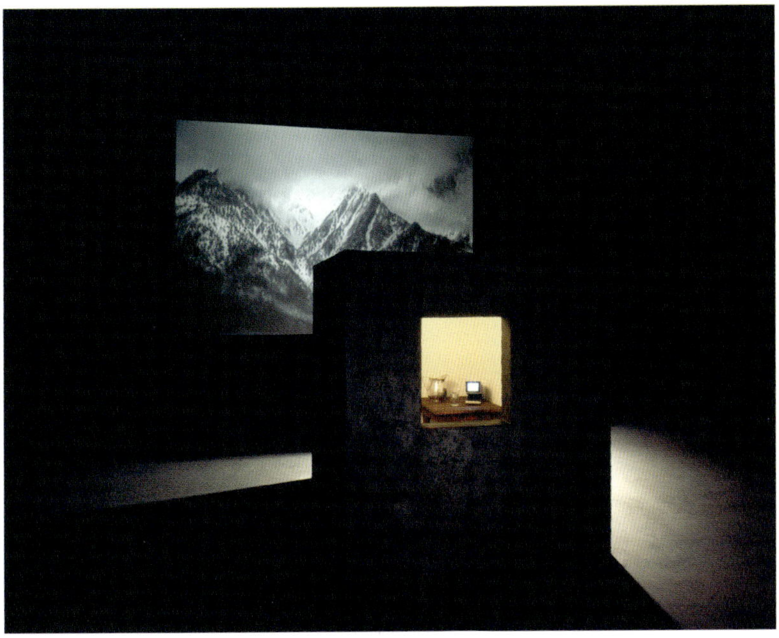

Installation view of Bill Viola's *Room for St. John of the Cross*, 1983. Video/sound installation.

"box." Similarly, photography was limited by its reliance on commercially available printing paper: until the eighties, most "art" photographs were between 8 × 10 inches and 20 × 24 inches, a size comparable to drawings and prints but small compared to most paintings. Only with the availability of much larger paper, and of labs dedicated to using it, did photography gain the same wall presence as painting—a phenomenon conveniently marked by the exhibition *Big Pictures by Contemporary Photographers* at the Museum of Modern Art, which appeared the same spring as the 1983 Whitney Biennial with Lucier's *Ohio at Giverny*.

Tina Barney, *Sunday New York Times*, 1982.

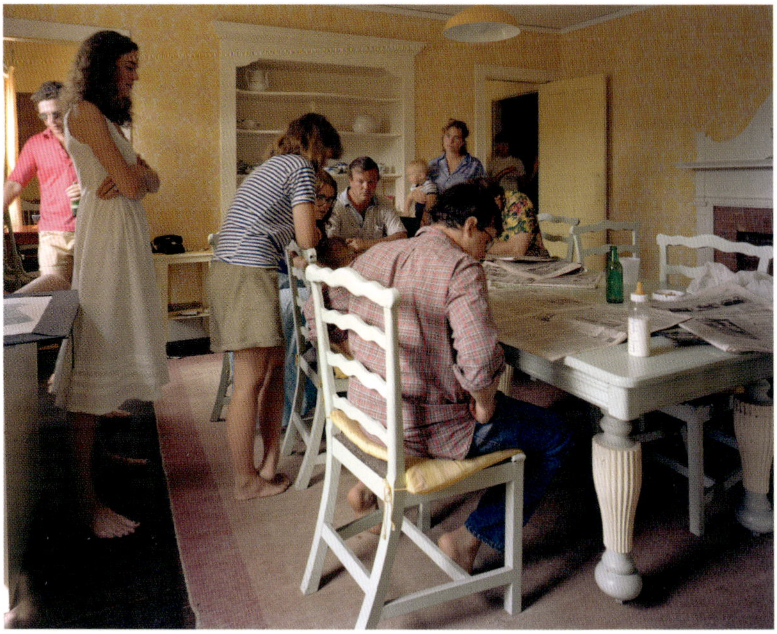

In reviewing *Big Pictures* for the *Times* ("Big Pictures That Say Little," May 8, 1983) I claimed that with the show the museum "for the first time publicly takes notice of the state of photography in the 1980s." Big was certainly part of it, but it wasn't the size itself that mattered, I argued:

> Considered as a survey of formal responses to the issue of large scale, however, "Big Pictures" is a big bore. There are just too many derivations of multiple-framing techniques, too many art-world grids, too many horizontal panoramas for anyone to emerge from this show convinced that we are seeing a demonstration of new formal possibilities. What we are seeing here, I think, are the last vestiges of photographic Modernism mixed rather confusingly with the early stages of Postmodernist practice, which conceives of scale in less formal terms and more in terms of impact and presence.

I went on to say that the show's standout image was a 4 × 5-foot color print by Tina Barney, *Sunday New York Times*, which I referred to as both snapshot-like and documentary. It was Barney's smash debut into the consciousness of the art world, and I enjoyed the great irony (perhaps meta-irony?) of calling it out in my review—since it happened to appear in the self-same newspaper that the family in her photograph was sitting down to read.

But more germane: My review pointed to something new in the practice and reception of photography, a hinge between the traditional frame hung around the art of photography and its new appearance in the world of art. (Just as Birnbaum's *Wonder Woman* could be said to mark a similar turn in video art.) I wasn't the first to use the terms, for sure, but in describing the sides of that hinge in the *Times* as Modernist and Postmodernist I was sticking my finger in photography's current sore spot. What could that mean, more than one reader wondered? What makes a photograph Postmodernist, or Modernist even? To know that, one had to have been paying attention not only to the newest contemporary art but also to the growing influence of cultural criticism and critical theory.

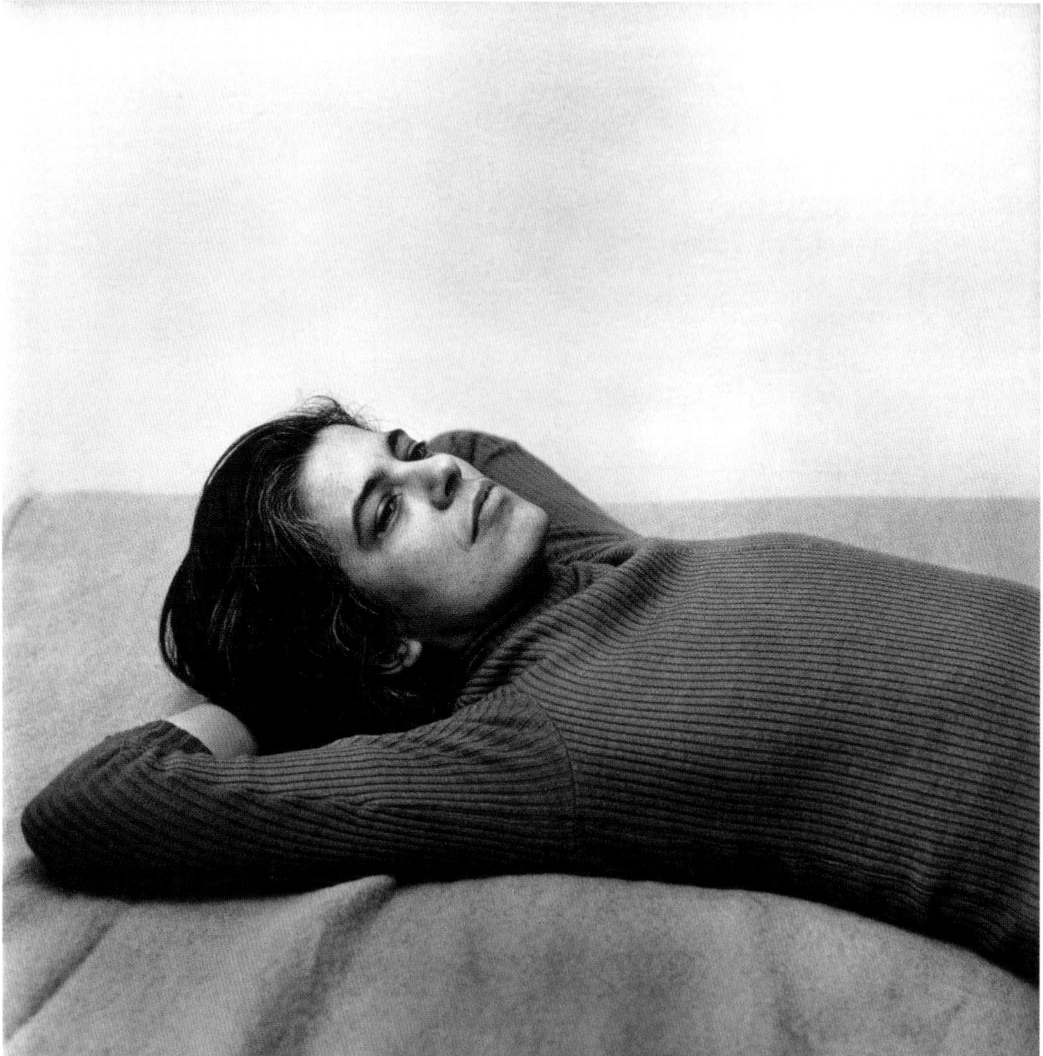

CHAPTER 9

Theory

Earlier much futile thought had been devoted to the question of whether photography is an art. The primary question—whether the very invention of photography had not transformed the entire nature of art—was not raised.

—Walter Benjamin, "The Work of Art in the Age of Mechanical Reproduction," 1936

For these artists and critics, art is not a timeless manifestation of human spirit, but the product of a specific set of temporal and topical, social and political conditions. The investigations of these conditions defines for us the activity of postmodernism.

—Rosalind Krauss and Annette Michelson, "Editorial," *October* 10, fall 1979

What exactly makes a photograph a work of art? The question became a central preoccupation of the seventies as more and more photographs were presented in museums and galleries, collected, sold at auction, and reviewed in the press. This led to a vast expansion of the medium's critical literature, initially from "insiders" like MoMA's director of photography, John Szarkowski, whose 1973 book *Looking at Photographs* convincingly suggested that the answer might be plural. Established photography-specific journals *Aperture* and *Image*, joined by upstarts like the Visual Studies Workshop's *Afterimage*, presented extended critical essays about photographers' work and also speculations about the nature of the medium as an instrument of creative expression.

I was an avid admirer of Szarkowski's book, which I enjoyed as much for the sophistication of its writing as for what it said about photographic aesthetics, and I regularly read the photographic journals, seeking out my own answers about what the art of photography might be. In part I was curious because I had an ambition to make photographs that could be considered art, and in part because in the midseventies I began to flex my critical muscles honed in literature and devote them to photography.

Peter Hujar, *Susan Sontag*, 1975.

But then there was the question of what photography criticism was, or should be. In a widely read 1975 essay A. D. Coleman, who wrote criticism for several publications in the early seventies, decried "the lack of a functional vocabulary for the criticism of photography,"[1] adding that "there is in fact nothing yet approaching a true critical dialogue taking place within photography."[2] The word *dialogue* is crucial here, since Coleman could easily have considered himself a one-man band. He started writing photography columns for the *Village Voice* in 1968, *Popular Photography* in 1969, and the *New York Times* in 1970—although he had parted ways with all of them by 1974.[3] Coleman's phrase *within photography* is also telling: his frame of reference was the universe of photographers and their "field," which he considered distinct from the realm of art and art criticism in general.

That other realm, however, already had created a dialogue about the nature of photography and its aesthetic claims. In addition to the several articles about Eadweard Muybridge's work generated by Conceptual artists, a book's worth of ruminative essays about photography was published in *Artforum* in the seventies. Among these were Max Kozloff's "The Uncanny Portrait: Sander, Arbus, Samaras," in June 1973; Jan Groover's "The Medium Is the Use," in November 1973; and Martha Rosler's "Lee Friedlander's Guarded Strategies," in April 1975. (It helped that *Artforum*'s editors at the time, John Coplans and Max Kozloff, had soft spots for the medium; after they left the magazine, they became exhibiting photographers.) The Conceptual artist Les Levine published "Camera Art" in *Studio International*, in the summer of 1975, in which he boldly announced, "Camera Art is a postcraft discipline."

At the same time, and more broadly, the extent of photography's cultural significance attracted curiosity across a spectrum of intellectual endeavors with no stake in whether a photograph could be considered art. What ultimately would prove a great deal more influential in terms of photography's future place in the art world came from writers assaying the medium from perspectives ranging from perceptual psychology and sociology to literature and linguistics. The opening thunderclap in this dense outpouring was Susan Sontag's series of essays published in the *New York Review of Books* starting in 1973, and collected in the book *On Photography* in 1977.

Sontag, whose reputation as a literary critic had been built on her essays in the books *Against Interpretation* and *Styles of Radical Will*, was inspired to examine photography phenomenologically in large part because of Diane Arbus's posthumous 1972 retrospective at the Museum of Modern Art. The show's mordant immediacy and emotional power fueled Sontag to survey the history of photography and its literature, producing a book that is as famous for its aperçus ("To photograph is to appropriate the thing photographed") as for its overriding premise, which is that photography is an agent of the surreal rather than a reflection of the real. "All that photography's program of realism actually implies is that reality is hidden," she writes, connecting its images to the project of surrealist art, which renders the world strange and therefore at one remove from what, in the Platonic sense, really matters: truth. Photography merely fixes the shadows cast on the wall of Plato's cave by the real world.[4]

The book's final chapter is titled, prophetically, "The Image-World," in which Sontag takes the medium to task as an agent of (capitalist) consumption—"As we make images and consume them, we need more images; and still more"—and as a perversion (again, Platonically) of reality itself: "images consume reality."[5]

The publication of *On Photography* had two, essentially contradictory effects on the photography field. It confounded and enraged photographers and their supporters because of its dim view of their enterprise as documenters of social reality or even as fine-art creators capable of seeing and depicting the world anew. But it also prompted attention to the medium in a much wider arena than had previously been the case. The dialogue that critic A. D. Coleman found so missing within the field had now been joined from without, which itself was annoying to many of the photographers I encountered at exhibition openings and lectures. I found their hostile responses puzzling: if you wanted the world to notice what you were doing, why not enjoy the attention? To me, it was a classic case of the PR truism, "There's no such thing as bad publicity."

As a largely pragmatic writer, I was more engaged by Sontag's argument as it applied to specific photographers whose work I found difficult to explain, notably Diane Arbus and Richard Avedon, and by its insistent focus on the camera's public role. Hers was not an aesthetic argument—certainly not of the sort I was used to, anyway—as much as a philosophical one. Indeed, there was an implicit philosophical basis for how she viewed photography, which she also used as a source for her criticism of literature: the so-called Frankfurt School of critical theory, the birthplace of neo-Marxist thought in the thirties and a key influence on American cultural critics ever since. Led by such thinkers as Max Horkheimer, Theodor W. Adorno, and Herbert Marcuse, the Frankfurt School was especially interested in the rise of mass culture, including art, film, and—most explicitly in Walter Benjamin's classic 1936 essay "The Work of Art in the Age of Mechanical Reproduction"—photography.

"The Work of Art in the Age of Mechanical Reproduction," part of a collection of essays (*Illuminations*) published in Germany in 1955 and made available in English translation in 1968, is divided almost equally between

Benjamin's analyses of photography and film. Both mediums he finds revolutionary instruments of representation, capable of reorganizing human consciousness in ways that can subvert the dominion of capitalism. Photography, only recently come into mass popularity via a postwar "picture press" that took advantage of the new technology of halftone reproduction (i.e., "mechanical reproduction"), he saw as transforming the very nature of art: famously, "That which withers in the age of mechanical reproduction is the aura of the work of art."[6] But he remained somewhat ambivalent about the result: the decline of the aura frees art from age-old tradition ("ritual," "uniqueness"), but it also seems to wither the possibility of transcendence (the "melancholy, incomparable beauty" of the faces in old portraits).[7]

Although Benjamin's ideas are not directly acknowledged by Sontag in *On Photography*, and there are no footnotes in any of its essays, she does quote his writing in her text and, in the book's coda, includes him in a section called "A Brief Anthology of Quotations," which is subtitled "[Homage to W. B.]." (Benjamin himself is legendary for having collected hundreds of quotes.)

Another writer of considerable import for Sontag's encounter with photography was Roland Barthes, a Frenchman whose work began appearing in English translation also starting in the late sixties. A critic and theoretician who himself would become preoccupied with photography in the seventies, Barthes looked at literature through a succession of frameworks: linguistic, semiotic (what he called semiology), structuralist and poststructuralist, and psychological. Sontag wrote an introduction for the American edition of his first book, *Writing Degree Zero*, published in France in 1953 and in the United States in 1968.

The first time I ever heard the word *semiotics* was in conversation with Bruce Wolmer, with whom, along with his partner, Denise Green, I had become friends soon after I moved to New York. Bruce and Denise shared a loft on Broome Street and together produced a comic strip for the *Herald*. Like the paper itself, the strip was in a category of its own, odd and arty, and I imagine it was partly inspired by the precedent of Ad Reinhardt's art cartoons for the old *PM* newspaper in the forties; in any case, it was a sideline for both, since Denise was a serious painter and Bruce was an art writer and editor. (He would later become the longtime editor-in-chief of *Art and Auction*, until shortly before his death in 2010.) Like me they hung out at Holly and Horace Solomon's 98 Greene Street Loft and showed up for poetry readings there and elsewhere.

Both were serious about criticism and loved to talk about the ideas circulating in the Soho art world. Denise, who came from Australia, became involved with the growing feminist movement and was part of a cohort of female artists who were involved in editing *Heresies*, an important feminist journal published in New York starting in 1977. Bruce, a native New Yorker, went in another direction, enrolling in a grad program at Johns Hopkins University in Baltimore. When I asked him what he was studying, he said, "semiotics."[8]

What I gleaned from Bruce opened a door into a world that soon would become impossible to ignore for anyone involved in writing about art. This was thanks in no small part to the quarterly journal *October*, to which I had an early subscription. Soon I, along with many others in the art world, was feverishly reading not only Roland Barthes but also Jean Baudrillard, Guy Debord, Jacques Derrida, Michel Foucault, Jacques Lacan, Claude Lévi-Strauss, and other semiotics- or poststructuralist-indebted "theorists" whose writings became available in English translation for the first time in the seventies and early eighties.

Two of these writers, Debord and Derrida, introduced terms into the art-critical conversation that by the eighties were inescapable. Debord's contribution was *the spectacle*, a concept he broached in his book *Society of the Spectacle* (published in French in 1967, and in English in 1970). Debord proposed that Western, postwar society had become addicted to the spectacle of images found in media and commerce, suggesting that this was a primary feature of our consumer capitalism. (Part of the French Situationist group, he took his cues on this from Karl Marx.) As would Baudrillard later, Debord argued that images had in effect replaced reality as we once knew it.

Derrida's major contribution to the discourse was *deconstruction*, a term that became so popular among critics and eventually the public that it soon lost all the subtleties of its original meaning. For Derrida, who as a philosopher looked at how writing delivered its meaning differently than speech, deconstruction was in essence a method of interpreting a text (a novel, a letter, whatever) by locating its internal contradictions. These usually involved dichotomies—man/woman, rationality/madness, self/other—that could be shown to be inherently unstable. What deconstruction achieved was to reveal a meaning unintended by, and usually at odds with, the author. Like all the thinkers who became known as poststructuralists, Derrida saw meaning as separate from authorship, and he reveled in the fluid "play" of written language.[9]

Derrida's book *Writing and Difference*, published in the United States in 1978, is often regarded as the urtext of deconstructive ideas, but he had already promulgated them as a lecturer and visiting faculty member at Johns Hopkins starting in 1967. (I imagine Bruce Wolmer may have sat in on his lectures while he was a student there, but I never asked him.) The appeal of deconstruction for those in the visual arts is not hard to grasp:

if existing images, like words, are not fixed representations but capable of being refashioned and reinterpreted to yield new, critical meanings, then the entire universe of pictures is a subject for artists—from Marlboro ads to Edward Weston photographs.

My reading list was formed mostly through the footnotes of articles in *October*, supplemented by talking with friends whose circles of friends included students at the Institute of Fine Arts and Columbia University, among other hotbeds of what was becoming known as "theory," often with a capital *T*. Denise, for example, introduced me to Sylvère Lotringer, founding editor of *Semiotext(e)*, a once-obscure publisher of the writings of Baudrillard.[10] I still have my worn copy of *Semiotext(e)*'s 1983 translation of *Simulations*, Baudrillard's most read and widely quoted piece, which introduced the idea that we live in a simulacrum of reality, not reality itself.

I was especially taken with Barthes, since he was particularly interested in talking about photography, viewing it as a producer of a particular and, in many ways, problematic kind of sign. A photograph, he famously wrote in "The Rhetoric of the Image" in 1964, is "a message without a code"—an exception to Ferdinand de Saussure's basic formula for linguistic signs. (Saussure, a turn-of-the-century Swiss linguist, was a founder of semiotics.) In a photograph, Barthes wrote, the signified and the signifier (the two parts of every sign, according to semiotic writ) are "quasi-tautological," making the image to a great extent overlapped with what it depicts.

The influential art critic Rosalind Krauss popularized Barthes's notion of the specialness of the photographic sign in a two-part article in two early issues of *October*, "Notes on the Index: Seventies Art in America." As the title indicates, Krauss looked to another founder of semiotic theory, C. S. Peirce, to explain the kind of sign system at work in photographs: they are indexical signs, she argued, inasmuch as they seem to contain a trace or direct imprint of what they show us. A portrait of Abraham Lincoln, for example, seems to contain a register of Lincoln himself at a particular time and place. "The connective tissue binding the objects contained by the photograph is that of the world itself, rather than that of a cultural system," she wrote. And, more controversially, she said, "As paradoxical as it might seem, photography has increasingly become the model for abstraction."[11]

The occasion for Krauss's ruminations on seventies art was the opening in May 1976 of a new artists' space, PS1, in an abandoned public school in Long Island City, Queens. At the time it was rare for Manhattanites to venture off-island to Brooklyn, much less Queens, but the arts impresario Alanna Heiss and her Institute for Art and Urban Resources lured us there by inviting an enviable cast of artists to create work that responded to, or altered, the building. Gordon Matta-Clark, always the smartest artist on the block when it came to architecture, cut door-shaped holes through the floors of the building, aligned one above the other to create a vertigo-inducing, four-story open shaft. Others riffed on the building's brick walls or crumbling plaster.

For Krauss, these interventions had the indexical qualities of a photograph, since the building and the artwork could be construed as inextricably linked.[12] For me, enjoying the opening on a fine spring afternoon with several friends, none of this was readily apparent. I understood the work only in terms of what I had seen at 112 Greene Street shows and what I knew about Gordon's trajectory. But theory would ingratiate itself to the art I was looking at soon enough. It would become indispensable in the eighties to the interpretation of a new aesthetic, Postmodernism. And as it happened, the first book I reviewed when I started writing for the *Times* was Barthes's last, *Camera Obscura* (1981), in which he once more tried to puzzle out the mysteries of the medium.[13]

In the winter of 1978 I traveled to the Corcoran Gallery of Art in Washington, D.C., to attend a symposium titled "Photography: Where We Are." If memory serves, this is where I first encountered Krauss and Sontag in person. The two-day weekend gathering was the brainchild of Jane Livingston, Harry Lunn Jr., and Sam Wagstaff on the occasion of a show of Wagstaff's collection, which the one-time contemporary-art curator had started a mere five years earlier.[14] Lunn was a powerful dealer of prints and photographs based in Washington, although his hands seemed to be everywhere. Livingston was the chief curator at the Corcoran and an early advocate of photography there.

I went to see a star-studded cast, which included Princeton photo historian Peter Bunnell, photographer Frederick Sommer, curator Van Deren Coke, French collector Andre Jammes, and the critics Hilton Kramer, Rosalind Krauss, Joel Snyder, and Susan Sontag. Thankfully the program was recorded, and transcripts were made of the audiotapes, so it is possible to gauge with better accuracy than memory the state of photography and photography criticism at the time. Still, I remember being impressed by how much seriousness of thought was involved in a medium just on the verge of being taken seriously by a museum-going general public.

Bunnell's kickoff talk celebrated photography's newly fashionable status as an art and bemoaned some of the consequences, including (without mentioning those present) "present day attitudes" seeded by Walter Benjamin and subsequent theorists. Photography, he insisted, was essentially "an imaginative enterprise." Bunnell was followed by Sommer, who discussed "pictorial logic" without as much as a nod to the corpus of semiotic thought.

The real intellectual firepower, and the conference's main draw for me, was the Sunday panel "Aesthetics and Criticism: Is Photography Sui

Generis?" Was photography its own distinct medium, as Bunnell already had suggested, with its own aesthetics and history and criticism, or was it a complex sign system inextricably embedded in the discourse of contemporary art, not to mention contemporary culture? Was it sui generis, unto itself and unique, or part of a broader picture-making universe that included the visual arts generally but also (like film, like television) exceeded them in the magnitude of its cultural presence?

In their individual presentations the panelists would only sneak up on an answer. Sontag began by admitting that she had already said what she had to say about photography in her book, so she spent the rest of her time lamenting the "remarkably low" level of photographic criticism and theory. The next three speakers essentially proved her wrong. Snyder, from the University of Chicago, focused on how the syntax of photographs made them distinct from the reality they depicted, presumably a counterweight to Krauss's already published notion of photographic indexicality.[15] Krauss talked about Alfred Stieglitz's *Equivalent* series and argued that photography recovers what Modernism had emptied out of art (recognizable subject matter, most obviously) while sharing its "stigma of fraudulence." Kramer, who had been writing in the *Times* about photography since the early seventies, talked about the medium's recent "museumization" and its (for him, mostly bad) consequences.

The group discussion afterward, moderated by Livingston, focused on "the trace," the idea that photographs contain some evidence of what they depict—a slightly scaled-back version of "the index," perhaps, and foreshadowing what Roland Barthes would later call, in *Camera Obscura*, the "having been there" essence of all photographs. Why is this important? For some, like Bunnell, thinking of the photograph this way challenged the orthodoxy that photographers are autonomous creative agents in the picture-making process, and thus the idea had to be resisted. For others, the linkage between tangible reality and the photograph was the marker of the medium's uniqueness, and thus held the key to its artistic status.

The "Sui Generis" presentations were remarkable for several reasons. Most simply, they demonstrated four diverging points of view about how photographs could be considered art—which retrospectively might be boiled down to two, photography as an imaginative enterprise (Snyder, Kramer) or photography as a palimpsest of contemporary life (Sontag, Krauss). Three of the four speakers came from outside the world of photography; only Snyder, an art historian of photography and cofounder of Chicago Albumen Works, an atelier that produced reprints of nineteenth-century photographs, could reasonably be said to be "within" photography. The level of thinking and discussion was far beyond the usual promotional efforts of photography writing found at that time in museum catalogs and photography journals.

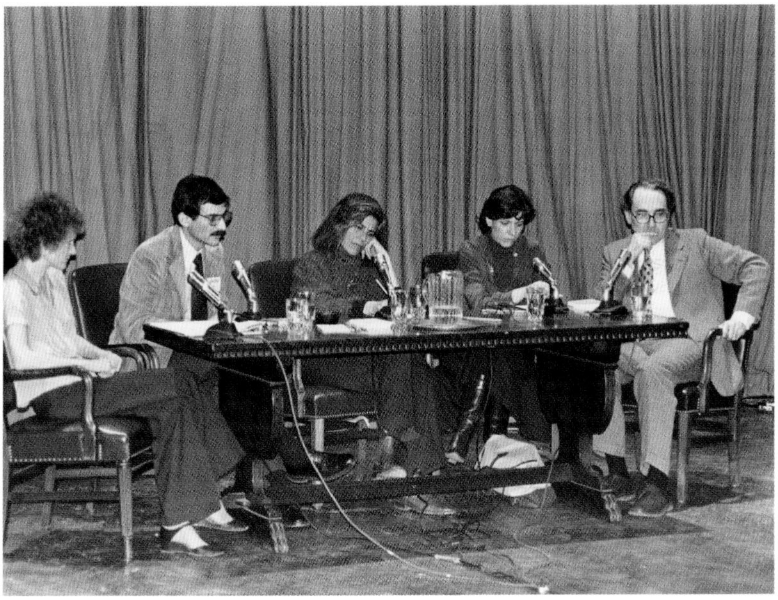

Panel discussion, "Aesthetics and Criticism: Is Photography Sui Generis?," during the symposium "Photography: Where We Are," Corcoran Gallery of Art, winter 1978. Left to right: Jane Livingston, Joel Snyder, Susan Sontag, Rosalind Krauss, and Hilton Kramer.

And, since the auditorium was packed to the gills, the conference showed that there was an audience for serious criticism of photography.

I felt strongly that Sontag had missed something: that the relative poverty of photographic criticism was fast being remedied, quantitatively and qualitatively. By decade's end, Gene Thornton had a regular slot for photography reviews in the Sunday *Times*, Ben Lifson was reviewing for the *Village Voice*, Shelley Rice wrote for the *Soho Weekly News*, and A. D. Coleman, Owen Edwards, and Phil Patton frequently appeared in mainstream monthlies. New talents like James Hugunin, Catherine Lord, and Michael Starenko were cutting their teeth at *Afterimage*, and on the West Coast Hal Fischer joined Joan Murray in reviewing photography for *Artweek*. (Like many critics of the time, Fischer was a practicing photographer; he published one of the great sleeper hits of the era, *Gay Semiotics*, the year of the Corcoran conference.) *Artforum*—required reading for anyone engaged with contemporary art—had devoted an entire issue to photography two years before the conference, with articles by A. D. Coleman, Nancy Foote, Max Kozloff, Aaron Scharf, and Colin Westerbeck.[16] Then there was the *October* contingent and its allies in theory: Benjamin Buchloh, Douglas Crimp, Hal Foster, Craig Owens, Martha Rosler, Allan Sekula, and Abigail Solomon-Godeau—all more or less of my generation.

Sekula was an especially important voice at the time because more than any of the others his work was read and absorbed by both the art world and the photography mainstream. Absorbed, but not always loved: Sekula's neo-Marxist ideology was more explicitly related to Marx and the Frankfurt School than *October*'s French-inflected, poststructuralist version, and his own photographs and those of his friends tended to focus on the circumstances of factory workers and other traditional laborers. But his writing was fueled not only by ardent conviction but also by good research and a fine nose for the pretensions of art photography. He made his mark first with a 1975 article in *Artforum*, "On the Invention of Photographic Meaning," in which he compared Alfred Stieglitz's canonical 1907 image *The Steerage* with Lewis Hine's 1905 *Immigrants Going down Gangplank, New York*, the Stieglitz being interpreted through what Sekula called a "symbolist esthetic discourse" while the Hine is "embedded in a complex political argument."[17]

His later essays were equally contentious, and included "The Traffic in Photographs" (*Art Journal*, 1981) and "The Body and the Archive" (*October*, 1986), the former debunking *The Family of Man* and its claims for both the universality of humanity and the supposed "universal language" of photography and the latter revealing the use of photography as an instrument of social control via criminal identification, eugenics, and motion studies. Virtually all the ideas Sekula broached in these essays, from the ready conversion of photographs from their original intentions into aesthetic objects to the role that archives play in our understanding of photographic meaning, continue to have resonance today.[18]

Sontag's complaint about the state of photography criticism also managed to ignore an obvious competitor of hers, Janet Malcolm, a *New Yorker* writer who in 1975 had begun a series of intelligent articles about the medium and its practitioners. These were collected in *Diana and Nikon: Essays on the Aesthetic of Photography* (1980), a book that did not quite raise the hackles of the photo community as much as Sontag's had but in many ways was just as trenchant. The jacket flap went so far as to identity Malcolm as "the photography critic for the *New Yorker*."

A wealth of earlier criticism and commentary on photography also existed, but its presence was not fully appreciated when Sontag gave her talk at the Corcoran. As if in answer, a trio of anthologies of photographic criticism appeared soon thereafter: the two-volume *The Camera Viewed: Writings on Twentieth-Century Photography*, edited by Peninah R. Petruck, in 1979; *Photography, Essays and Images: Illustrated Readings in the History of Photography*, edited by Beaumont Newhall and published by MoMA in 1980; and *Photography in Print: Writings from 1816 to the Present*, edited by Vicki Goldberg, in 1981. Together, these collections of commentaries helped make Lady Elizabeth Eastlake, Peter Henry Emerson, Sadakichi Hartmann, László Moholy-Nagy, and Walter Benjamin required reading for anyone presuming to understand the medium's aesthetic traditions.

As for me, my start as a working critic with a regular deadline came the next year after the Corcoran symposium, when Gerald Marzorati asked me to write reviews for the *Soho Weekly News*. The *Soho Weekly News* was a fledgling "alternative" weekly started on a wing and a prayer in 1973 by Michael Goldstein, a rock music publicist, with the intention of becoming the next *Village Voice,* and in an effort to appeal to the downtown set it featured extensive coverage of the arts, especially music and the visual arts. For me, it was reminiscent of the boundless raw energy of the *Herald,* albeit with a much better marketing plan.

My first column for the paper, at the end of March 1979, covered shows of Ray Metzker (at Light Gallery) and Robert Adams (at MoMA). Two weeks later it was Bruce Davidson (at the International Center of Photography), Lynn Davis and Robert Mapplethorpe (also at ICP), and Robert Mapplethorpe solo (at Robert Miller Gallery). Although Robert Miller was an art gallery that largely showed painters and sculptors, I naturally tended to focus my attention on photography-specific spaces, in part to stay out of the way of John Perreault and William Zimmer, who were the paper's other art critics, and in part to support what then were financially marginal operations.

The critics at the *Times* followed much the same script, with Gene Thornton designated to write about museum and gallery shows of photography while Hilton Kramer and John Russell covered the rest of the art world. This critical division was the rule at the time, including at the *Village Voice* and across the country. But as my confidence grew, and the marketplace for photography did the same, I also regularly stepped outside photo-gallery territory, reviewing shows at Castelli, Sonnabend, and Marlborough.

In my *Soho Weekly News* reviews I wrote about movements and tendencies I discerned at the start of a new decade, from the decline of formalism as a means of securing photography's art status to the rise of color photography. I wrote not one but two long articles about Joel Meyerowitz and his *Cape Light* series of luminous, large-format beach pictures. I mentioned Helen Levitt's career in color whenever I had the chance (including a show she had at Sidney Janis Gallery) and reviewed Light Gallery's exhibition of Harry Callahan's new color photographs. And I reported on the annual conference of the Society for Photographic Education, held at a faded resort hotel in the Catskills, where I was part of a panel on photography criticism. Apparently my contribution was to complain about the anticriticism, anti-intellectualism I felt was rampant among photographers at the time.[19]

Although none of my reviews had anything much to do with the critical theory I was reading at the time, it is clear from my *Soho Weekly News* clips that I sensed a fundamental transition happening in regard to photography's place in the art world. Seconding Douglas Davis, the art reviewer of *Newsweek* who seemed increasingly focused on photography, I suggested that the "photo boom" was over—prematurely, one might say, since this was in 1980—and considered the possibility that the medium's fortunes, literally and figuratively, were fading. But I also sensed a momentum building at ground level in what young photographers were up to. A group show that Marvin Heiferman put together at Castelli Graphics in the summer of 1980 offered one clue, as did a show that fall at Artists Space curated by Cindy Sherman.

Marvin Heiferman's show, *Likely Stories*, asserted the importance of narrative in the new photography. Sometimes this was a matter of multiple images literally telling a story, as in Allan Sekula's "novel" about the plight of poor workers, but I was more interested in the single-image contributions that claimed narrative status more obliquely: Sandy Skoglund's manufactured interior scene of a drab woman in a drab housecoat, or Brian Weil's radically enlarged section of a pornographic film frame. The "likely" of the title referred to the wide-open spaces such pictures created for interpretation by a viewer. The curator's intention went even further, judging from his press release: "[The show] reflects a growing idea that art photography need not restrict itself to the mimicry of modernism's formal conceits. Photography's strength is as a medium of communication, a fact better understood—until recently—by commercial photographs [sic] than by university-trained photographers." As I said in my review, "These are fighting words, to be sure."[20]

Cindy Sherman's show, which appeared a few months later at Artists Space sans title, featured seven photographers. Some she had known in Buffalo and some she had met in New York or had seen their work by virtue of her job at Artists Space. I pointed out in my review that all made pictures that engaged with "cultural clichés and stereotypes," used cinema or fashion as reference points, and seemed to favor fifties pop culture, including movies, television, and comics. "All these attributes, not surprisingly, are true of Sherman's own photographs, in which she costumes herself to appear as the starlet in what look to be movie stills circa early Ann-Margaret," I wrote, obviously referring to her *Untitled Film Stills* series. In a burst of enthusiasm, I also said, "It's the most refreshing show of the year, and possibly years."[21]

As good as the show was, none of its artists ever achieved Sherman's level of success, although Pat Place became famous as the guitarist of the Bush Tetras and Brian Weil left a lasting mark as an AIDS activist and founder of a New York City needle-exchange program. René Santos died of an AIDS-related illness in 1986, one of a number of his generation to have promising careers sadly cut short. Mostly, they demonstrated that the concerns of the Postconceptual, Postmodern generation of artists then remaking the downtown scene were widely shared and not just the province of Sherman, Richard Prince, Sherrie Levine, and a few other soon-to-be-famous people. And while Santos had studied with Rosalind Krauss, so he was at least on speaking terms with critical theory, he and the rest were responding to their life experiences as much as to the art around them. Theory might adopt them, as it most definitely did Sherman and Levine, but it did not direct them.

My first-ever review of Sherman's own work appeared in my last column of the year for the *Soho Weekly News*—December 17, 1980—with the title "Lies for the Eyes."[22] The occasion was her first show at Metro Pictures. Splitting the then relatively small quarters on Mercer Street with Jack Goldstein, Sherman showed brand-new color pictures in which she appears as various female characters in front of scenes provided by rear projection. "Self-conscious fictionalizing may well be the hallmark of vanguard photography," I noted at the time.

I might also have mentioned that her work was a cogent example of the kind of art Metro Pictures was showing, and that the gallery's roster of artists represented a new consideration of camera images in contemporary culture.[23] Theory, it turned out, was about to give these artists an importance that helped put them at the center of the art world's conversation. To give the full picture of this nascent scene, however, I would have had to trace its origins back to Southern California and Buffalo, New York.

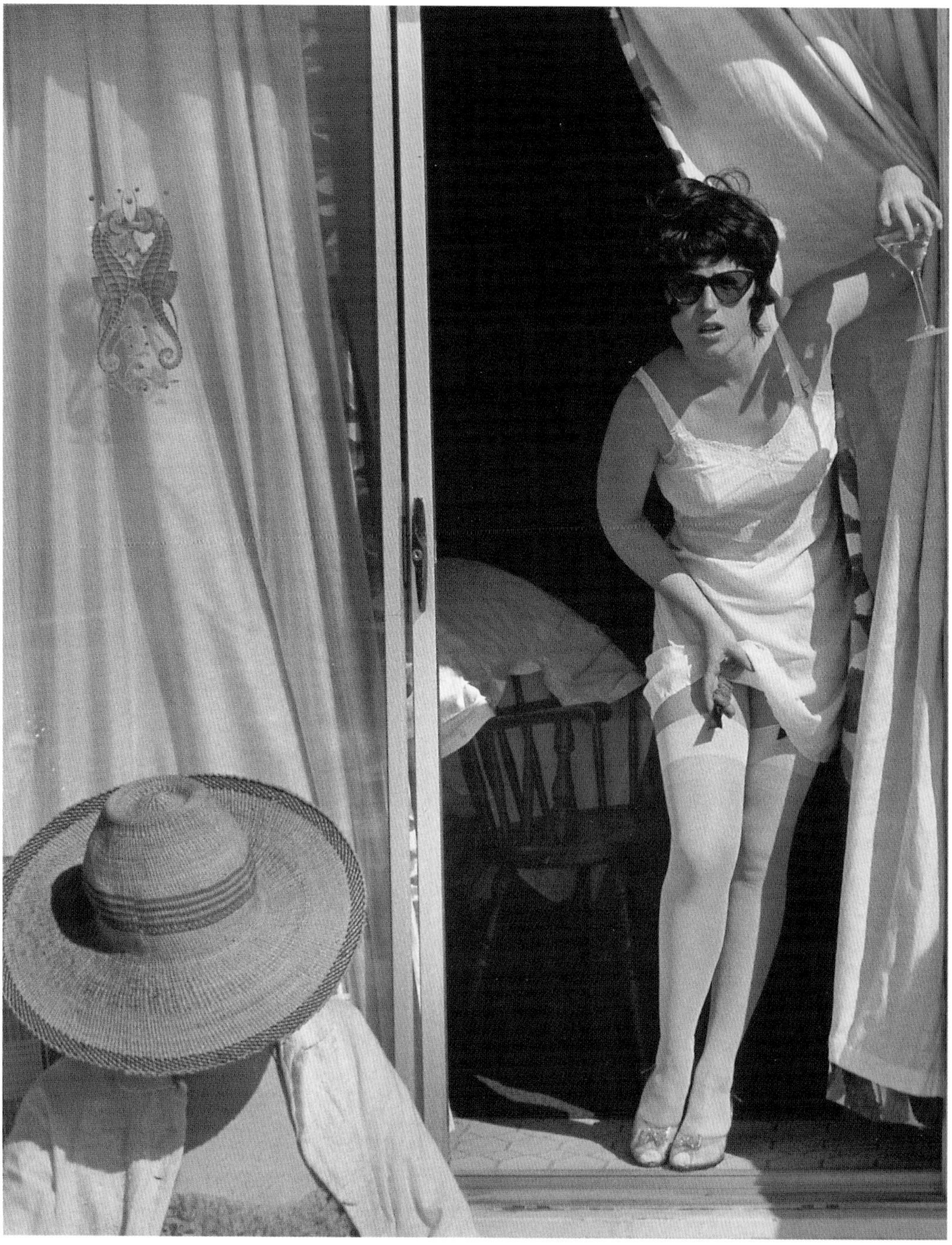

CHAPTER 10

The Image World Meets the Art World

"Quotation," "appropriation," "image-scavenging," "age of simulacra" . . . For several years now these words have filled the air as we have tried to explain to ourselves what has been happening in recent art. They are such complex words. They provoke a certain nostalgia for the clear brightness of slang. Sometimes, when thinking about quotational art, I call such works "After Art"—works that are openly *after* other pieces.

—Thomas McEvilley, "Marginalia: The Original Sin," *Artforum*, October 1985

When the eighties arrived it was clear that a new generation of artists had landed in New York and that they had brought with them a new attitude toward photography's place in contemporary art. Like me, these artists had grown up as television natives and were totally visually literate in terms of their exposure to advertising and other commercial functions of the medium. The world of images in which we all were swimming was not the antithesis of what art should be; it was their art's primary subject.

Many had been students at two hotbeds of new art. One was CalArts, formally known as the California Institute of the Arts, which was formed by Walt Disney via a merger of an existing music conservatory and the Chouinard Art Institute. Officially opened on a brand-new campus in the L.A. suburb of Valencia in 1971, the school had an interdisciplinary curriculum and featured a radical visual-arts faculty that included John Baldessari, Allan Kaprow, Nam June Paik, and Miriam Schapiro. Baldessari, who had moved up from San Diego, established a now-legendary class called "Post-Studio Art," while Kaprow promoted his trademark Happenings and Schapiro, together with Judy Chicago, started the Feminist Art Program.

Many of the students who ended up studying with Baldessari—Ross Bleckner, Barbara Bloom, Troy Brauntuch, Eric Fischl, Jack Goldstein, Matt Mullican, David Salle, James Welling—would come to New York to live after finishing their coursework. Goldstein said of Baldessari's class, "Students didn't get much hands-on education, but we learned a whole new attitude

Cindy Sherman, *Untitled Film Still #7*, 1978.

about what art could be—not expression but investigation, investigation of picture making by mimicking movies or cartoons or propaganda or advertising."[1]

Baldessari also invited New York artists like Joan Jonas, Sol LeWitt, Robert Morris, and Lawrence Weiner to CalArts to talk to his classes, which drew students from throughout the program. Not surprisingly, students gleaned that being in New York was then a key to artistic success. Since this slightly older generation had already colonized Soho, most of the CalArts group ended up living in Tribeca or elsewhere downtown below Canal Street.

The second cocoon for the new generation was Buffalo, New York. Other than the presence of the Albright-Knox Art Gallery and the propinquity of the Visual Studies Workshop in Rochester, the declining manufacturing city had little reason to become a center for new art. But thanks to Charles Clough, Robert Longo, and Cindy Sherman, it did.

As Longo has recalled, he was studying at a "mediocre art school," Buffalo State College, and living with Sherman, an art-education major at the same college, when he met Clough and the three of them moved into an abandoned ice factory.[2] There, in an unused hallway, Clough and Longo created Hallwalls, an impromptu exhibition space that morphed into an alternative space roughly modeled on Artists Space in New York. Starting in 1974 they invited nationally known artists like Vito Acconci, Dan Graham, and Robert Irwin to be visiting artists, which usually entailed a show at Hallwalls, a lecture at Buffalo State, and hanging out with the Hallwalls group, which also included Diane Bertolo, Nancy Dwyer, and Michael Zwack. The group mounted shows of their own work, including Sherman's first real body of photographs, *A Play of Selves*, featuring paper doll–like cutouts of herself as various characters.

Hallwalls sometimes collaborated with a nearby photography alternative space, CEPA (Center for Exploratory and Perceptual Arts), which had produced the *Metro Bus Show* series with Sherman's and Ellen Carey's work.[3] The scene also benefitted from the 1975 arrival at the Albright-Knox of Linda Cathcart, a young and ambitious contemporary-art curator who knew the New York art world from working for Marcia Tucker at the Whitney.[4]

The original, inspiring cast of the Buffalo scene didn't stay long; the lure of New York was too irresistible. Hallwalls denizens Dwyer and Zwack moved to the city in 1976, Longo and Sherman in 1977, and Clough in 1978. Part of the inspiration for the timing of this exodus was a show of Hallwalls artists mounted at Artists Space at the end of 1976. The collaborative counterpart to an exhibition of CalArts artists earlier that year at Hallwalls, the exhibition at Artists Space introduced the Buffalo artists to a vanguard art audience in New York and cemented an alliance between the CalArts and Hallwalls contingents.[5]

The glue that brought what came to be called "the CalArts mafia" and the Hallwalls crew together—and in a larger sense introduced what we now know as the "Pictures Generation" into the world—was Helene Winer. Winer started her chain of influence as a gallery director at Pomona College in California, a job that allowed her firsthand access to Los Angeles–based artists like Baldessari, Bas Jan Ader, Chris Burden, and William Wegman as well as to the studios of ambitious art students like Goldstein, a graduate of Chouinard who went on to the new grad program at CalArts. Winer gave Goldstein a show at Pomona, and they became romantic partners soon thereafter. In 1974 they moved to New York. In the fall of 1975 Winer became director of Artists Space, a pioneering alternative (i.e., noncommercial) gallery space founded three years earlier by the art historian Irving Sandler with a mission to show emerging artists. Soon after she took the job, the organization decamped from Wooster Street in Soho to Hudson Street, near where the Holland Tunnel emerges from New Jersey.

Goldstein and Winer's downtown apartment became a meeting place for many of the CalArts grads who moved to New York soon after graduating, including Troy Brauntuch, Matt Mullican, and David Salle. She arranged for shows of their work at Artists Space, apparently sometimes to the dismay of Sandler, who was worried that her aesthetic tastes violated the organization's founding ethic of being open to the curatorial impulses of young artists.[6] Among the audience for these shows were Longo and the Buffalo artists associated with Hallwalls, who were impressed enough to invite the CalArts artists to exhibit there.

Besides returning the favor, Winer invited a young art-history graduate student, Douglas Crimp, who was studying at the Institute of Fine Arts with Rosalind Krauss, to organize a show of the new art she believed in, and she took him with her to Buffalo to visit Hallwalls. He also scouted the artists he knew in Tribeca, where he lived. The result—impossible to imagine without Winer's influence on Crimp—was a show called *Pictures* at Artists Space in the fall of 1977. Its artists included Troy Brauntuch and Jack Goldstein from CalArts, Robert Longo from Hallwalls, and two artists from outside the dyad, Sherrie Levine and Philip Smith. Levine, who had studied art at the University of Wisconsin, Madison before moving to New York in 1975, and Smith, who was a writer and editor for the magazines *Interview* and *GQ* as well as a visual artist, were part of the downtown scene in which Crimp and the others swam.[7]

In retrospect one of the most remarkable things about the *Pictures* show, given its reputation as the *ursprung* event of the art "ism" that would flourish well into the nineties, is how many of the artists now known as "Pictures artists" were not included. This omission includes most prominently Cindy Sherman, of course, whose work Crimp had seen but chose not to include, as well as Sarah Charlesworth, Barbara Kruger, Louise Lawler, Matt Mullican, Richard Prince, David Salle, Laurie Simmons, and James Welling.[8] Sherman's absence was somewhat rectified when Crimp amended his original curatorial introduction to the show and wrote an expanded essay for the spring 1979 issue of *October*, again called "Pictures," in which he discussed her work.[9]

Significantly, in terms of what would play out in the art world over the next ten years, Crimp's "Pictures" essay in *October* makes the claim that the work of the artists he discusses takes a step away from Modernism to become something else: "It remains useful to consider recent work as having effected a break with modernism and therefore as postmodernist." He locates this break in the multiplicity of media employed, and in the "processes of quotation, excerptation, framing, and staging" the artists use.[10] While not overtly reliant on continental critical theory—Crimp quotes Roland Barthes but once, and aims most of his guns at the American critic Michael Fried's "Art and Objecthood" essay from a 1967 issue of *Artforum*—the "Pictures" essay is clearly informed by his mentor Krauss's evolving ideas about photography as a radical model for a new art that signals the end of Modernism and moves past it. Crimp's contribution is to insist that this new art, which he explicitly calls "Postmodernist," contains a radical critique of all that came before it. In theoretical terms he is saying, in effect, that Postmodernist art serves to deconstruct Modernism.[11]

Like the *New Topographics* exhibition, *Pictures* has had an outsized influence compared to the relatively small audience that saw it. Most accounts attribute this to the republication of Crimp's essay in *October*, a year and a half after the show, but Winer's evangelism for the movement and its ideas also played a crucial role. She arranged for it to travel, the first time an Artists Space show had gone on the road, and the catalog was also a first for the organization.[12]

And as has always been true, it is not a matter of how many people see a show (or read its catalog essay) but who they are, and Winer made sure the "thought leaders" of the day found out about Brauntuch, Goldstein, Longo, and the rest. Among Winer's friends was Regina Cornwell, a critic of art and film, who introduced her to Michael Klein, who recently had moved to town after working at the Walker Art Center in Minneapolis. Klein had taken a job with Max Protetch, who was moving his gallery from Washington, D.C., to West 57th Street. Klein subsequently introduced me to Winer and to her collaborator Janelle Reiring, after the *Pictures* show but well before the two opened their gallery, Metro Pictures.

I remember visiting them late in the day at Reiring's loft on North Moore

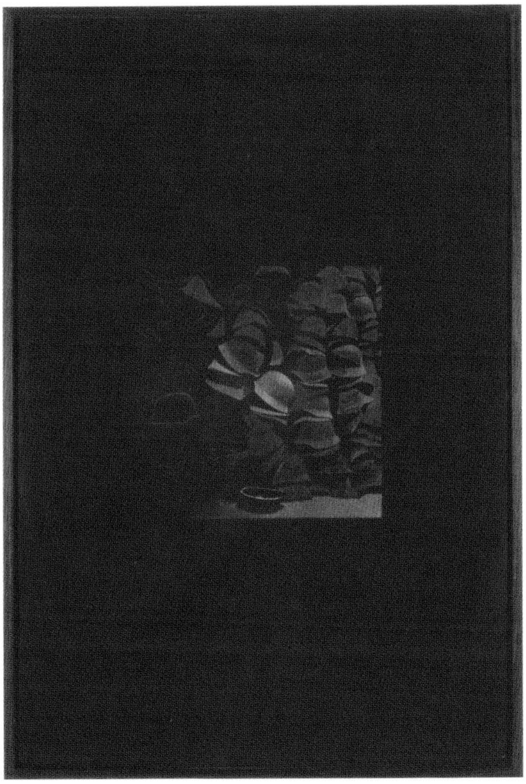

Troy Brauntuch, *Untitled (Hats)*, 1981. Pencil on paper.

Street in Tribeca, where the art of Brauntuch, Goldstein, and several others was on display. Reiring had been working at Leo Castelli's gallery in Soho, alongside Louise Lawler, when she met Winer, who invited her to organize a show at Artists Space. That exhibition, *Four Artists*, took place in September 1978 and included Lawler, Sherman, Adrian Piper, and Christopher D'Arcangelo. Notably, it was the first-ever exhibition of Sherman's *Untitled Film Stills*, which she had started making the year before.[13] Not long thereafter Reiring left her job at Castelli and Winer quit hers at Artists Space. Their plan was to open a gallery of their own, featuring the artists they had on display in the loft. The name they chose, Metro Pictures, both echoed the title of the Artists Space show Crimp had organized and evoked a Hollywood film studio.

The evening I met them they showed me Brauntuch's and Goldstein's new paintings; I felt myself in over my head but did my best to fake knowingness. I was familiar with New Image painting, where the images were abstracted and vaguely symbolic, as if floating in a Color Field painting, but the images in these paintings were photographic and more akin to history painting. Indeed, Brauntuch's were history paintings of a sort: his source materials were photographs from the Third Reich taken by Adolf Hitler's chief photographer, Heinrich Hoffmann, and others employed by the Nazis.

Goldstein's were less specific but more spectacular, looking like photographs of lightning or fireworks.

Knowing that photographs were central to the new art that Reiring and Winer were promoting made me intensely curious. I was especially curious about the work they intended to feature at Metro Pictures that *was* photography, especially Cindy Sherman's and Laurie Simmons's. Here I felt somewhat less derailed, not only because photography was my field of expertise but also because I already had seen some of their work, thanks to Michael Klein.

Klein had a great nose for the new and already had a sense that Reiring and Winer were on to something. He even beat them to the punch in terms of showing some of their stable of artists, mounting an exhibition called *Re:Figuration* at Max Protetch Gallery in December 1979, almost a year before Metro Pictures opened. *Re:Figuration* included Brauntuch, Longo, Sherman, and Simmons, among others. Despite Protetch's protests—"I'm not showing photography in the gallery," Klein remembers him saying—the show did well, with megacollector Charles Saatchi buying all the Longo and Sherman work on view.[14]

Since I had been writing reviews for *Art in America*, as well as taking pictures of artwork for the gallery, Klein decided I could be a sounding board for the new photo-based art he was seeing. Once, after I had finished photographing some drawings by Richard Fleischner in the gallery's back room, he asked me what I thought of two Laurie Simmons photographs he had hung on the wall. One showed a dollhouse figure seated in a miniature living-room set, and the other was of two cowboy figures astride plastic horses in a patently fake Western outdoors.

At first I was nonplussed. Photographers of my generation and a generation earlier had long ago decided that "tabletop photography" was the province of amateurs with too much time and too little talent—and that included any form of miniature setups like Simmons's. Tabletops were tantamount to model railroading—why not go out and ride a real train? Plus, the figures Simmons used were utterly familiar: my sister had played with a similar dollhouse while I was growing up, and I probably had similar cowboy figures lurking in my childhood toy box.

It turns out this was exactly the point. As Klein explained it, the artist was re-presenting the scenes with a critical eye, asking viewers to reflect on the fantasies they were allowed (and encouraged) to construct during childhood. Girls were shown what middle-class mothers were supposed to look like, and boys were supplied with mythic, hypermasculine models of adult men. I was somewhat prepared, then, to understand Sherman's *Untitled Film Stills* when Klein pulled a few from a flat file.

Klein left Protetch after four years and went on to open his own gal-

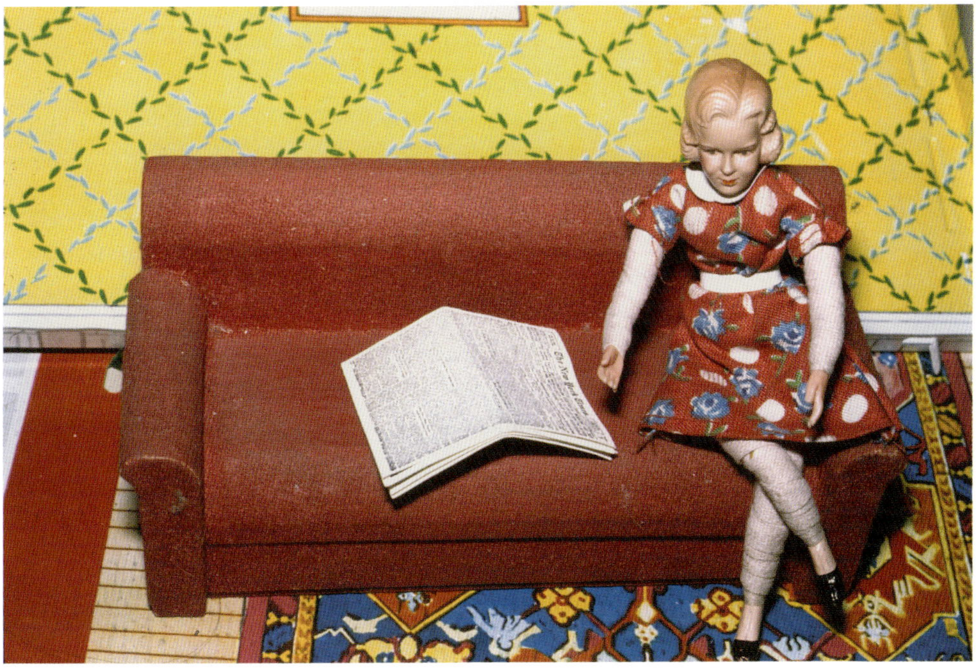

Laurie Simmons, *Woman with Red Chair*, 1978.

lery, where he continued to introduce me to new work he admired. Among the vanguard artists he represented then were Marina Abramović and Ulay (Frank Uwe Laysiepen), her romantic partner and artistic collaborator at the time. Abramović and Ulay were supplementing their confrontational performances with tall, life-sized Polaroids depicting themselves as mythic figures or engaged in enigmatic interpersonal actions. Although they came from Europe, they seemed to me to come from another planet.

Klein also began to represent James Casebere, whose work I had seen before but not fully appreciated. Casebere was manufacturing scenes for the camera, most of them involving houses and other architecture, and photographing them so as to look almost real. They were easily decoded as not the real thing, though, since they were made of foamcore board, plaster, and paste. Though not strictly a part of the CalArts and Hallwalls aesthetic, his work was equally derived from prior representations and was even more "tabletop"—literally—than Simmons's work. It was close enough to the Metro Pictures sensibility that it was included in a photography group show at the start of the gallery's second season, in the fall of 1981.[15]

Klein was not alone in recognizing the new art coming from downtown as something to herald. Marvin Heiferman, who had left Light Gallery and become director of photographs at Castelli Graphics in 1975, organized a summer show there in 1979 called *Pictures: Photographs*. With its titular borrowing from Crimp's Artists Space show and article, the exhibition of ten color pictures by as many artists included soon-to-be Metro Pictures

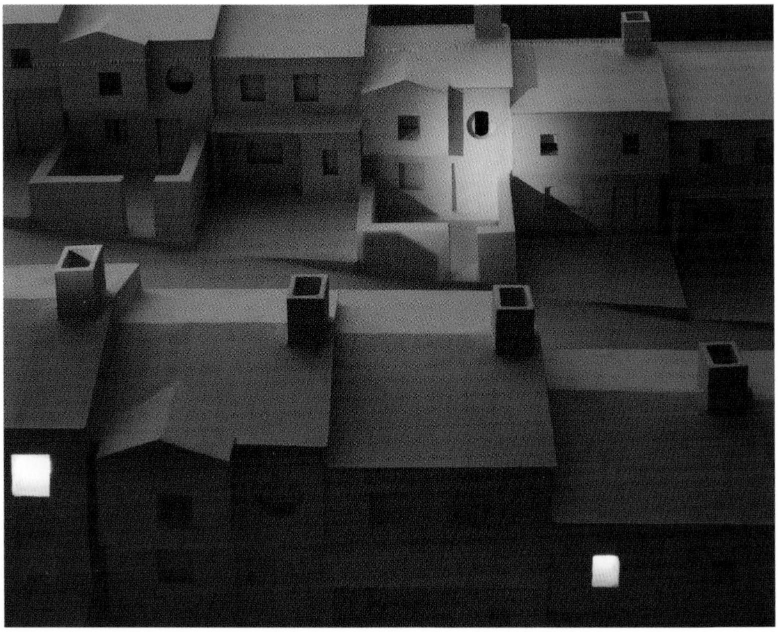

James Casebere, *Subdivision with Spotlight*, 1982.

regulars Sherrie Levine and Richard Prince. Otherwise, though, it diverged from Crimp's program by including set-up photographs by Steve Collins, Bernard Faucon, and Sandy Skoglund and snippets from real life by Brian Hagiwara, Len Jenshel, Arnold Kramer, Sharon Smith, and one Nancy Goldin—now known as Nan.

Sherrie Levine at the time was making simple collages using photographs cut out of fashion magazines—famously, her *Presidents* series of the silhouetted profiles of the country's founding fathers. These not only combined fashion and politics, two realms usually thought to be exclusive of each other, but also linked images of women, depicted as accessories of beauty, to those of men, represented (even in their ghostly absence) as figures of authority and power. This series came after the work that put her in the *Pictures* show, which consisted of silhouettes painted on graph paper, depicting members of a stereotypical family, a dog, and President Kennedy.

Shortly thereafter, though, Levine dropped her X-acto knife in favor of a camera, taking pictures of well-known pictures she found in art-history textbooks and artists' monographs, and thus began the practice that would make her simultaneously famous and notorious. This "re-photography," or unapologetic appropriation of someone else's photograph (and later, painting as well) was easily mistaken for the original if one did not look carefully enough to decipher the dots and other signs of the reproduction process that supplied Levine with her "original" subjects.

Richard Prince's photographs were just as puzzling, if slightly less offensive to photography collectors and other purists. Starting in 1977 he

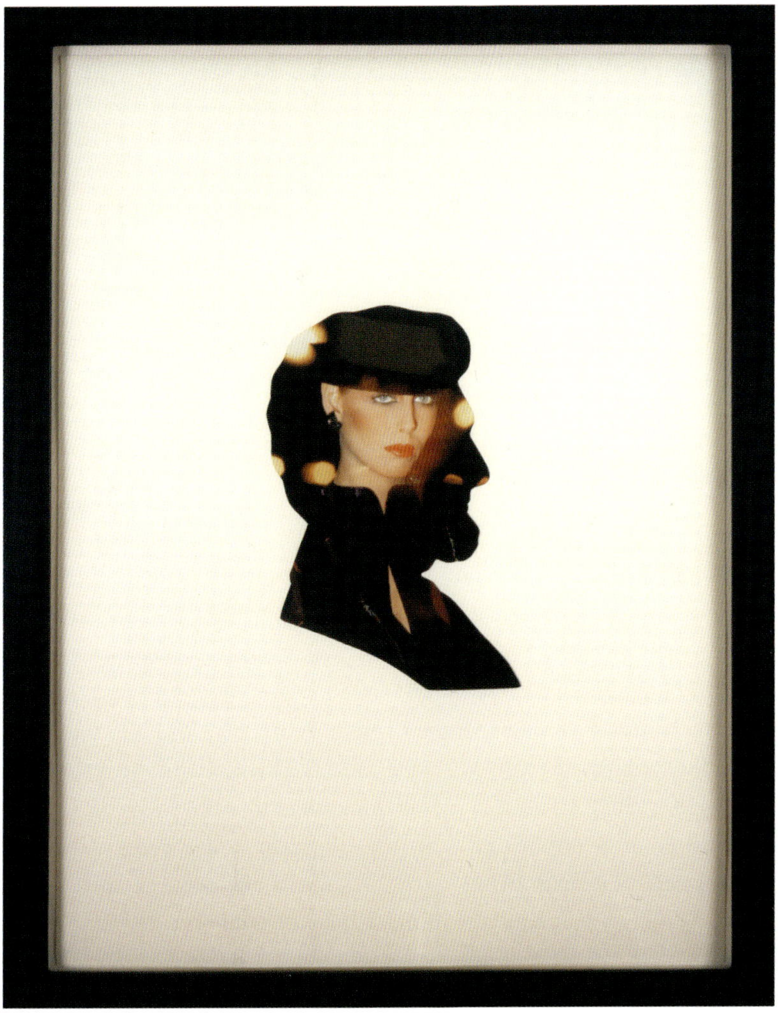

Sherrie Levine, *Untitled (President Collage: 4)*, 1979. Collage on paper.

re-photographed glossy advertisements, some of which he came across as part of his job at Time-Life, where he worked as a clip man cutting out articles from magazine pages. Often he presented these in groups of three or four, showing how certain poses were used repeatedly, as if a cultural contract demanded conformity. The triptych *Untitled (three men looking in the same direction)* shows three models with their heads turned to their left; *Untitled (three women looking in the same direction)* does the same, only they are looking to their right. Most famously, in the early eighties he re-photographed Marlboro cigarette advertisements, focusing on the mythic notion of the male cowboy and the unspoiled American West, as well as a widely circulated picture of a ten-year-old Brooke Shields emerging naked from a bathtub. Prince titled his version, from a photograph taken by Gary Gross, *Spiritual America* (1983), a reference to the title of Alfred Stieglitz's notorious image of a gelded horse.[16]

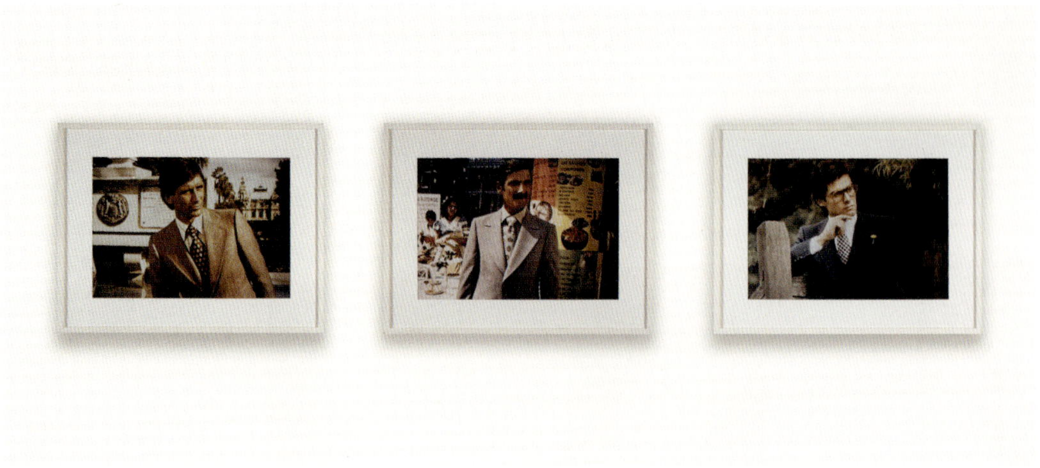

Richard Prince, *Untitled (three men looking in the same direction)*, 1978.

Plenty of folks in photography were less than sympathetic to Heiferman's championing of Prince and Levine, and to the attention given to the new Pictures artists generally.[17] Although I was not particularly intent on thumbing my nose at traditional art photography, I was captivated by this new approach to the medium. I recognized as my own the experience of understanding the world through images. These artists and I shared a history of early television, of picture magazines and the slick commercial advertising photography that came with them, of Hollywood productions in black-and-white and "living" color, of roadside billboards and pin-up calendars and anti–Vietnam War posters. We were the offspring of the sign language of the camera lens, and we fancied that we could read the signs better than most.

The opening of Metro Pictures gallery in mid-November of 1980, in a retrofitted, relatively narrow former bar on Mercer Street between Prince and Houston, was an art-world event that drew much of the Soho and Tribeca crowd. One could say it marked the official beginning of contemporary art in the eighties. Twelve artists were in the show, seven showing paintings or sculpture (Brauntuch, Goldstein, and Longo, plus Michael Harvey, Thomas Lawson, William Leavitt, and Michael Zwack) and five showing photographs (Levine, Prince, Sherman, Simmons, and Welling). It was, in a sense, a more broadly populated and refined version of the *Pictures* show three years before.

The work on view by Prince, Sherman, and Simmons was familiar to me, having seen versions of it in the shows at Protetch, Castelli Graphics, and a few noncommercial spaces like PS1. Sherman hung a group of color pictures with backgrounds supplied by rear projection, Prince some rephotographed magazine ads featuring watches and jewelry, and Simmons

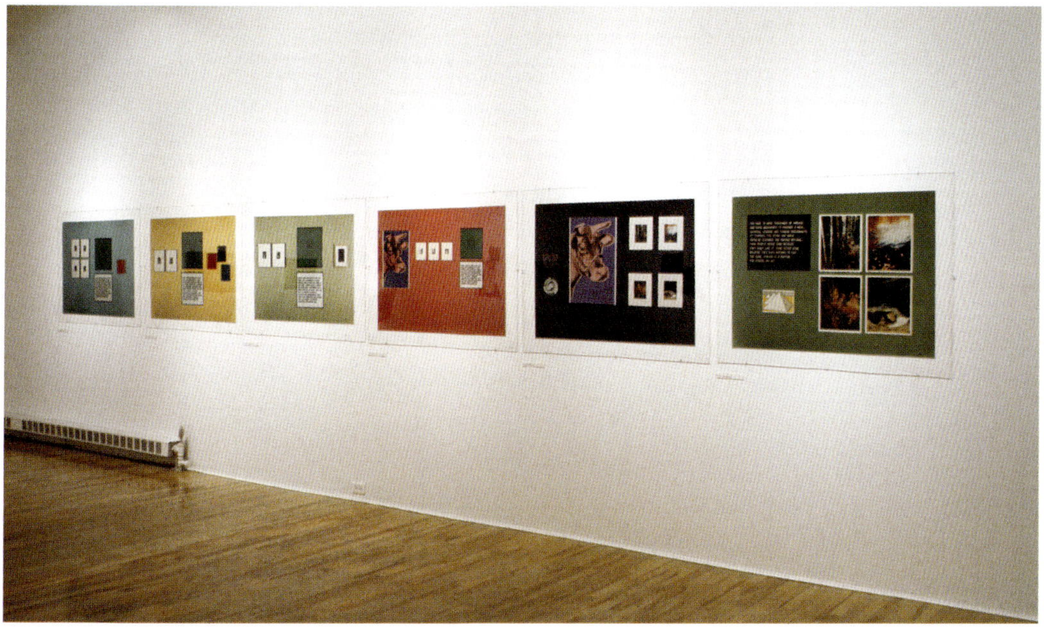

Installation view of Louise Lawler's exhibition *Arrangements of Pictures*, Metro Pictures, New York, 1982.

color photographs of underwater swimmers. Levine's work, though, took the most radical step: she showed the first in a long series of bald appropriations of another artist's images, in this case Edward Weston's.

Levine's "versions" of Weston's torso of his son Neil caused expectable controversy, not only because of the image's glorified status as an icon of Modernist photography but also because of her affront to the hallowed institution of authorship. Like almost all her appropriations, the six images Levine presented were copies she had made of poster and art-book illustrations; in other words, the "Neil" I was looking at in the gallery (multiple times) was simply one final link in a chain of such images that led back to the subject before Weston's camera. (Final, that is, until some smart aleck chose to appropriate Levine.) Or, as Crimp would argue in that spring's issue of *October*, Levine's pictures pointed to a chain that led past Weston and past photography all the way back to classical sculpture.[18] Soon, however, the Weston estate came knocking at Levine's door to assert its copyright, which led her to switch to images in the public domain, prominently Walker Evans's.

James Welling's work in the opening Metro Pictures show was even more confounding: five examples of 4 × 5-inch contact prints of crumpled aluminum foil. These enigmatic images take advantage of our natural yearning to organize visual stimulation into some sort of meaning, creating emotions or feelings that have no specific source, but unlike Alfred Stieglitz with his cloud photographs, Welling was not hoping to evoke music or raise our spiritual consciousness. The pictures remain obdurately mute.

After the opening group exhibition Metro Pictures settled into a pattern of showing two artists at a time, one in the front room and one in back; often paintings were paired with photography, as was the case in December when the gallery featured Goldstein's and Sherman's work. There were some exceptions, notably the next month when Robert Longo's *Men in the Cities* sculptural wall pieces and drawings had the space all to themselves. Another exception, on the occasion of the gallery's second anniversary, was Louise Lawler's exhibition, *Arrangements of Pictures*, for which the artist installed paintings and photographs by the gallery's other artists in the front room and hung her own photographs of their work as she found it "arranged" in art collectors' homes. Not exactly appropriation and something more than curation, Lawler's interventions then and now focus on how context determines what we see as art and how we interpret it.

All of this activity attracted plenty of critical attention, especially from downtown writers for progressive publications like *Flash Art*, but the gallery still had to struggle to sell enough work to get by. All this would change over the course of the eighties. Metro Pictures moved into much more spacious digs on Greene Street in 1983, before eventually migrating to Chelsea, as the market for many of the Pictures artists it represented skyrocketed.

As important as Metro Pictures was in establishing a beachhead for new art that became tagged as Postmodernist, its artists were representative of a broader phenomenon. Other artists, at other galleries, were mining the same territory and were part of the same social circles. This was especially true of the women artists whose interest in the feminist movement paralleled their interests in the shaping power of representation. The work of Sarah Charlesworth and Barbara Kruger, in particular, was as much a part of the conversation as that of Sherman, Simmons, and Levine.

Charlesworth was one of the few artists of the Pictures Generation already versed in critical theory while making their work in the seventies.[19] She became an important part of the circle of women artists gathered around Metro Pictures and, despite her absence from the Pictures pantheon as erected by Crimp, in many ways was as influential.

Charlesworth had studied with Douglas Huebler when she was a student at Barnard College in the late sixties. Afterward she fell in naturally with the downtown Conceptual Art crowd and began a long relationship with Joseph Kosuth, of *One and Three Chairs* fame. When she began to make Conceptual-style photoworks in the midseventies she found an audience first in Europe, where many of the important collectors of Conceptual Art lived; her first solo show in the United States was in 1978, at a small gallery in Tribeca called C Space. This was the launch of a series of artworks that made her reputation, collectively titled *Modern History*.[20]

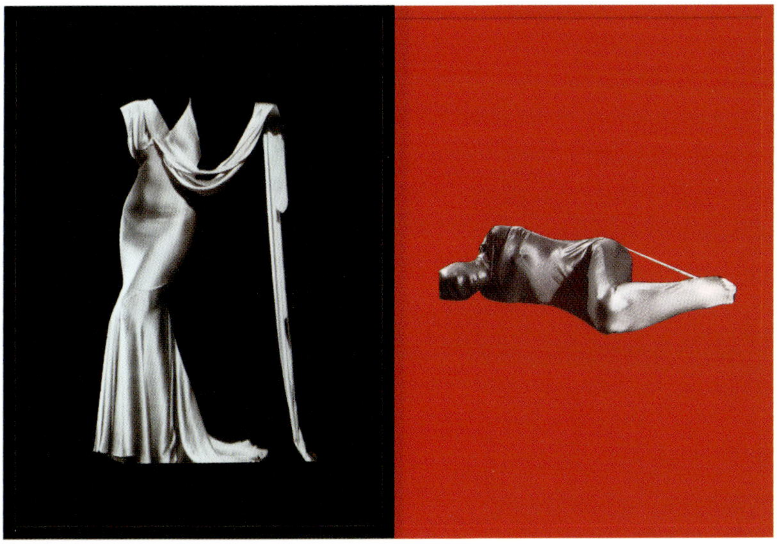

Sarah Charlesworth, *Figures,* 1983, from the series *Objects of Desire*.

In that show, against a plain brick wall, Charlesworth hung twenty-six framed, same-size reproductions of all the front pages of the *International Herald Tribune* published during the month of September 1977. She removed all the headlines and text except for the masthead, leaving only the photographs. A slightly later, more well-known piece using the same strategy, *April 21, 1978*, reproduces the front pages of forty-five newspapers from around the world on that date, all of which carry a picture of the kidnapped Italian prime minister Aldo Moro. The repetition is part of the point, as is the variety of ways in which the one image appears.

These pieces demonstrate, in a practical way, Barthes's notion of the rhetoric of the image, as photography is enlisted by the news media as an instrument for bolstering stories in print and simultaneously creating supplementary meanings of its own. Cropping, positioning, and sizing all determine how the photograph is read, and how much importance viewers give it—as, of course, do captions, but here they have disappeared along with all other text. By her simple act of elimination, Charlesworth opened journalistic convention to question.

The pictures that I remember most vividly are from a later series, *Objects of Desire*, begun in 1983, which I first got a glimpse of in a group show that fall at no less an elegant uptown venue than Marlborough Gallery—a sign of how quickly the allegedly oppositional Postmodernists had cracked the top end of the marketplace. Each picture featured a black-and-white image, culled from a halftone reproduction, against a vivid monochrome—either red or black. Now the image was silhouetted but otherwise left intact—floating within the picture space much like the falling bodies of her earlier *Stills* series, which appropriated news photographs of individuals leaping from tall buildings. The *Objects of Desire* pictures, which focus on materialism, consumerism, and the influence of the male gaze on women, were printed using the then-new Cibachrome process, giving them a high-gloss finish akin to varnish. Long gone were the days when Conceptual photography took pains to look deskilled.

That an establishment gallery like Marlborough was presenting a show of photographs by young artists—besides Charlesworth, they were Mac Adams, Ellen Brooks, James Casebere, David Levinthal, Laurie Simmons, and James Welling—was remarkable at the time. The gallery had asked Abigail Solomon-Godeau, a critic aligned with the Pictures artists and *October*'s aesthetics, to organize the exhibition, which she titled *In Plato's Cave*, and to write an essay for its catalog. Marlborough's calculation in showing these young turks was not a huge risk: just that spring the Whitney Biennial had featured Charlesworth as part of a cohort of photo-based Postmodernists, including (for the first time in a Biennial) Casebere, Kruger, Levine, Prince, Sherman, and Simmons. Pictures art was firmly on the contemporary art world's horizon.

I reviewed *In Plato's Cave* for the *Times*, together with concurrent exhibitions of Sherman's work at Metro Pictures and of Prince's at Baskerville and Watson, which was a few doors down 57th Street from Marlborough. It was an occasion for me to work out what I had begun to sense of late: that the concurrence of Pictures art and *October*'s theoretical superstructure in support of it was delaminating, in large part because the art was being embraced by the very institutions to which it was nominally opposed. I wrote:

> Post-Modernist photography, and all Post-Modernist art, is positioned politically, that is, against the ruling assumptions of the art world and the culture as a whole. While very few of Post-Modernism's practitioners and theorists embrace any sort of dogmatic political system, most believe that politics permeates all of our reactions, including our responses to visual art. What are we to think, then, when Post-Modernist photography's relation to the existing cultural power structure becomes one not of critical opposition but of apparent collusion? When it becomes part of not only the power structure of the existing art world but also the commercial worlds of publishing, advertising and fashion?[21]

I added: "One possible answer to the questions posed above is that the critical theory that has defined and promoted Post-Modernist photography is becoming increasingly out of phase with the realities of today's art world, if not the world itself." I fancied that I was choosing to prioritize art practice

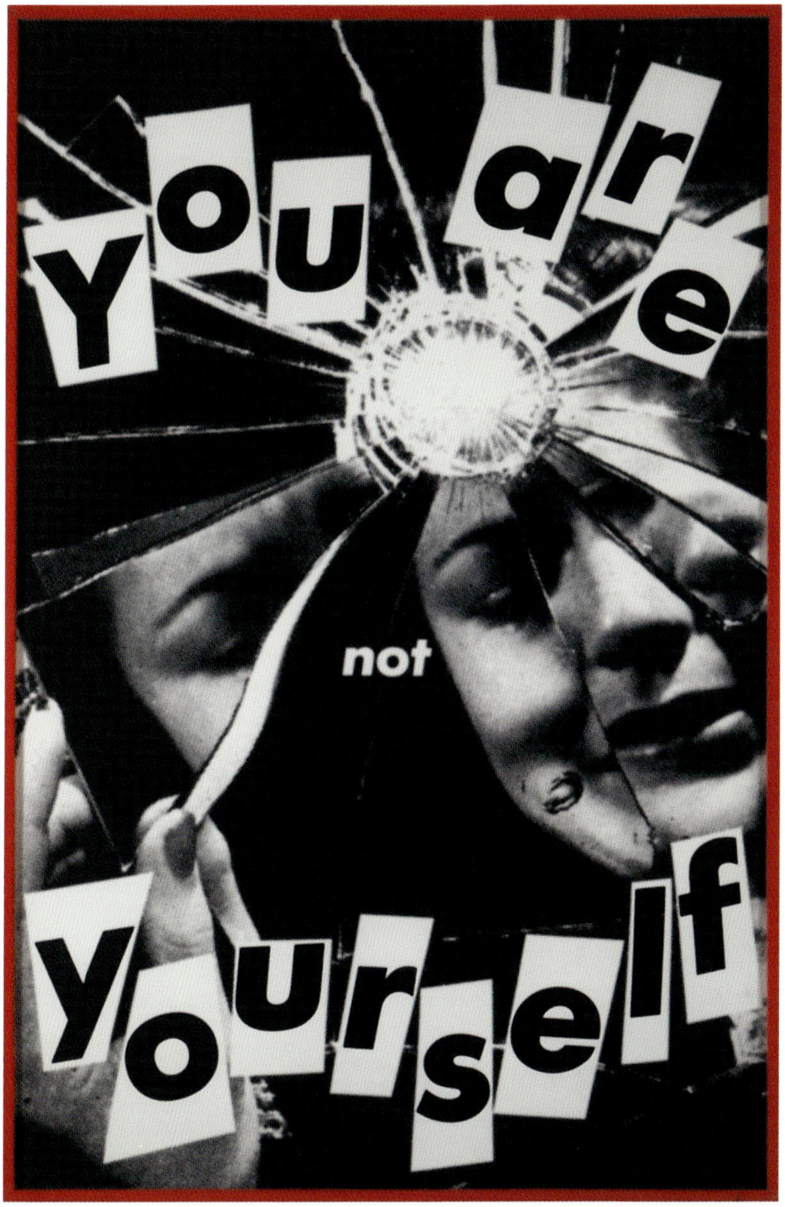

Barbara Kruger, *Untitled (You Are Not Yourself)*, 1982. Glenstone Museum, Potomac, Maryland.

over theory, but that didn't stop me from continuing to read, and quote from, critical theorists in the years to come.

Like Charlesworth's, Kruger's artwork finds its location at the intersection of image and text, but hers features text as a coequal component of the photographic image. Essentially, Kruger would take existing photographs, crop and enlarge them, and combine them with utterances or sayings that were never originally intended to be seen together. "You are not yourself," "Your manias become science," "Your body is a battleground," "When I hear the word culture I take out my checkbook."

Like most young artists in New York, Kruger first showed her work at noncommercial, "alternative" places like PS1. (Before that, she was an art director at *Mademoiselle*, a Condé Nast magazine, which undoubtedly influenced her flair for image/text collages.) In the early eighties she showed with Annina Nosei Gallery, at a space on Prince Street that famously had a basement used by Jean-Michel Basquiat early in his career, and her work was included in a number of important shows of Postmodernist photography, such as *Image Scavengers* at the Institute of Contemporary Art in Philadelphia, in 1982. That show was divided into two parts, one for painting and one for photography, with a large cast that included Goldstein, Lawson, Longo, and Salle in the painting section and Kruger, Levine, Prince, Sherman, and Simmons in the photography part. But by this time, the relations of photography and painting had become quite contentious.

When Metro Pictures opened its doors, painting was a resurgent medium. A young and ambitious gallerist named Mary Boone had opened a gallery directly across West Broadway from Castelli and Sonnabend in the winter of 1979 and devoted it to painters roughly the same age as the Pictures artists, starting with Julian Schnabel, who burst onto the scene with paintings brimming with human figures and other representational subject matter. Even more shocking, he slathered his paint onto canvas—or onto broken plates embedded within the canvas, or onto black velvet—in crusty thick gobs, dispensing once and for all with the lingering influence of thinned out Color Field painting.

Soon he was coupled in the art world's imagination with several European painters whose work was shown at the 1980 Venice Biennale, the Germans Georg Baselitz and Anselm Kiefer and the Italians Sandro Chia, Francesco Clemente, and Enzo Cucchi. Together with Schnabel, they were labeled Neo-Expressionists.[22]

The Neo-Expressionists were seen by many as the antithesis of the Pictures artists assembled around Metro Pictures, being a uniformly male cohort engaged in self-expression and proudly wearing the accoutrements of artistic genius. A form of critical warfare sprang up, in which the theory-based critics of *October*—Benjamin Buchloh, Crimp, Hal Foster, Craig Owens—derided Neo-Ex painting as a recidivist gesture or last gasp of Modernism, while other, less doctrinaire critics and curators saw it as the long-awaited liberation of contemporary art from idea-driven Conceptual Art and its derivatives.[23]

The enthusiasm for Neo-Expressionism and the much-hyped fashionable lives of its practitioners and dealers allowed a previously repressed antipathy toward photography to emerge in clear view. Richard Hennessy, a painter whose work resembled Neo-Ex painting in spirit if not in ambition, was permitted to give early voice to the antiphotography forces in *Artforum* in a May 1979 article titled "What's All This About Photography?" In Hennessy's opinion, the answer was much ado about nothing. "Photography," he said, in an epic insult, "bears the same relationship to fine art that figure skating does to ballet." Its major point of difference and major problem, for Hennessy, was its lack of evidence of the artist's hand. Whereas a painting's depiction on close inspection becomes brush marks on a surface, a photograph's appearance, he wrote, is seamless and impersonal. Like Charles Baudelaire, Hennessy saw photography as a representative of industrial society, responsible for a "decline in artistic taste."[24]

Among those who saw photography's new place in contemporary art as a good thing, revivifying both contemporary art and photography, Hennessy's complaint seemed anti-intellectual and jejune, perhaps a last peep of resistance to a medium definitely on the rise. But it appeared in *Artforum* and thus had the attention of those who mattered in the art world, many of whom resented Postmodernist practice and theory and the politics of the journal *October* more than they did photography.

Unintentionally, the revival of painting in the form of Neo-Expressionism and the backlash against what was being called "photo-based art" had a positive effect. The Postmodernist artists associated with Metro Pictures now had a clear antagonist against which to compete, and arguments about which was the real vanguard of contemporary art served to thrust them even more into the spotlight. And the ranks of young artists focused on the role of photographic representation continued to grow, expanding out beyond Soho and Tribeca to the East Village, where a new art scene was in its infancy.

By the time Metro Pictures had moved over to Greene Street, galleries that were sympathetic to the Pictures aesthetic and what was being called photo-based art were springing up almost daily on the narrow streets of the neighborhood known as Alphabet City—the avenues east of First Avenue that were named A, B, and C. By 1983 the twenty-square-block, down-at-the-heels area held more than a dozen storefront galleries, among them Civilian Warfare, Fun Gallery, Gracie Mansion, Pat Hearn, International with Monument, and P.P.O.W. Arts writer Carlo McCormick opined in the *East Village Eye* that October that "East Village galleries are multiplying like rats."[25]

Many in the now-expanded ranks of Postmodernist artists had their first shows in galleries like Leslie Tonkonow's Art City, Colin de Land's Vox Populi, Lisa Spellman's transplanted 303 Gallery, Tim Greathouse's Oggi Domani, and Peter Nagy's Nature Morte. I was introduced to this scene by Helene Winer, who one day suggested we walk over to Nature Morte after we had lunch in Soho, and soon the East Village became a regular destination on my critic's route. There I saw, for the first time, work by Vikky Alexander, Alan Belcher, Silvia Kolbowski, Annette Lemieux, and David Robbins.

The East Village scene, at least in terms of upstart galleries, did not last long; by 1988 it was essentially over. But by then the whole notion of Postmodernism and the photo-based art through which it defined itself was no longer on the margins—geographically or critically—of contemporary art. The oft-cited marker of Postmodernist artists taking their place in the thick of the Soho marketplace was the 1987 move of Barbara Kruger and Sherrie Levine to the Mary Boone Gallery, whose MO had been Neo-Expressionist painting. Boone had lost her first and most popular Neo-Ex artist, Schnabel, to Pace in 1984, but she still represented Ross Bleckner, Eric Fischl, David Salle, and the German artists Georg Baselitz, A. R. Penck, and Sigmar Polke. She also had recently been criticized by the Guerrilla Girls for having an all-male stable of artists. As for Kruger and Levine, who had been represented by two midtier galleries, Annina Nosei and Baskerville and Watson, joining Boone meant a big step up in visibility and marketing.

In a long piece I wrote for the *Times* about the move—"When Outs Are In, What's Up?," July 26, 1987—I saw it as a signal of Postmodernist art's acceptance; "The work of these two artists, which was once consigned to the outskirts of the marketplace, now occupies the symbolic center of popular and commercial success." And I noted that Postmodernism's most doctrinaire proponents, among them Yve-Alain Bois and Hal Foster, were none too happy. Bois wrote that they had "abandoned themselves to the seduction of what they claim to denounce" and Foster plaintively asked, "What has happened to the dialectic between modernism and mass culture?"[26]

One answer might be that mass culture had won the day. But a better one, more in keeping with a Marxist idea of dialectics, is that something else—a third term, embedded within a wider view of Postmodernism than *October* condoned and without an ax to grind against Modernism—had been produced: an art that reflected wryly and often critically on contemporary culture without distinguishing between its traditional, conventional "high" forms (read painting, drawing, sculpture) and its "low" and middlebrow ones (read photography, film, video, comics, etc.).

While Brauntuch, Longo, Lawson, and Salle continued throughout the eighties to make paintings and drawings based on photographs, much of Postmodernist art was taking the form of photography—photographs about photographs, and about photography's place in the world. This seemed to me fundamentally different from the appearance of photographs in most Conceptual Art, with their insistently anticraft qualities; the photographs these Postconceptual artists were making were sleek and attractive by comparison. And it was fundamentally different from the independent activity of photographers working in or against the medium's own art tradition. As much as I had been enamored of the contemporary experimental work shown at Light Gallery during the seventies, I felt that a page had been turned.

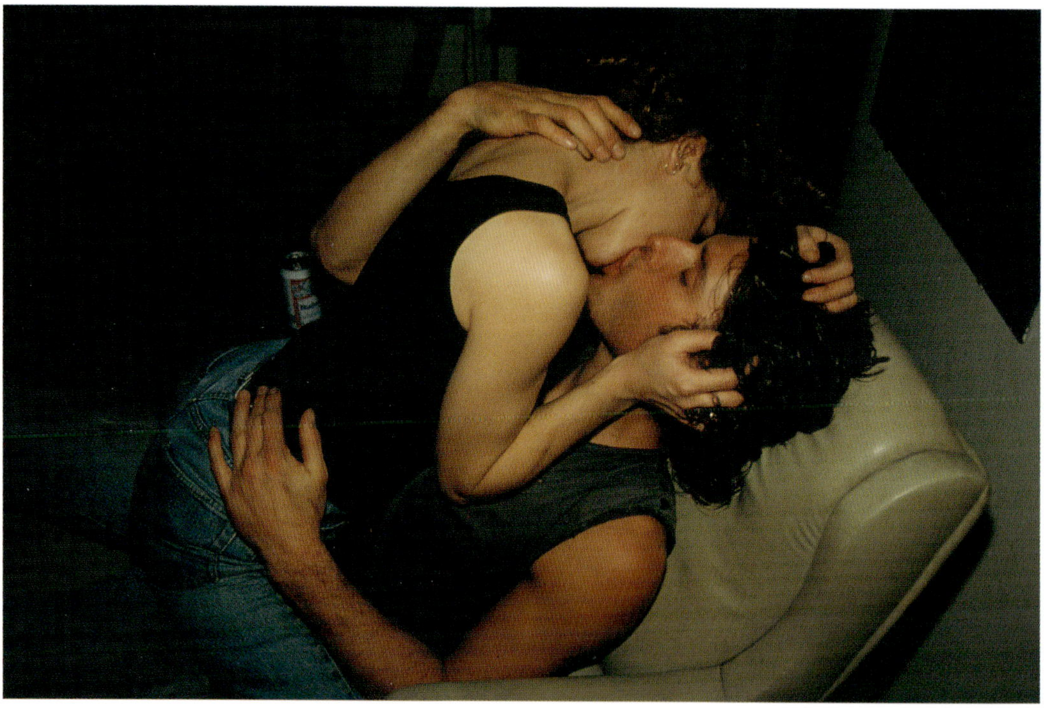

CHAPTER 11

Essentials for the Eighties

My first review for the *New York Times* appeared May 10, 1981, and focused on a show of Tod Papageorge's work at Daniel Wolf Gallery on 57th Street, one of a number of new galleries opened in the late seventies devoted exclusively to showing photographs. It was, let us say, not an entirely complimentary review of the established photographer, although I hope not a hatchet job either. I managed to positively note the visual ironies his pictures capture and to suggest that he was trying to combine the candid qualities of Walker Evans's 35mm work with the seamless detail of Evans's better known 8 × 10 view camera pictures.[1] The lead, though, was written under the influence of Hilton Kramer, who urged me to dwell on how powerful Papageorge's presence was within contemporary photography. I did my best to inflate the man so that I could then put a pin in him, oblivious to whatever consequences this might have on my future in the profession. I heard later that Papageorge was not pleased by my attention, and my reception at the Wolf Gallery became palpably frosty for months afterward.

Whatever its flaws, my debut review announced my independence from the reigning order of art photography. Having watched with enthusiasm the development of a new generation of artists using photography from my perch at the *Soho Weekly News*, I was not about to revert to the Museum of Modern Art's vertical version of who and what mattered in contemporary photography. I set about, only half consciously, to straddle the different worlds represented by photography galleries on the one hand and art galleries on the other—and, if possible, to bring them together.

My first year of writing for the *Times* included discussions of a cornucopia of practitioners: classic nineteenth-century landscapist Timothy O'Sullivan; Surrealist-inflected Modernist Frederick Sommer, experimentalist Robert Heinecken, documentarian Danny Lyon, and newcomer Joel Sternfeld. I also wrote about Robert Rauschenberg's photographs for the Sunday *New York Times Magazine* and reviewed books by photojournalist Susan Meiselas (*Nicaragua*), poststructuralist Roland Barthes (*Camera Lucida*), and *New Topographics* alum Robert Adams (*Beauty in Photography*).

And that fall I reviewed Cindy Sherman's second one-person show at Metro Pictures, a review that was printed with the provocative title, "Cindy

Nan Goldin, *Rise and Monty Kissing, NYC*, 1988.

Sherman: A Playful and Political Post-Modernist." Granted, writers for newspapers don't get to write their own headlines—that's the prerogative of the editors, who tailor them to exactly fit a given space—but the introduction of the word "Post-Modernist" to the readers of the *Times* was apparently a feat. *Artforum*, in a 2003 issue devoted to reassessing the art of the eighties, wrote in its chronology, "The term 'postmodernism' migrates into the fine-arts discourse, for Andy Grundberg's 'Cindy Sherman: A Playful and Political Post-Modernist' . . . Perhaps the first time 'postmodernism' in the *October*-ish sense appears in the newspaper of record."[2]

In my review, I dove into the deep end of post-ness without hesitation:

> Today it is clear that photography's isolationist preoccupation with its unique formal properties—its reflexive urge to prove itself a fully modernist art—has run its course. Why worry over modernism when modernism itself is in such disarray throughout the arts? Painters have turned to representation and Realist styles despite photography's presence; architects have taken to decorating their edifices with columns and curlicues culled from the past; dancers have left the lofts and sidewalks to return to the proscenium stage. We are, many believe, in the throes of a post-modernist age, which entails not only a passage beyond modernism, but also an active rejection of its historical imperatives. . . .
>
> By focusing exclusively on conventionalized, almost stereotypical forms of representation, Sherman seems to question our assumptions about originality in art. By borrowing from popular culture rather than high culture, she questions the vitality of the fine-art tradition. By fragmenting her own identity into a series of performing personae, she deflates our image of the artist as a glamorized, Nietzschean superhero. And, in photographic terms, she moves past the investigation of formal syntax to take up questions of content.[3]

The pictures in question—now officially enumerated *Untitled #85* to *Untitled #96*, but commonly known as the "centerfolds"—were commissioned by the editor of *Artforum*, Ingrid Sischy, as an artist's project intended for publication. But at the last moment Sischy apparently thought better of it, so the exhibition was their first appearance. Each wide-screen image, proportionally a double-page magazine spread, shows Sherman positioned on a bed, couch, or floor, usually prone but in some cases sitting up on them. She wears bedclothes or slightly disheveled outfits and gazes out into an indeterminate space that shows no awareness of the camera's, or viewer's,

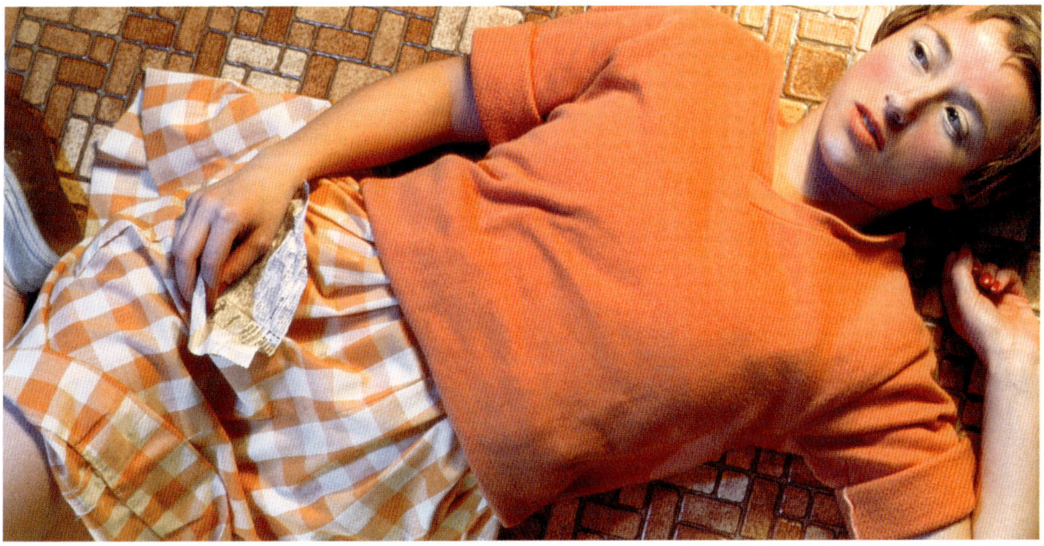

Cindy Sherman, *Untitled #96*, 1981.

presence. (One exception: she stares directly at a telephone next to her shoulder, as if awaiting a call.)

Overall, the centerfolds show several versions of a young woman in a suspended state of what looks like dread or expectation; either something has just happened to her (in one she is soaking wet, in another her skirt is turned up) or is about to. They are an invitation to create one's own narrative, determined in large part by one's gender. The woman is alone in the pictures, but her look suggests another presence: possibly, a male beholder like the one who is the unspoken audience for conventional magazine centerfolds.

If the *Untitled Film Stills* are what Sherman is best known for today, the centerfolds propelled her into the center of contemporary art's conversation at the time. While my review was nothing but laudatory, feminist critics reacted differently. According to Eva Respini, who organized a Sherman retrospective at MoMA in 2012, "The centerfolds provoked debate about the victimization of women because in many of the pictures viewers look down at the model, a vantage point that evokes a male point of view and suggests the woman's passivity and vulnerability." Laura Mulvey and Roberta Smith were two of the critics Respini cites who saw the figures in the pictures as victims. Nonetheless, or perhaps because of such reactions, "Commercially and critically, this provocative body of work ushered in a new era in Sherman's career, catapulting her to art stardom and engendering a new round of vigorous critical debate."[4] For the rest of the eighties, and beyond, she was the "It Girl" of Postmodernism.

Sherman's pictures, and I suppose my response to them in the widely circulated Sunday *New York Times*, also spurred a different critical debate, one that took place within the increasingly defensive photography world. Some felt that Sherman was a flash in the pan, too young to warrant all the attention her pictures were getting. Some felt that what she was doing—setting up scenes and posing herself in costumes—was not what the art of photography was or should be about. In any case, I had just exacerbated the conflict between a traditionalist, photography-as-art contingent identified with John Szarkowski's ideas and a contemporary, art-as-photography scene that had been bubbling up since Robert Rauschenberg, Edward Ruscha, and Andy Warhol.

In retrospect I realize I spent much of my time straddling these two territories in my writing for the *Times,* often of a mind to explain one to the other. The week after my Sherman piece the *New York Times Book Review* ran my review of Robert Adams's book *Beauty in Photography: Essays in Defense of Traditional Values,* a traditionalist manifesto if ever there was one. While I made a case for his devotion to the Platonic ideals of truth and beauty, I noted that "post-structuralists and postmodernists are likely to find them irritating."[5] Earlier, in the summer, I had observed that what ostensibly was an aesthetic contest was also a shift in status: "Photography galleries were born of a specific need back when photographs were still somewhat suspect as art objects. Photography galleries showed photographs, and so-called art galleries did not. But today the art galleries are much more amenable to photographs; Sonnabend, OK Harris, Zabriskie, Marlborough, Holly Solomon all show them."[6]

Finances were involved, too. At the time of Sherman's show it was clear that several photography-only galleries, Light Gallery included, were having financial difficulties, and the National Endowment for the Arts was ending its special programs for photography exhibitions, catalogs, and surveys. However, given that art galleries were picking up the slack, I wrote that this shift didn't mean that the interest in photographs as art objects was waning.[7] For the rest of the eighties the majority of my reviews covered museums and art galleries showing photography and not medium-specific galleries.

As a result of my continued interest in Postmodernist artists, I was asked by David Featherstone of the Friends of Photography in Carmel, California, to organize a show of their work for the group's gallery. The Friends of Photography had been founded by Ansel Adams and his friends and was primarily interested in West Coast "straight" photography; however, they also wanted to stay abreast of contemporary practice. *Masking and Unmasking: Aspects of Post-Modernist Photography* opened in Carmel in March 1984 and included the work of Eileen Cowin, Louise Lawler, Richard Prince, Cindy Sherman, Laurie Simmons, and James Welling. I borrowed most of the work, Cowin's excepted, from Metro Pictures, which had just moved to its larger quarters on Greene Street. After I had sent in a checklist of the photographs I wanted in the show, Featherstone called me from the Friends and asked how the prints would be delivered. I had assumed this was his problem, but I asked how most of their shows were shipped. "Through the mail," he said. When I relayed this, it bemused Helene Winer, since the pictures in question were all framed and weren't about to be dismounted for shipping in an envelope. Out of the goodness of the gallery's heart a crate was built to house all the works, which were then trucked to Carmel. I'm not sure who ultimately paid the freight.

I was invited out for the opening and to give a lecture about the show.[8] Ansel Adams, whom I had first met a few years before, didn't show up for the talk, but Berenice Abbott, who was there to receive a distinguished achievement award from the Friends, did, which contributed to my already high anxiety. Fortunately she soon fell fast asleep in her chair, which helped me relax a bit. Ansel, it turned out, was in bad health, and he died at home a few weeks later at age eighty-two, while the show was still up. I like to imagine that it was the last photography exhibition he saw, if he ever did, in which case I hope the sight of where photography was headed didn't contribute to his demise.

Lecturing in Carmel in the company of masters of modern photography was oddly fun, but for the rest of the eighties I felt like the designated punching bag for photographers who saw Cindy Sherman as an existential threat to their profession. As a thirty-something New York critic writing about and thus helping to make reputations for those outside the traditional photo axis, I wasn't acting out of any perverse pleasure or need for revenge. I felt, with something like a missionary's zeal, that the photography world was missing a paradigm shift in what the medium's art purpose could and should be. Converting the unconverted, to no surprise, was no easy sell.

Sometimes I was in friendly territory, as when I gave a lecture the night that Sherman's first big-league traveling museum show opened at the Akron Art Museum, in June 1984. Sherman, her parents from New Jersey, her gallerists Janelle Reiring and Helene Winer, and several collectors of her work were in attendance, which gave me more stage fright than I would have had anyway, but the response was all positive, including from the artist.

Not so when I gave essentially the same talk at the Visual Studies Workshop in Rochester, where the workshop's founder, Nathan Lyons, was known to be skeptical about the importance of the Postmodernism movement's impact on photography. (Part of the problem also was Rochester's proximity to Buffalo, where Sherman had gone to school. Some of the audience remembered her as a neophyte whom they deemed unlikely to succeed; others were just envious.) I got the same kind of aggrieved reaction, and worse, when I gave the same talk in Washington, D.C., Philadelphia, and Boston. This led me to develop my theory of inversely proportional hostility: the closer the lecture was to New York, the more negativity I got from the crowd. When I traveled to Lawrence, Kansas, or Des Moines, Iowa, my audiences seemed more interested than offended.

By this time Sherman had moved on from the film stills and centerfolds and was making work that mixed designer fashion with the grotesque. In 1985 she made a series of fairy-tale pictures that look like gruesome versions of the tales of the Brothers Grimm, using prosthetic attachments to alter her own appearance; fans of her Hollywood starlet look were justifiably appalled. She followed these with a series of truly repulsive scenes of what looks like vomit or fresh garbage, in which the artist is barely visible.

In all of this progression, Sherman seemed to cannily respond to the critical responses the previous work had received and against the expectations for her next moves. When feminist critics thought the centerfolds showed passive victims, Sherman countered with variously angry, ebullient, and seemingly deranged women wearing high-end fashion. When critics argued that these women were slaves to the designer clothes they modeled, Sherman dispensed with any hint of luxe in the fairy-tale series. Finally, when still other critics noted that the through line in all her work was the visible presence of the artist, she virtually eliminated herself from view.

In reacting to how her work was received, Sherman was playing with her audience on her own terms; paradoxically, portraying herself as the product of so many cultural roles served to empower her and to assert her autonomy as a self-defining artist and woman. In effect, and in quintessential Postmodern fashion, she was able to create an individual identity by disappearing into the myriad of identities available to her.

Sherman was not the only Postmodernist woman artist of the eighties to take on issues of female identity that were central to the conversations of feminists, but the prominence of her work within feminist criticism, its centrality to Postmodernist theorizing, and its popularity with a large swathe of the art world made her a model for the next generation of young women artists, many of whom took up the camera under her influence. However, her strategy for using photography to address her identity as a woman was not the only one at play during the decade. Two other female photographers, from far outside the Postmodernist, Pictures orbit, figure nearly as large by taking quite different paths: Nan Goldin and Francesca Woodman. Together with Sherman they represent three major influences on photography today.[9]

"What Robert Frank's 'The Americans' was to the 1950s, Nan Goldin's *The Ballad of Sexual Dependency* is to the 1980s," I declared in the *Times* at the end of 1986, when Aperture published a book of 130 of her pictures.[10] But as I pointed out in the review, the *Ballad* was not really a book, or even a show of prints from the book, but a multisensory, slide-show-and-sound

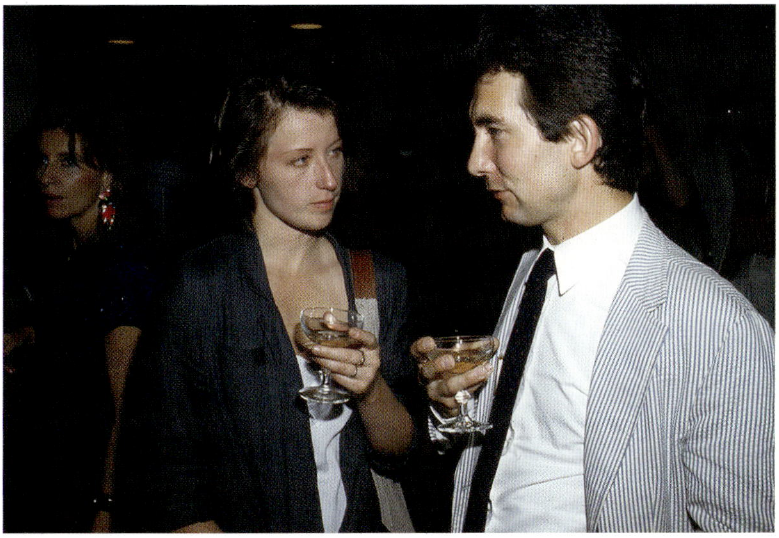

Cindy Sherman and the author at the opening of *Cindy Sherman*, a 1984 retrospective exhibition at the Akron Art Museum, Ohio.

experience of some seven hundred pictures, orchestrated and animated by the presence of the artist.

Individually, Goldin's photographs resemble snapshots in terms of composition, lighting, and color, although they are much more sophisticated than today's surfeit of selfies. Like a snapshot album, the *Ballad* also has a recurring cast of characters—Goldin's friends and lovers, Goldin herself—whose lives and physicality become central to the narrative of the whole. And it has "chapters" of pictures about similar themes: men posing as hypermasculine; women grooming themselves and others; heterosexual couples falling in love, having sex, getting into fights, dealing with AIDS. All of this makes the *Ballad* emotionally immediate and, ultimately, harrowing, given that there is no happy ending. One is left with the sense that individual happiness and social intimacy are two quite different things.

Goldin had first "performed" the *Ballad* in its embryonic stage at the Mudd Club in lower Manhattan in 1979, but as she continued to photograph in the early eighties and expand the number of slides in the show—eventually, it took at least nine slide trays to hold them all—the *Ballad* became deeper, richer, and totally absorbing. As I noted in my review, "the pictures examine nearly all permutations of human interactions with an obsessive attention. Women with women friends, men with men friends, parents with their children." I added that the overall message was the insufficiency of intimacy as a cure for a pervasive sense of individual isolation. Despite the sobering message, seeing the *Ballad* in person was a pleasure, with moments of hilarity and an irresistible mix track of aptly chosen music performed by the likes of the Velvet Underground, the Supremes, and James Brown, plus a Maria Callas aria and the theme song from *The Good, The Bad and the Ugly*.[11]

Goldin was not much talked about by feminist art critics of the time, perhaps because of the *Ballad*'s title or because she, as the major protagonist of the piece, frequently appears as a victim of male aggression, most famously in a picture of her staring at the camera through a black eye. Still, there is a sense of female agency discernible in the *Ballad*, and the women we see have a much broader emotional range, including a deep sense of camaraderie with other women, than the men.

If Sherman showed future generations of young artists—women, people of color, immigrants, LGBTQ folk, and others—that they could try on various personae in their work and critique both mass-media stereotypes and the conventional gaze by turning the camera back on itself, Goldin demonstrated that one could document one's life close-up, warts and all, and cumulatively create a narrative that spoke to a wider cultural condition. Both were attractive options to art-school students well into the next century. And there was a third popular option: one could transform oneself into a mythic but embodied figure that peeled away contemporary culture like so many clothes to get at something more compelling, profound, and self-reflecting than everyday reality. This was the territory of Francesca Woodman.

Woodman was a prodigy, a too-brief flash of intense artistic energy starting at age thirteen and ending with her suicide at age twenty-two, in early 1981. The child of two artists, George and Betty Woodman, she lived her life almost entirely for the sake of her art, producing some eight hundred photographs in less than a decade.[12] By the time she got to art school at the Rhode Island School of Design she had fixed the direction and method of her work: alone (with some exceptions) and usually partly or completely nude, she posed with props or interacted with walls, floors, and furniture. Frequently she used a slow shutter speed to blur all or parts of her body and often homed in to show just her torso or breasts.

Her oeuvre is a tour de force of self-portraiture, and although she does not pretend to be anyone else but herself she imbues the pictures with such metaphoric potential that one reads her figure not as a specific individual but as a more generic presence, a Freudian or perhaps Jungian embodiment of the female. As a result, her work has attracted feminist art critics starting with Rosalind Krauss and Abigail Solomon-Godeau. Unfortunately, all the attention and adulation has come posthumously. When Woodman fell to her death from a Manhattan rooftop she felt unrecognized and underappreciated.

Woodman had moved to New York in 1979 after finishing school and spending time in Rome, and she aimed to forge a career quickly enough to support herself. She made the rounds of galleries and museums, without much success, and at one point decided she might do fashion photography to make ends meet. (She went as far as trying to make work samples that

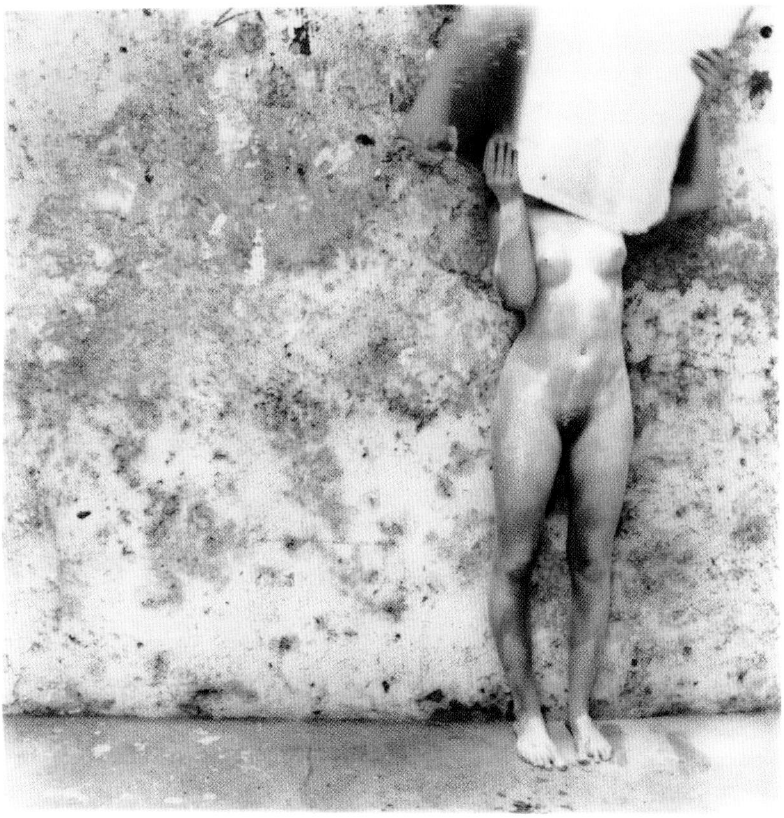

Francesca Woodman, *Self-Deceit #4, Rome, Italy*, 1978.

looked like fashion photography, even hiring models to pose, but the pictures only look like more "Woodmans."[13]) She even knocked on the doors of photography magazines.

When Woodman dropped off her portfolio at *Modern Photography*, where I was still working as picture editor, I was impressed enough to invite her back to the viewing room when she picked up her work, so we could talk about it together. But after chatting I gave her my standard response when a photographer seemed promising: we can't use anything right now, but I'm interested, so come back in a year and show me your new work then.

This response had worked out well with Joel Sternfeld, whose pictures I had discovered in a similar way and eventually did publish, so I felt it was a good line, but Woodman definitely didn't. She argued stridently that the work was already good enough to be published right away. In retrospect perhaps she was right, but despite her beguiling charm at the time I was annoyed that someone just out of art school (with an undergraduate degree, at that) should expect me to give her an instant career boost. She seemed in a great hurry to make her mark, and thus more than a bit pushy. I didn't expect to see her again, and I didn't. She committed suicide a few months later.

When I heard about her death I felt terrible, imagining that if I had rushed some of her pictures into print, tragedy might have been averted. But almost every editor and curator I knew and talked to had a story like mine to tell; Woodman had been indefatigable in making the rounds of the photography "establishment," of which by this time I had become a part. We all had failed to live up to her expectations, as unreasonable as they may have been.

The subsequent validation of Woodman's career, and the beginning of her reputation as photography's version of Sylvia Plath, began with a 1986 exhibition mounted at the Wellesley College Museum and Hunter College Art Gallery by Ann Gabhart, *Francesca Woodman: Photographic Work*, to which Krauss and Solomon-Godeau contributed catalog essays. Solomon-Godeau argued that Woodman's work was essentially a feminist critique of what she called the construction and inscription of femininity. Her work, said the critic, is "a living testimonial, a valuable bequest to other women."[14]

What I had taken to be a romantic, even sophomoric fascination with props such as garter belts, cantaloupes, and calla lilies, Solomon-Godeau apprehends as the construction of fetishes, but fetishes that are "overdetermined" in the work. "Ultimately," she wrote, "the power of Woodman's photographs lies not in wresting new meanings from the lexicon of fetishism (much less in redeeming them), but, rather, in re-presenting that very lexicon so as to effectively block its automatic consumption and acceptance."[15] That Woodman was innocent of any such critical intention for her work Solomon-Godeau readily acknowledged, nor did the work's insistent narcissism bother the critic or any of the curators, critics, and art students who have lionized the artist since. She was, in their view, a Postmodernist, but a different sort than Cindy Sherman.

Sherman's work bites the hand that feeds it, in the sense that it rebukes the viewer, and thus the art world, at the same time that it proffers enjoyment. By contrast Woodman's is almost blatantly ingratiating. Both, though, at least in the beginning of Sherman's career, are equally adept at visual seduction. By which I mean not only that they foreground a young and attractive woman who intentionally displays herself to the camera (and yes, mine is a male gaze) but also that they use our associations with the photographic medium to signal pleasure: the anticipation of going to the movies, say, in the case of Sherman's *Untitled Film Stills*, and the erotic frisson of nineteenth-century daguerreotype nudes, with Woodman.

Woodman had a beautiful body that was classically proportioned and served as a counterpoint to her fondness for the decrepit and decaying interiors with which she typically interacted. These classical proportions are essential to a series she did less than a year before her death in which she imitated Greek caryatids and other sculptural figures for a projected *Temple* installation at the Alternative Museum. The pictures, printed six feet tall using a commercial process similar to blueprints, link her work to a history of representations of the female form long before the invention of photography. They also open what could have been a new chapter in her career. Caryatids represent women who carry the weight of the temple roof, forever supporting the (presumably male) ambitions of the architecture. She might have been hard at work on these new pictures when I saw her, but I don't remember that she mentioned them. I would have been interested.

Almost forty years later, Sherman's and Goldin's work continues to seem vital and contemporary while Woodman's has an historical, somewhat nostalgic affect much like that of Pre-Raphaelite art for twentieth-century viewers. That doesn't mean Woodman has been any less influential, however. Her decision to represent herself, to deal with her own body on her own terms, and at the end to invoke a whole history of male representations of the female (and, per Solomon-Godeau, the female fetish) was undeniably brave and certainly inspiring to new generations of artists wanting to address their sexual and gender identities. While not unprecedented—female performance artists Ana Mendieta, Adrian Piper, Carolee Schneemann, and Hannah Wilke all courageously used their bodies to challenge traditional, male ideas about women's subjectivity and subjecthood—Woodman's work seems one of a kind.

Together, the three women's work—which began virtually simultaneously—suggests how deeply the consciousness of being a woman in a man's world informed the art of the eighties. And it shows how broad the territory for photography had become at the start of what should be remembered as the decade in which photography became not only a full member of contemporary art but also, to an unprecedented degree, its aesthetic driver.

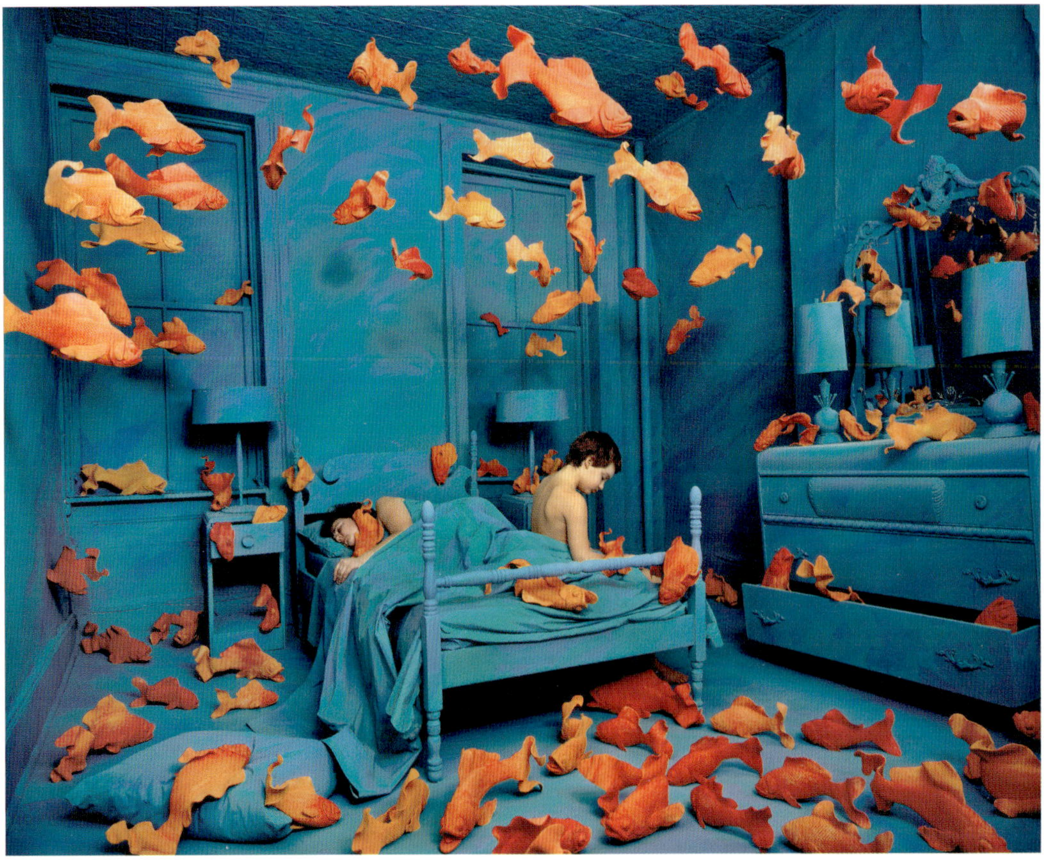

CHAPTER 12

Inventions of Pure Imagination

The special genius of photography depends on the seamless coherence of its description; the camera shows us a particular cone of space during a specific parcel of time. This makes it a perfect tool for visual exploration and discovery, but a rather clumsy one for realizing the inventions of pure imagination.

—John Szarkowski, "A Different Kind of Art," *New York Times*, 1975

But the camera's status as a mechanical recording instrument does not mean that its images are necessarily any more innocent of bias than [Jacques-Louis] David's pigments. This is especially obvious today, when everyone from politicians to post-modernists is aware of how media images can be fabricated to serve specific ends. In our century, the camera's ability to refashion the world is a given.

—Andy Grundberg, "Photojournalism: A Blend of Artifice and Actuality," *New York Times*, 1988

The artistic triumph of the Pictures Generation certainly changed contemporary art, but I doubt it alone would have permanently vanquished the art world's lingering doubts about photography as an equal of painting and sculpture if the art of photography had not been changing radically at the same time. By the eighties the hegemonic, stand-alone aesthetic influence of John Szarkowski and the Museum of Modern Art's photography department was cracking apart like an eggshell no longer able to contain its maturing contents. "Straight" photography, street or otherwise, was being superseded by a taste for images designed for the camera by the artist/photographer, as fashion and other forms of commercial photography always had been. Such pictures were made, not taken, in many ways just like those of the Pictures artists.

As much as the 1977 *Pictures* show at Artists Space has come to mark the entry of Postmodernism into the art world, it was but one of the watershed

Sandy Skoglund, *Revenge of the Goldfish*, 1981.

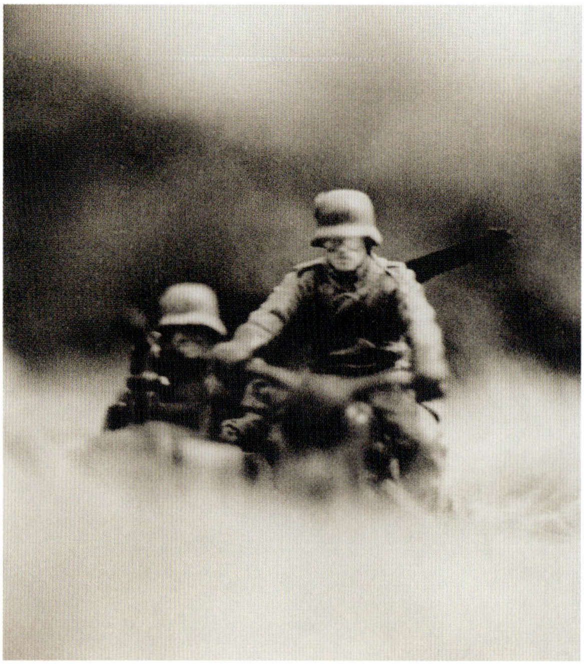

David Levinthal, *Untitled*, 1974. From the book *Hitler Moves East*, 1977.

events that year that presaged photography's broadened acceptance in the precincts of art. I've already discussed the critical impact of Susan Sontag's dystopian collected essays *On Photography*, published in book form in 1977, but not two other books published the same year that had lasting artistic influence. They were David Levinthal and Garry Trudeau's *Hitler Moves East* and Larry Sultan and Mike Mandel's *Evidence*. While unconnected to the CalArts and Hallwalls art scene, and receiving nowhere near the public attention of Sontag's book, these quirky, collaborative artists' books sketched out—in vitro, as it were—the territory for a major transformation of photography in the eighties.

Hitler Moves East: A Graphic Chronicle, 1941–43 is an earnest-seeming account of the ill-fated German military invasion of the Soviet Union during World War II, considered by many historians the undoing of Adolf Hitler's grand plan of conquest and ultimately of his Reich. It has illustrations and quotes, sourced from actual archival sources, in addition to introductory chapter texts written by Trudeau. But the mainstay of the book is its photographs of toy soldiers and props (tanks, railroad tracks, bridges), devised mainly from HO-scale train accessories and children's playsets, cunningly arranged on a card table in Levinthal's apartment.

Levinthal and Trudeau, then students in Yale's art program, contrived the scenes to look realistic—based, of course, on photographs of World War II that themselves look realistic. Levinthal, the photographer, used a wide aperture to throw most of the background and foreground out of focus.

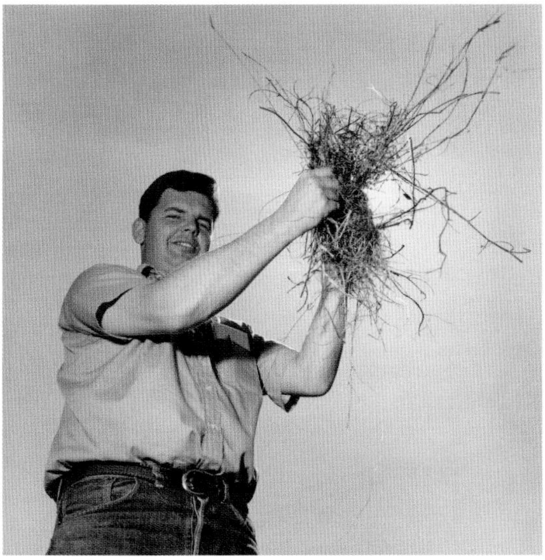

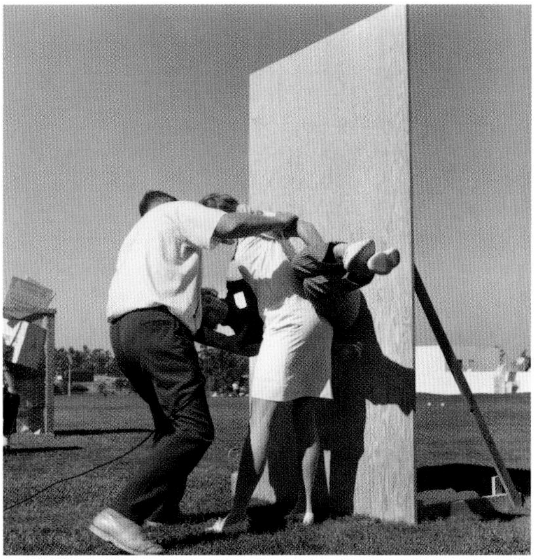

Mike Mandel and Larry Sultan, untitled, undated facing photographs. From the book *Evidence*, 1977.

To make it seem to be snowing, the two tossed flour in the air. These devices afford the images a degree of believability, but at the same time the camera's implacable descriptiveness belies their authenticity. The stiff, stilted poses and the plastic features of the figures give the game away. The result is a conundrum: pictures that evoke the reality of war by reminding us of other pictures we have seen, yet are patently, more or less obviously, fake.[1]

None of the ambiguity of the visual information supplied in *Hitler Moves East* is disclosed: the book may be a parody of war photography, but it takes itself, and its subject, seriously. Viewers then have to discover for themselves the ruse, if one can call it that. As with Troy Brauntuch's paintings in the *Pictures* show, Levinthal and Trudeau's photographs are reliant on our familiarity and associations with images embedded in history—specifically, World War II—and like Cindy Sherman's *Untitled Film Stills* they are photographs that approximate and thus evoke earlier photographs; they do not copy or appropriate them directly.

Levinthal went on to devote his entire career to making quasi-believable and sometimes controversial scenes from miniature figures and props, ranging from Japanese sex dolls to Western cowboys, eventually returning to Hitler in the 1996 series *Mein Kampf*, which includes tabletop re-creations of Nazi death camps. (Trudeau, of course, devoted his career to cartooning, creating the popular strip *Doonesbury*.) But it is hard to overstate the radicality of *Hitler Moves East* at the time it appeared, when the vast majority of photography being presented as art relied on the medium's inherent documentary qualities. The subsequent popularity throughout the eighties of what came to be called tableau or fabricated photography blurred the distinction between artists like Laurie Simmons, who was at Metro Pictures and thus seen as a Pictures artist, and someone like Ellen Brooks, who had started making scenes with doll figures at about the same time as Simmons while living in California but whose identity in the marketplace was as a photographer.

Sultan and Mandel's book *Evidence*, by contrast, was about the contingency of meaning of photographs that were devised and intended to be seen as factual—and about the ineffability and indeterminacy of lens-made images generally. By figuratively dumpster diving in corporate, research, and government files of once-useful photographs, the two photographers assembled a trove of mysterious and absurdist pictures that spoke to Sontag's assertion of photography's inherent surrealism. More to the point, Sultan and Mandel selected, edited, and arranged the pictures to create a cumulative meaning that their individual image makers surely never intended. The artists were, in brief, demonstrating Roland Barthes's poststructuralist assertion of the death of the author, an author no longer in control of the meaning of her or his work.[2] Appropriation, yes, and in advance of both Sherrie Levine and Richard Prince, but Sultan and Mandel did not pretend to author the individual images they reproduced, only the work in which they were assembled.

The pictures in *Evidence* show explosions, crime scenes, measuring devices, hunks of plastic foam, and the like, their unifying motif being human intervention. Hands appear from the edges of the images, holding a piece of rope, a ruler, a monkey; figures (usually white men in white shirts) stand next to centrifuges or on desolate highways, providing scale for those who might need it. *Evidence* as a whole could be read as a meditation on industrial technology, as an exposé of a society bent on controlling both nature and human beings . . . or as a commentary on the uneasy status of photography's recognition as a form of art. Its appearance coincided with a widely read article by Hilton Kramer about the "museumization" of photography, in which he compared Alfred Stieglitz's self-consciously aesthetic pictures to the work of Jacob Riis, who documented life in New York's urban slums in the 1880s. Kramer noted the paradoxical relationship of a photograph's documentary origins and its (usually much later) aesthetic recognition, a paradox that Sultan and Mandel exploit and make obvious.[3]

Evidence could be considered an extension into serial or book form of the *Blasted Allegories* of John Baldessari, since both usurp existing pictures and refashion them into new contexts and meanings. Sultan and Mandel's usurpation is more like pure appropriation, however, since they do not excerpt or adjust the images at all; as with Sherrie Levine's work, the images stand as nakedly as the day they were born. Sarah Charlesworth, Silvia Kolbowski, Barbara Kruger, Paul Laster, Annette Lemieux, Sherrie Levine, Richard Prince, and other artists of the eighties whose work centered on found or repurposed camera images all produced their own kind of "evidence" by following, wittingly or not, the example of *Evidence*.

Taken together, *Hitler Moves East* and *Evidence* suggest that the *Pictures* show was but one manifestation of a new generation's approach to photographs. Also, and just as important, the two books show a growing awareness that camera images were shaping our understanding of ourselves and of the world, and that this awareness was taking place across the erstwhile divide between contemporary art and photography. Postmodernism, however it might be defined as oppositional in the visual arts, was aligned with what some in photography were already thinking and doing. In this sense Postmodernism can be thought of as a response prompted by felt experience, not an ideological demonstration of critical theory or an egregious example of what the dandy "New Journalist" Tom Wolfe cynically called "the painted word."[4]

For photographers the urtext for the shift in contemporary taste from "straight," documentary modes like street photography to openly fictional and reflexive forms that involve building sets and manufacturing scenes in studios was A. D. Coleman's 1976 article in *Artforum*, "The Directorial Mode: Notes toward a Definition."[5] Coleman had noticed that much of the new work he was seeing dispensed with any pretense that photographs showed the world in situ. His prime exhibits were Duane Michals and Les Krims, but he included a long list of fellow travelers that ended with Edward Ruscha, William Wegman, Robert Cumming, and Bruce Nauman—all artists putatively from the other side of the photography/contemporary art divide.

In coining the term *directorial mode* Coleman invoked the cinema, where conventions of fiction are assumed, not contested. The film director, as an auteur, creates a reality that is convincing on its own terms but made only of celluloid. Something about this appealed to Michals, Krims, and others on Coleman's list, such as John Pfahl and Arthur Tress. Most staged their pictures in their studios or apartments—except Pfahl, who was essentially a landscape photographer. In his popular midseventies series *Altered Landscapes*, Pfahl painstakingly intervened in the usually picturesque scenes before his camera and inserted material that mimicked or extended the natural world's features (although occasionally the central figure was man-made, as in his picture of a pile of hay reconfigured as an ice-cream cone).

Although it dealt with the landscape and was akin to Earth Art, Pfahl's work became affiliated with what soon was a widespread practice of tableau and tabletop arrangements for the camera, one that attracted the attention of galleries and museums. Van Deren Coke, the curator of photography at the San Francisco Museum of Modern Art at the time, originated his own term for such work, *fabricated to be photographed*, the title of a 1979 group show he organized that included Pfahl along with Ellen Brooks, James

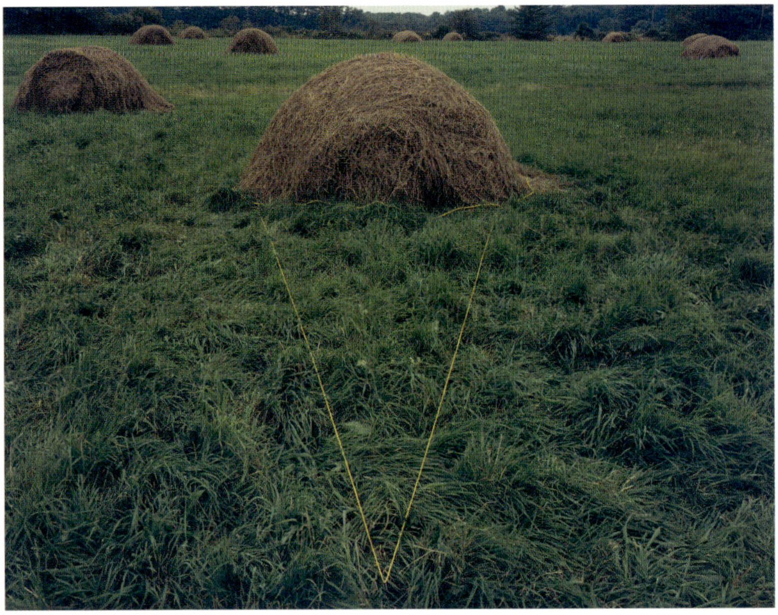

John Pfahl, *Haystack Cone, Freeport, Maine*, 1976, from the series *Altered Landscapes*.

Casebere, Robert Cumming, Les Krims, and others. While noting that, "There have been objects fabricated for studio and table-top photography for at least a hundred years," Coke argued that a new generation of photographers was seeking total control of the image surface as a way of getting across an idea, much like Conceptual artists.[6] Neither he nor Coleman in "The Directorial Mode" mentioned another possibility: that these photographers were familiar with patently staged images not just from art history but from having grown up in an inescapable milieu of advertising and commercial photography.

By 1981 the trend toward photographs that manufactured an imagined world rather than described the existing one had sufficiently evolved that my favorite magazine of the time, a glossy, oversized photography quarterly simply called *Picture*, published an issue titled "Tableau Photography."[7] The issue featured a baker's dozen of contemporary photographers whose pictures were fashioned in studios or constructed in darkrooms, from the veteran Jerry Uelsmann to Postmodernist Cindy Sherman. Their new work was contextualized by the inclusion of reproductions of artistic precursors: Julia Margaret Cameron and Henry Peach Robinson, in the nineteenth century, as well as William Mortensen, Lejaren à Hiller, George Platt Lynes, and Angus McBean. The latter four qualified as footnotes at best in twentieth-century photography, having been virtually cast from view by the proponents of straight photography, most notably Ansel Adams.[8]

Several of the young and up-and-coming artists in the issue were from California, including Brooks, Eileen Cowin, and Patrick Nagatani. Brooks's

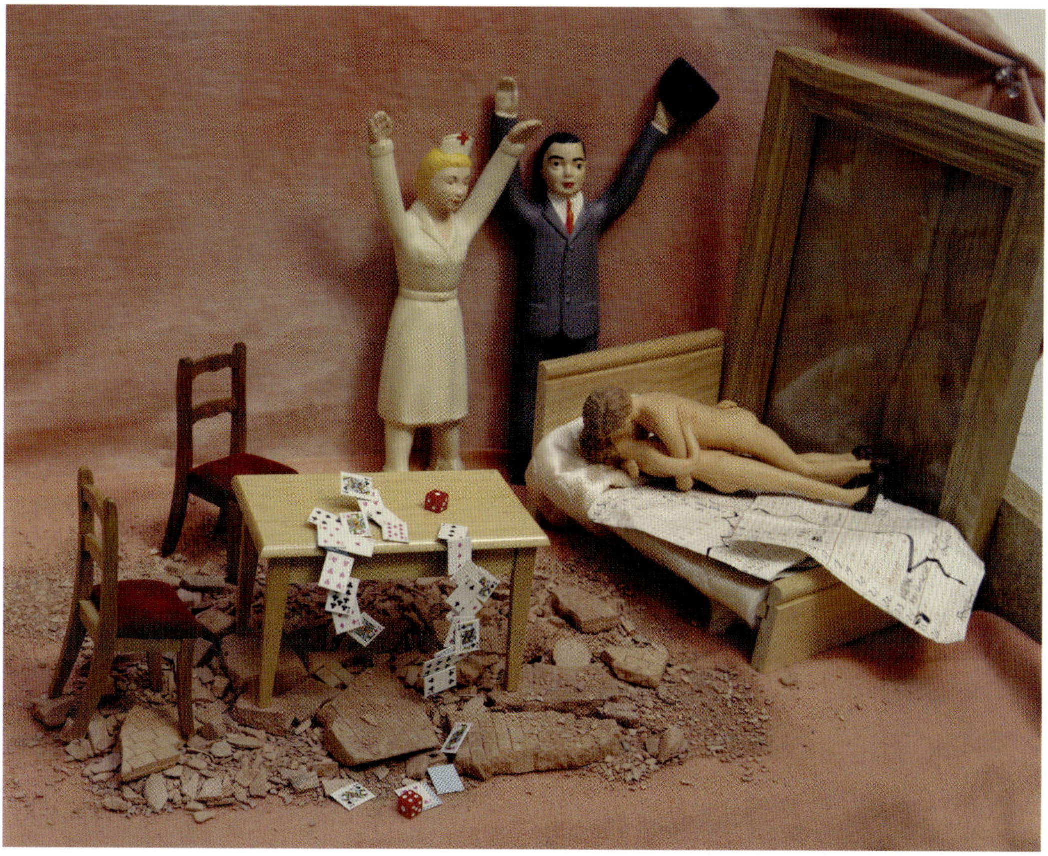

Ellen Brooks, *Untitled [Doctor and Nurse]*, 1978.

work bears a passing resemblance to Laurie Simmons's, involving scenes in which dollhouse figures interact amid dollhouse furniture, but the psychological intensity of the encounters Brooks devised made them less about stereotypes than about a dystopic gender warfare. Cowin's pictures were similar to Brooks's in their concentration on how heterosexual couples relate, but her staged family dramas used real-life actors—her husband, daughter, an identical twin sister, and herself. Nagatani's contribution in the issue was from a series he called *Chromo-Therapy*, faux medical images in which his "patients" are exposed to various parts of the electromagnetic spectrum, purportedly as a healing regime.

Missing from *Picture*'s pages was one of the early pioneers of the mode in California, John Divola. In 1974 Divola had started work on a black-and-white series called *Vandalism*, which recorded his graffiti-inspired, spray-paint mark making on the inside of abandoned houses in Los Angeles. But his real breakthrough came with his 1977–78 series *Zuma*, done in color. The *Zuma* pictures were all taken within an abandoned Malibu beach house, and like the *Vandalism* images they featured Divola's spray-painted additions on the walls, ceilings, and floors; however, they were in color, giving them a

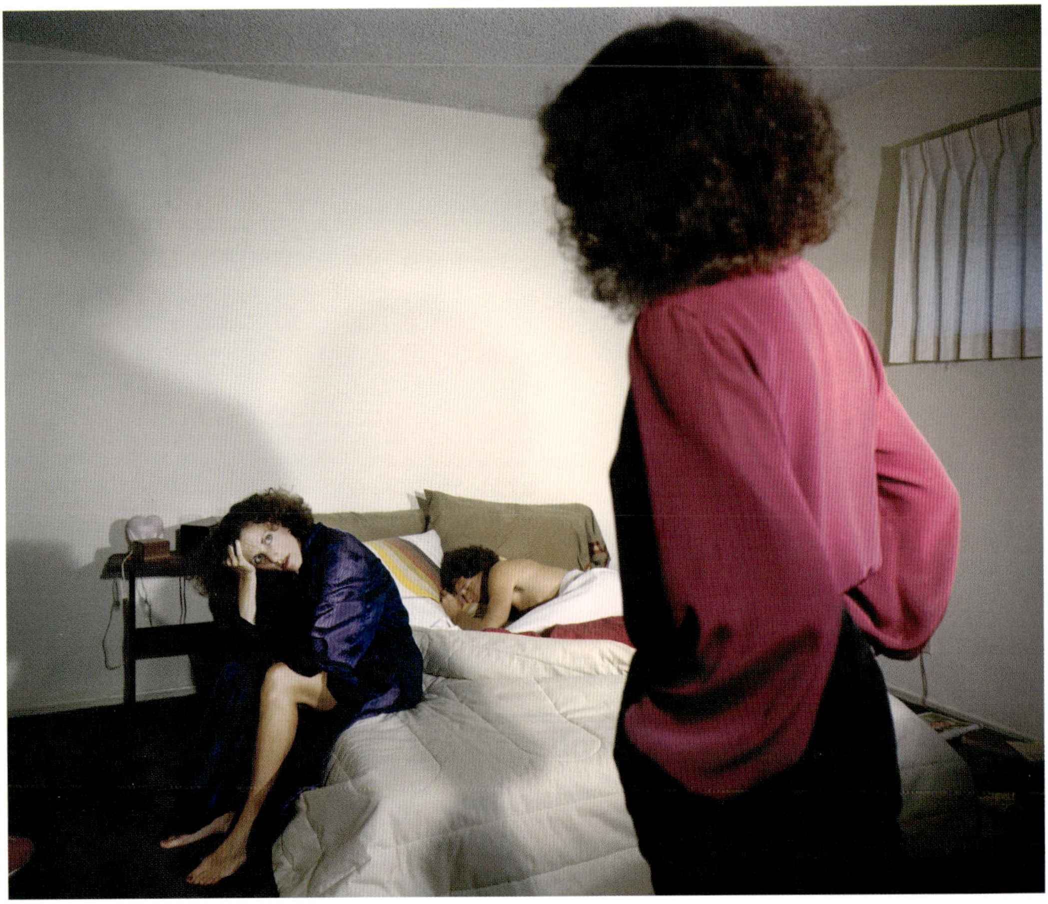

Eileen Cowin, *Untitled*, 1980–83, from the series *Family Docudrama*.

decorative touch at odds with the decay they depicted. Eventually the house was set on fire and demolished, ending the series, but not before Divola embellished the burnt interiors and took more pictures.

Divola's work was shown widely in the late seventies in California and at photo outposts like the Visual Studies Workshop in Rochester and the Center for Creative Photography in Tucson, and the *Zuma* series debuted in New York in 1980 with a one-person show at the Robert Freidus Gallery. But it was the next spring's Whitney Biennial exhibition that really put him on the map . . . and put photography's mark on the map of contemporary art as well.

From the early thirties until 1973 the Whitney Museum of American Art had been presenting annual exhibitions of contemporary American art, with sculpture and painting being presented alternately;[9] in 1973 the format was changed to a biennial but the focus remained on painters and sculptors, now mixed together. Only a few photographers occasionally slipped in—Duane Michals and Lewis Baltz made the cut in 1977—until the 1981 installment blew the doors wide open. Besides Divola, that Biennial included Robert

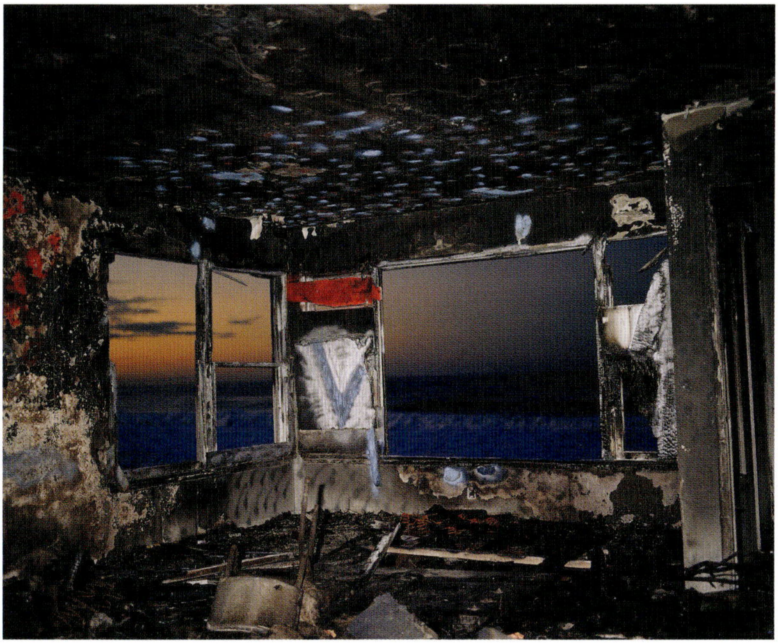

John Divola, *Zuma #29*, 1978, from the series *Zuma*.

Adams, Harry Callahan, Larry Clark, Robert Frank, Jan Groover, David Haxton, Robert Mapplethorpe, Joel Meyerowitz, Duane Michals, Richard Misrach, Leland Rice, and more than a half dozen other photographers among the show's 115 artists. It seemed that the museum was making up for lost time.

Over the course of the rest of the eighties photography became a noticeable and integral component of the Biennial exhibitions, which because of the show's notoriety (it is known as the show critics love to hate) gave the medium art-world credibility that it hadn't seen before. The selection of photographers in 1981 was purposefully catholic and arguably representative: *New Topographics*–style landscapes, gritty black-and-white documentation, formal studies arranged for the camera, and Mapplethorpe's elegant portraits, nudes, and still lifes. Two of the artists, Groover and Haxton, were part of Sonnabend's growing roster of photographers. Haxton's work consisted of color views of what looked to be a photographer's studio, with the backdrop paper folded, cut, and lit in ways that created an intriguing ambiguity of both space and subject matter; what nominally would serve as the background was forced into the foreground and became the apparent subject of the image.[10]

The shining star of the 1981 Whitney Biennial, and the artist of the year altogether as far as photography was concerned, was Sandy Skoglund. Skoglund's *Revenge of the Goldfish* premiered at Castelli Graphics that winter as a one-photograph, one-person show, and it quickly caught the attention of critics, curators, and collectors. (It also marked the establishment of Castelli Photographs as a division within Castelli Graphics.) Part of what made the exhibition noteworthy was an installation in the gallery that effectively redid the photograph in three dimensions, complete with ceramic goldfish, but the photograph by itself was remarkable enough. It soon became the poster child for tableau photography in the minds of many—an easy step, since it was printed as a poster to promote the show.

Skoglund, an erstwhile sculptor, filmmaker, and Conceptual artist, had converted a Lower East Side apartment into a photography studio a couple of years earlier and started to use the entire space as a set utilizing human figures and sculptural multiples she created. I had mentioned some of these pictures when I included her in a fall *Soho Weekly News* article devoted to up-and-coming artists:[11] *Hangers*, in which a man wearing yellow pajamas peers into a room with yellow walls that are adorned with floor-to-ceiling plastic coat hangers (which also fill the pink-painted floor); *Ferns*, an all-beige room with all-beige occupants and green plastic ferns patterning the walls; and *Radioactive Cats*, showing a gray room inhabited by an older couple and a large herd of acid-green cat sculptures, which had been handmade by the artist.

Revenge of the Goldfish was a similar construction, with bright-orange goldfish that Skoglund had modeled and cast hanging in an all-blue bedroom above a boy and a woman on a blue double bed. The flesh of the boy's torso and the other figure's (his mother's?) face and arm bring a disconcerting note of real life to the otherwise surreal scene, which may explain why Skoglund consistently used live models. This element was missing in the gallery reconstruction of the image; instead of human presence, it made do with a pile of the goldfish occupying the bed. Gene Thornton, in reviewing the show in the *Times*, suggested the goldfish may have been "taking an after-dinner nap."[12] Whatever their motives, and the nature of their revenge, the two-foot-long creatures were also offered for sale; like the photograph, their numbers were limited by the gallery as an edition. But the tangibility of the goldfish and the physical presence of the gallery installation were less satisfying than the photograph, which with its human occupants and untouchable surface seemed to inhabit a different, more complicated aesthetic dimension.

At the time, Skoglund's pictures were printed on 30 × 40-inch paper, not that large by today's standards but big enough to seem large at the time. To traditionalist photographers they may have seemed swollen in an attempt to compete in the art market; to the rest of the art world they could "hold the wall" in a white-cube gallery and hold their own in a room with much larger paintings. Since Skoglund used a large-format camera, like most studio-based photographers and landscape photographers at the time, her prints

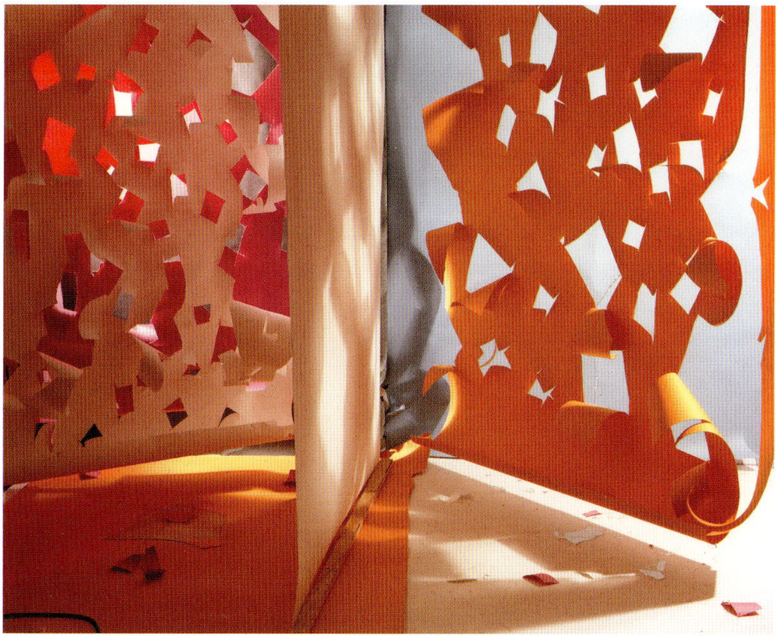

David Haxton, *No. 160, Division with Irregular Squares in Magenta and Orange*, 1980.

contained a wealth of precise detail even at that scale (and kept it even when later she enlarged them to 4 × 5 feet). This separated them from painting and paradoxically heightened their unreality.

The trend toward large color prints in the work of tableau photographers like Skoglund was soon noticed by curators, which led to the 1983 exhibition at the Museum of Modern Art, *Big Pictures by Contemporary Photographers*, which marked the debut of Tina Barney. The list of the thirty-three artists in the show also included David Hockney, Sol LeWitt, Robert Rauschenberg, Kenneth Snelson, and William Wegman, whose reputations exceeded photography. But as much as I would have expected to like the show, I dismissed *Big Pictures* as "a big bore," primarily because much of its supposed bigness was a matter of multiple images or collage rather than a single integral image printed large.[13]

Some had even stronger negative reactions to *Big Pictures*. Marvin Heiferman, who in 1981 had left his job overseeing photography at Castelli Graphics to work independently on books and shows (and to represent Nan Goldin), was moved to organize an exhibition for the Queens Museum that was in every sense a direct response to MoMA's show. Archly titled *The Real Big Picture*, and presented in 1986, it included fifty works by as many artists, only a few of whom had been in the earlier show. In a brief essay, Heiferman explained why his show was different:

> Much attention has been directed toward the art of photography over the past two decades: some museums collect and exhibit with

fervor, galleries and periodicals specialize in art photography, universities grant advanced degrees in photography as an art. But an intellectual and economic chasm separates this photography world from the community of contemporary art, where artists largely untrained in photography have captured the public imagination and critical attention with brash photographic pieces and big prices.

> In the art world, the "art photography" subgroup maintains photography's status as art by encouraging a formal approach to the medium, one that emphasizes connoisseurship and downplays the blue collar nature of most of the pictures we come in contact with. But while photography is a part of our daily experience, art photography isn't; it thrives in a self-imposed exile, separated from the humble snapshot, the blunt news picture, the slick ad or the X-ray that proves to the larger public that the good picture gets a job done. While art photographers often choose to avoid this perception, artists recognize the promiscuity of the medium and exploit it; they study the various come-ons and adopt the visual ploys. Artists use photography rather than revere it. They make pictures—not photographs, objects—not images. It's no surprise that artists' photographs attract attention.[14]

To buttress his case that big pictures and big ideas lived together on the artists' side of the ledger, Heiferman included John Baldessari, Bernd and Hilla Becher, Chuck Close, Jan Dibbets, Gilbert and George, David Hockney, Douglas Huebler, Joseph Kosuth, Bruce Nauman, Robert Rauschenberg, Edward Ruscha, Andy Warhol, and a dozen other artists of contemporary currency. He borrowed from Ronald Feldman, Gladstone, Marian Goodman, Metro Pictures, Annina Nosei, Holly Solomon, Sonnabend, and John Weber—all galleries known for showing cutting-edge contemporary art.

But despite his insistence that the show's focus was "artists' use of photography," many of the younger artists included were known solely for their photography: Lewis Baltz, Tina Barney, Ellen Brooks, James Casebere, Nan Goldin, Boyd Webb, Brian Weil, and, of course, Cindy Sherman and Laurie Simmons. What made them "not-photographers-but-artists" and not a part of the " 'art photography' subgroup" is an intriguing question that the show did not answer; however, the exhibition made another point by including them: the once-distinct worlds of art and photography had collided and merged, as in a Venn diagram in which two circles are almost coincident, with only a small sliver of each retaining a discrete identity.

The Real Big Picture, from today's perspective, was just one of a number of photography exhibitions and books that merged what had been separate spheres of activity into one, in the process eliding the aesthetic and marketplace distinctions between Postmodernist "Pictures artists" and studio-based "tableau photographers." This made some sense, since many tableau photographers were trained as artists and chose photography as their medium afterward, as had most photo-oriented Pictures artists and, before them, Conceptual artists. On the other hand, there was still a distinct difference between photography galleries, with a constant diet of photo shows, and art galleries, which generally took on one or two photographers at most. For one, art galleries charged higher prices for photographs than did photography galleries.

Sally Eauclaire's book *The New Color Photography* (Abbeville Press, 1981) was an early example of the eighties urge to mix together photographers and artists-using-photography without noting any real differences between them. It reproduced Groover, Haxton, Hockney, and Webb, all represented by Sonnabend, and Lucas Samaras, represented by Pace, in a book dominated by a cast of traditional photographers like William Eggleston, Joel Meyerowitz, and Stephen Shore. Anne H. Hoy's exhibition and book *Fabrications* (Abbeville Press, 1987), coming near the end of the enthusiasm for the tableau mode, included artists like Eleanor Antin and Christian Boltanski in the company of photographers like Jo Ann Callis and Robert Fichter.

I contributed to the mash-up of photography-as-art myself, with an exhibition and book I coproduced with Kathleen McCarthy Gauss of the Los Angeles County Museum of Art called *Photography and Art: Interactions Since 1946* (Abbeville Press, 1987). Like Hoy, Gauss and I erred on the side of the encyclopedic, producing a huge traveling show that in retrospect was too big for its britches; however, we did organize the material so that Conceptual artists' photographs were in a section separate from photographers' contemporaneous experiments in form, and Postmodernist pictures were in a different chapter than tableau studio constructions.[15]

By that time it seemed that museums couldn't wait to get on the bandwagon to reveal that photography belonged to artists. The Ringling Museum of Art in Sarasota, Florida, produced *This Is Not a Photograph: Twenty Years of Large-Scale Photography, 1966–1986*, the same year that *Photography and Art* opened; it included most of the same artists and introduced a new one: Jeff Koons. The Walker Art Center in Minneapolis organized *Cross-References: Sculpture into Photography*, a show that included photographs and an installation by each of its six artists (Casebere, Skoglund, and Webb among them). And as if to sum things up, at the end of the decade the Smithsonian's National Museum of American Art launched *The Photography of Invention: American Pictures of the 1980s*, a huge show of studio and tableau photography by ninety makers, some of them known as artists and others as plain photographers. The exhibition and catalog made no attempt to distinguish them.[16]

While this melding of art-world and photo-world interest in the artificiality and cultural influence of photographic representation was taking place, photography of the sort that birthed a market in the early seventies was in retrenchment mode. Daniel Wolf closed his 57th Street gallery in 1987, the same year that Light, after reviving from an earlier hiatus in 1983, shut down for the final time. But optimistic newcomers arrived to fill the gap, including Howard Greenberg, who opened up shop in Soho after operating a gallery in Woodstock for several years, and Catherine Edelman in Chicago. And museums continued to add photography as a new curatorial department, most notably the J. Paul Getty Museum in Los Angeles, which in 1984 caused a quake-worthy tremor by announcing its move into photography with the purchase of at least five major private collections and the hiring away of Met curator Weston Naef. Given the Getty's legendary resources, the new department quickly became a major player in the marketplace, although its original collecting purview extended only into the fifties.

Nor did traditional photography suddenly disappear. The influence of the *New Topographics* exhibition continued to be felt in work that insisted on the virtues of traditional documentary transparency, notably in Joel Sternfeld's 1987 book *American Prospects*. Modeled roughly on the sort of on-the-road survey of America familiar from Walker Evans's *American Photographs* and Robert Frank's *The Americans*, *American Prospects* managed to be both witty and dismaying, a tragicomic narrative suggesting the end of the American dream.

Meanwhile, much of the downtown gallery and collecting scene had become preoccupied with other forms of art making. If photography was essential to the "post" aesthetics of Postmodernist artists and those who followed in their wake, it was largely absent in the "neo" aesthetics that revitalized the practices of painting and sculpture in the eighties—first Neo-Expressionist painting as exemplified by Julian Schnabel, then the Neo-Geo movement, which prominently featured Ashley Bickerton, Peter Halley, Jeff Koons, and Haim Steinbach.[17] Halley produced paintings, but the rest made sculptural assemblages. Bickerton covered his vaguely sinister industrial concoctions with corporate logos; Koons encased vacuum cleaners and basketballs in Plexiglas vitrines; Steinbach put boxes of corn flakes on custom, Minimalist shelving. Although they started their careers in the East Village, in 1986 they became the center of attention in Soho, as Sonnabend Gallery gave them a group show and soon was representing several of them individually.

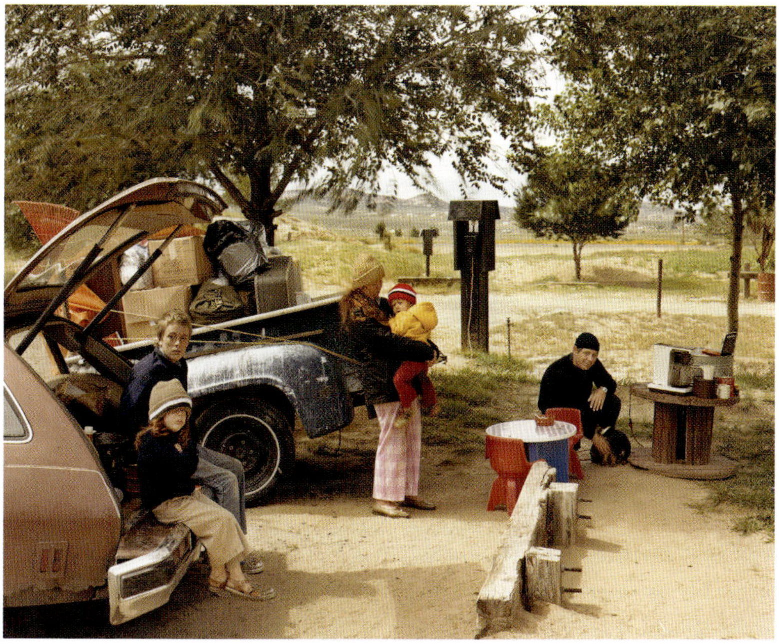

Joel Sternfeld, *Red Rock State Campground, Gallup New Mexico*, 1982.

Neo-Geo was criticized in some quarters as a marketing gimmick, and the artists were accused of being slick careerists—especially Koons, who veered off into photography in 1989 with the series *Made in Heaven*, which depicted him having sex with his future wife, an Italian porn star named Ilona Staller.[18] But it was also new, and expanded in inventive ways on Warhol's fascination with commodity culture and advertising, topics that were also a focus of many Postmodernist artists.

The tension between the "Post" and the "Neo" positions in the art world cried out for resolution, and it arrived in Soho not long after Neo-Geo did, via Boston. Two identical twin brothers, Mike and Doug Starn, photography students at the School of the Museum of Fine Arts there, had been introduced in a 1985 group show called *Boston Now: Photography*, at the city's Institute for Contemporary Art, and in a solo (technically, duet) show that followed at Stux Gallery in Boston. Their pictures were radically new for photography: instead of using a single sheet of paper for each image, they fashioned their images from many pieces of enlarging paper and taped or pinned them together in improvised, overlapping fashion onto plywood supports. Many of the prints were toned or stained, and often they were displayed in rough, homemade frames.

When Stefan and Linda Stux opened a space in Soho the next year and showed the Starns, the work created an immediate stir. Gary Indiana, a critic for the *Village Voice*, told readers to "run, don't walk, don't miss it: it's brilliant."[19] Soon big-time collectors like Eugene and Barbara Schwartz, Don and Mera Rubell, and Charles Saatchi were buying everything the Starns could make.

The coronation of the Starn brothers as hot artists of the moment came in spring 1987 when their work was included in the Whitney Biennial. There they showed several examples of their breakthrough work, including a dramatic double self-portrait with one figure right side up and one upside down like a playing card, a large piece that confronted viewers getting off the elevator on one of the Biennial's floors. As if taping and stapling their images together weren't enough, they installed the work as a salon hanging—pictures were grouped together to fill the entire wall, not strung out in single file in classic photo-art style. The crowds loved it, even if some critics worried that the twins were overly hyped.

Doubling was an early Starns trope; besides the self-portrait, they depicted a chair, a flight of stairs, and the *Mona Lisa* two times each in a single work, as if each twin had to see things for himself. They mixed images of subjects that they had taken themselves—the chair, the stairs, a flower, portraits of friends—with images of paintings they appropriated Sherrie Levine–style, although in most cases they photographed the artworks on site in museums. The Leonardo da Vinci was photographed at the Louvre on a student trip to Europe in 1984. *Double Rembrandt with Steps* (1987–88), made after the Biennial, combines the two sources, a doubled figure painted by Rembrandt van Rijn (and presumed to be the artist's father), photographed by the Starns at the Art Institute of Chicago, surrounded by a border of steps photographed outside the museum near Lake Michigan. *Double Rembrandt* is one of the first pieces for which the brothers used large sheets of photographic film as well as printing paper, adding another layer of complexity to its construction.

The Rembrandt image was shown in a two-part show in Soho in 1988, when the Starns were all of twenty-seven years old and barely three years out of art school. Their work held center stage simultaneously at Stux Gallery, where *Double Rembrandt* was hung, and within the main space of Castelli Gallery on West Broadway. There they showed another remarkable picture, an image of the dead Christ as originally painted by Philippe de Champaigne. Covering more than one piece of plywood, the large image verged on becoming sculpture, with sections of wood arranged to suggest a frame and a piece of Plexiglas propped up on blocks and leaning into the picture. The image itself consisted of hundreds of blue-toned sheets of photo paper, with one odd brown-toned piece on the right incongruously depicting a seascape. Not since showing Rauschenberg's photo silkscreen paintings had Leo Castelli devoted so much room to camera images.[20]

In one way, what the Starns supplied was a final confirmation that pho-

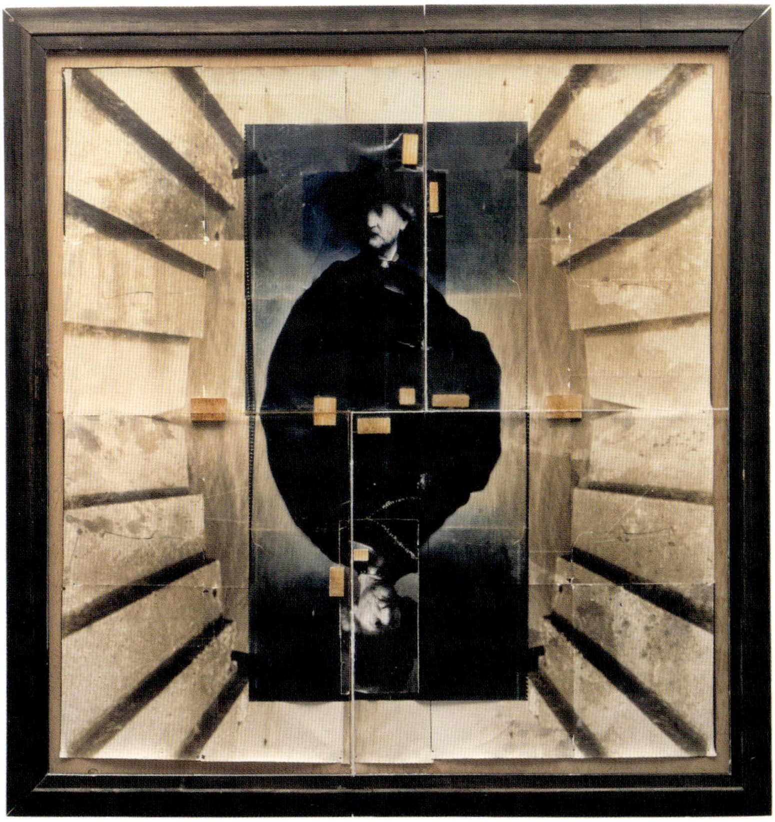

Mike and Doug Starn, *Double Rembrandt with Steps*, 1987–88. Toned black-and-white prints, toned ortho film, wood, adhesive, and Plexiglas.

tography could function in the vanguard of contemporary art. The savvy among us may have known this already, at least since Sherman's *Untitled Film Stills* were shown ten years earlier, but even devotees of painting still claiming that photographs were too mechanical to be art could look at the Starns' work and see ample evidence of an artist's hand (well, four hands, actually). Perhaps more germane to the moment, the Starns' work offered a resolution to the apparently irreconcilable camps of Neo- and Post-. It was photography, often used appropriated images already in the cultural memory bank, and actively deconstructed the classic tropes of Modernist photography, thereby marking its allegiance with Postmodernist practice. But it also was produced intuitively with hands-on élan, reflected the twinned identity of its makers by doubling up on art-historical images, and aspired to metaphysical themes by using the figure of Christ and alluding to history.

If this was a resolution, it was also a conclusion. After the Starns appeared on the scene, and certainly by the arrival of the nineties, the critical urgency of much of eighties art dissipated. Postmodernism was no longer new. The founders of the Pictures Generation continued to forge successful careers, often veering away from photography in the process, but the succeeding generation seemed to dwindle as the East Village gallery scene faded away.

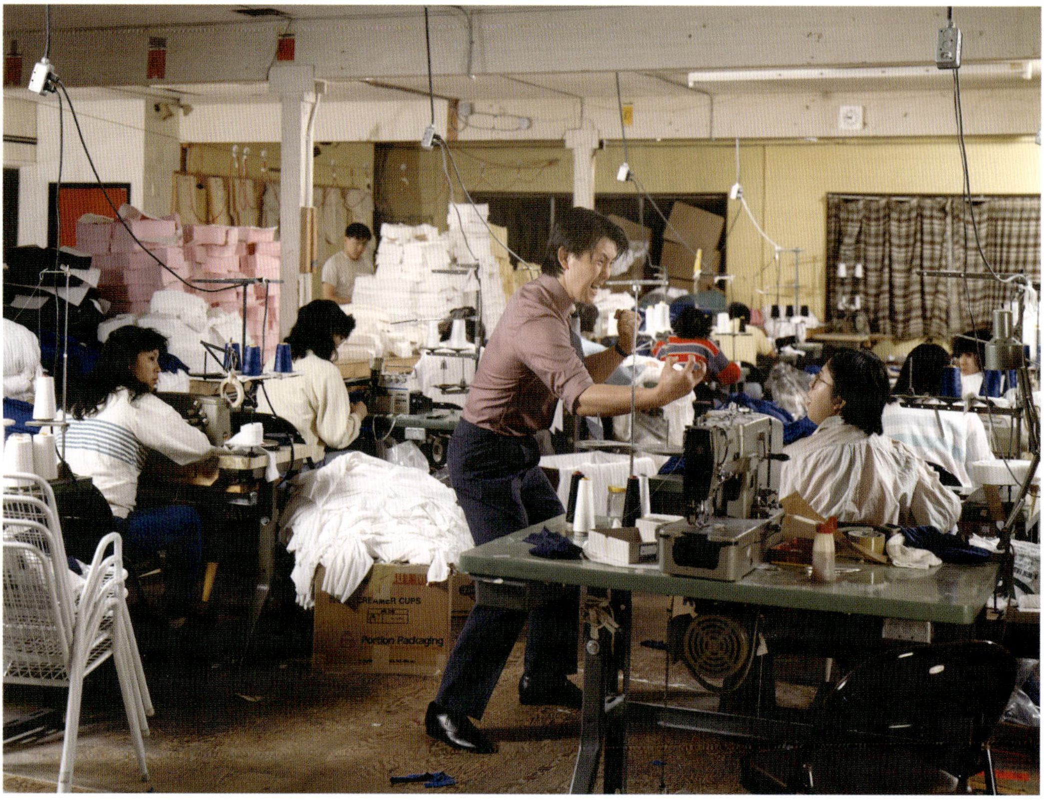

Jeff Wall, *Outburst*, 1989.
Transparency in lightbox.

Critically, *October* continued to support the theory and practices that had fueled Postmodernism's rise, but the French theorists on whom its founding mission relied died or faded away. Even though "Theory" had become an art-school subject unto itself, it now was received knowledge and thus something a young student would want to rebel against. As my headline writer at the *Times* cleverly put it for an article I wrote in September 1990, "As It Must to All, Death Comes to Post-Modernism."

The situation for Neo-Expressionists and Neo-Geo artists was similar, although they had never theorized their existence. As artists like Schnabel became rich and established, they left their Soho roots (Mary Boone, in Schnabel's case) to become cosmopolitan artists of the world, venturing into new ventures like fashion and film. Among the Neo-Geo artists, the indisputable star was Jeff Koons, and his arch re-creations of cultural disposables increasingly seemed neither Neo nor Geo. What emerged from the obsession with Neo was not a new generation of rule-breaking art but a new fixation: celebrity. What Andy Warhol had started at the Factory, and Ingrid Sischy had suffused in her editorial tenures at *Artforum* and *Interview*, was an art world focused less on any avant-garde than on the manufacture of artists as cultural superstars.

The era of tableau photography was over by the nineties, but its influence lingered in the work of upcoming artists like Jeff Wall and Gregory Crewdson, who fashioned quasi-documentary scenes with a sense of control worthy of feature films. Most remarkably, in retrospect, the genre's willingness to bend the camera image to its maker's intention appears to have anticipated what happened to photography once digital image-making and digital editing tools became available in the nineties. True, the notion of using the camera as an instrument of the imagination flowered once the medium forsook film, but its roots were in a predigital era when the ubiquity of personal computers and cell phones was still decades away.

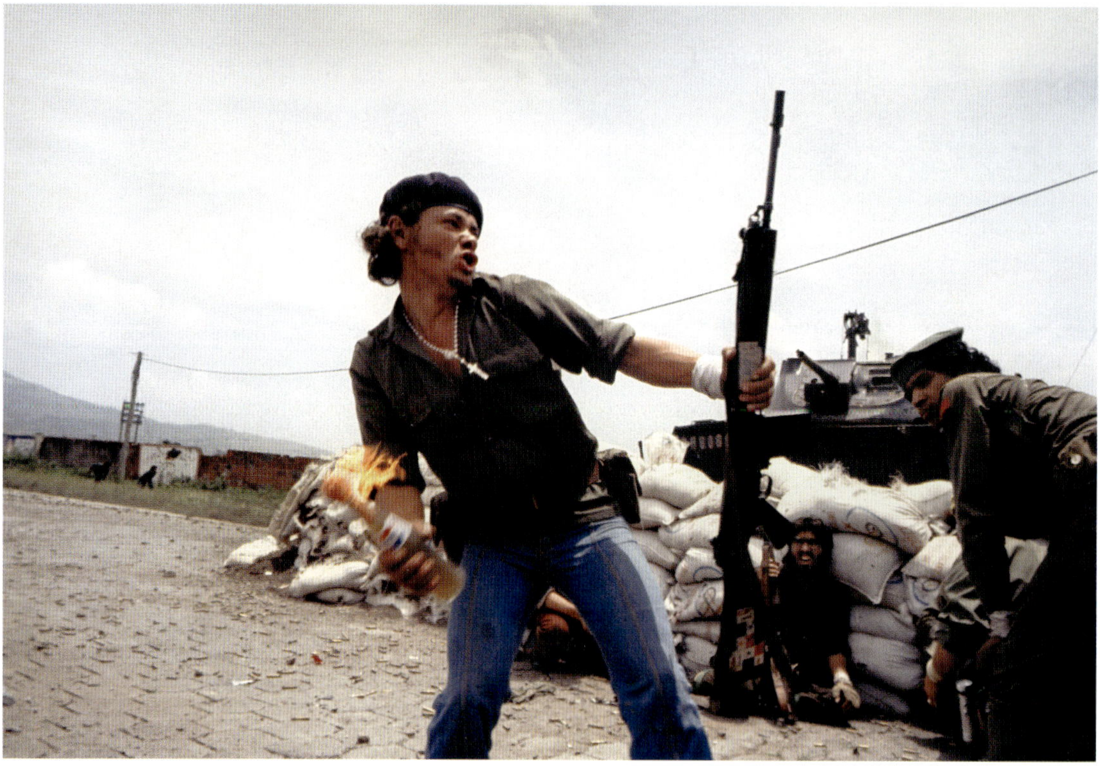

CHAPTER 13

Expanded Terrain

It is clear that photography is too multiple, too useful to other discourses, ever to be wholly contained within traditional definitions of art. Photography will always exceed the institutions of art, always participate in non-art practices, always threaten the insularity of art's discourse.

—Douglas Crimp, "Appropriating Appropriation," *Image Scavengers: Photography*, 1982

If the first review I wrote for the *Times* in 1981 irked much of the photography establishment, the second nearly got me fired. It covered two exhibitions, a group show of trendy new work at PS1 in Queens, organized by a friend and colleague, Carol Squiers, and a one-person show at Castelli Graphics of the work of Mary Ellen Mark. My take on Mark, it turned out, caused a big internal kerfuffle, if I can believe what Hilton Kramer told me over a long lunch afterward.

Mark was a photojournalist and Magnum Photos veteran already well known for her pictures of a West Coast mental hospital and of teen runaways living on the streets of Seattle. She also had once been in a relationship with Ralph Gibson, whose work Castelli represented. The show I saw was devoted to recent color pictures she had taken of prostitutes in Bombay, India (now Mumbai), which just had been published in the book *Falkland Road*. Ever heedless and surprisingly oblivious to the ramifications of reputation, I slammed the show for the hyperintensity of the color prints, which I felt had the effect of glamorizing their subjects much like fashion photography does—the color "gives the world's oldest profession something of a make-believe, Alice-in-Wonderland aura that surely is out of keeping with its grim reality"—and more generally for exoticizing a far-off culture without telling us much about it. (The prostitutes were not going to leave the profession for better lives because Mark's photographs revealed their oppression, I remember thinking.)

Little did I know that Mark had been to dinner a week or two earlier with Arthur Gelb, the powerful arbiter of the paper's cultural coverage and Kramer's immediate boss. Apparently she was an attractive and amiable guest and impressed her host with her enthusiasm for photographing in

Susan Meiselas, *Estelí*, 1979. From the book *Nicaragua*, 1981.

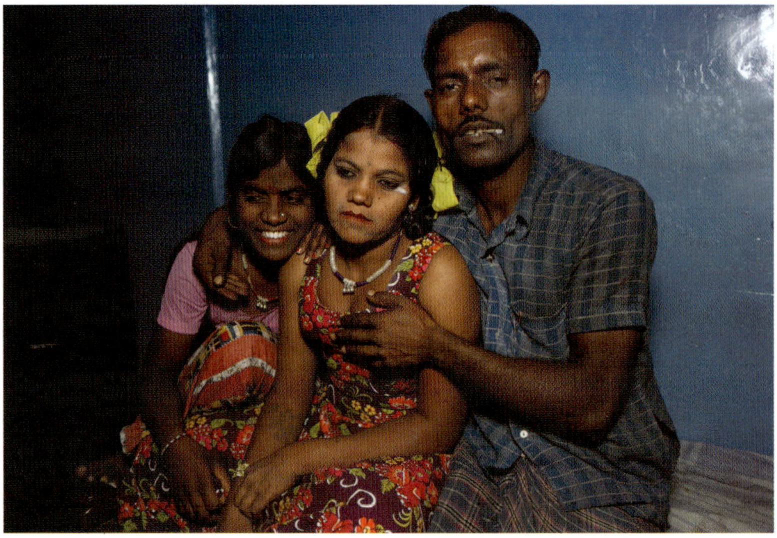

Mary Ellen Mark, *Falkland Road, Bombay, India*, 1978. From the book *Falkland Road*, 1981.

India, for when Gelb read my column before it headed off to the typesetter he decided to "spike" it. He called in Kramer and asked who this new critic was to write so negatively about such well-intended pictures by a famed photographer whose work had been published by the *Times* in years prior.

Kramer, to his eternal credit, averred that it would be unfair to kill my piece and abruptly end my tenure as a *Times* critic without having seen the exhibition and judging for themselves if my opinions had any merit. So off went Kramer and Gelb uptown to the gallery where, apparently, my opinions were discovered to have some justification. On Sunday my piece appeared in the paper as written. This did not end all my problems, though. Once the piece was published I received an indignant call from my friends Charles Harbutt and Joan Lifton, who had just recruited Mark away from Magnum to join their new breakaway photo agency, Archive. Their complaint required sessions of mediation to restore our friendship, though I'm not sure Mark ever forgave me. But the paper's decision to publish confirmed my faith in its ultimate virtue. Or, better said, bearing in mind Arthur Gelb's position, my faith was tempered without being destroyed.[1]

The idea that photojournalism like Mark's could be shown as prints framed on the wall of a gallery or museum was not new in 1981. Eight years earlier the Museum of Modern Art had mounted a show of newspaper photographs culled mainly from the files of the *New York Daily News*, as part of John Szarkowski's career-long quest to incorporate vernacular and commercial pictures into the aesthetic tradition of the medium. (The research had been done in part by Diane Arbus, whom Szarkowski hired for the purpose.) And in 1974 Cornell Capa had opened the International Center of Photography in a converted mansion on the Upper East Side to showcase the work of "concerned" photographers like Capa's brother, the famous photojournalist

Robert Capa, Henri Cartier-Bresson, David Seymour (known as "Chim"), and others, most of whom were associated with the cooperative photo agency Magnum.

This validation of reportage and its permutations as endeavors worth being seen as art was part of a larger expansion of the boundaries of art as a whole during the second half of the twentieth century. Photography was certainly a large fraction of this phenomenon, but it was not alone. The ground had been prepared by the Pop, Conceptual, performance, and installation artists who transgressed first the hierarchy of abstract painting and sculpture and then the very idea of painting and sculpture as the recognized signifiers of art. If it could be a work of art to be shot in the arm, as Chris Burden had done, or to sing and play violin in a gallery, as Laurie Anderson had done, why couldn't a picture of wounded Marines fighting a pitched battle in Vietnam be art as well?

Photographs, however, are particularly susceptible to being retrospectively recognized as art—even when their makers had absolutely no aesthetic intentions. Since interesting, even fascinating pictures often emerge from cameras operated by robots or unthinking humans, one needn't be identified as a conscious artist to produce something that can be hung on a gallery wall. Indeed, the history of photography would be a quick read were it not for the reconsideration and recategorization (or, sometimes, "discovery") of commercial portraitists like Nadar; geological survey employees like Timothy O'Sullivan; and odd ducks like E. J. Bellocq, who photographed prostitutes in New Orleans, and Jacques-Henri Lartigue, who did his best work as a preadolescent.

The seventies was full of examples of the work of small-town commercial photographers recuperated and re-presented as artistically meaningful. Charles Van Schaick, a turn-of-the-century portraitist in a small Wisconsin town who figured in John Szarkowski's 1964 show *The Photographer's Eye*, became a cult hero with the publication of *Wisconsin Death Trip* by Michael Lesy (Pantheon, 1973). Mike Disfarmer, a near-recluse working in remote Heber Springs, Arkansas, had his portraits of townsfolk exhibited at the International Center of Photography and published in the book *Disfarmer: The Heber Springs Portraits, 1936–1946* (Addison House, 1976).[2] A Boston photographer, Barbara Norfleet, assembled pictures from sixteen photo studios around the country for a book neatly titled *The Champion Pig* (David R. Godine, 1979). All three books received broad—and largely favorable—critical attention.

By the eighties the tendency to view photography as a source of unlikely, even unintended aesthetic titillation meant that photographers practicing in the fields of photojournalism, fashion, and other functional, work-for-pay genres like advertising were fair game to be considered artists and to have their work exhibited and published as art. It also meant that curators and dealers were set free to explore territory outside the framework of the established Modernist canon, and to raise questions about the sources of photography's newly popular aesthetic appeal.[3]

At this time the International Center of Photography had grown to become a welcome shelter for working photographers and others who had been left out of MoMA's orbit or who felt that the art world was too snobbish for their tastes. Not only did the center exhibit the work of elite Magnum photographers like Cartier-Bresson and idiolect spot-news lensmen like Weegee (Arthur Fellig), it opened a school that served a growing population of New Yorkers whose sights were largely set on black-and-white documentary photography. Cornell Capa, an immigrant from Hungary with an impish mien and a beguiling twinkle in his eye, charmed enough donors to finance the place and had the wisdom to hire smart young people to run it. The first head of the exhibition program that I remember was Bill Ewing, who came in 1977 and left in 1984; Miles Barth joined him in exhibitions a couple of years later and stayed much longer. The talents of Phil Block, Willis "Buzz" Hartshorn, Anne H. Hoy, and Charles Stainback would later combine to put the place firmly on the map, with shows and lectures that explored a range of contemporary issues.

Capa let his young curators follow their instincts even when they made no sense to him; I remember many times at openings or press previews when he would signal his lack of enthusiasm for a show—sometimes he was subtle, but not always. He was happiest when there was a big crowd and celebrities were on hand, never more so than when Jacqueline Kennedy Onassis was the star of an opening reception. Once I got to shake her hand on my way upstairs to the galleries; at another event I spoke briefly with Margaret Mead. These were occasions when Capa was in his element, and his gruff demeanor would give way to unmasked pleasure.

ICP even in the seventies had not confined itself to photojournalism, branching out into fashion photography and New York street photography that was not strictly documentary. (There was, for example, a show in 1978 of pioneering fashion pictures by Martin Munkácsi.) That fashion photography would be displayed in a museum seems as radical as showing photojournalism, but the ground for that had been broken well before ICP was established.

Richard Avedon, who with Irving Penn was the preeminent fashion photographer of the postwar years, was a pioneer. His photographs were shown on the walls of the Smithsonian in 1962—in a hallway, unframed, at the institution's history museum—and more importantly at the Minneapolis Institute of Art in 1970, in a one-person exhibition organized by Ted Hartwell. Hartwell, who became the museum's curator of photography only after

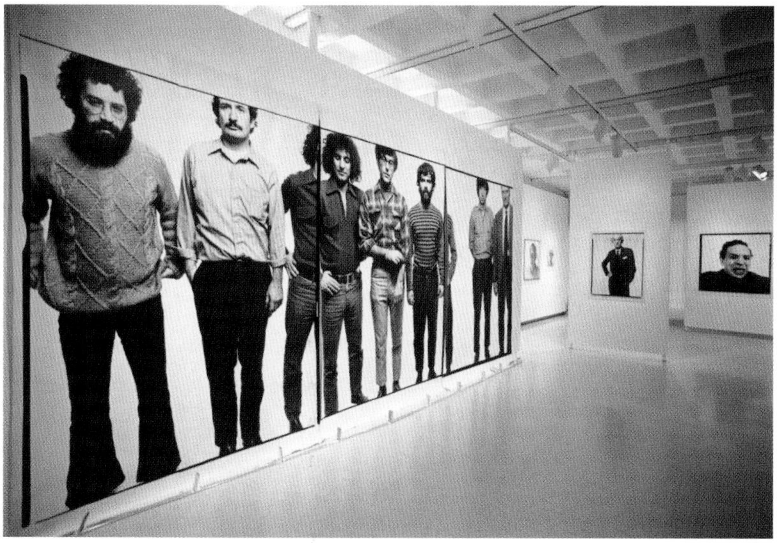

Installation view of Richard Avedon's *Portraits* exhibition at the Marlborough Gallery, New York, 1975. Foreground: *The Chicago Seven*, 1969.

the Avedon show, emphasized Avedon's "personal" pictures over his fashion images. The show included a wall-filling, mural-print version of Avedon's three-panel portrait of the members of the Chicago Seven, who had been accused of inciting riots at the 1968 Democratic convention, as well as individual portrait images, many of which had appeared in *Nothing Personal*, the 1964 book that was a collaboration between photographer Avedon and the writer James Baldwin.[4]

In 1974 at MoMA, Szarkowski organized the first Avedon museum exhibition in New York, a small, eight-print show devoted to photographs of Avedon's dying father, Jacob Israel Avedon. I remember this as deeply moving, since it documented in unflinching detail the decay of a man in the last eighteen months of his life. The extent to which Avedon's lens seemed objective and unmoved was also disturbing; it was as if he had taken the phrase "nothing personal" to heart. I also saw Avedon's first commercial art-gallery show a year later, at the posh Marlborough Gallery on 57th Street. Focused entirely on portraiture, it included mural-print versions of the Chicago Seven, Andy Warhol and his Factory crew, and the Vietnam Mission Council. The show later toured to museums on the West Coast and in Japan.

It would take the Metropolitan Museum of Art, in 1978, to plunge into untested waters and mount a show devoted solely to Avedon's fashion photographs, the vast majority of which were taken as part of his job as a photographer for *Harper's Bazaar* and *Vogue*. The popular exhibition was a breakthrough for the museum, for fashion, and for photography. At the Met, photography had no home until 1971, when the Department of Prints became the Department of Prints and Photographs; Weston Naef, the museum's first real photography expert, was hired the same year. Fashion

Irving Penn, *Deli Package, New York,* 1975.

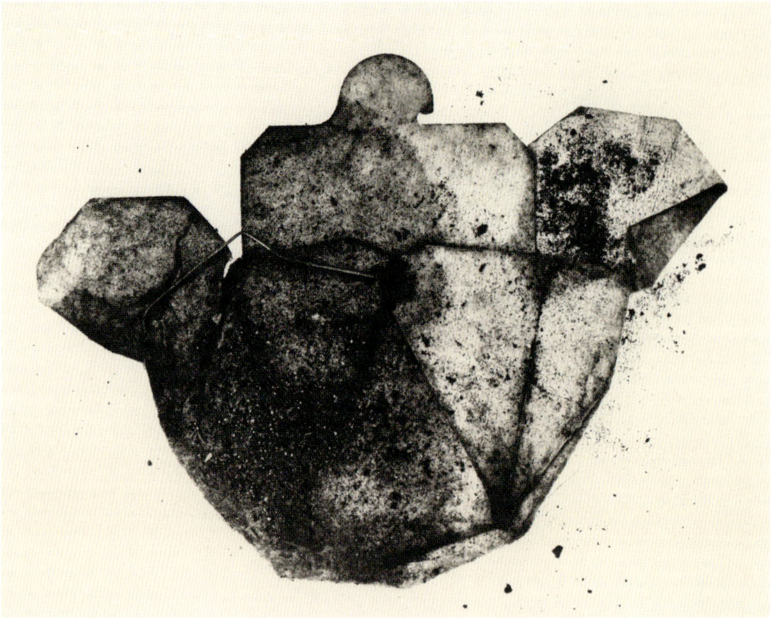

had been incorporated earlier, in 1959, when the vaunted Costume Institute became a formal department within the museum, but then it was not considered on the same plane as the departments devoted to art. Oddly but significantly, Colta Ives, a print curator and head of the prints and photographs department, was credited with "supervising" the Avedon show. (With Avedon, curators mostly sat back and watched as he designed and installed the installation himself.)

For all the attention to his fashion pictures and portraits, Avedon still felt underrecognized as an artist of the camera, which may have prompted him to accept a commission from the Amon Carter Museum of American Art in Texas, in 1979, to produce a series of portraits of noncelebrities. For the show, *In the American West*, which opened in Fort Worth in 1985 and was accompanied by a book of the same name, he photographed coal miners, drifters, grifters, casino dealers, beekeepers, and assorted other mostly economically challenged denizens of the West, using the same merciless style, clinical in its detail, that characterized much of his celebrity portraiture.

The work was controversial in Texas and environs: self-identified Westerners thought he had missed the cross section of the West they were expecting (people like themselves, presumably) and overemphasized the poor and bizarre; others saw him as disrespecting the disadvantaged people he had convinced to pose. But *In the American West* was well received in the art world when it toured the country, and it got plenty of attention in the *Times*. In the *New York Times Book Review*'s annual holiday photography book roundup I made it my lead, saying, "It is his most emotionally chilling series of pictures since his portraits of his dying father taken in the early 1970's." A week later in the Arts and Leisure section my colleague Gene Thornton wrote a glowing review of a twinned New York gallery exhibition of the pictures, at Pace and Pace/MacGill.

Like Avedon, Irving Penn had seen his pictures included in a variety of group exhibitions put on by MoMA's photography department in the fifties and sixties, including the blockbuster *The Family of Man.* His first one-person museum show was organized by John Szarkowski at MoMA in 1975, a year after Avedon's debut there, and consisted of fourteen large platinum prints of half-squashed cigarette butts. Controversy ensued. Szarkowski insisted that the pictures were of a piece with Penn's fashion work—"It might therefore seem that the new pictures represent a break with Penn's work of the past, but it is more likely that they represent a further advance"[5]—but others, including myself, saw them as a glamorization of inconsequential gutter trash.[6] The platinum process Penn adopted, once widely used by Pictorialist photographers at the beginning of the twentieth century, required hand mixing of chemicals and hand coating of paper, and it connoted both the presence of the picture maker's hand and luxury.

What Penn did with cigarette butts, which was to make them iconic and oddly beautiful, he proceeded to do to all manner of street debris, resulting two years later in a one-person exhibition at the Metropolitan Museum of Art. *Irving Penn: Street Material,* subtitled *Photographs in Platinum Metals, 1975–76,* was organized by no less than the museum's curator of modern art, Henry Geldzahler. A companion show of platinum images appeared at the Marlborough Gallery the same year, which included portraits and fashion pictures reprinted from older negatives, followed in 1980 by a Marlborough show of platinum prints depicting fleshy, corpulent female nudes.[7] From that point on, and as Penn continued to reprint a career's-worth of images that were mostly taken for *Vogue*, galleries and museums made no real distinctions between his fashion and nonfashion work, including in a major retrospective in fall 1984 that Szarkowski organized at MoMA.

A younger batch of fashion photographers was making its mark at the same time, both on the pages of *Vogue* and *Harper's Bazaar* and in the art world. Helmut Newton, Deborah Turbeville, and Bruce Weber were the vanguard of the moment, each breaching the boundaries of conventional fashion in his or her own way. Newton specialized in hints of sadomasochism and fetishism, Turbeville in anomie and what later would be called "heroin chic," and Weber in superhero physiques and gay sexual suggestiveness. Reflecting the growing interest in fashion photography among collectors, a gallery devoted to it opened in Soho in 1981, run by Etheleen Staley and Taki Wise.

In March 1982 I reviewed a Staley-Wise group show of nudes by

David Robbins, *Talent*, 1986.

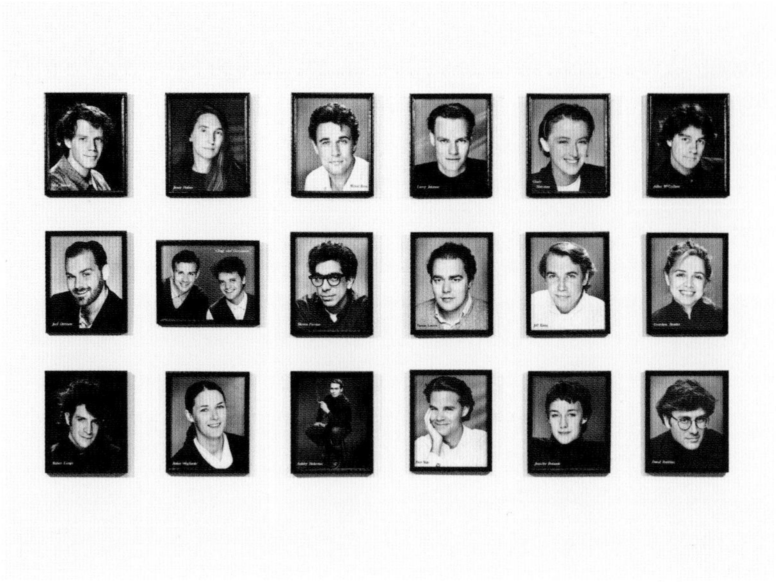

twenty-seven fashion photographers along with a larger and more attention-grabbing exhibition at Marlborough, which was doubling down on its commitment to showing photographs. The highlight of Marlborough's exhibition of Helmut Newton's work was a set of nearly seven-foot-tall prints of nearly seven-foot-tall female models, nude and walking toward the camera. While these works from Newton's *Big Nudes* series seemed to recognize the power of women, they also conveyed a more subliminal message, which was that ultimate power belongs to the camera and the man behind it. Despite a few glimmers of an ironic and mildly comic stance on Newton's part, I found the whole enterprise distasteful. "His nudes are the epitome of fashion," I wrote, "they merely wear the emperor's new clothes."[8]

As mentioned earlier, Szarkowski can be held at least partly responsible for the widespread entry of fashion, photojournalism, and other "commercial" genres of photography like advertising photographs and Hollywood celebrity portraiture into the discourse of the art world. His aesthetic insisted that new photography makes use of old photography, by which he meant the medium's entire tradition. This was once again clear when, in 1984, MoMA reopened after an expansion and the photography department unveiled the reinstallation of its permanent collection gallery; in a review, I complained about its formalist mentality, which operated to the exclusion of a great deal of current photographic practice, including Postmodernism. Cindy Sherman, Barbara Kruger, and Richard Prince were not among those with work in the show.

Outside MoMA, and downtown, the idea that new photography could be inspired by the old was being demonstrated in spades, but with an atti-

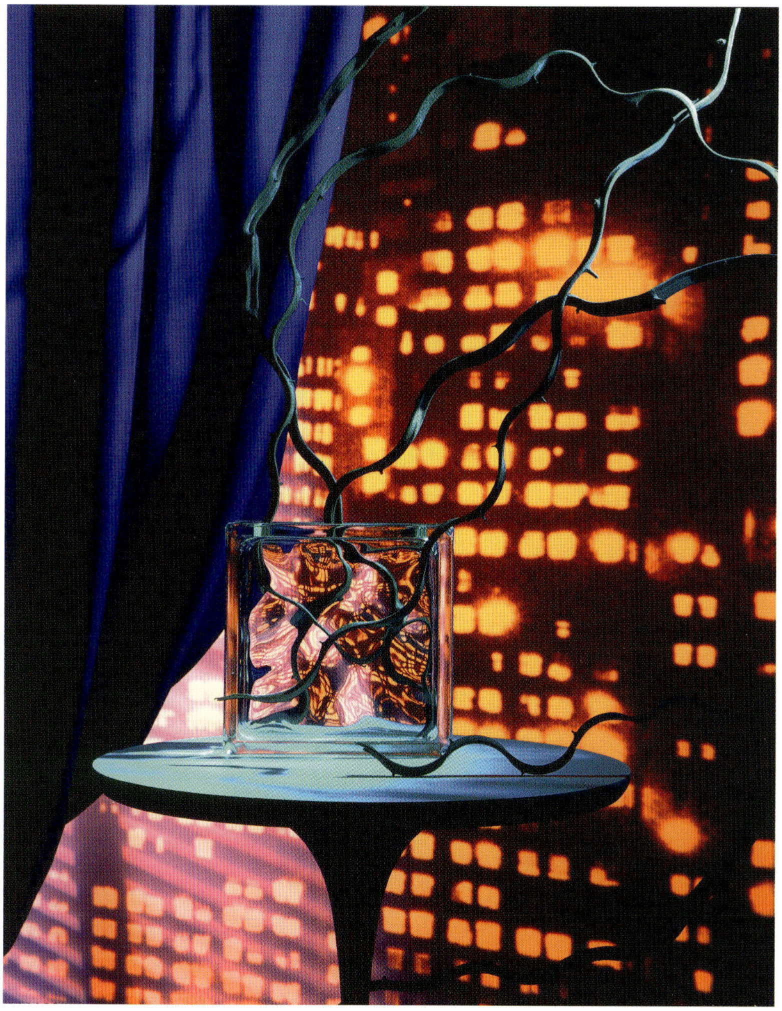

Frank Majore, *Interior*, 1989.

tude bent on revelation, not elevation. There was, of course, Prince's notorious appropriation of Marlboro cigarette ads, the *Untitled (cowboy)* series, which was followed by Silvia Kolbowski's totems of images rephotographed from fashion magazines, Ken Lum's flat-footed studio portraits of Canadian families that he gussied up with invented graphic logos, and Allan McCollum's *Perpetual Photo* series, blowups of artwork seen in the background of the sets for television shows. One of my favorite works of the East Village era, David Robbins's *Talent*, was based on a type of commercial studio practice common in New York, the promotional "8 × 10 glossy," made to be handed out by aspiring actors, musicians, and models at auditions and go-sees. It was first shown at Nature Morte gallery in 1986.

Talent consists of eighteen portrait photographs of young artists—among them Ashley Bickerton, Jenny Holzer, Jeff Koons, Thomas Lawson, Robert Longo, Cindy Sherman, and Robbins himself—in an edition of one hundred, 8 × 10-inch, black-and-white prints. Robbins commissioned the portraits from a Times Square commercial photographer whose business was making "glossies" in bulk, and he induced the artists to visit the studio and be "styled" appropriately. The result is a hilarious send-up of the notion of artistic celebrity and, in retrospect, an unexpectedly poignant memorial to the potentials of artistic community.

The idealized, souped-up hyperreality of advertising photography and Hollywood portraiture attracted other artists to manufacture their own versions, albeit ones lacking in brand recognition. Frank Majore's glamorous simulations of modern interiors, marked by spectral light sources and intense colors, included Trimline phones (retro even then), cut-glass ashtrays, and strands of pearls as objects of desire, although whose desire was left unclear. In reviewing his work in January 1986, shown in simultaneous exhibitions at ICP, 303 Gallery, and Nature Morte, I suggested that "it was perhaps inevitable that the most unabashedly commercial, mass-marketeering genre of all—advertising photography—should come to hold the ultimate fascination. For today's photographers and artists using photography, it is as seductive as the apple was for Adam and Eve."[9]

Nine months later I seemed like a genius at prognostication, as ICP put on a show called *Art and Advertising: Commercial Photography by Artists*. The exhibition included Majore's work along with that of Postmodern regulars Cindy Sherman and Laurie Simmons and others, like William Wegman and Robert Mapplethorpe, whose work was never intended to critique media culture. The show's organizer, Willis "Buzz" Hartshorn, paired their artwork with images they had taken for clients—in Majore's case, the client was Sony—to demonstrate how their styles carried over into the commercial realm. Not everyone was thrilled to learn that artists and the advertising industry were complicit, nor comfortable with the implication that art itself was an industry that markets its wares by advertising style.

At the same time, a revival of interest in classic Hollywood portraiture done by the likes of Bruno of Hollywood (yes, he used the name), Clarence Sinclair Bull, and George Hurrell was shadowed by its Postmodern counterpart in the form of Neil Winokur's candy-colored studio portraits of art-world denizens, seemingly done tongue in cheek, and Timothy Greenfield-Sanders's ultradetailed, black-and-white, more pulled-back portraits of many of the same folk, mixed in with celebrities from the worlds of music, theater, and politics. Winokur's pictures were shown in Soho at the Barbara Toll Gallery, which otherwise specialized in painting, until Janet Borden opened her photo-specific gallery in 1988. Greenfield-Sanders was a regular at Marcuse Pfeifer's photo space uptown until branching out downtown in the second half of the decade with shows at Castelli and Mary Boone.

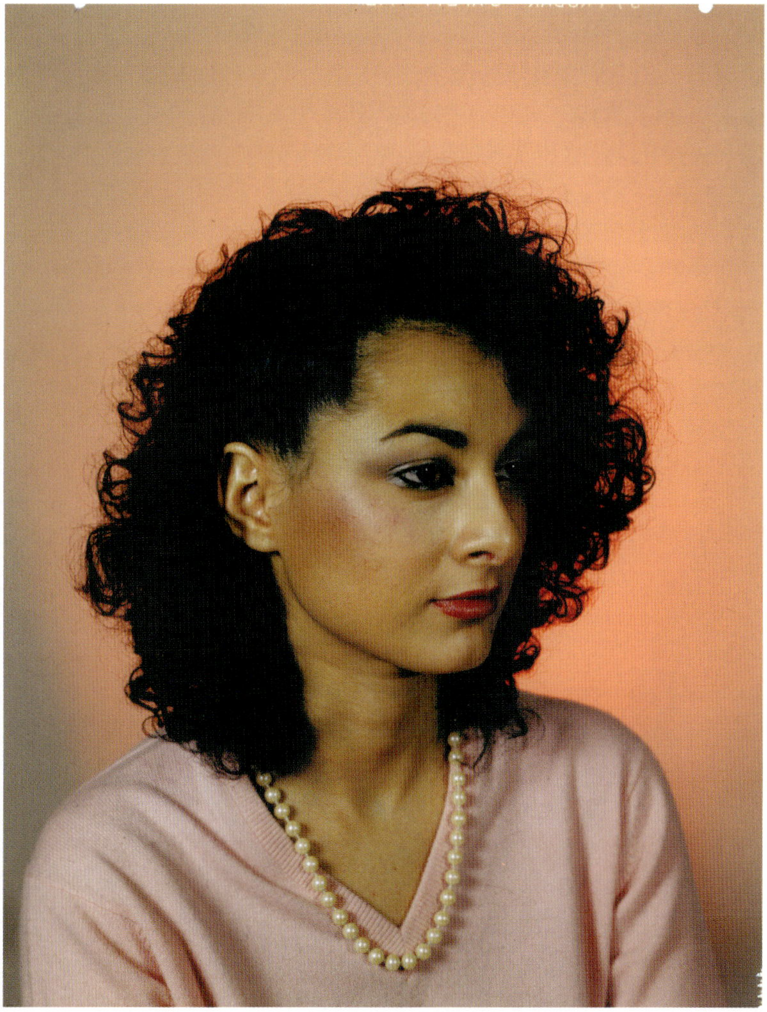

Neil Winokur, *Mary Boone*, 1983.

The rapid and seemingly unchecked expansion of the territory of photographs-deemed-eligible-to-be-displayed-as-art by this time had created a backlash, which I was moved to write about in 1983. My piece was headlined, "Two Camps Battle over the Nature of the Medium":

> The field of photography has never been one big happy family—to start with, it has never been that big—but, increasingly, it seems to consist of two families, and feuding ones at that. The issue that both divides and frames current photographic thinking is not (blessed relief) whether photography can be considered an art, but what kind of an art it is. Is it an art like painting or drawing, with the same esthetic claims and standards, or is it an art form unto itself, so inextricably interconnected with social and political values that to call it "art" in the conventional sense requires quotation marks?

> The lines are drawn between those who think of photography as a relatively new and largely virgin branch of art history, and those who rebel at the very notion of photography being "estheticized." The former welcome the medium's elevation to the realm of the museum, the marketplace and traditional art-historical scholarship, while the latter argue that photography's "museumization" (Hilton Kramer's neologism of a few years back) robs it of its real importance—that is, its social meanings. Never mind that one finds the antagonists of photography's estheticization performing essentially the same tasks as its proponents, teaching art history, assembling exhibitions and writing criticism; the split is real and the rhetoric is fierce.[10]

I named the two camps the "connoisseurs" and the "contextualists," and concluded that "If we follow the contextualist camp's own dialectical logic, it is the contextualists who will wither away." My argument was that as photography was supplanted by newer means of recording images—electronic media being the beast on the horizon—its functional uses would wither and die, leaving only aesthetic reasons for its existence. But I hedged:

> In practice, however, I suspect that the contextualist way of thinking will continue to exert a strong oppositional influence as long as the impulse remains to convert photography into an adjunct of painting, drawing and sculpture. Photography's distinction has always been its connection to the world outside the imagination, and it traditionally has been practiced not in the artist's garret but on the streets or battlefields or mountaintops. A photograph traces something real, and it is the mission of the contextualists to open our ideas about art to accommodate this fact.

What I failed to mention about this split, but what seems noticeably ironic in retrospect, is that connoisseurs and contextualists alike were busy opening the photographic gates to all corners of the photographic enterprise—the contextualists just didn't want to call it art. In 1983 Allan Sekula, one of the contextualists I had in mind, wrote an essay about a Cape Breton, Nova Scotia, studio photographer from the fifties and sixties, Leslie Shedden, whose work recorded the lives of Canadian coal miners in straightforward, if not to say pedestrian, fashion. Sekula framed the work as an archive "between labor and capital," in the words of his title, carefully avoiding any aesthetic claims for it, but the book in which his essay appeared was published by the Press of the Nova Scotia College of Art and Design and edited by two of the school's teachers, Robert Wilkie and Benjamin Buchloh.[11] So while the author may have wanted to avoid calling it art, his audience was the art world.

My reference to streets, battlefields, and mountaintops as locales of photographic practice in my "Two Camps" article was likewise not hypothetical. In all likelihood I was thinking about a new wave of contemporary photojournalists that had piqued my interest. My generation had grown up in the shadow of Vietnam and had seen war photographs that exceeded the ambitions of those from World War II and Korea. There was Eddie Adams's widely published image of a South Vietnamese brigadier general executing a Viet Cong suspect with a point-blank bullet to the head, and Nick Ut's of a naked, burned, and screaming village girl running toward his camera—both won Pulitzer Prizes as news photos—but I found myself most engaged by Larry Burrows's color pictures of wounded Marines, which I saw when they were published in *Life* in the sixties. Their color was not incidental; it seemed to have been how Burrows composed the pictures. Burrows's work was followed by the equally indelible color photos of an Army photographer, Ron Haeberle, that when published in *Life* and other publications at the end of the decade told the world about a massacre by American troops of several hundred Vietnamese civilians in My Lai. All of which was prelude to what became one of the most-talked-about photography books of the eighties, Susan Meiselas's *Nicaragua*. Published by Pantheon in 1981, *Nicaragua* is a record of that country's civil war as seen by Meiselas in 1978 and 1979. Although she photographed with one of her cameras loaded with black-and-white film, all the pictures in the book are in color. As with Burrows's combat scenes, Meiselas's pictures seem composed to exploit our attraction to certain colors, or conversely to mute that attraction by coupling it with horrific subject matter. That is to say, they have an aesthetic sensibility that is impossible to ignore.

When I reviewed *Nicaragua* shortly after I started writing for the *Times* I noted that the subject matter was deeply disturbing, including bodies "blown to stumps, swollen in the sun, burning under a blanket of tires," and yet the photographs often were intensely beautiful. The book was haunting "precisely because of the precarious balance between the beauty of its pictures and the horror of what they depict." But I took issue with the format: the pictures were printed alone on the page, with their captions in the back of the book, so at first one couldn't be sure what one was seeing. Are those government soldiers, or rebels? Which side has killed those children? I saw this as photojournalism's failure to ever fully tell a story, but it could also be construed as a purposeful ambiguity: if the good guys and bad guys are indistinguishable, then war is a kind of hellish chaos. Which it apparently is.[12]

Meiselas was a young member of Magnum Photos when the book

appeared, having joined in 1976. Together with Gilles Peress and Alex Webb, Meiselas became identified as one of the young turks of the agency. Their interests lay less with the news cycle, in getting their images immediately into print, and more with controlling the contexts in which they were shown. Peress's book *Telex Iran: In the Name of Revolution* (Aperture, 1984), a black-and-white record of the Iranian revolution, and Webb's *Hot Light/Half-Made Worlds: Photographs from the Tropics* (Thames and Hudson, 1986), of color pictures taken on trips to the Caribbean, Mexico, and India, can be read as artists' books, not photojournalism. Both show a world that is mysterious and inchoate, using complex framing in Peress's case and saturated color in Webb's. In all three cases, the authorship of the images is never in doubt.

These young Magnum members went on to show prints of the images in their books at photography-specific exhibition spaces and in museum group shows. One of the best of these, *On the Line: The New Color Photojournalism*, opened at the Walker Art Center in Minneapolis in 1986 and toured to mid-sized museums for two years afterward. *On the Line* seemed well timed to capture the renewed spirit in photojournalism, featuring twelve photographers, including Meiselas, Peress, and Webb, a well-printed catalog, and an essay by Adam Weinberg, who organized the show at the Walker. (Weinberg went on to become a highly successful director of the Whitney Museum of American Art in New York.) Weinberg put the issue quite neatly:

> What unites this generation of photographers, now in their 30s and 40s, is not simply their use of color photography but their position vis-à-vis the field of art photography and photojournalism. They are "on the line" between two worlds. Not easily classified as simply art photographers or photojournalists, these are among a significant number of hybrid photographers whose work defies strict categorization and points to the inadequacy of labels used in the history of photography.[13]

In the best case, the new photojournalism mediated between the camps of the connoisseurs and the contextualists, walking the line as Weinberg suggests. Or, to cynics, it was another example of the aestheticizing of images intended to help explain the real conditions of the world. In either case, it breathed new life into a field that had been in danger of being vestigial.

Another large part of photography's social functioning, one that entails both commercial and vernacular images, deserves equal mention: pornography. The largely underground genre has a rich tradition throughout the history of photography, so it, too, was ripe for Postmodern appropriation. It also represents a side of photography that is covert, disreputable, and in some cases illegal, and thus seldom discussed by art historians. But it was much discussed by politicians in the eighties.

A national Commission on Obscenity and Pornography was established by President Lyndon Johnson in 1968, but the report it issued in 1970 was repudiated by his successor, President Richard Nixon, who called its social science–based research and nonjudgmental conclusions morally bankrupt. Flash ahead fifteen years and President Ronald Reagan appointed a new panel, the Attorney General's Commission on Pornography, headed by Edwin Meese. In its 1986 report the Meese Commission recommended a law-enforcement assault on the pornography "industry," concluding that viewing pornographic films and photographs harms adults and children and can lead to rape. At the same time conservatives in Congress, egged on by fundamentalist Christian lobbying groups, were launching an attack on the National Endowment for the Arts, which they saw as promoting liberal cultural values. Thus began the "Culture Wars" of the late eighties.

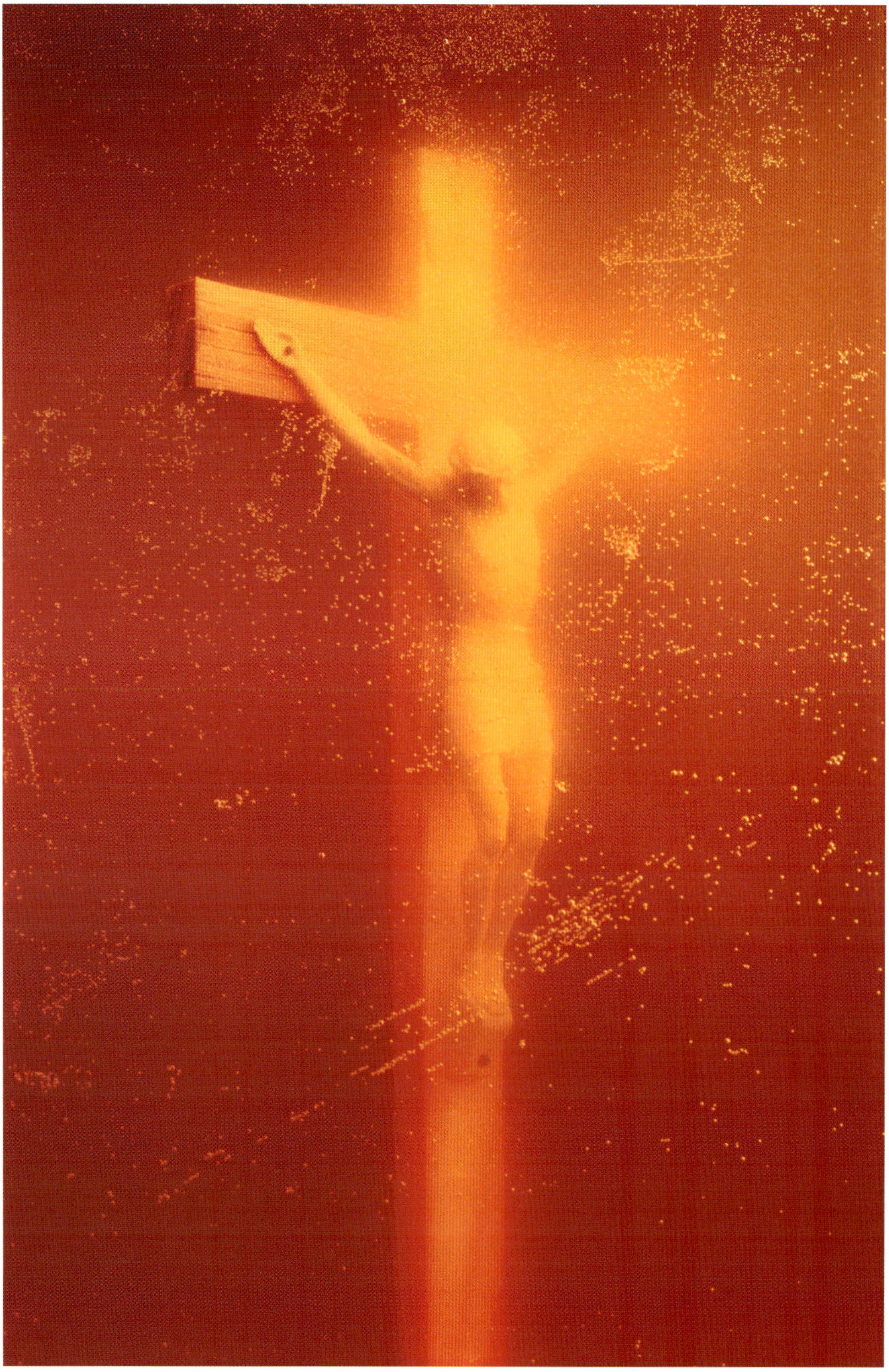

CHAPTER 14

Culture Wars

I do not know Mr. Andres Serrano, and I hope I never meet him. Because he is not an artist, he is a jerk.

—Senator Jesse Helms, 1989

Gradually, the real enemy begins to take shape—not a few "dirty" pictures, but the whole corpus of modern avant-garde art.

—Robert Brustein, "Art Wars," *Reimagining American Theatre,* 1991

In late September 1990 I found myself sitting in a courtroom in Cincinnati, Ohio, at the obscenity trial of Dennis Barrie and the institution he directed, the Contemporary Arts Center. I was there at the behest of the defense, as a possible witness; Barrie was there because his museum had the temerity to present a retrospective exhibition of Robert Mapplethorpe's photographs, *The Perfect Moment.*

The show had been organized by the Institute of Contemporary Art in Philadelphia, a part of the University of Pennsylvania, and after opening there it had toured to Chicago, without incident, and to Washington, D.C., where its scheduled presentation at the Corcoran Gallery of Art was abruptly canceled by the museum, which feared political reprisals. Instead, the exhibition was shown at the Washington Project for the Arts, a local artists' space, where many of the eventual fifty thousand visitors stood in line for hours waiting to get inside. After that, it was seen in Hartford, Berkeley, and Boston, all without incident, and finally Cincinnati.

The ostensible reason for the trial was the presence in the exhibition of seven photographs, five images of gay men engaged in sexual activity or some semblance of it and two pictures of young children, one a frontal nude of a boy and the other a girl in a dress but in a pose that revealed she was not wearing any underwear.[1] According to the city police chief, the county sheriff, and the prosecutor, these were patently offensive, appealed to the prurient interest, and had no artistic value, and thus were criminally obscene.[2] Among the gay sex pictures included in the indictment: a man urinating into another's mouth, a man's fingertip inserted in his penis, and most famously

Andres Serrano, *Piss Christ,* 1987.

Robert Mapplethorpe, *Self-Portrait*, 1978.

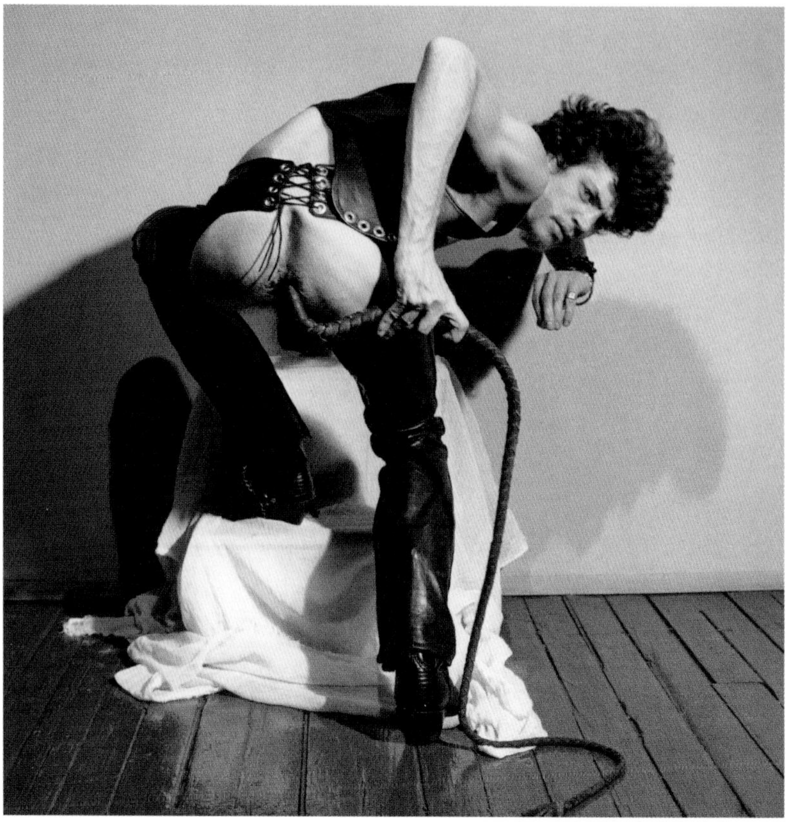

Mapplethorpe's self-portrait with a bullwhip in his anus. Otherwise, the show consisted mainly of elegant portraits of art-world notables and friends of the artist, classical nudes, and quite beautiful still lifes of calla lilies and other flowers, all photographed with classical precision and printed with exquisite care.

Mapplethorpe had died earlier that year of AIDS-related causes, so he was not there to defend himself. That task was left to the art-world experts, including the show's curator, Janet Kardon, directors of museums in Philadelphia and Minneapolis, and critics like myself. I ultimately wasn't asked to testify; my notion that Mapplethorpe was appropriating pornography, not making it, probably was deemed too dense and Postmodernish by the defense. Instead, curator Kardon and other witnesses who took the stand ignored the subject matter of the works in question and focused exclusively on their formal qualities—how beautiful the lighting was, how careful the poses and framing, how the highlights and shadows created intertwined positive and negative spaces, and so forth—and how these qualities related to classic aesthetic values prized as far back as the Romans and the Greeks. I heard this and squirmed in my chair, believing that such formalist arguments for photography's status as an art mercifully had been tossed aside by the midseventies, when Mapplethorpe was starting his career. But the jury was sufficiently impressed: after two hours of deliberation, it acquitted Barrie and the museum of all charges.[3]

Robert Mapplethorpe: The Perfect Moment created a perfect storm around the issues of censorship, obscenity, sexuality, and government support for the arts, but the controversy that surrounded its appearance had been brewing for years. The alleged proliferation of visual pornography had become an agenda item for conservative politicians going back to Richard Nixon's presidency in the early seventies and became a fixation of the Reagan years; in 1986 the Meese Commission on Pornography issued a report that linked visual images to sexual behavior and urged prosecutors to vigorously pursue producers and sellers of pornographic pictures. A year earlier Tipper Gore, the wife of then-senator Al Gore, created the Parent Music Resource Center to lobby Congress for hearings on rock music lyrics, some of which she considered obscene. Christian evangelists Jerry Falwell, Pat Robertson, and Donald Wildmon created and oversaw "family values" lobbying organizations such as the American Family Association as a political means of forwarding their antiabortion, antihomosexual, and antipornography agendas.[4]

Homosexuality was particularly anathema to such Protestant fundamentalist Christian groups. The decade of the eighties had started with an ebullient gay liberation movement that had many men coming out of the closet and ended with the scourge of AIDS decimating the gay communities in New York, San Francisco, and everywhere else. Many religious conservatives concluded that AIDS was a "gay disease" brought on by what they considered immoral behavior. But the so-called Moral Majority didn't stop there; they also saw the news media, Hollywood, and the art world as hopelessly immoral and permissively liberal. And they wanted the government to be their morals police.

Starting in 1983, the President Ronald Reagan–appointed chair of the National Endowment for the Arts, Frank Hodsoll, began to second-guess the work of the expert peer panels that juried almost all of the NEA's grants. That year he vetoed panel-approved funding for a series of talks by Hans Haacke, Suzanne Lacy, Lucy Lippard, and Martha Rosler, all progressive artists and critics. In 1986 he vetoed a panel-approved grant for a mobile signboard by Jenny Holzer that would have displayed messages near the White House and Congress. In both cases the stated reason was a shortcoming of "artistic merit," but the anti-Reagan politics of the artists (and the pro-Reagan politics of Hodsoll) seemed a more likely explanation. And if these were efforts to insulate the Endowment from criticism from the right, they didn't succeed: Hodsoll let stand a $30,000 grant to the Institute of Contemporary Art to support the Robert Mapplethorpe show, as well as a grant to the Southeastern Center for Contemporary Art, which used some of the funds to support an exhibition that included the work of Andres Serrano, a photographer living in New York. Hodsoll resigned in 1989, the year the Cold War ended and the work of these photographers hit the fan.

Serrano's photographs started it—or one photograph in particular. Though thoroughly ambiguous to look at, it showed a crucifix afloat in a wash of intense red and yellow Cibachrome color, and it bore the title *Piss Christ*. That was enough to set off Wildmon and his organization, who took the opportunity to call for an end to government funding of "blasphemous" art. On the floor of the Senate in May 1989, Senator Alfonse D'Amato (R-N.Y.) angrily tore up the catalog that reproduced *Piss Christ*, an act followed by Senator Jesse Helms (R-N.C.), who told his fellow legislators that Serrano was "not an artist, he is a jerk."

Serrano's *Piss Christ* was soon described by antagonists and supporters alike as showing Christ "submerged in a vat of urine," as if the Son of God himself had been defiled in a dunk tank. In fact, I longed to tell the New York Senator, who represented me at the time, the photograph depicts no such thing. It shows a plastic crucifix, a familiar Christian icon sold in novelty stores, in an indeterminate space with a few bubbles. Not to quibble, but the artist's intention, as made clear by his other work in the series, which was exhibited but not reproduced in the catalog, was to transpose the iconography of his upbringing into a corporeal realm by using his own bodily fluids—a strategy bizarrely reminiscent of God's decision to have his emissary to humanity take the form of flesh, as the New Testament tells it. Clearly Serrano was working out his own problems stemming from his Catholic childhood, but collectively the work speaks to a struggle, not to satire or blasphemy.

There also is an autobiographical struggle related to a Catholic upbringing to be seen in Mapplethorpe's work, which became the bone of contention in Congress less than a month after Serrano's. This time it was the House of Representatives, with one hundred of its members led by Dick Armey (R-Tex.) writing to the NEA to criticize its support of *The Perfect Moment*. With government funding for the NEA the subject of current Congressional debate, the Corcoran Gallery of Art's director, Christina Orr-Cahall, and its Board of Trustees decided five days later to cancel the museum's long-scheduled showing of the exhibition. The move had limited success: Congress eventually renewed the NEA's funding at $2 million more than the prior year's but included a prohibition on grants for anything that could be considered obscene.[5]

Attacks on the Endowment continued even after the budget battle for the agency was over. In November 1989 a new chair of the NEA, John Frohnmayer, appointed by George H. W. Bush, revoked a $10,000 grant to

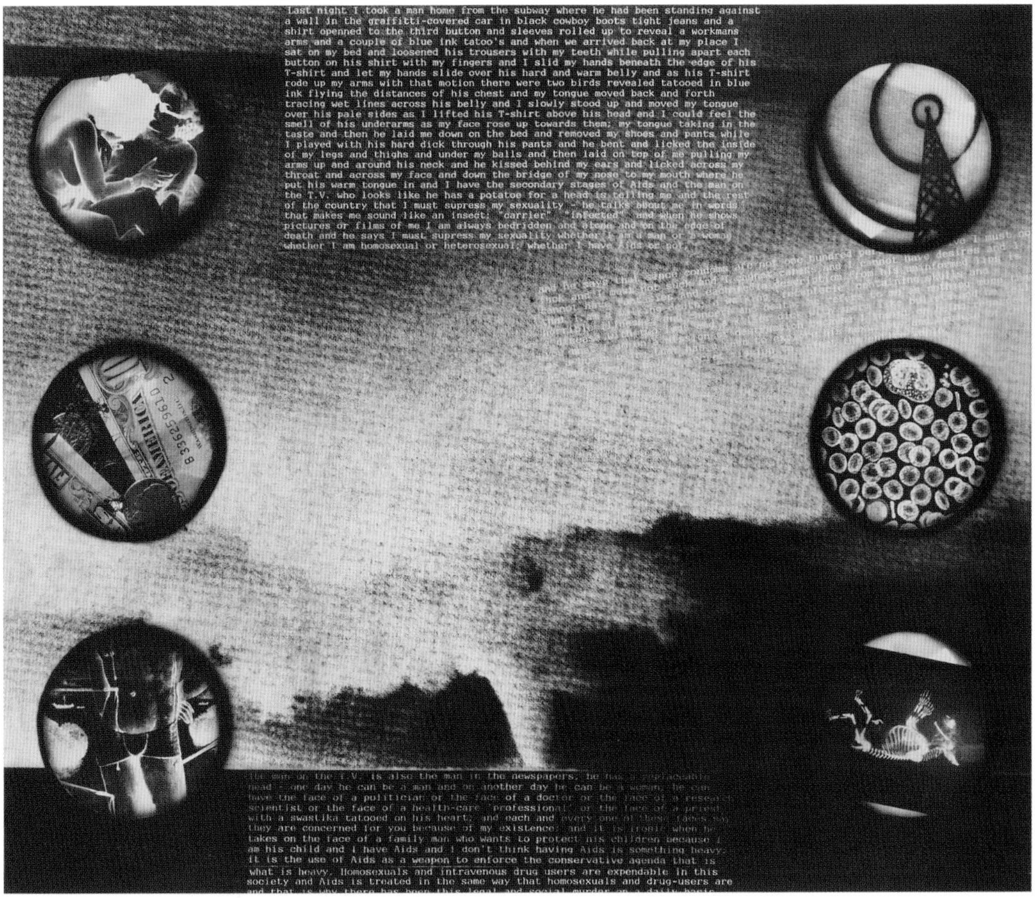

David Wojnarowicz, *Untitled*, 1988–89, from the *Sex Series (for Marion Scemama)*.

Artists Space for a show called *Witnesses: Against Our Vanishing*. The show was about the impact of AIDS on the art community, but since AIDS was (mistakenly) seen by fundamentalists as a gay man's disease it had the potential to provoke the same forces as before. Explaining his action, Frohnmayer singled out the catalog and an essay by David Wojnarowicz, an openly gay artist whose work was in the exhibition. Wojnarowicz's essay lashed out at Senator Helms and others who had been blatantly homophobic in attacking the arts.

Wojnarowicz's work was as angry as his essay but mitigated by his obvious flair for incorporating collaged materials and his use of personal, pained testimony. Wojnarowicz, who had been a male hustler much of his brief adult life and was HIV positive, appropriated visual and written materials from magazines—including gay porn magazines—and after collaging them together photographed the result. The *Sex Series* of 1988–89 includes small circles of porn shots, blood cells, and U.S. currency that flank an overall landscape overlaid with text. His most widely reproduced image, an untitled work from the same time period, shows buffalo falling headfirst off the edge of a mesa, again referencing the AIDS crisis. To make it he simply photographed a diorama at the Smithsonian's National Museum of Natural History in Washington, D.C.

How the art world responded to its critics during this period, now known as the "Culture Wars," is a matter of public record, since art journals and newspapers were filled with articles defending the right of artists to make art of any sort they wanted, even if it offended. Artists organized rallies against what they saw as government censorship. I weighed in with an article in the *Times* defending the right of critics to dislike art of any sort they wanted, even if it was under attack by idiots who knew nothing about art; it ran as the lead on the front page of the Arts and Leisure section that week.[6]

I had been following Mapplethorpe's career, and reviewing exhibitions of his work, for more than a decade, but I was never an unalloyed fan. I found him in equal measure challenging and troubling. As with Serrano, who was still an emerging artist when his work was caught up in the Culture Wars, Mapplethorpe seemed to love shock value a bit too much for my taste. On the other hand, he also seemed eager to please, making his portrait subjects look great and adding fancy frames and luxe fabric panels to his photographs of nudes and flowers. I thought the portraits and flowers were potboilers; what I considered his important work were the male nudes and the early homoerotic sex pictures, sampled in the *X Portfolio*, which indeed verge on pornography.

Mapplethorpe's early, transgressive gay sex pictures were shown at the Kitchen in 1977 and a year later at the Robert Samuel Gallery on Broadway in the Village. Opened by Samuel Hardison in 1978, the gallery specialized in showing photography of the male figure, often taken by openly gay artists such as George Dureau, Robert Giard, Peter Hujar, and Arthur Tress. By then Mapplethorpe had a gallery uptown, Robert Miller Gallery on Fifth Avenue, but it professed interest only in the portraits, flowers, and classical nudes, so at first Mapplethorpe relied on Hardison to show his hard-core work. I remember seeing it and being shocked and amazed: the S&M gay scene was much written and talked about at the time, but I had never seen visuals describe it so graphically. Still, the studio settings and technical niceties of most of the images made it clear that Mapplethorpe was creating tableaux based on sadomasochistic bondage, not documenting it in any cinema verité sense.

I first saw the notorious *X Portfolio* in the back room of the Robert Miller Gallery, in conjunction with a show of his more palatable prints, which suggests that after a year the gallery had retracted its initial reticence about showing any sex pictures. I reviewed the exhibition soon after I started writing for the *Soho Weekly News*, at the end of March 1979:

> Left to his own devices, as he seems to have been in his exhibition at the Robert Miller Gallery, Mapplethorpe tends to go on a bender. His homoerotic, heavy leather, sadomasochistic images overshadow the pictorialist flowers, foggy landscapes and plain portraits also included in the show. One strong example of the former category is a diptych picturing a man's genitals bound to some sort of rack, then squashed. To some this is shocking and therefore execrable; to others it is shocking and therefore the cat's meow. (To still others it is none of the above.)[7]

I went on to observe that Mapplethorpe had hedged his bets by including in the main part of the show pictures with Art Deco–derived frames and mirrors, coyly invoking more mainstream formal "issues," and that his portraiture on its own had much to recommend it. "One can see a future in which Mapplethorpe functions as a contemporary, Gotham-style Bruno of Hollywood," I predicted. For those unfamiliar with Bruno of Hollywood's oeuvre, suffice it to say that my remark was not an unalloyed compliment.

With the encouragement and tutelage of his lover, the pioneering photography collector Sam Wagstaff, Mapplethorpe continued to build his reputation by offering cool beauty to some and erotic thrills to others. (I was part of a parade of influencers to be invited to Wagstaff's posh 1 Fifth Avenue apartment around this time to meet the artist and see his new pictures.) By 1983 he was recognized enough in the art world to have three simultaneous shows: sculptures consisting of photographs flanked by framed mirrors and cloth panels in the shapes of crosses and stars, at Robert Miller; nude images of the female bodybuilder Lisa Lyon, at Castelli Gallery's Greene Street annex; and erotic sex scenes of a heterosexual kind, at Robert Samuel, which had recently been renamed Samuel Hardison Gallery.

In addressing all three shows in the *Times* I floated the idea that Mapplethorpe might be a Postmodernist, trying to deconstruct pornography the way that Richard Prince was deconstructing magazine advertising, but concluded that the pictures were too much like pornography to be seen as commenting on it: "Rather than addressing the conventions of pornography, they are pornography," I wrote in a declarative mode.[8] While legally not obscene, Mapplethorpe's transgressions were real, in other words, but they were also made to be seen as art.

All of the focus on photography that the Culture Wars created seemed full of irony to me. To start with, the medium only recently had found its way into the art world and was attracting more and more contemporary support just at the moment when politicians chose to identify it as the embodiment of all that was corrupt and salacious about art. Surely some artists, gallerists, and critics at that point must have had second thoughts about welcoming photography into their fold. Moreover, artists and photographers had just spent a decade demonstrating that a photograph is a construction, intentionally or not, and not a slice of real life. Cindy Sherman's self-portraits were not really portraits of the self, after all, but stand-ins for prior forms of representing women. Even the revitalization of a traditional realist style by Nan Goldin in her *Ballad of Sexual Dependency* took the form of a construction—it was performed realism, a kind of documentary theater of the real, complete with sound track, so clearly not the real thing.

Politicians like Helms, D'Amato, and Armey had not been paying attention to developments in downtown art, however. It was clear from their descriptions of what offended them that photographs were real to them. In Serrano's case, it wasn't a plastic crucifix, but Christ himself who had been bathed in the artist's urine; in Mapplethorpe's, it wasn't a staged version of the artist's erotic desires, but real sex among homosexuals. The theatricality of contemporary photography—and specifically the heightened variety found in Serrano's and Mapplethorpe's work—apparently eluded them. So did the nature of picture taking. One of the highlights of the obscenity trial in Cincinnati was the prosecutor's attempt to show that the composition of Mapplethorpe's picture of the nude young boy was intentionally designed to direct the viewer's gaze to his genitals—because, formally speaking, he observed, the inside lines of his legs led directly to his crotch. Perhaps the DA should have put anatomy on trial.

But if all the politics around photography and pornography seemed perversely ironic, it was a dangerous irony that profoundly disrupted the lives and livelihoods of artists and would-be artists across the country. In Virginia, New Jersey, and Ohio, photography students and weekend amateurs had their negatives flagged by photo processors as possible child porn, simply because they had taken pictures of their own children nude. Police arrested mothers, searched parents' homes, and sent their kids off to protective custody.[9] In 1990 Jock Sturges, a widely exhibited California photographer known for his pictures of young and attractive French nudists, had his work confiscated by police and the FBI and his studio searched after a local photo-processing lab called authorities to report his processed film.

Sally Mann, who in 1988 published a book of her photographs of preteen girls in preternaturally mature poses, *At Twelve*, managed to avoid any overt encounters with the law, but she still had to worry about reactions from the unofficial police of childhood sexuality—including a surprising faction of feminists. Shortly before she published *Immediate Family*, an even more controversial book containing nude pictures of her young son and two daughters, in 1992, she took both the prints and her family to meet a child-porn investigator with the FBI, essentially to find out if he thought she would be arrested when the book came out. He assured her she wouldn't be, and she wasn't, but her work soon became the center of an art-world debate about what should and shouldn't be photographed when it comes to women's and children's bodies.[10]

Here's what I wrote in 1989, in the midst of all this pornography panic, and what I think remains true today, even in our digital world:

> It is not entirely happenstance that photographs are at the center of the stormy political dispute brought on by indirect Federal support of works by Robert Mapplethorpe and Andres Serrano. Much more than paintings, sculptures, plays, novels and poems, camera images seem to bring the world directly to our doorstep. When the world they bring is distasteful or repugnant, it is easy to blame the medium for the message.
>
> Like it or not, photography's seemingly inherent realism makes it especially vulnerable to a criticism based solely on the contents of an image. It is the most stylistically transparent of the visual arts, able to represent things in convincing perspective and seamless detail. Never mind that advertising has taught us that photographic images can be marvelous tricksters: what we see in a photograph is often mistaken for the real thing. More to the point, the subject matter of photographs is often mistaken for their meaning and value.[11]

An even greater irony than the persistence of photographic realism may be that while Mapplethorpe's and Serrano's photographs were being pilloried in Congress and denounced by the evangelical right, photography itself was partying like it was 1999—but ten years early. The year 1989 marked the 150th anniversary of the announcement of the medium's invention, and a sesquicentennial celebration had been planned for years. Several major museums that had established photography departments within the past two decades joined together to present enormous surveys of the medium's history, including one shown at the Museum of Fine Arts, Houston, which partnered with the Royal Academy of Arts in London, and another organized jointly by the Art Institute of Chicago and the National Gallery of Art. The latter show, *On the Art of Fixing a Shadow: One Hundred and Fifty Years of Photography*, was on view in Washington, D.C., when the Corcoran canceled its showing of the Mapplethorpe exhibition.[12]

On the Art of Fixing a Shadow included Mapplethorpe's work as well as a number of photographs by artists, among them Chuck Close, Jan Dibbets, David Hockney, and Anselm Kiefer; however, there was scant evidence of

Postmodernism (one Sherrie Levine, one Cindy Sherman) and virtually nothing of then-current tableau photography (no James Casebere, David Levinthal, or Sandy Skoglund). This made for a rather peculiar celebration, one that took for granted photography's place within the constellation of art-world institutions—the museum, the auction house, the art gallery—but almost ignored its most vital presence, which was within contemporary art of the moment. And the idea that the medium might have interacted with contemporary art in ways that had changed contemporary art profoundly and irrevocably—for better or worse—was nowhere considered.

The Culture Wars unfolding next door to *On the Art of Fixing a Shadow* showed photography's current impact on art much more clearly. The politics of the Culture Wars were at heart a reaction to contemporary art's long penchant for making its audience uncomfortable, expressed in this case with images that challenged existing mores related to religion and sexuality—and images that had the veracity of photographs. Of course it also could be said that the conflict was a more general expression of resentment about the perceived liberal elitism of the arts, and a reaction to giving government dollars to increase the pleasure of a mostly urban, well-heeled cultural audience. That, and homophobia.[13]

In one sense photography was an odd culprit to choose for a war on elitism, since it was and is the most widely dispersed method for making images that we have and thus familiar to everyone. But its familiarity may have worked against it. The widespread notion that photographs are easily made and readily understood made them handy targets for criticism in a way that paintings were not, since commenting on the latter seemed to require some interpretive expertise.[14] Performance was an easy mark, too, given its even closer ties to real life. In 1990 four performative artists—Karen Finley, John Fleck, Holly Hughes, and Tim Miller—had their proposed NEA fellowship grants vetoed by John Frohnmayer, based on their transgressive, "political," content.

Thankfully the Endowment survived, albeit neutered by the constant threat of controversy. When I served on the 1993 peer panel for photography fellowships, we voted to fund applications from Merry Alpern, Barbara DeGenevieve, and Andres Serrano. Our recommendations were overridden by the then-chairwoman, the actor Jane Alexander, for reasons that seemed to us extraneous, dismaying, and annoyingly vague. Alpern had photographed prostitutes, vaguely visible through a window across the street from the photographer's studio; DeGenevieve's collages involved images of women's bodies; Serrano's pictures happened to be of dead bodies in a morgue. Alexander, who had recently been appointed by President Bill Clinton, insisted that they all lacked sufficient artistic quality, an individual if inarguable critical judgment. Three years later, with Alexander still at the helm, the Endowment was forced by Congress to cancel all its individual artist fellowship programs, except for the one for writers.

Photography, on the other hand, because of or despite being at the forefront of the Culture Wars, continued to flourish in the art world. Its politicization mirrored the politicization of all of contemporary art by the conservative right, and this provoked an equal and opposite reaction: more and more artists in the nineties made work that was explicitly political. Using photography became a sign of being woke.

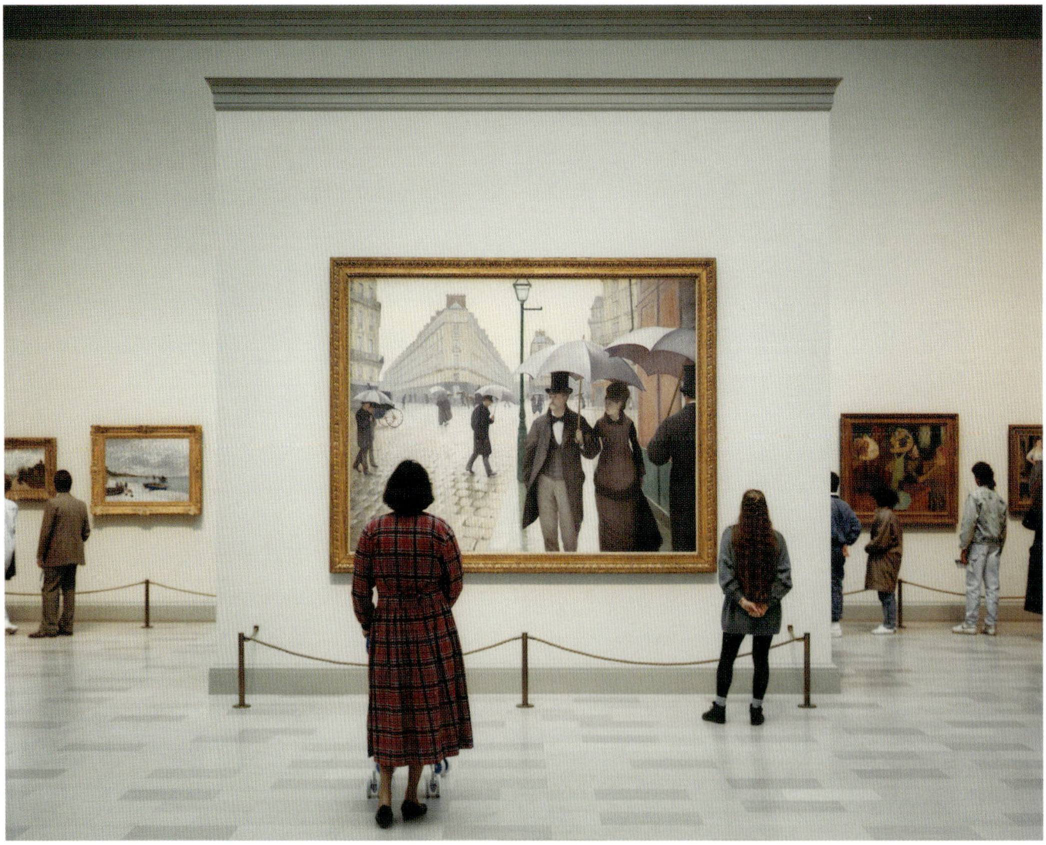

CHAPTER 15

Moving On

A few months into 1991 I announced that I was leaving New York and ending my tenure as a critic and columnist for the *Times* to move to San Francisco, where I had been offered a job with the Friends of Photography. Although the organization had been the brainchild of Ansel Adams and operated a museum called the Ansel Adams Center, its mission was to support contemporary photography. I would be in charge of curating the kind of exhibitions I felt needed to be done, as well as running its publishing program, and I hoped I could put my experience and contacts to full-time use.

I arranged to have a series of good-bye lunches, including one with John Szarkowski, who had announced in January that he was leaving his prominent position at MoMA. Although I had been on his case for years about his hesitancy to consider photographs from outside his comfort zone, like those of Cindy Sherman and Nan Goldin, I thought we at least shared a good sense of timing our departures. In his case, he was just coming off an ambitious project, *Photography Until Now*, a history of photography published as a book and exhibited at the museum in the winter of 1990.

Photography Until Now did include a color picture by Sherman, along with equally recent work by Robert Cumming, Lucas Samaras, and William Wegman, but in his text Szarkowski could barely manage to sound lukewarm about it.[1] When I interviewed him one last time for an Arts and Leisure feature I tried to make the case that Sherman deserved more credit; I opined that she and like-minded others were "what was happening" in contemporary photography. Szarkowski's reply was dismissive but also amazingly predictive of photography's future. "What's happening? People are taking three million photographs a year of their cats," he said. "That's what's happening." The developers of Instagram were less than ten years old at the time, but they could have been listening.

Peter Galassi, who had worked under Szarkowski at MoMA for ten years and who graciously came to my departure party at Janet Borden's Soho gallery, would take over the department and help deossify its outlook. (He organized a show of Sherman's *Untitled Film Stills* in 1997, and got the museum to add the entire set to its collection.) The transition was a sign of a new era at the museum, and also for the medium: MoMA's reign as the

Thomas Struth, *Art Institute of Chicago 2, Chicago*, 1990, from the series *Museum Pictures*.

ultimate tastemaker and portal to success for photography had ended—in truth, even before Szarkowski left the building.[2]

By 1991 it was clear that photography's status had changed irrevocably in the almost thirty years since Andy Warhol and Robert Rauschenberg had first silk-screened news photographs onto canvas, Edward Ruscha had assembled his own photographs into a proto-Conceptual artist's book, and Carolee Schneemann had had herself photographed as an embodiment of her expressionist paintings. Photographs now were hard to avoid if you visited a museum or crawled the galleries downtown and even uptown. Color was no longer remarkable but the rule, and print sizes had begun to exceed even the 4 × 5-foot limit of most commercial processing machines. But the real difference lay in the assumptions and intentions of the contemporary artists who used the medium. Making and exhibiting photographs was no longer either an act of defiance toward painting or a sign of allegiance to photography's distinct traditions; instead, photography had become simply a medium of choice for many young artists who wanted to express themselves in relation to the external world—even if that relation was one of hermetic rejection.

Photographs and videos were now being made by thousands of artists and would-be artists, and they were being shown (along with performance and its permutations) as prevalent parts of museum and gallery exhibition schedules, complementing exhibitions of painting and sculpture and surpassing those of prints and drawings. Contemporary art's aesthetic basis also had been fundamentally transformed. The notion of a single, dominant avant-garde, like the allied idea of a hierarchy of distinct mediums, had dissipated, replaced by a focus on interdisciplinarity and "issues" of concern to an individual artist and her or his colleagues. Pluralism, the short-lived buzz term of the seventies that signaled the existence of several simultaneous and competing aesthetic directions, seemed back in vogue, although the word was never uttered.

Postmodernism, which had so captivated the eighties and set the terms of discussion for photography's singular status as a singular kind of sign, was no longer on everyone's lips. As Hal Foster noted in his 1996 book *The Return of the Real*, "treated as a fashion, postmodernism became démodé."[3] Either it had succeeded so thoroughly that now all art was essentially Postmodern, or it had had its moment and passed the aesthetic-vanguard baton. Confoundingly, if the latter is true, no new "ism" or other label appeared. Neo-Expressionism and Neo-Geo were yesterday's news. It was as if Postmodernism's most lasting accomplishment was to eliminate the need for a unified vanguard style or aesthetic—hence the lack of any "isms" since.

Life in New York had changed as well. For an aspiring middle-class person like myself the city may have begun to be a more livable place, but any optimism this might have produced was shadowed by the absence of many people I had known or admired. The toll of AIDS kept rising: Robert Mapplethorpe, prominently, in 1989, two years after his paramour Sam Wagstaff, who died the same year as Peter Hujar. A few months after Mapplethorpe, Scott Burton, my first editor at *Art in America* and a fabulous artist whose sculpture assumed the forms of Minimalist furniture. The next year Jimmy DeSana, whose strange studio setups and portraits were beloved by downtown artists. Tseng Kwong Chi, who photographed himself as a Chinese tourist in a Mao suit and also documented the beginnings of Keith Haring's career. Haring himself. And many others less well known.

We were all consumed by the AIDS crisis. I was volunteering at Gay Men's Health Crisis and on the board of Photographers and Friends United Against AIDS, an organization started by Joseph Hartney Jr., a photographer's rep, to foster awareness of AIDS and raise money for research and care. A fellow board member of Photographers and Friends, my friend Marvin Heiferman, spearheaded a benefit exhibition the group organized. *The Indomitable Spirit: Photographers and Artists Respond to the Time of AIDS* opened in the winter of 1990 at the International Center of Photography and ended with a benefit auction.[4] It counted as doing something, at a time when drugs had not yet been developed to effectively combat the disease.

Downtown, Soho as I knew it was emptying out. Clothing and shoe stores were replacing storefront galleries, and it seemed increasingly unlikely that I would encounter any surprising or unexpected new art. The East Village scene was pretty much over, too, and Chelsea—home of today's New York art scene—was just getting started. I would still run into intrepid collectors making their rounds of Soho as I made mine—Arthur and Carol Goldberg were my favorite collecting couple, and we seemed always to cross paths on Prince Street—and I could stop in to see Helene Winer and Janelle Reiring at Metro Pictures on Greene Street, or bring a coffee from Dean and DeLuca to Janet Borden on Broadway. Castelli and Sonnabend still were doing exciting shows of their artists' work at 420 West Broadway, as was Mary Boone across the street. But I had a sense that a chapter was about to close.

I also had to face my dissatisfaction with continuing to live full-time in New York. I wasn't alone: many of my friends and acquaintances were heading out of town, quitting downtown lofts for underused (and cheap) studio spaces in upstate New York, or more radically pulling up stakes for Europe. Jan Groover and Bruce Boice moved to Bordeaux; Joan Simon and her family went to live in Paris. Seeing them go was a sign: after twenty years in New York, maybe I had done what I needed to do.

My career as a critic seemed at an apex and at a juncture. I was writing two or three times a week for the *Times*—covering photography shows, reviewing photo books, writing obituaries and the weekly Camera column—and increasingly involved with exhibition and book projects on the side. The biggest of these had been the sprawling exhibition *Photography and Art: Interactions Since 1946*, which traveled for two more years after opening at the Los Angeles County Museum of Art in June 1987.

Following the *Photography and Art* exhibition I did a show for the gallery at Moore College of Art in Philadelphia about recent advertising photography, featuring Annie Leibovitz, Wayne Maser, Denis Piel, and Bruce Weber.[5] The blurring of the boundaries between art and commerce whetted my appetite for more of the same. Then my Cornell friend Sarah Bodine commissioned me to write a book about the influential *Harper's Bazaar* designer Alexey Brodovitch, and a year later Mike and Doug Starn asked me to write for their eponymous first book, published in 1990.[6] And I signed a contract with Aperture to publish a collection of my critical writing, *Crisis of the Real*, which also came out in 1990.

No doubt my track record as a critic was getting me lots of other work, but I still worried about earning a living over the long term. The *Times* had never put me on staff, despite my pleas and complaints from the *Times* writers guild to management that I was writing as much as a full-time staffer. The publishing powers that be at the paper seemed more concerned with trimming costs than in keeping the union or me happy. I was now in my mid-forties and starting to worry—probably for the first time—about my future.

I might have put up with such a pragmatic concern if I hadn't had a sense that my preoccupation with photography's inside/outside status in the art world, which had propelled my career from its beginnings, no longer was necessary. No longer did a critic need to promote photography as a visual medium of aesthetic potential, or to announce its currency as a great cultural influencer. In fact, critics with résumés in painting and sculpture now were regularly writing about photography and video as if it had been a part of their purview forever. With camera images naturalized within galleries, museums, art schools, auction houses, and art magazines (with relatively few exceptions), the sense of struggle that I had implicitly enjoyed had vanished.

Photography and video had not just become normal fare within the art world, they had acquired considerable cachet. Contemporary and historical exhibitions of photographs were now favorites at most museums across the country, both because they brought in large new audiences and because they were relatively inexpensive to produce and to travel compared to shows of paintings and sculpture. Video, relishing the development of new computer-driven tools for editing and for achieving a cinema-like presence, attracted more and more artists interested in installation and narrative. (Video projection had become better than cinema in galleries; thanks to high-definition digital projectors, the room did not need to be that dark.)

Then there was the déjà vu I experienced in reviewing the 1991 Paul Strand retrospective at the National Gallery of Art. Strand has long been presented as a founding father of photography's Modernism, someone whose early work took cues from Cubism and nestled comfortably within the aesthetic of Precisionist painting. He also made documentary films and adopted a different style for his later still photography, one akin to (but arguably better than) Socialist Realism, so he was in essence two photographers in one. I found this fascinating when I saw his retrospective at the Philadelphia Museum of Art in 1971 and again at the Metropolitan Museum of Art in 1973, and in the eighties I wrote in the *Times* about shows of his work at Zabriskie Gallery and the New York Public Library.

I was hopeful that the National Gallery show, the first since his 1976 death, would finally address the contradictions of Strand's career.[7] Instead, the exhibition was essentially hagiography, declaring all his work to be of equal greatness—a requirement, perhaps, given that many of the prints in the show were promised gifts. It was, to my mind, a recapitulation of the same Strand narrative I already knew. I reviewed the show for the *Times* in January 1991 and soon afterward had a waking nightmare: if I stayed on my current path, I would be condemned to a lifetime of reviewing essentially the same shows over and over again.

Not everything was a final chapter, however. Postmodernism might have been over, Szarkowski might have retired, and I might have gotten a bit jaded with photography's success, but the nineties were ushered in by a flurry of new work and new ideas born of the late eighties. Some artists were responding directly to issues posed by Postmodernism, such as the argument that all pictures are representations held at one remove from what they portray, and seeking to restore our faith in photographic authenticity. Others took the issues and approaches of Postmodernism—such as the idea that images reflect implicit cultural biases—and used them to speak to their own culturally heterogeneous identities.

Like all developments in art that are perceived as new, these reactions had precursors in the period from which they sprung. In the case of photographs dealing with cultural identity, one could start with Tseng Kwong Chi, or Kwong Chi as he was familiarly known in the seventies. At roughly the same time that Cindy Sherman was at work on her *Untitled Film Stills*, he dressed himself up as an emissary of the Maoist regime, posed in front of stereotypical Western tourist sites like the Eiffel Tower and the Golden Gate Bridge, and made early versions of what we now know as selfies. (Tseng was born in Hong Kong and grew up in Canada, so performing a Chinese stereotype was purposely ironic.) Shown widely downtown, these photographs set an example for much of the work of the late eighties and early nineties.

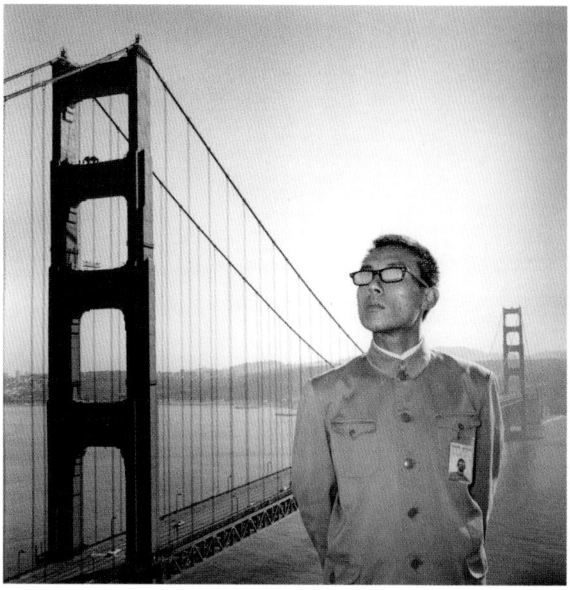

Tseng Kwong Chi, *San Francisco, California*, 1979, from the series *East Meets West*, 1979–89.

The Japanese artist Yasumasa Morimura took up the image of a cultural "other" with a series in which he cast himself as the lead figure in various canonical European paintings. While an unlikely candidate to play the role of Édouard Manet's nude Olympia or a heavily bandaged Vincent van Gogh, he was able to create eerie near-doppelgängers of the originals. His first solo show in the United States, in 1991 at Luhring Augustine in Soho, was a smash hit, and soon his good-humored cultural transpositions seemed to be everywhere. Tseng had shown himself as an Asian man standing in front of Western culture; Morimura managed to put himself into the thick impasto of it.

In a similar vein, Dinh Q. Lê, a Vietnamese artist living in the United States at the time, literally wove himself into the Western canon of painting by combining strips of two separate color photographs into a form of tapestry. Lê, who was a student in the MFA program at the School of Visual Arts when he first started showing his *Portraying a White God* series (I was teaching there at the time), was descended from a family of traditional weavers; his woven-together pictures combine a traditional craft culture from Asia with the modern Western technology of color photography as the means of inserting his image into icons of European art. In the series Lê, in briefs, appears interspersed with a variety of painted Christ figures, the "white god" whom he, as an Asian in America, was attempting to model—albeit ironically.

The sense of "otherness" these Asian and Asian American artists conveyed could also be shown to exist within American society, in terms of both race and gender. Starting in 1986 Lorna Simpson produced pointed and

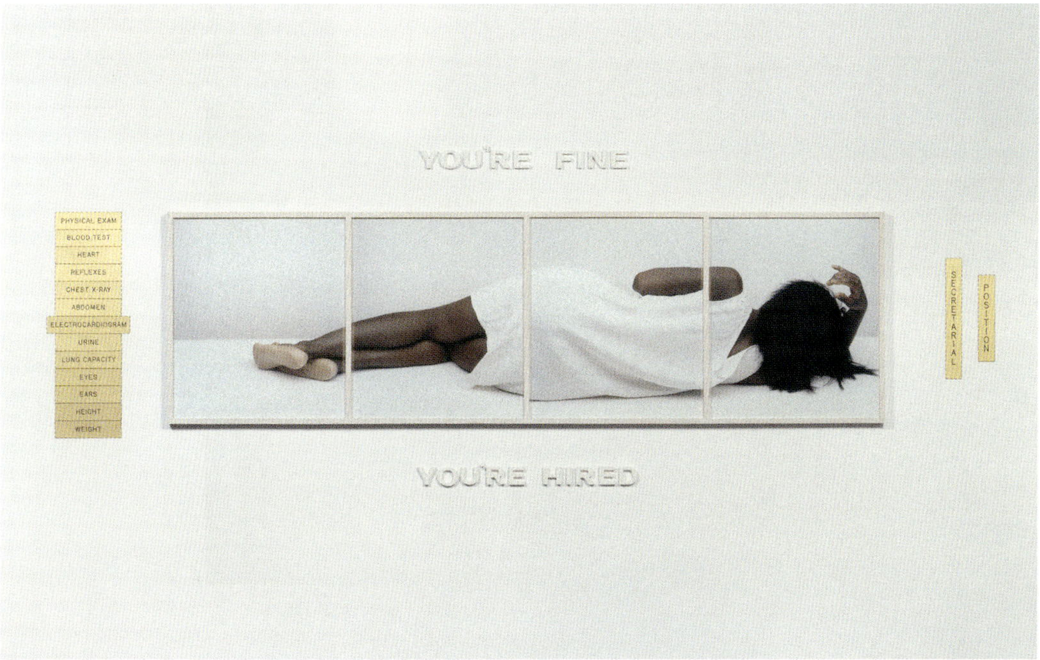

Lorna Simpson, *You're Fine*, 1988. Four Polaroid prints in one frame, fifteen engraved plastic plaques, and ceramic letters.

discomfiting work that juxtaposed photographs and text to make powerful statements about how African American female bodies were vulnerable not only to stereotyping but also to manipulation by those in positions of power. Simpson used models instead of herself, never revealing their faces but depicting them in plain white smocks against plain backgrounds in a way that suggested a clinical setting. Below or alongside the pictures were plastic plaques of the sort once used to label offices and classrooms, with anodyne lettering that evoked an institutional voice.

You're Fine of 1988 is a classic example, combining four 20 × 24-inch Polaroid prints of a prone black woman seen from the back, raised lettering that conveys the title, and plaques on the left side that list the checkoffs for a physical examination. On the right the vertically arrayed words *secretarial* and *position* suggest both a job title and the applicant's submissive role. In linking a medical exam with a job application, the artist showed how female bodies—and specifically African American ones—are objectified and often sexualized in oppressive fashion.

Californian Carrie Mae Weems appeared on the New York scene at about the same time, and she has proved to be one of the most influential of those artists who adopted the methods of Postmodernist and tableau photography to address their particular places in the world. Essentially, she melded the idea of self-portrait as performance familiar from Cindy Sherman's work with the specifics of racial and gender differences as addressed in Adrian Piper's performance pieces in the sixties.

Carrie Mae Weems, *Untitled (Woman and Daughter with Makeup)*, 1990, from *The Kitchen Table Series*.

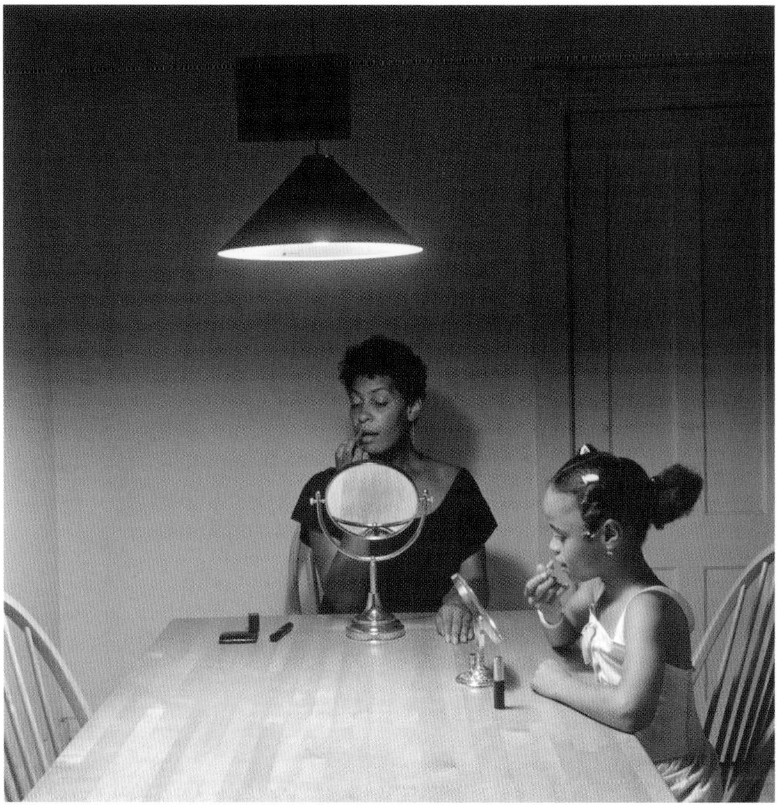

An African American woman and single parent, Weems in her landmark *The Kitchen Table Series* (1990) staged herself at the end of a table in her Oakland apartment as she confronted a changing cast of characters: her daughter, her boyfriend, her girl friends. When shown together, as intended, the series of some twenty images was accompanied by narrative text panels that sharpened the pictures' points. *The Kitchen Table Series* followed on the heels of the *Colored People* series, in which Weems used colored gels over her straightforward portraits of African Americans to address racially determined stereotypes. The two bodies of work led to her being shown at P.P.O.W. Gallery in New York and, in 1991, included for the first time in a Whitney Biennial.

Weems then went on to probe more deeply into her origins, making work that followed the trail of African American experience back to slavery and hence back to Africa. In 1991 and 1992 she photographed on the Sea Islands of South Carolina where isolated former slaves preserved parts of African culture after the Civil War, and in 1993 she visited Africa's so-called Slave Coast, producing pictures that show the architecture of the slave trade. Perhaps most notoriously, in 1995–96 she made copies of daguerreotypes of slaves commissioned by Harvard's Louis Agassiz and, in her series *From*

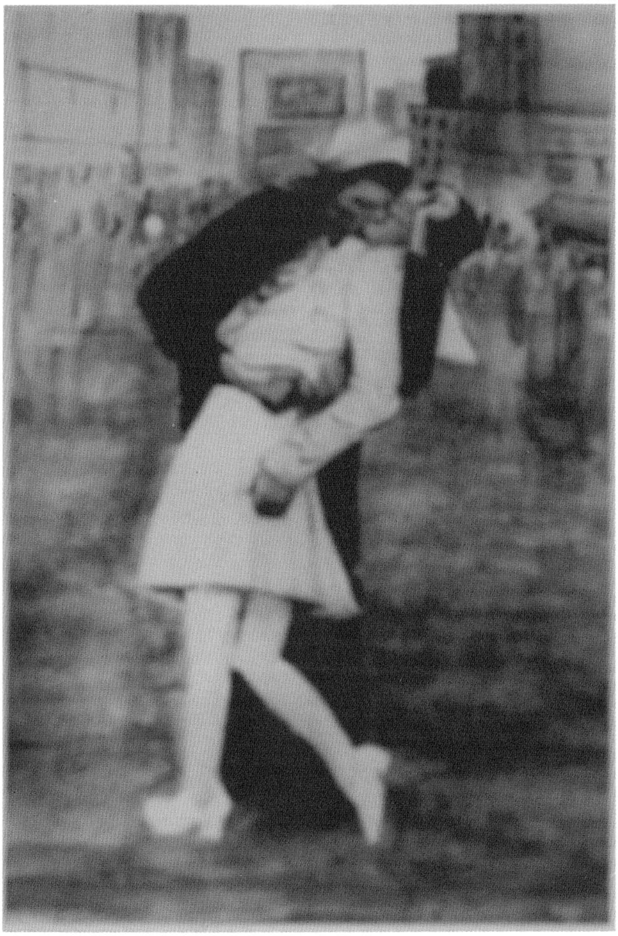

Vik Muniz, *Memory Rendering of Kiss at Times Square*, 1990, from the series *The Best of Life*.

Here I Saw What Happened and I Cried, put them behind color gels surprinted with text. "You became a scientific profile" one reads, over an image of a naked female standing sideways with downcast eyes.[8]

The urge to examine one's cultural heritage and the contradictions between it and society's putative norms, so central to Weems's work and that of the other artists mentioned above, propelled a new wave of what is often called, in art-world shorthand, "identity art." Much of it reflects on oppressions suffered by the artists on account of their races, genders, sexual preferences, and countries of origin. Photography did and continues to play a large role in such work, as does video, not only because of its place in the lives of these artists and its documentary qualities but also because Postmodernism showed it to be a medium of critical agency. And then there is its less salubrious use historically as an uncritical instrument of ethnography, anthropology, and discredited fields such as eugenics.

Even work that seemed to stick to the Picture Generation's text often revealed itself to have a cultural subplot. Vik Muniz, a Brazilian-born artist who showed his first work at Stux Gallery at the same time as Mike and Doug Starn, produced a series of "memory renderings" in a process that starts and ends with photography. Recalling news photographs that the newly emigrated artist had seen in *The Best of Life,* a book he had bought but then lost, Muniz literally drew them as he remembered them; he then photographed the drawings through a halftone screen so that the final pictures read on first glance as news photos. Most depict only the bare bones of the original image, and some are flipped side to side, but enough of the original survives to make them instantly recognizable.

The artist has explained that he started the series (known as *The Best of Life*) because the pictures—of the "tank man" in Tiananmen Square, the VJ Day kiss in Times Square, the dead student at Kent State—helped him acclimate to the country to which he had moved in 1983. Muniz went on to elaborate on this photograph-drawing-photograph process in many ingenious ways, using alternative drawing materials including wire, chocolate, sugar, ketchup, dust, diamonds, and more recently junk from a Rio de Janeiro landfill. He also regularly reproduces artworks other than photographs, such as Old Master paintings, although he works from reference photographs of them.

If some artists dealing with their cultural heritage or sense of cultural dislocation took the lessons of Postmodernism and ran with them, other artists were seeking to turn back the clock and reassert the medium's relationship to reality—to the "trace" or "index," in Rosalind Krauss's analysis. There has been, since photography's Day One, the sense that the medium captured something real—Nature, say, in the case of landscapes, or the Soul, in the case of portraiture. What better way to refute the hegemony of the simulacrum than to return to that moment of origin, to what might be called the ontological essence of the photographic process?

British artists were at the heart of the originalist movement early on. Susan Derges, Adam Fuss, and Garry Fabian Miller all began experimenting with cameraless photograms, pinholes, and other "primitive" techniques in the late eighties—coincidentally, since Fuss by this time was in New York while Derges and Miller lived in the English countryside. They were joined by like-minded Londoners Christopher Bucklow and Steven Pippin, each of whom engineered unusual pinhole cameras to make their equally unusual pictures.

The first exhibition of Fuss's work that I remember seeing in New York, at Massimo Audiello Gallery in Soho in 1990, consisted of a series of apparently solid black rectangles. Initially puzzled, I stared at them long enough to realize that they held portraits of people, but printed so darkly that only a barely perceptible silhouette remained. The printing process was what made

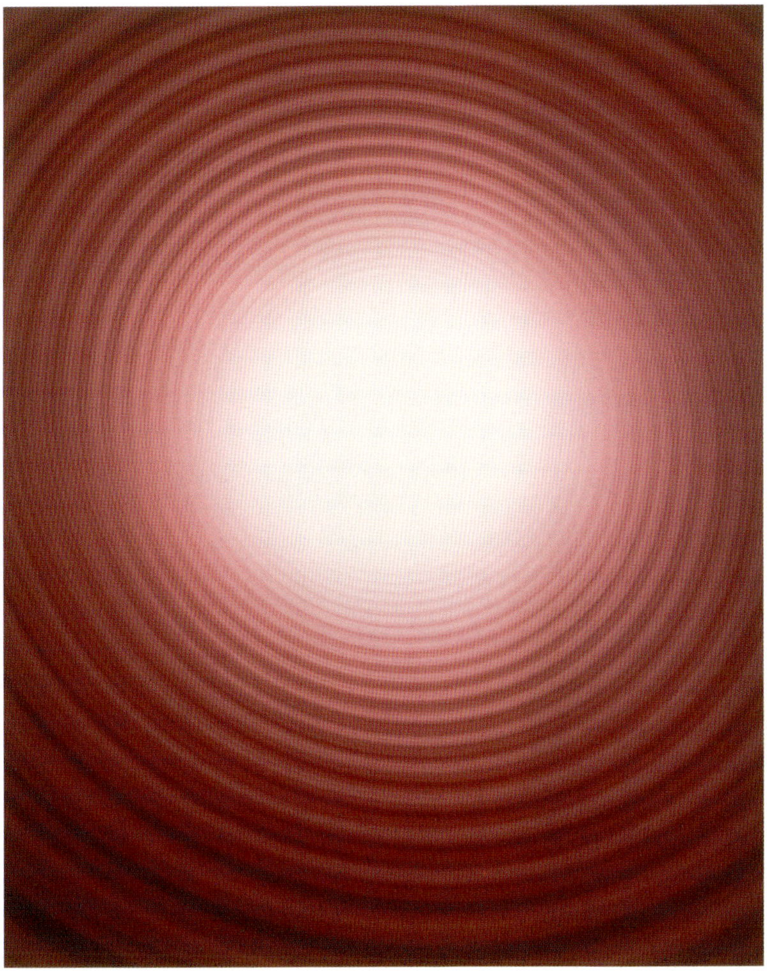

Adam Fuss, *Untitled*, 1990.

them unconventional; otherwise, they were enlarged from regular camera negatives.

At the same time, Fuss was experimenting with cameraless pictures, producing photograms of light spirals on black-and-white photo paper and, thanks to the existence of Cibachrome, a direct-positive process, in monochromatic color. These pictures, done by suspending a flashlight as a pendulum over the printing paper while working in the dark, have a mesmerizing effect and are both documentary (they record the passage of light in time) and abstract (the "subject," light, is in essence ephemeral).

Fuss would go on to produce a remarkable series of color photograms featuring eels, babies, and notably, in the 1992 image *Love*, a pair of eviscerated rabbits. Later he learned to make daguerreotypes, the first publicly available process for making photographs and one known for the fragile, reflective surfaces of its unique images, which in Fuss's case have included self-portraits, birds, butterflies, and translucent children's smocks.[9]

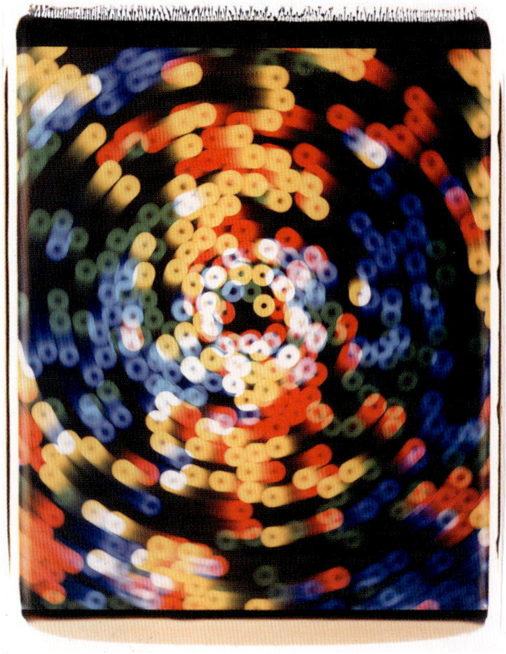

Ellen Carey, *Color Theory*, 1995.

Bucklow, Derges, and Miller had a similar evolution, making color photograms that record the direct action of light. Bucklow's *Guest* series was particularly ingenious and complex, a series of portraits of visitors to his studio consisting of thousands of tiny circles, or sun spots, created by pricking holes in a piece of aluminum foil to produce a life-size silhouette of the person's head and body and then exposing the foil to daylight with sensitized paper behind it.

Pippin, trained as an engineer, started making oddball cameras that actually produced pictures in the mideighties. One of the first, in 1986, was a vacant house, which took a picture through a hole in its front door of a man (the artist) standing in front of the houses across the street. In 1991 he created a laundromat camera. By blacking out the door of a front-loading washer and placing the photo paper inside, he could take a picture of what the washing machine, if it had eyes, would be looking at. The machine's water supply allowed him to process and wash the image on the spot. Several years later he elaborated on the process by turning a row of twelve washers into adjacent cameras and riding a horse through the laundromat, thus replicating Eadweard Muybridge's nineteenth-century motion studies.

The urge to rediscover a sense of photography's origins in its essential materiality was not limited to Britain; in the United States Ellen Carey and Abelardo Morell produced important work that reflected on the medium's first principles. Together with later revivalists like Jerry Spagnoli, a master of the daguerreotype; Sally Mann, who adopted the archaic wet-plate collo-

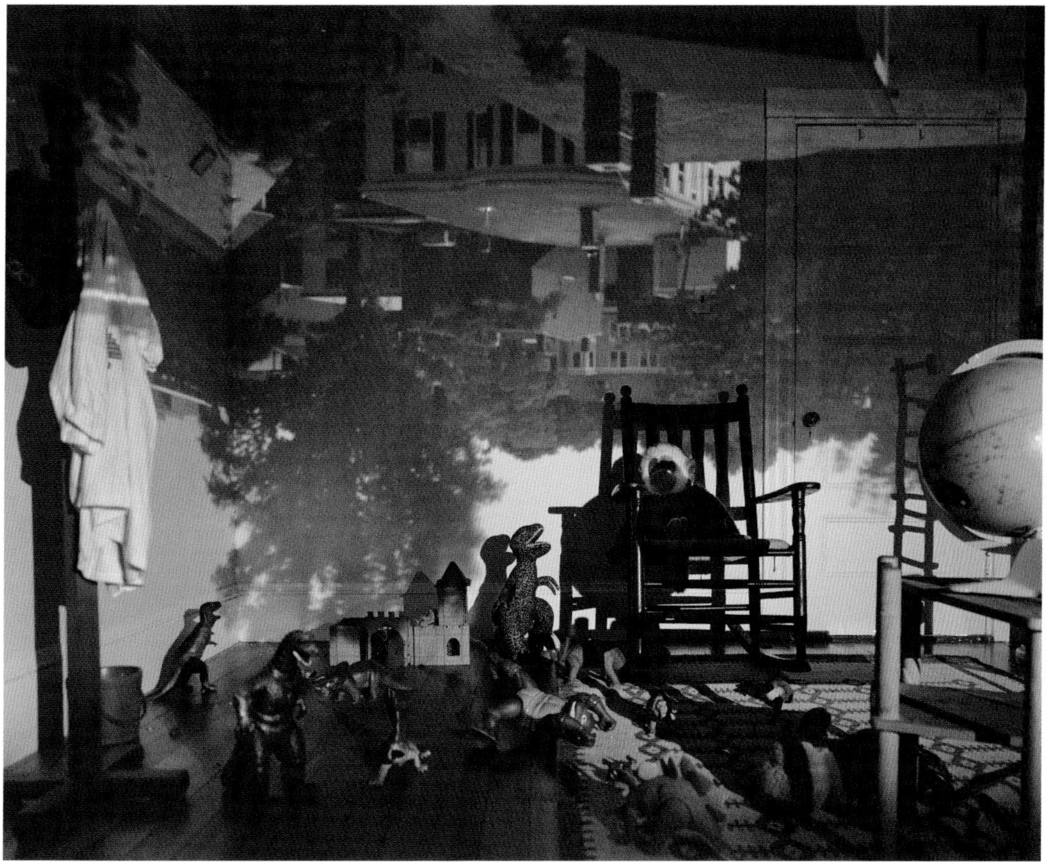

Abelardo Morell, *Camera Obscura View of Brookline from Brady's Bedroom*, 1992.

dion method for photographing Civil War battlefields; and Vera Lutter, who created large pinhole negatives and showed them as the final work, these artists found ways to discover new possibilities in techniques that predate photography's association with photomechanical reproduction.

As a student Carey had been in Buffalo in its artistic heyday; she had equal billing with Cindy Sherman in CEPA's now-legendary *Photo Bus Show*, and in 1978 her master's thesis exhibition of painted self-portraits hung in Hallwalls. Soon, like many photographers of the time, she became entranced by Polaroid. When Polaroid introduced its 20 × 24-inch color camera in 1980 and set up studios for it in Boston and New York, Carey abandoned paint in favor of overlays of geometric forms, which either covered her face or fragmented it into multiples, not unlike a kaleidoscope.

By 1988 her interest in the circular and spiral forms in these pictures led her to abandon self-portraiture in favor of purely abstract elements. Using marbles and other round objects, she began to make color and black-and-white photograms with the large Polaroid material. And in the midnineties Carey abandoned even marbles, producing photograms on long strips of Polaroid materials that are solely artifacts of light striking the light-sensitive surface and of the chemical agents that develop it. She calls her work in this vein "photography degree zero"—a riff on Roland Barthes's 1953 book *Writing Degree Zero*.

Born in Cuba and raised in New York City, Morell started taking pictures as a teenager and pursued a career as a more-or-less conventional street photographer and portraitist. It wasn't until he had a son and turned forty that his work took an unconventional direction. Noticing the wonder with which his son, Brady, interacted with the world, and especially the world of light and shadow, Morell began to make images that are about the workings and wonders of light. In 1992 he embarked on the pinhole project that has preoccupied him ever since. For one of the first in the series, he covered the window of his son's bedroom with black plastic to turn it into a literal camera obscura, and then photographed the room using a long exposure. This produced a simultaneous image of inside—with Brady's toy dinosaurs on display on the floor—and outside. The view looking across the street at the neighbor's yard is upside down, making the picture nominally about how camera lenses work. But more profoundly it suggests the tension between the imaginative wonders of childhood and the external, adult reality that intrudes on and eventually replaces it.

Ironically, technologically modern "straight" photography was having its own revival at the same time that photograms, pinhole cameras, and obsolete processes were enjoying second acts. In large part this revival was a consequence of another, more important development in the art world: New York, and the United States in general, was no longer the alpha and omega of contemporary art, either in terms of its making or its reception. The enthusiastic appreciation of German and Italian painting that was key to the rise of Neo-Expressionism (Francesco Clemente, Anselm Kiefer, Sigmar Polke, et al.) opened Americans' eyes to contemporary art in Europe, which soon expanded well beyond one medium and two countries. In 1988, for example, Damien Hirst organized an exhibition of his work and that of his fellow art students in London that gave birth to the movement known as the Young British Artists (or YBAs). Simultaneously aggressive and transgressive, the YBAs made work in many mediums including, most famously, Hirst's formaldehyde tanks filled with dead animals.

In New York the adulation of Walker Evans and a growing appreciation of the *New Topographics* photographers were keeping traditional photography alive within photographic circles, but a far more decisive factor in terms of its acceptance within contemporary art was the mounting influence of the German artists Bernd and Hilla Becher and the coming-of-age of a remarkable generation of their students: most prominently, Andreas Gursky, Candida Höfer, Thomas Ruff, and Thomas Struth.[10]

These artists, some of whom also had studied with the painter Gerhard

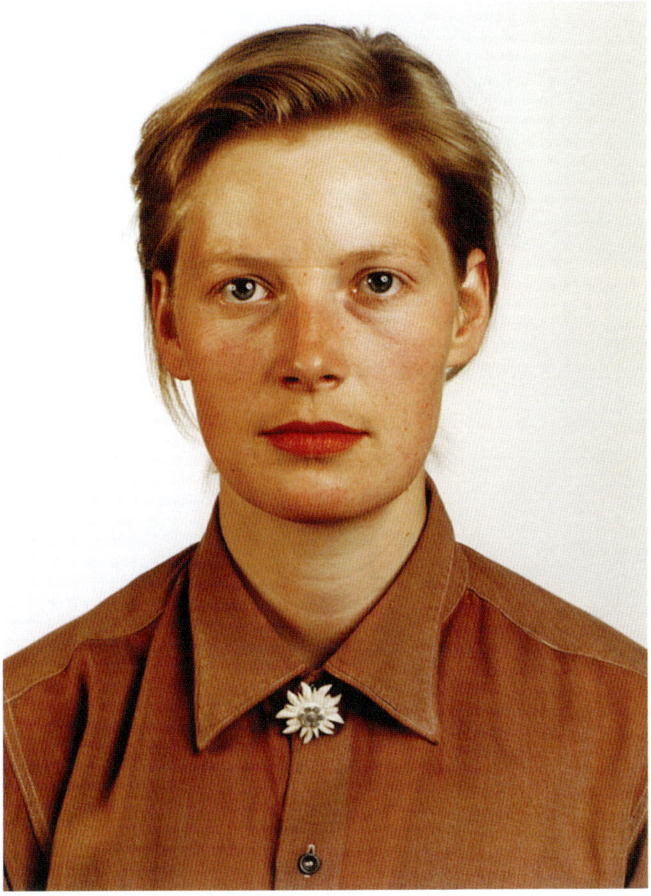

Thomas Ruff, *Porträt (P. Stadtbäumer)*, 1988.

Richter while at the Düsseldorf academy of art (Staatliche Kunstakademie, Düsseldorf, to be precise), began showing in New York in 1989 and 1990 and quickly became stars in the contemporary art firmament. The Bechers, of course, were already well known as Conceptual artists because of their catalogs of photographs of water towers and other structures begun in the sixties. Richter, for some students an equal influence, had been painting from photographs since defecting from East Germany in the fifties, as well as collecting news pictures and his own snapshot images, which he grouped together and assembled as an archive called *Atlas*. (His landmark series of paintings of Baader-Meinhof terrorists made from police photographs of their suicides, *October 18, 1977*, was created in 1988 and first shown in the United States in 1990.)

However the relative influences of the Bechers and Richter are parsed, the graduates of the Düsseldorf school maintained the same cool, almost disembodied approach to photographing as their teachers, used a typological method that required sustained attention to repeating similar subjects, and presented their work without explaining their intentions. What they did differently than their mentors, most obviously, was take advantage of new color printing technology that allowed their photographs to take on the size of paintings.

Thomas Ruff's larger-than-life portraits of his fellow art-school friends were the first to get my attention. Seemingly simple—head-and-shoulders, passport-style frontal images that reflect the direct gazes of their subjects—the portraits are incredibly complex from the viewer's point of view. There are no smiles or facial tics or backgrounds to distract from the confrontation of one person looking back at you, unblinking, limned in precise detail, and much larger than you are. They draw you in when you enter their space, and despite being strangers they invite you to stare.

Ruff had started making portraits in 1981 while still a student and continued after he left school in 1985, at which point the prints became much bigger. They were, for the time, quite large at about 4 × 5 feet, which was the size of Tina Barney's color print in the 1983 *Big Pictures* show at the Museum of Modern Art, only his were photographed vertically. At that size they made Ruff's portrait subjects literally larger than life and seemingly totems of their generation (stuck as it was between the Baby Boomers and Millennials), and they held the wall in a way that earlier single photographs rarely did. Even in a room full of paintings they tend to be the first thing you see.

Ruff soon was making even bigger prints for his next series, *Stars*, which was shown at 303 Gallery in the fall of 1990. Although printed in color, these pictures were essentially black fields with tiny white spots in them, made from negatives from an observatory telescope documenting constellations in the night sky. That fall marked a breakthrough for other young German photographers: while Ruff's *Stars* pictures were up at 303, Candida Höfer was having her first exhibition in New York at Nicole Klagsbrun, and Thomas Struth's work was being presented at Marian Goodman Gallery on 57th Street.

Struth's early black-and-white prints had been shown in New York back in the late seventies, when he was in residence for a student year at PS1 in Queens, but the show at Goodman of his *Museum Pictures* made his career.[11] Taken at the Louvre in Paris, the Galleria dell'Accademia in Venice, the Art Institute of Chicago, and other museums, the large color prints (even bigger, by several inches, than 4 × 5 feet) record the display of widely popular paintings and the spectators gathered to gaze at them. Since we are looking at lookers who, based on the perspective of the image, are nearly life size, Struth makes us self-conscious about our own roles in viewing art, putting us into a metaphoric picture within a picture if we imagine someone with a cellphone camera standing behind us.

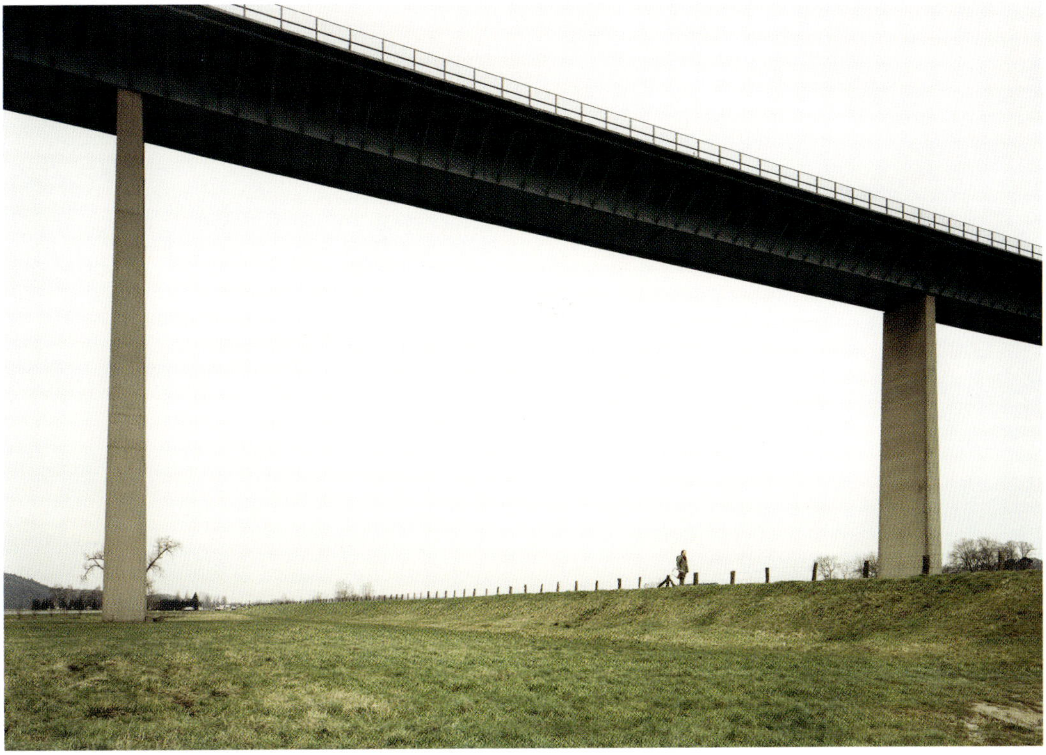

Andreas Gursky, *Ruhr Valley*, 1989.

Andreas Gursky had had his debut in New York a year earlier at 303 Gallery, albeit with color prints not yet as large as Ruff's or Struth's. (That would come later.) Gursky, whose student years roughly coincided with Ruff's, specialized in precisely rendered landscapes in which small human figures often appeared as footnotes to nature. One, *Ruhr Valley* (1989), shows a lone pedestrian on a walking path underneath an elevated rail bridge; the sky, subsuming much of the picture, is eerily blank.

While I was looking at this picture 303 Gallery's director, Lisa Spellman, came out of her office to explain that the blankness was in part due to the artist's intervention; apparently, some electric or telephone wires were visible in the original negative but had been erased by a process that involved digital retouching. This was the first time I had heard of such a thing in an art context, and I wasn't sure what to think about it. That Gursky wanted his postindustrial view of the Ruhr to look spare and emptied out I understood, but he had violated the what-you-see-is-what-was-there compact on which almost all photography relies. I remember leaving feeling somewhat queasy, not knowing that at that moment a pair of ingenious software coders were busy writing a program that would become Adobe Photoshop, which would allow anyone and everyone to mess with photographic reality. Gursky, for his part, would go on to make even larger color pictures, some as large as

Nancy Burson, *Androgyny (6 Men + 6 Women)*, 1982.

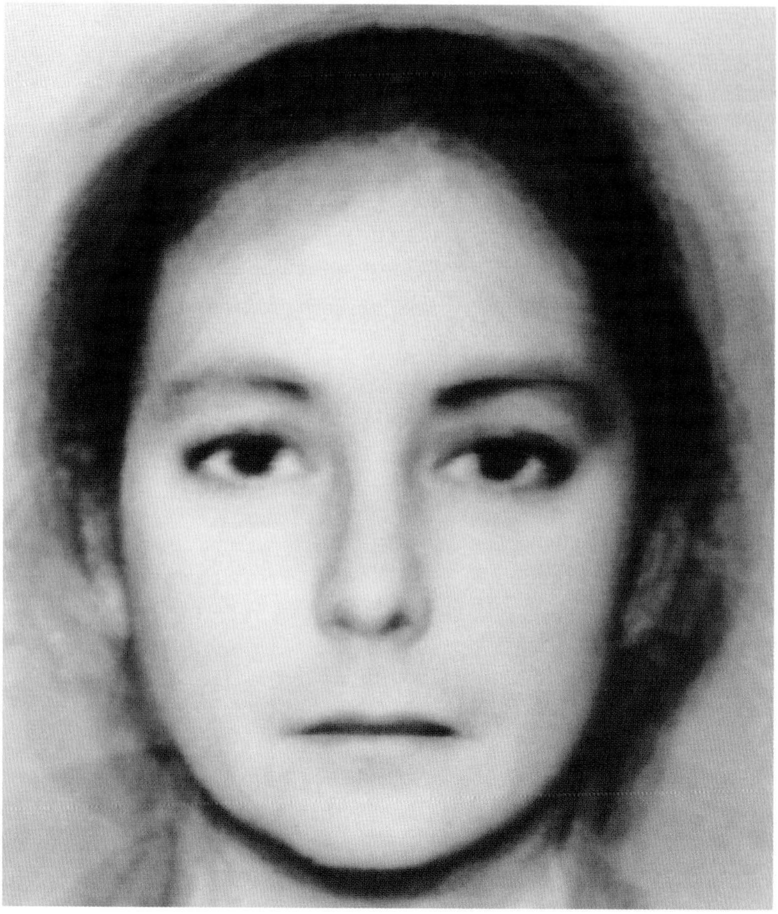

the average wall, and to perfect his image-alteration skills to imperceptibly extend the display of products in a 99¢ store and the number of floors in a hotel atrium.

Of course I wasn't totally naive about the possibilities for fiddling with photographs to make them show something that wasn't. The journalistic world of photography had already seen plenty of examples of image manipulation, most famously in the Soviet Union during the Stalin era. Whenever a government official fell from favor (Leon Trotsky, prominently) his presence in official photographs would be airbrushed out of existence. Newspapers loved the airbrush as well, graying out background information to make the featured subject stand out more clearly. But computerized manipulation seemed to be of another order. *National Geographic* had done it (and later regretted it) with a 1982 cover showing two Giza pyramids, which the editors moved closer together to better fit the magazine's format.

Also in 1982 the artist Nancy Burson began a collaboration with two software engineers to make "composites"—her term for her portraits that show more than one person's features. *Warhead I*, for example, shows a single, imposing face that consists, according to the artist's caption, of 55 percent Ronald Reagan, 45 percent Leonid Brezhnev, and less than 1 percent each of Margaret Thatcher, François Mitterand, and Deng Xiaoping—the percentages being based on the number of nuclear warheads each world leader controls. She also digitally combined the faces of movie stars, men and women, different racial and ethnic types, and a cat and a dog. These pictures quickly made their way into the art world; by 1990 they had been seen at Holly Solomon Gallery, the International Center of Photography, Boston's Institute of Contemporary Art, and MIT's List Visual Art Center.[12] The notion that computers could do the things Burson and her collaborators made them do was scary, but at the same time it was rather obvious; no one was going to be fooled into thinking that her composite of six men and six women (*Androgyny*, 1982) was a real person. That kind of sleight of hand would come much later.

In the nineties the technical methods of photography—and to some minds, the medium itself—truly were transformed, and in radical ways that not everyone anticipated. This transition included a gradual but intensifying shift from silver salts and chemistry to electronics. Over the next fifteen years analog gave way to digital and 35mm film succumbed to CCD chips and hard drives, following the lead of video. In early 1990 Adobe introduced version one of Photoshop for the Mac, the first image-processing program that allowed someone with a home computer to improve the exposure, colors, and tonalities of her or his digital photographs, as well as to add and subtract subject matter more or less at will. The art world took the digitization of photography in stride—color prints at galleries, which already had gotten big, got even bigger—but for photographers it was a paradigm shift. Some declared the word *photography* obsolete, seeking to displace it with *imaging*.

I covered the beginning of this shift in my role as Camera columnist for the *Times*—my potboiler gig covering new cameras, film, and other innovations. Toward the end of 1989 I attended what was an annual holiday presentation for the photographic press put on by Eastman Kodak in New York, a kind of we'll-wash-your-hands-if-you-wash-ours event with free lunch, free drinks, and free swag bag on the way out, all to let us know what Kodak was innovating in far-off Rochester. The big news that year was that Kodak had acquired Verbatim, a floppy-disk maker. This in itself seemed underwhelming, but the context made it astounding: the company founded a hundred years before on the technology of flexible photographic film had seen the future and was preparing to shift itself into the digital age. As you might imagine, based on how long floppy disks were the ne plus ultra of computer storage, this shift didn't turn out so well for Kodak, but the company did see it coming.

What I remember most about the presentation, and remarkably distinctly at that, is hearing that Kodak scientists and futurists had projected that by the first decade of the twenty-first century most photography would be digital. Audible gasps arose from the audience of cynical writers and editors. And by the second decade of the century, the spokesman continued, the resolution of digital images would exceed that of Kodachrome, the company's most advanced and admired color film. Even I gasped at that, since at the time digital resolution was so bad the pixels could be counted on the nose of a portrait subject in an 8 × 10-inch print. Eventually, the spokesman concluded, with the development of new forms of image chips the resolution limit of digital photography could be molecular. Applause broke out throughout the room.

Sadly, if that is an adequate word for what happened to Kodak, the company missed the digital wave and found itself in bankruptcy some twenty years later, a miserable pale shadow of the hulking industrial giant it once had been. A very similar fate awaited Polaroid, a newer and more glamorous powerhouse technology company devoted to instant photography, which had its heyday in the seventies and eighties. Polaroid executives produced strategic documents starting in the mideighties showing how it would position itself in the middle of the digital imaging revolution, and its engineers devised some impressive high-end digital scanners, but the company bet all its chips on the future centrality of the photographic print—what company diagrams of the time called "hard copy."[13]

Shortly before the Kodak press luncheon I was called in to meet with the deputy publisher of the *New York Times*—the first and last time I would encounter the soon-to-be-anointed chieftain of the most influential newspaper in the country. The son of the legendary Arthur Ochs "Punch" Sulzberger, whose family had owned the paper for generations, Arthur Jr. (or "Pinch," to wags) was thinking about what present he could give his main lieutenants as a holiday gift, and he wanted my opinion about a novel new camera he had heard about, the Canon Xap Shot, which didn't use film to record pictures.

My first advice was to pass; I knew that more advanced and capable cameras were in the pipeline at various Japanese manufacturers, and that both Kodak and Polaroid had taken an interest in the digital imaging future. But then again, I offered, if Sulzberger's intent was to demonstrate how forward-thinking and prescient the *Times* needed to be as new digital technologies made themselves felt in the newspaper business, then making early adopters of his top administrators and editors might be a smart strategy. I believe he followed my first piece of advice and found another gift, but the digital transformation of photography was soon paralleled by another digital transformation, that of the newspaper business itself. The *Times* managed it better than Kodak, thank goodness, but many other newspapers did not.

The contemporary art world, on the other hand, was poised to become an even bigger and more successful business in the next century—a business in which photography would be both highly visible and, ironically, to the extent that it was now thoroughly embedded in artistic discourse and practice, largely unremarkable.

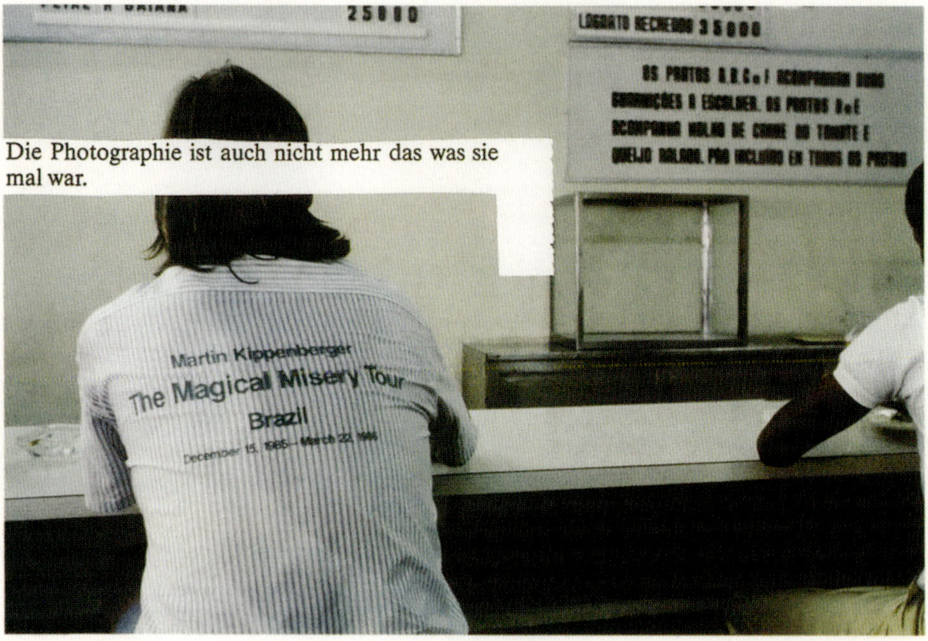
25000
35000
Die Photographie ist auch nicht mehr das was sie mal war.
Martin Kippenberger
The Magical Misery Tour
Brazil

Epilogue

It is tempting to conclude my account of photography's rise within contemporary art by asserting that its recognition and acceptance was a fait accompli by the beginning of the nineties. Or, for the benefit of any doubters, say by the end of the century. But it may be more accurate to say that its recognition is recursive. Every generation, it now seems, gets to discover photography's importance anew, just as it gets to reinvent contemporary art itself.

In 2003 I saw a photography show in London at the Tate Modern titled *Cruel and Tender*. The exhibition was billed as a survey of the documentary strain of twentieth-century photography, as its subtitle, *The Real in the Twentieth-Century Photograph*, suggests. It was also, according to the press release for the show, a breakthrough for the museum:

> Although photography has been included in a number of previous exhibitions at Tate, and regularly features in Collection displays, this is the first major exhibition at Tate dedicated purely to the medium. As such, it signals Tate's acknowledgement that photography is a key component of contemporary visual culture and will continue to feature in Tate's exhibition programmes.[1]

Since the Tate Modern had opened its doors for the first time in May 2000, the lag in mounting a photography exhibition might not be egregious, but the museum's need to announce its "acknowledgement" of photography's importance seemed to me a bit behind the times.[2] That said, the show did announce something else: that the art world's understanding of photography had evolved to the point that it could retrospectively recognize the efforts of twentieth-century photographers to make pictures as works of art. The artificial separation of "photographs as art" and "artists making photographs" seemed to be put to rest.

Cruel and Tender, which was organized by German curator Thomas Weski with Emma Dexter of the Tate, conveyed this message by including huge chunks of the photography tradition and knitting them seamlessly

Martin Kippenberger, color photograph of the collage *Die Photographie ist auch nicht mehr das was sie mal war* (*Photography isn't anymore what it used to be*), 1986, pasted in the artist's book *Sand in der Vaseline* (*Sand in the Vaseline*), 1986. The original collage reproduced is paper on a photograph by Ursula Böckler taken in Brazil.

together. August Sander's portraits of the twenties and thirties and other examples of German Neue Sachlichkeit photography preceded Bernd and Hilla Becher's industrial typologies and the Bechers' students Andreas Gursky, Thomas Ruff, and Thomas Struth. Walker Evans's Depression-era images were presented as the origin of a similar American vein, from Robert Frank through William Eggleston. Bodies of work from John Szarkowski's 1967 *New Documents* exhibition (Diane Arbus, Lee Friedlander, and Garry Winogrand) and from William Jenkins's 1975 *New Topographics* show (Robert Adams, Lewis Baltz, Bernd and Hilla Becher, Stephen Shore) recapitulated for the Tate's art audience the photography world's own understanding of its aesthetic legacy. At last, at least for the summer of 2003, the divided consciousness that distinguished photography from art was reconciled.

Of course this was not the final cure for the neurosis that causes the inexorable question, "What makes photography art?" In a commentary on the exhibition commissioned by the Tate, critic Carter Ratcliff wrote, "We are living through a protracted epidemic of confusion about the difference between artworks and documents. A border is being blurred."[3] In his sights, the differences between art and document remain irreconcilable, despite the Tate exhibition. I would counter that it has been precisely this tantalizing conundrum that has fueled the responses by and to many artists, starting (arguably) in the sixties with Pop Art, Earth Art, Conceptual Art, Performance Art, and the rest.

Due to *Cruel and Tender*'s theme, the Tate's account of photography's presence in contemporary art omitted any sense of the widespread critique of "the real" that underpins the work of several crucial artists who fully emerged in the nineties. To cite two well-known examples: Sophie Calle and Thomas Demand, like Vik Muniz, employ photography as a fictional foil, pointing out the contingency and subjectivity of its presumed documentary evidence. Calle's career began in the eighties when she hired a private eye to create a surreptitious photographic record of her peregrinations through Paris, starting her on a path that often focuses on the seductive and narrative qualities of surveillance. Demand makes works that begin with photographs, but he re-creates them as three-dimensional sets in his studio and then returns the models to the condition of photographs. Jeff Wall and Gregory Crewdson also produce realistic scenes that are as staged as any Hollywood production.

By virtue of its scope, my story omits a fuller account of these influential artists as well as of many others who made photographs a vital presence in art at the turn of the century. The same is true of the many artists using video during those years, including Matthew Barney, Douglas Gordon, and Steve McQueen. But in a sense all were the beneficiaries of those who in the sixties and seventies seized on photography and video as the tools of a revolution in the very nature of art, and of those who in the eighties helped make camera images and their cultural presence a central subject of art.

Also, I have chosen in my narrative not to concentrate on the marketplace impact of photography within the art world, but it may be worth noting here that since photography auctions began in the early seventies the top prices for photographs have gone from five figures to seven. True, there remains a two-tiered market, one selling photographs understood traditionally and the other selling photographs seen as part of contemporary art—a division still apparent in Chelsea where specialized photography galleries coexist with art galleries that sell photographs for far more money. But prices for all forms of photography have risen with the art-world tide, which has encompassed all mediums.

In the fall of 2011 Andreas Gursky's *Rhein II*, a 6 × 9-foot picture even more blank than the *Ruhr Valley* image I puzzled over in 1990, was hammered down at Christie's in New York for $4.33 million, making it (temporarily, to be sure) the most expensive photograph ever sold. The price surpassed Gursky's previous auction record of $3.35 million, set five years earlier, as well as the $3.89 million paid for a single Cindy Sherman image the previous spring.

These transactions happened at contemporary art sales; photography-only auctions usually involve smaller amounts—although a Man Ray vintage print fetched $3.12 million at a photography auction in Paris in 2017. (Compare this to 1993, when another Man Ray picture, *Glass Tears*, set an auction record for a single photograph at under $200,000.) As for auctions of contemporary art, prices now reach into the eight figures (a Jeff Koons sculpture, made in 1986, sold for $91.1 million in spring 2019) and often surpass the prices paid for Impressionist and Old Master paintings. All this attention to contemporary art has made the intimate art world I experienced in my first years in New York irretrievably obsolete.

Turn-of-the-century worries that photography also would become obsolete in the digital age now seem laughably perverse. The opposite has happened: the world's archive of pictures has grown geometrically since the insertion of cameras into cell phones. The invention of ways to share digital images across the Internet has made photographs and videos integral parts of social communication. This can have benign consequences, as in most social media exchanges, or less salutary ones, as in the uploaded pictures of Iraqis being abused by their American jailers at the Abu Ghraib prison.

The superfluity and superfluidity of images have attracted the attention of a generation of artists who have little or no memory of photography before cell phones and cloud storage. These artists also have no memory of photography as an independent medium trying to be an art while excluded from its discourses. Progress, no doubt, but all the more reason to honor the artists who preceded them and enabled photography to become contemporary art.

Photography's role in instigating the Image World in which we now live is taken for granted by most of today's artists and critics, and in that sense its centrality to the art of the last quarter of the twentieth century was a one-time event. Other roles that photography has come to play—in social media, policing, the news, drone warfare—continue to attract and deserve artistic attention, but without the single focus once encapsulated by that now-unfashionable word, Postmodernism. The same is true of contemporary art, which has become so capacious in terms of aesthetic ambitions over the last twenty-five years as to seem beyond categorization and even critical comprehension.

What today's artists and their audiences may not fully appreciate is the extent to which photography is greatly responsible for the current landscape of contemporary art. Starting with its uses in the revolt against Abstract Expressionism and its documentary roles in Earth, Conceptual, and Performance Art, photography brought tokens of the real world into galleries and museums. So did film and video, its sister, camera-based mediums. Today their presence in any art fair, biennial, or gallery tour may represent only a fraction of all the works on view, but the real world is apparent throughout, in the form of exhibits and artworks that touch on gender identity, class, race, colonialism, geopolitical issues, and relational and community-based projects. Art is no longer seen as a refuge or respite from everyday life, but as a means of coping with it.

In short, one could say that photography's influence has spread far beyond its technical presence or its marketplace share. Contemporary art has become photography, if by that we mean not the medium itself but its function as a messenger of contemporary life.

Notes

INTRODUCTION

1. This omission was not fully corrected until 1986, after H. W. Janson's death, when his son Anthony added a chapter on photography to the book's third edition. Douglas C. McGill, "Janson's Son Revises Classic Art Text," *New York Times*, March 12, 1986, https://www.nytimes.com/1986/03/12/books/janson-s-son-revises-classic-art-text.html.

2. *La Gazette de France*, Paris, Jan. 6, 1839, in Beaumont Newhall, *Photography: Essays and Images; Illustrated Readings in the History of Photography* (New York: Museum of Modern Art, 1980), 17. Newhall mentions that the writer's byline was "H. Gaucheraud." For information about Talbot's process, see Helmut Gernsheim, *The Origins of Photography* (New York: Thames and Hudson, 1969), 77–81.

3. Newhall, *Essays and Images*. Newhall's reference to Eastlake's article in his history of photography is the primary reason it has remained influential among photographers.

4. See, most prominently, Josef Maria Eder, *History of Photography* (New York: Dover, 1978). Eder's *History* was first printed at the turn of the century and revised in 1932; the revised version was translated into English by Edward Epstean in 1945.

5. The 1859 Salon was reviewed by the poet and critic Charles Baudelaire, who famously took issue with its inclusion of photographs. He wrote that the photograph, a work of a machine, was the enemy of art, a work of the imagination. Yet simply by including photography and taking its claims to be art seriously, Baudelaire's review suggests how much the art world of the time was being disrupted by the new medium's presence. See Vicki Goldberg, ed., *Photography in Print: Writings from 1816 to the Present* (New York: Touchstone, 1981), 121–126.

6. A complete list of exhibitions at 291 is in William Innes Homer, *Alfred Stieglitz and the American Avant-Garde* (New York: New York Graphic Society, 1977), 295–298.

7. Edward Steichen and Edward Weston were curators of the American section of *Film und Foto*, which might explain their inclusion. Keith Davis, *An American Century of Photography: From Dry-Plate to Digital* (Kansas City, Mo.: Hallmark Cards; New York: Harry N. Abrams, 1995), 103–104. The exhibition did not travel to the United States, but two allied publications, *Foto-Auge/Photo-Eye* (by Franz Roh and Jan Tschichold) and *Es kommt der neue Fotograf!* (by Werner Gräff), spread its influential message.

8. Suzanne E. Pastor, "Photography and the Bauhaus," *Archive* (Center for Creative Photography, University of Arizona, Tucson), no. 21 (March 1985): 12.

9. Many of the photographs on view took the form of collage, or were merely documents of paintings the museum could not borrow. The checklist is available on the Museum of Modern Art's website, https://www.moma.org/documents/moma_master-checklist_325071.pdf.

10. Irving Sandler, *The Triumph of American Painting: A History of Abstract Expressionism* (New York: Harper and Row, 1976).

11. However, and sadly, I arrived too late to experience Limelight, a precursor to the commercial galleries of the seventies that existed from 1954 to 1961. The brainchild of Helen Gee, it functioned as a coffee house in Greenwich Village but had serious gallery space in back, mounting shows of photographs by Berenice Abbott, Ansel Adams, W. Eugene Smith, and other major names in addition to younger talents such as Rudy Burckhardt, Robert Doisneau, Elliott Erwitt, Louis Faurer, Leon Levinstein, Gordon Parks, and Dan Weiner. Although her gallery had closed, Gee was often at photo openings I would attend at Witkin and other galleries and museums. A shorter-lived gallery that proved influential in retrospect was Roy DeCarava's A Photographer's Gallery, which he ran in his Upper West Side apartment from 1955 to 1957. DeCarava later cofounded and ran the Kamoinge Workshop, which supported (and still supports) exhibitions and publications of black photographers, most of whom lived in Harlem.

12. Irving Sandler, *Art of the Postmodern Era: From the Late 1960s to the Early 1990s* (Boulder, Colo.: Westview Press, 1998).

CHAPTER 1
PRELUDE, 1962

1. Thomas Crow, "Social Register," *Artforum* 47, no. 1 (September 2008): 426–431, https://www.artforum.com/print/200807/thomas-crow-42044.

2. See "Chronology," *Robert Rauschenberg* (Washington, D.C.: National Collection of Fine Arts, Smithsonian Institution, 1976), 31.

3. Douglas Crimp, "On the Museum's Ruins," *October* 13 (summer 1980): 56.

4. Walter Benjamin, "The Work of Art in the Age of Mechanical Reproduction," in *Illuminations*, ed. Hannah Arendt (New York: Shocken, 1969).

5. Sylvia Wolf, "Nostalgia and New Editions: A Conversation with Ed Ruscha," *Ed Ruscha and Photography* (New York: Whitney Museum of American Art; Göttingen, Germany: Steidl, 2004), 263. Ruscha's choice of twenty-six may also have had something to do with the number of letters in the alphabet.

6. The phrase is the title of an article by John Szarkowski in the *New York Times Magazine*, April 13, 1975.

7. Nathan Lyons gives his own account of the conference, called the Invitational Teaching Conference, in a 1997 interview with Maria Antonella Pelizzari. "Nathan Lyons: An Interview," in *Nathan Lyons: Selected Essays, Lectures, and Interviews*, ed. Jessica S. McDonald (Austin: University of Texas Press, 2012), 251–253.

8. This was typical of the time. Ted

Hartwell became the first curator of photography of the Minneapolis Institute of Art in 1972 by virtue of having worked for ten years as the museum's photographer of artwork. Van Deren Coke, who taught photography at the University of New Mexico in the sixties and became curator of photography at the San Francisco Museum of Modern Art in 1979, was a photographer first, having studied at the Clarence H. White School of Photography in New York. Today's photography curators are more likely to have credentials as PhDs in art history.

CHAPTER 2
ARRIVAL

1. The 112 Greene Street space was owned and opened by the sculptor Jeffrey Lew and presented some excellent large-scale sculptures of a Postminimalist sort, by Richard Nonas and Jene Highstein, among others. Later 112 Greene Street morphed into White Columns, a not-for-profit alternative space, which still exists at a different address.

2. From a chronology, compiled by Tina Kukielski, in *Gordon Matta-Clark: You Are the Measure*, ed. Elizabeth Sussman (New York: Whitney Museum of American Art; New Haven, Conn.: Yale University Press, 2007), 209.

3. From a letter sent by the artist to Judith Russi Kirshner, curator, quoted in Briony Fer, "Gordon Matta-Clark's Color Cibachromes," in Sussman, *Gordon Matta-Clark*, 138. Not everyone was as enthusiastic about the photographs as Gordon was; his fellow artist Lawrence Weiner later said of Gordon, "He liked photography a lot. I think it was one of his weaknesses," echoing a common Conceptualist complaint about anything even vaguely decorative. Interview with Joan Simon, in *Gordon Matta-Clark: A Retrospective*, by Mary Jane Jacob (Chicago: Museum of Contemporary Art Chicago, 1985), 141.

CHAPTER 3
DOWN TO EARTH

1. The Whitney Museum of American Art's website provides images and a cogent summary of the work: http://collection.whitney.org/object/29487.

2. Ada Louise Huxtable, "'Megalopolis' Show: Artists and the Urban Scene," *New York Times*, Oct. 31, 1972, https://www.nytimes.com/1972/10/31/archives/megalopolis-show-artists-and-the-urban-scene-hans-haackes-exhibit.html.

3. Based on what I've found out since, I believe the construction outside the museum was probably a piece by David Medalla, which was executed without his presence, or else Michael Heizer's entry-in-progress, which was never finished and thus left out of the exhibition catalog.

4. A digital record of the catalog of the *Earth Art* exhibition is available on the website of Cornell University's current art museum, the Herbert F. Johnson Museum of Art, at http://museum.cornell.edu/earth-art-1969.

5. Virginia Dwan mounted *Earthworks*, which may count as the first show of Earth Art, at her gallery in New York in October 1968, several months before Willoughby Sharp's show at Cornell. Dwan was a supporter of Walter De Maria, Michael Heizer, and Robert Smithson, and financially backed their most ambitious work, including *Double Negative* and *Spiral Jetty*. See Dana Micucci, "Uncommon Ground," *Art and Antiques* 35, no. 3 (April 2012): 76, http://www.artandantiquesmag.com/2012/04/land-art-earthworks-postwar-american-art/.

6. Willoughby Sharp, "Foreword," *Earth Art* (Ithaca, N.Y.: Andrew Dickson White Museum of Art, Cornell University, 1970), np, https://babel.hathitrust.org/cgi/pt?id=coo.31924020514380&view=2up&seq=22&size=125.

7. An innovative 2017 show at the Grey Art Gallery, *Inventing Downtown: Artist-Run Galleries in New York City 1952–1965*, organized by Melissa Rachleff, surveyed many of these early spaces. See Melissa Rachleff, *Inventing Downtown* (New York: Grey Art Gallery, New York University; Munich: DelMonico Books/Prestel, 2017).

8. See Michael Kimmelman, "Sol LeWitt, Postwar Artistic Innovator and Master of Conceptualism, Dies at 78," *New York Times*, April 9, 2007, https://www.nytimes.com/2007/04/09/arts/design/09lewitt.html.

9. For Smithson's early take on the site/non-site distinction, see "A Provisional Theory of Non-Sites," 1968, in *Robert Smithson: The Collected Writings*, ed. Jack Flam, 2nd ed. (Berkeley: University of California Press, 1996), https://holtsmithsonfoundation.org/provisional-theory-nonsites.

10. "The Monuments of Passaic" was published as an article, with Smithson's text, in the December 1967 issue of *Artforum*. For a complete survey of Smithson's uses of photography, see Robert A. Sobieszek, *Robert Smithson: Photo Works* (Los Angeles: Los Angeles County Museum of Art; Albuquerque: University of New Mexico Press, 1993).

11. *Spiral Jetty* is archived by Electronic Arts Intermix and described in detail on its website, https://www.eai.org/titles/spiral-jetty.

CHAPTER 4
GETTING THE CONCEPT

1. For the full story of *Fountain* and the significance of Stieglitz's photograph, see Thierry de Duve's series of articles about Duchamp and contemporary art published in *Artforum* in 2013–14, starting with "Pardon My French" in October 2013 (https://www.artforum.com/inprint/issue=201308&id=43117). The specifics of the photographic evidence and the fate of the original *Fountain* are discussed in the second installment, "Don't Shoot the Messenger," in November 2013 (https://www.artforum.com/inprint/issue=201309&id=43534).

2. Functionally, Stieglitz's picture of Duchamp's *Fountain* is a precursor of the French artist Yves Klein's legendary *Leap into the Void*, a photograph that was taken in 1960 by Harry Shunk and János Kandor that seems to show Klein diving off the roof of a two-story building in a Paris suburb. In fact, the picture is a composite of two negatives, in one of which Klein leaps into a tarpaulin held by friends. Klein had the picture made so that he could reproduce it in a fake Sunday newspaper he had printed and then distributed on Parisian newsstands. Like Duchamp, Klein was manufacturing a news event that announced a new way of thinking about art—in Klein's case, one in which the artist is a key performer.

3. De Duve, "Pardon My French."

4. Sol LeWitt, "Paragraphs on Conceptual Art," *Artforum* 5, no. 10 (summer 1967): 79–83.

5. Kosuth used the same strategy in a companion piece made the same year,

Clock (One and Five), English/Latin Version, now in the collection of the Tate, https://www.tate.org.uk/art/artworks/kosuth-clock-one-and-five-english-latin-version-t01909.

6. Huebler's piece now is owned by the Museum of Modern Art and viewable online at https://www.moma.org/collection/works/147060?locale=en.

7. Jeff Wall, "'Marks of Indifference': Aspects of Photography in, or as, Conceptual Art," in *Jeff Wall: Selected Essays and Interviews* (New York: Museum of Modern Art, 2007), 157.

8. See Joshua Shannon, "Uninteresting Pictures: Photography and Fact at the End of the 1960s," in *Light Years: Conceptual Art and the Photograph, 1964–1977*, ed. Matthew S. Witkovsky (Chicago: Art Institute of Chicago; New Haven, Conn.: Yale University Press, 2011), 90–91.

9. The idea of "dematerialization" was first broached by Lucy Lippard and John Chandler in a jointly written article, "The Dematerialization of Art," in *Art International*, February 1968. It reappears in Lippard's book *Six Years: The Dematerialization of the Art Object from 1966 to 1972* (Berkeley: University of California Press, 1973), a valuable compilation of artists' and critics' writings and a timeline of activities during the period.

10. See "Biography," Sol LeWitt Prints Catalogue Raisonné, https://www.sollewittprints.org/biography. *Human and Animal Locomotion* became much more popular with artists and photographers after Dover Publications published two abridged editions, *The Human Figure in Motion* and *Animals in Motion*, in 1955 and 1957, respectively. One of these may have been the book that LeWitt discovered in the apartment.

11. The most comprehensive account of Muybridge's career can be found in Philip Brookman, *Helios: Eadweard Muybridge in a Time of Change* (Göttingen, Germany: Steidl; Washington, D.C.: Corcoran Gallery of Art, 2010); see in particular Brookman's essay that addresses Muybridge's motion studies, 77–88. My introduction to the book broaches the topic of Muybridge's influence on LeWitt and others, notably Mel Bochner and Hollis Frampton. Bochner wrote about Muybridge's influence on his art for *Artforum* in 1967, and Frampton wrote about Muybridge's career, again in *Artforum*, in 1973.

12. "Biography," Sol LeWitt Prints Catalogue Raisonné.

13. *Muybridge I* is reproduced and discussed in Witkovsky, *Light Years*. It also was a center of controversy when it appeared in 1991 at the National Museum of American Art, Washington, D.C., as part of a traveling show, *Motion and Document—Sequence and Time: Eadweard Muybridge and Contemporary American Photography*. The museum's director, Elizabeth Broun, ordered that the piece be omitted from the exhibition on the basis that it was "degrading to women" but quickly relented after the curators cried censorship and other artists in the show threatened to withdraw their work. See Barbara Gamarekian, "Yielding on Nude in a Box, Museum Returns It to Show," *New York Times*, July 16, 1991, http://www.nytimes.com/1991/07/16/arts/museum-restores-a-nude-to-show.html.

14. "LeWitt was also interested in Russian Constructivism, with its engineering aesthetic and the idea of making utilitarian art in an industrialized age. However, the work that influenced him the most was Eadweard Muybridge's serial photography. . . . LeWitt's three dimensional structural works from the mid to late 1960s—such as *Serial Project, Three Part Variations on Three Different Cubes*, and hundreds of sculptures made of open white cubes—grew out of this interest in the serial." See "Biography," Sol LeWitt Prints Catalogue Raisonné.

15. For the quote and an image of the work, see *Serial Project, 1 (ABCD)* on the Museum of Modern Art's MoMALearning website, https://www.moma.org/learn/moma_learning/sol-lewitt-serial-project-i-abcd-1966.

16. Presumably these were plates from the original editions of the work, since the republication of *Locomotion* in full-plate format did not happen until 1979. The plates were offered for sale at a bookstore on Lexington Avenue called the Weyhe Gallery, which specialized in art prints. LeWitt, in a phone call a year before his death, told me that he would go by occasionally to purchase individual plates for himself or for friends.

17. Dan Graham, "Muybridge Moments: From Here to There?," *Arts Magazine* 41, no. 4 (February 1967): 23–24, 65.

18. Dan Graham, "Homes for America: Early 20th-Century Possessable House to the Quasi-Discrete Cell of '66," *Arts Magazine* 41, no. 3 (December 1966–January 1967): 22. This was the issue immediately before Graham's piece on Muybridge was published.

19. The entire article is three pages long, with illustrations of six photographs of "pithead gears," a single water tower, and a grid of nine water towers. The full-page single photograph is an anomaly for the time, although it prefigures how the Bechers would later show the work more flexibly. Carl Andre, "A Note on Bernhard and Hilla Becher," *Artforum* 11, no. 4 (December 1972): 59–61, https://www.artforum.com/print/197210/a-note-on-bernhard-and-hilla-becher-36170.

20. Joe Masheck, "Unconscious Formalism: A Response to Andre's Note on the Bechers," *Artforum* 11, no. 7 (March 1973): 24–25, https://www.artforum.com/print/197303/unconscious-formalism-a-response-to-andre-s-note-on-the-bechers-37441.

21. It is important to note that Ileana Sonnabend was showing photographs by many of these artists, although not the Bechers, in Europe before 1972. The Galerie Ileana Sonnabend opened in Paris at the end of 1962, with a show of paintings by Jasper Johns; Sonnabend Gallery, New York, opened in September 1971 with a performance by Gilbert and George as *Singing Sculpture*. See Charles Stainback, "No Ideas Have Entered This Introduction," in *From Pop to Now: Selections from the Sonnabend Collection*, ed. Margaret Sundell (Saratoga Springs, N.Y.: Tang Teaching Museum and Art Gallery at Skidmore College, 2002), 7–14.

22. Quoted in Coosje van Bruggen, *John Baldessari* (Los Angeles: Museum of Contemporary Art; New York: Rizzoli, 1990), 29.

23. Ibid., 214.

CHAPTER 5
PERFORMERS, BODIES, CAMERAS

1. On Burden's photo book, see Sydney Stutterheim, "Deluxe Photo Book," *Gagosian Quarterly*, May 10, 2018, https://gagosian.com/quarterly/2018/05/10/deluxe-photo-book-7173. For evidence

of how Burden's reputation arrived in New York, see Peter Plagens, "Art in California: He Got Shot—For His Art," *New York Times*, Sept. 2, 1973, https://www.nytimes.com/1973/09/02/archives/he-got-shotfor-his-art-art-in-california-he-got-shotfor-his-art.html.

2. True, there were women Earth artists even in the heyday of Earth Art—Nancy Holt (who was married to Robert Smithson and with whom she sometimes collaborated), Alice Aycock, Mary Miss—but their reputations were overshadowed by the men. That changed somewhat in the eighties. See Sarah Gottesman, "Ten Female Land Artists You Should Know," Artsy, July 18, 2017, https://www.artsy.net/article/artsy-editorial-10-female-land-artists. Ana Mendieta, whose work is discussed in this chapter in terms of Performance Art, is also considered a Land artist of a slightly later vintage. As for Conceptual Art, one of the only women artists to achieve contemporaneous recognition was Hanne Darboven, a German artist who lived in New York in the midsixties.

3. Pamela M. Lee, *Chronophobia: On Time in the Art of the 1960s* (Cambridge, Mass.: MIT Press, 2004), 202.

4. *Meat Joy* premiered in May in Paris and was presented in London in June, before making its way to the Judson Memorial Church in November. "Performance Chronology," http://www.caroleeschneemann.com/bio.html.

5. Thirteen of Anthony McCall's photographs of *Interior Scroll* were issued in a limited-edition portfolio in 2009, indicating that by the twenty-first century the art world had come to recognize the value of performance photography. They were sold as the work of the artist, Carolee Schneemann, not the photographer. See https://www.artbasel.com/catalog/artwork/53501/Carolee-Schneemann-Interior-Scroll. In the same manner, the photographs in Edward Ruscha's *Twentysix Gasoline Stations*, the pioneering artist's book of 1963, were reprinted and sold as a limited-edition portfolio in 1989.

6. A retrospective of Piper's work, *Adrian Piper: A Synthesis of Intuitions 1965–2016*, organized by the Museum of Modern Art, New York, and the Hammer Museum, Los Angeles, appeared at MoMA in 2018 and made clear the artist's long reliance on photographs and video. *Catalysis IV* was one of a series of public actions Piper undertook from 1970 to 1973, all titled *Catalysis*.

7. Press release, "Projects: 100 Boots by Eleanor Antin," Museum of Modern Art, May 30, 1973, https://www.moma.org/documents/moma_press-release_326846.pdf.

8. A 2009 show at the Susan Inglett Gallery in Chelsea focused on the entire incident. For details, see Roberta Smith, "Art or Ad or What?: It Caused a Lot of Fuss," *New York Times*, July 24, 2009, http://www.nytimes.com/2009/07/25/arts/design/25benglis.html.

9. There is the tantalizing possibility that Gordon Matta-Clark's and Ana Mendieta's paths may have crossed at 112 Greene Street, where Mendieta had a show while she was still living in Iowa. Matta-Clark could have seen her installation *Ñáñigo Burial* and films that were screened there in the winter of 1976, although by then he was often out of town working on his own projects; she also had a piece in a group show at 112 Greene Street the year before. I have not been able to determine if she visited New York while the show was up.

10. Judith Wilson, "Ana Mendieta Plants Her Garden," *Village Voice*, Aug. 13, 1980, 71. Quoted in Stephanie Rosenthal, "Ana Mendieta: Traces," *Ana Mendieta: Traces*, by Julia Bryan-Wilson, Adrian Heathfield, and Stephanie Rosenthal (London: Hayward Publishing, 2013), 16.

11. Ana Mendieta, introduction to the *Dialectics of Isolation: An Exhibition of Third World Women Artists of the United States* catalog (New York: A.I.R. Gallery, 1980), reproduced in Bryan-Wilson, Heathfield, and Rosenthal, *Ana Mendieta: Traces*, 205.

12. Quoted by Julia Bryan-Wilson, "Against the Body: Interpreting Ana Mendieta," in Bryan-Wilson, Heathfield, and Rosenthal, *Ana Mendieta: Traces*, 32.

CHAPTER 6
BOOM YEARS

1. One of the last attempts I remember to come up with something aesthetically concrete enough to qualify as an "ism" was Ronny H. Cohen's usage of *Energism* in a September 1980 *Artforum* article titled "Energism: An Attitude" (https://www.artforum.com/print/198007/energism-an-attitude-37720). The art dealer Michael Findlay noted in his letter in response, "It is no mean feat to coin such a pronounceable epithet so lacking in definition that it cannot be misapplied."

2. *Photography Year: 1973 Edition* (New York: Time Life Books, 1972), 146.

3. Ibid., 150. The birth of a modern market for photographs is often attributed to an earlier rise in the market for prints by contemporary artists, which by the seventies had soared in price to the extent they were no longer affordable for beginning collectors. According to this analysis, photographs became the "starter kit" for a new generation of entry-level art collectors—although in my experience print collectors and photography collectors are two different breeds.

4. *Life* was brought back to life in 1978 as a monthly and persevered in that form until 2000; it later became a newspaper supplement that was killed, one hopes for good, in 2007. After *Life* was shut down as a weekly news magazine, Time-Life embarked on a series of books and exhibitions highlighting its magazine's legacy of photographs and photographers, starting with *The Best of Life* (1973). *Great Photographic Essays from Life* (1978) contains what in many respects is the essence of the magazine's contributions to the art of photography.

5. Noted in Keith Davis, *An American Century of Photography: From Dry-Plate to Digital* (Kansas City, Mo.: Hallmark Cards; New York: Harry N. Abrams, 1995), 294. Outside of New York a number of influential gallerists were showing photography as well: Harry Lunn Jr. in Washington, D.C.; Carl Siembab in Boston; Helen Johnston in San Francisco; G. Ray Hawkins in Los Angeles; and Tom Halsted in Birmingham, Michigan.

6. Ibid.

7. A recent example: Peter Moore's pictures were a mainstay of the visual material assembled for the Museum of Modern Art's exhibition about the Judson Dance Theater in the fall of 2018. His work was shown at Paula Cooper Gallery in Chelsea at the same time.

8. The first Witkin Gallery, from March 1969 to July 1971, was at 237 East 60th

Street; its second address, from September 1971 to January 1976, was three doors away, at 243 East 60th Street. Witkin then moved to 41 East 57th Street, a more spacious and professional-looking space in the Fuller Building, which housed several art galleries, such as Zabriskie—a sign of success for the gallery as well as an indication of the burgeoning of the collecting market for photographs. The first two shows on 57th Street, in the winter of 1976, were devoted to photogravure plates from Stieglitz's early twentieth-century journal *Camera Work*. Information from "Complete List of Shows at the Witkin Gallery, March 1969–March 1979," a photocopied handout provided by the gallery at the time of its tenth anniversary. Lee Witkin died in 1984; the gallery, under the leadership of Evelyne Daitz, persevered, eventually closing in 1999.

9. For an unalloyed negative review of Stephen Shore's first Light Gallery show, see A. D. Coleman, "American Yawn, Irish Wail," *Village Voice*, Oct. 5, 1972, http://stephenshore.net/press/VillageVoice_Oct_72.pdf.

10. Harold Jones's professor Van Deren Coke was director of what was then called the International Museum of Photography at George Eastman House (now the George Eastman Museum) at the time Jones worked there. Coke was on leave from his job at the University of New Mexico—an indication of how small the photography world was then.

11. Marvin Heiferman supplemented my memory of who worked at Light in the early years. Interview with Marvin Heiferman, October 24, 2018, New York, New York.

12. Conversation with Harold Jones, October 18, 2013, Tucson, Arizona.

13. Harry Callahan, it is worth noting, had a one-person show at Witkin in the fall of 1970, before Light Gallery opened. See "Complete List of Shows at the Witkin Gallery." Callahan also had received major exposure in New York in 1964 when his work was featured in the second show of the Hallmark Gallery at 720 Fifth Ave. The Hallmark Gallery, which regularly showed photography until its closing in 1973, was one of the first corporate art galleries in New York. See Keith Davis, *The Big Picture: The Hallmark Photographic Collection at the Nelson-Atkins Museum of Art* (Kansas City, Mo.: Nelson-Atkins Museum of Art, 2018), 14–18.

14. According to the Archives of American Art website, 420 West Broadway was originally a "share space" leased by André Emmerich, Leo Castelli, Ileana Sonnabend, and the legendary Earth Art dealer Virginia Dwan; it opened as a gallery building in 1971. "A Finding Aid to the André Emmerich Gallery Records and André Emmerich Papers, 1929–2009," Archives of American Art, Smithsonian Institution, http://sova.si.edu/record/AAA.andremmg. Ealan Wingate confirmed this in our interview of June 20, 2018, but added that Dwan was replaced by John Weber prior to the opening.

15. Bruce Nauman's first show at Castelli happened at the uptown (4 East 77th Street) gallery in 1968; the next year he had another one-person show featuring his holograms and videotapes. See "Castelli, Exhibitions, 4 East 77 (1957–1976)," https://www.castelligallery.com/exhibitions/past/4-east-77-1957-1976.

16. See "Castelli, Exhibitions, 420 West Broadway (1971–1999)," https://www.castelligallery.com/exhibitions/past/420-west-broadway-1971-1999.

17. Ealan Wingate has suggested that one of the contributions of Conceptual artists was to free up the medium of photography to be something new; he also noted that at the gallery "it was rare to have people interested in the work." Conversation with Ealan Wingate, June 20, 2018, Washington, D.C.

18. See Charles Stainback's brief history of the gallery in "No Ideas Have Entered This Introduction," in *From Pop to Now: Selections from the Sonnabend Collection*, ed. Margaret Sundell (Saratoga Springs, N.Y.: Tang Teaching Museum and Art Gallery at Skidmore College, 2002), 7–14.

19. Years later a group of New York art directors asked me to write a book about Alexey Brodovitch as part of a new series called *Masters of American Design*, which was edited by my friend Sarah Bodine. The result was *Alexey Brodovitch*, published in 1989 by Harry N. Abrams. László Moholy-Nagy's book, titled *Malerei, Fotografie, Film* when it appeared in German in 1925, was volume 8 in the *Bauhausbücher* series. The paperback edition I saw (and bought) was an English translation published by MIT Press in 1973.

20. Thomas Barrow was not alone in his interest in this new copying technology. His use of the Verifax machine was preceded by that of Wallace Berman, a California artist admired for his wildly experimental work of the sixties, and simultaneous with that of Robert Fichter, who, like Barrow, was in Rochester in the last years of the decade. See Kathleen McCarthy Gauss and Andy Grundberg, *Photography and Art: Interactions Since 1946* (New York: Abbeville Press, 1986), 117.

CHAPTER 7
CROSSING OVER

1. Eastman House's official name in the seventies, since dropped due to its unwieldy nature, was the International Museum of Photography at George Eastman House; today it is simply the George Eastman Museum.

2. William Jenkins, *The Extended Document: An Investigation of Information and Evidence in Photographs* (Rochester, N.Y.: International Museum of Photography at George Eastman House, 1975), 1–2.

3. Cumming's "crossover" was not without problems for some, however. A 1974 lead article in the *New York Times*'s Arts and Leisure section by Roy Bongartz, headlined "Question: How Do You Buy a Work of Art Like This?," highlighted how photographs were not always meant to be seen or heard in contemporary art. Bongartz told the story of a gallerist (Susan Gibson, John Gibson's wife) refusing to allow Cumming's work to be shown in a group show with a section devoted to photography: "Mrs. Gibson insisted Cumming's work go into the fine arts section because he was not showing photographs, but conceptual art. The reply was, well, we hope this is what photography will become. 'Too late,' said Mrs. Gibson. 'This is what fine art has become.' It was a standoff—no show for Cumming." *New York Times*, August 11, 1974, https://www.nytimes.com/1974/08/11/archives/question-how-do-you-buy-a-work-of-art-like-this-buying-conceptual-a.html.

4. Britt Salvesen, "New Topographics," in *New Topographics*, by Britt Salvesen and Alison Nordström (Tucson, Ariz.: Center

for Creative Photography; Göttingen, Germany: Steidl, 2009), 12. "Looking back from the perspective of the twenty-first century, we can see *New Topographics* as a bridge between the still-insular fine-art photography world and the expanding, post-conceptual field of contemporary art," she adds.

5. In William Jenkins, "Introduction," in *New Topographics: Photographs of a Man-Altered Landscape* (Rochester, N.Y.: International Museum of Photography at George Eastman House, 1975), 5. About 2,500 copies were printed and are now considered rare; a more readily available version can be found within the 2009 catalog *New Topographics*, noted above, which accompanied a traveling exhibition that reconstituted the original show.

6. This was not the first time the Bechers' photographs were seen at the Eastman House. Museum records indicate that they were shown in 1972 in a single-artist show organized by Robert Sobieszek, who was the museum's curator of nineteenth-century photography.

7. David L. Shirey, "Prints and Photographs on View at Metropolitan," *New York Times*, Feb. 24, 1971, http://stephenshore.net/press/NYT_Feb_71.pdf. Also, Gene Thornton, "Is It Necessary to Ask What They Mean?," *New York Times*, March 7, 1971, stephenshore.net/press/NYT_Mar_71.pdf.

8. Light Gallery's early exhibitions are listed in *The Light Gallery Catalogue of Contemporary Photographs*, published by the gallery in 1976 when Victor Schrager was director, and also in *Light*, a catalog in celebration of the gallery's tenth anniversary in 1981, when the director was Charles Traub.

9. The term *paradigm shift* has been used by Britt Salvesen, for one: "When, how, and why did *New Topographics*—not some other exhibition, group, or approach—come to be seen as marking a turning point or even a paradigm shift for photography?," she asks in her essay "New Topographics," 55.

10. Salvesen, "New Topographics," 54. Salvesen's essay reveals much about the origins and intentions of the exhibition and is highly recommended.

11. Salvesen, "New Topographics," 49.

12. Interview with Janet Borden, February 13, 2018, New York, New York.

13. Interview with Roger Bruce, May 9, 2018, Rochester, New York.

14. Interview with Charles Hagen, April 21, 2018, Sperryville, Virginia.

15. See Walter Hopps, "The Bricoleur," in *William Christenberry*, foreword by Elizabeth Broun, essays by Walter Hopps, Andy Grundberg, and Howard N. Fox (New York: Aperture; Washington, D.C.: Smithsonian American Art Museum, 2006), 16–17.

16. Judging from the press release, the show, which opened in May, seems to have been untitled, or perhaps called "Color Photographs by William Eggleston." *William Eggleston's Guide* refers only to the book. See press release, "Color Photographs by William Eggleston," Museum of Modern Art, May 25, 1976, https://www.moma.org/momaorg/shared/pdfs/docs/press_archives/5391/releases/MOMA_1976_0051_40.pdf.

17. Hilton Kramer, "Art: Focus on Photo Shows," *New York Times*, May 28, 1976, https://www.nytimes.com/1976/05/28/archives/art-focus-on-photo-shows.html.

18. Ibid.

19. In addition to curating the Ernst Haas show, John Szarkowski organized a show of Helen Levitt's color slides in 1974, two years before the William Eggleston exhibition. His untitled Eggleston essay seems to reject Haas's approach out of hand: "The second category of failure in color photography comprises photographs of beautiful colors in pleasing relationships. . . . Such photographs can be recognized by their resemblance to reproductions of Synthetic Cubist or Abstract Expressionist paintings." (*William Eggleston's Guide*, 9). Untitled press release for "Ernst Haas: Color Photography," Museum of Modern Art, August 21, 1962, https://www.moma.org/momaorg/shared/pdfs/docs/press_archives/3043/releases/MOMA_1962_0102_99.pdf, and press release, "Color Photographs by Helen Levitt," Museum of Modern Art, September 26, 1974, https://www.moma.org/documents/moma_press-release_326909.pdf.

20. A selection of the *Cape Light* pictures was exhibited at the end of 1977 at Witkin, which represented Joel Meyerowitz.

21. For a lucid and critical account of Polaroid's adventures in the land of art, see Peter Buse, *The Camera Does the Rest: How Polaroid Changed Photography* (Chicago: University of Chicago Press, 2016).

22. Sally Eauclaire, *The New Color Photography* (New York: Abbeville Press, 1981).

23. The article got its title, "100 Years of Color," because of the pioneering efforts of Louis Ducos du Hauron, a Frenchman who developed a three-color process in the 1860s and used it to take a photograph, dated 1877, of the town of Agen. The photograph is in the collection of George Eastman House, where I went once again to do research for the article. I also found that the museum had an extensive collection of mid-twentieth-century color work by Nickolas Muray, made using a color carbro process not far removed from Ducos du Hauron's. Kodachrome, the first "integral" color film and grandfather of all modern color emulsions, was introduced by Eastman Kodak in the late 1930s and early 1940s. Mary O'Grady also researched "100 Years of Color," and was credited as the article's third author.

24. For a fuller account of Christenberry's photographs and their relation to his other art, see my essay "Orders of Memory: Photography in the Art of William Christenberry," in *William Christenberry*, 178–187.

25. Jeff Perrone, "Jan Groover: Degrees of Transparency," *Artforum* 17, no. 5 (January 1979): 42–43, https://www.artforum.com/print/197901/jan-groover-degrees-of-transparency-35903.

CHAPTER 8
VIDEO, THE OTHER NEWCOMER

1. Gene Thornton had once shared photo critic duties with another writer, A. D. Coleman, who wrote for the *Times* regularly from 1970 to 1974. Coleman was also a reviewer for the *Village Voice* and *Popular Photography* during these years. A. D. Coleman CV, The Nearby Café, http://nearbycafe.com/artandphoto/photocritic/wp-content/uploads/2010/07/ADColeman-CV-20104.pdf.

2. The establishment of the Kitchen followed on the heels of Anthology Film Archives, a showplace and repository for independent films, many of them

experimental, founded in 1970. Anthology's primary founder was Jonas Mekas, a seminal downtown figure for decades until his death in 2019.

3. See, for example, the description of the work on the Museo Nacional Centro de Arte Reina Sofia website, http://www.museoreinasofia.es/en/collection/artwork/three-transitions.

4. Kathy O'Dell, "Performance, Video, and Trouble in the Home," in *Illuminating Video: An Essential Guide to Video Art*, ed. Doug Hall and Sally Jo Fifer (New York: Aperture, 1990), 147.

5. Ibid., 142. Kathy O'Dell notes that Joan Jonas thereafter resisted showing her video works in commercial galleries, preferring "rough" loft spaces that reflected video's marginal status in the art world of the time.

6. Castelli-Sonnabend Videotapes and Films, which offered both sales and rentals of artists' works, officially existed from 1974 to 1985, although the galleries continued distribution into the nineties. Its offerings were first advertised in the May/June 1974 issue of *Avalanche*, the editor of which, Willoughby Sharp, had made video interviews with several of the galleries' artists. Joyce Nereaux and Nina Sundell first ran the enterprise. Currently the Whitney Museum of American Art is working to reconstitute all the video offerings included in the project's catalog and add them to the museum's permanent collection.

7. The video camera and recording equipment Bruce Nauman used were on loan from Leo Castelli, his dealer, who later let Richard Serra and other of his artists use it as well. Constance M. Lewallen, *A Rose Has No Teeth: Bruce Nauman in the 1960s* (Berkeley: University of California Press, 2007), 88.

8. Elizabeth Baker and Joe Raffaele, "The Way-Out West: Interviews with Four San Francisco Artists," *Artnews* 66, no. 4 (summer 1967), quoted in Lewallen, *A Rose Has No Teeth*, 82.

9. Lewallen, *A Rose Has No Teeth*, 112, note 68.

10. If I were to pick my favorite Nauman video, using sheer perversity as a ranking tool, it would have to be *Clown Torture*, done in color in 1987, an installation which consists of multiple monitors, two video projections, and sound speakers in a single darkened room. On the screens a clown in a striped jumpsuit sits on the floor and screams and yells hysterically and loudly as if someone (the video maker? the audience?) were inflicting great physical or emotional pain. Critic Christopher Knight has written in the *Los Angeles Times*, "*Clown Torture* is a poignant elaboration on the expressive possibilities of making buffoonish faces at a camera. Its devastating depiction of a garishly painted man as an angry, frustrated public fool chronicles the artist as emblematic lost-self for contemporary society." Knight, "Working Well with Whatever Works: Bruce Nauman's Rich Retrospective Shows an Artist Comfortable in Any Medium," July 19, 1994, https://www.latimes.com/archives/la-xpm-1994-07-19-ca-17274-story.html. Those with an acquired clown-phobia will find their fears well justified, needless to say.

11. Today William Wegman's and John Baldessari's videos are cataloged and distributed by the Video Data Bank of the School of the Art Institute of Chicago; https://www.vdb.org/. Wegman donated a collection of his videotapes to the Metropolitan Museum of Art in 2018.

12. Both *Media Burn* and *The Eternal Frame* are archived by Electronic Arts Intermix and described in detail on its website: https://www.eai.org/titles/media-burn and https://www.eai.org/titles/the-eternal-frame. The tapes themselves are available on DVDs from EAI or the Video Data Bank of the School of the Art Institute of Chicago.

13. Marita Sturken, "The Whitney Museum and the Shaping of Video Art: An Interview with John Hanhardt," *Afterimage* 10, no. 10 (May 1983): 4–8. Available online at http://www.experimentaltvcenter.org/whitney-museum-and-shaping-video-art-interview-john-hanhardt.

14. Barbara London, "Video: A Brief History and Selected Chronology," in *Transmission: Theory and Practice for a New Television Aesthetics*, ed. Peter D'Agostino (New York: Tanam Press, 1985), 308.

15. Ibid., 309–312.

16. John Russell, "Why the Latest Whitney Biennial Is More Satisfying," *New York Times*, March 25, 1983, https://www.nytimes.com/1983/03/25/arts/why-the-latest-whitney-biennial-is-more-satisfying.html.

CHAPTER 9
THEORY

1. A. D. Coleman, "Because It Feels So Good When I Stop," *Camera 35*, October 1975, reprinted in *Light Readings: A Photography Critic's Writings 1968–1978* (New York: Oxford University Press, 1979), 213.

2. Ibid., 208.

3. Ibid., 204.

4. Photography "is the one art that has managed to carry out the grandiose, century-old threats of a Surrealist takeover of the modern sensibility," Sontag wrote in the section titled "Melancholy Objects," adding "the mainstream of photographic activity has shown that a Surrealist manipulation or theatricalization of the real is unnecessary, if not actually redundant. Surrealism lies at the heart of the photographic enterprise: in the very creation of a duplicate world, of a reality in the second degree, narrower but more dramatic than the one perceived by natural vision." Susan Sontag, *On Photography* (New York: Farrar, Straus and Giroux, 1977), 51, 52. These ideas have a familiar ring: they echo forward to the approach to photography developed a few years later by Postmodernist artists and their critical supporters, and backward to Frankfurt School and poststructuralist thinking about images—see Walter Benjamin, Roland Barthes, Jean Baudrillard, Jean-François Leotard, et al., most of whose work existed at the time only in French.

5. Sontag, *On Photography*, 179.

6. Walter Benjamin, *Illuminations*, trans. Hannah Arendt (New York: Harcourt, Brace and World, 1968), 221.

7. Ibid., 223–226.

8. Actually, Bruce Wolmer might have said "semiology," which is the study of semiotics, but my memory has been fuzzed by a contretemps I got into later with an academic who objected when I wrote something in the *Times* about "semiology" when I should have used *semiotics*. Mea culpa.

9. Jacques Derrida's fascination with "play" in writing is in part responsible

for making his essays notoriously laborious to read. Terry Eagleton's book *Literary Theory* (Minneapolis: University of Minnesota Press, 1983) does a good job of explaining Derrida and poststructuralism in general and helped smooth my plunge into theory. Eagleton's take on deconstruction is especially useful: "Deconstruction . . . had grasped the point that the binary oppositions with which classical structuralism tends to work represent a way of seeing typical of ideologies. . . . Deconstruction tried to show how such oppositions, in order to hold themselves in place, are sometimes betrayed into inverting or collapsing themselves, or need to banish to the text's margins certain niggling details which can be made to return and plague them. . . . The tactic of deconstructive criticism, that is to say, is to show how texts come to embarrass their own ruling systems of logic." (133).

10. I say "once-obscure" because in 1997 *Semiotext(e)* published Chris Kraus's *I Love Dick*, a hybrid memoir/novel that became a cult hit and more recently a streaming series on Amazon TV. Kraus is married to *Semiotext(e)* publisher Sylvère Lotringer, who, as "Sylvere," is a character in her book.

11. Rosalind Krauss, "Notes on the Index: Seventies Art in America, Part 2," *October* 4 (fall 1977): 60, 58. "Notes on the Index: Seventies Art in America, Part 1," appears in *October* 3 (spring 1977).

12. "In each of these works it is the building itself that is taken to be a message which can be presented but not coded," she wrote, echoing Barthes's "message without a code" formulation for the photograph. Krauss, "Notes on the Index, Part 2," 65.

13. I reviewed *Camera Obscura* for the *New York Times Book Review* ("Death in the Photograph," August 23, 1981) and averred that it was less useful as a guide for analyzing images than as a sign of Barthes's divorce from the methodology of semiotics; https://www.nytimes.com/1981/08/23/books/death-in-the-photograph.html.

14. This is according to the transcript of the collecting panel held on Saturday afternoon. This, together with transcripts of all the talks and recordings of the event, are part of the Corcoran archives housed in the Gelman Library of the George Washington University, accessed January 10, 2018.

15. Some two years earlier Joel Snyder had written, with Neil Walsh Allen, an article for *Critical Inquiry* that broached this subject. "Photography, Vision, and Representation," *Critical Inquiry* 2, no. 1 (Autumn 1975): 143–169.

16. *Artforum*, "Photography Issue," 15, no. 1 (September 1976). In addition to articles on Nadar (Kozloff) and Étienne-Jules Marey (Scharf), the contents included A. D. Coleman's much-anthologized "The Directorial Mode: Notes Toward a Definition," and a survey of artists-using-photography (Foote) that illustrated photographs by Vito Acconci, John Baldessari, Bernd and Hilla Becher, Jan Dibbets, Hamish Fulton, Michael Heizer, Douglas Huebler, Richard Long, Dennis Oppenheim, Edward Ruscha, Robert Smithson, and . . . because of his Leo Castelli connection . . . the photographer Lewis Baltz.

17. *Artforum* 13, no. 5 (January 1975).

18. I wouldn't meet Allan Sekula until well into the eighties, but I became acquainted with the woman who would become his wife and intellectual partner, Sally Stein, in 1978, when she brought slides of Farm Security Administration color photography she had just discovered to *Modern Photography*. I was her editor in publishing these photographs and their hidden story for the first time, "FSA Color: The Forgotten Document," in the January 1979 issue of *Modern Photography*.

19. A possible artifact of my contribution to the SPE panel, and possibly a response to the Corcoran conference before it, was my article "Toward a Critical Pluralism," published in *Afterimage* in October 1980 and reprinted two years later in the anthology *Reading into Photography: Selected Essays, 1959–1980*, ed. Thomas Barrow, Shelley Armitage, and William Tydeman (Albuquerque: University of New Mexico Press, 1982). In it I describe the varieties of criticism of photography then in play and argue that the era of photographic formalism (such as it was) was ending. I also contest the notion that photography requires the invention of a new form of criticism suited to it, as A. D. Coleman once proposed.

20. Andy Grundberg, "Fairy Tales," *Soho Weekly News*, July 23, 1980, 33, 41.

21. Andy Grundberg, "(New) Wave at the Camera," *Soho Weekly News*, Nov 19, 1980, 15.

22. I did write about Sherman earlier for the *Soho Weekly News*, in a September 17, 1980 profile called "Artbreakers: Cindy Sherman."

23. The Metro Pictures initial roster of artists, as indicated by the cast of its opening group show in November 1980, consisted of Troy Brauntuch, Jack Goldstein, Michael Harvey, Thomas Lawson, William Leavitt, Sherrie Levine, Robert Longo, Richard Prince, Cindy Sherman, Laurie Simmons, James Welling, and Michael Zwack. These artists were all featured in the gallery's first year of exhibitions while others, like Louise Lawler and Walter Robinson, were to be added later. Source: "Metro Pictures Exhibitions, 1980–1981 Season," typescript, Metro Pictures Gallery.

CHAPTER 10
THE IMAGE WORLD MEETS THE ART WORLD

1. Jack Goldstein, "Early Days at CalArts," in *Jack Goldstein and the CalArts Mafia*, ed. Richard Hertz (Ojai, Calif.: Minneola Press, 2003), 55.

2. Robert Longo, "Reflections," in Hertz, *Jack Goldstein*, 167.

3. Heather Pesanti, "Wish You Were Here: The Buffalo Avant-Garde in the 1970s," in *Wish You Were Here: The Buffalo Avant-Garde in the 1970s*, by Heather Pesanti et al. (Buffalo: Albright-Knox Art Gallery, 2012), 36–37.

4. Ibid., 23.

5. Douglas Eklund, *The Pictures Generation, 1974–1984* (New York: Metropolitan Museum of Art; New Haven, Conn.: Yale University Press, 2009), 100, and Pesanti, *Wish You Were Here*, 34–36.

6. Jack Goldstein, "Helene Winer: Artists Space and Metro Pictures," in Hertz, *Jack Goldstein*, 89.

7. For an almost full description of the *Pictures* show, along with the background influences of CalArts and Hallwalls, see Eklund, *Pictures Generation*. I say "almost full" because his exhibition and catalog left out one of the five original artists in the 1977 Artists Space show, Philip Smith. Curator Douglas Eklund subsequently explained that he found Smith's work aesthetically insuf-

ficient to include in the 2009 Metropolitan Museum of Art show, even though Douglas Crimp had found it sufficient to include in his. See also note 9.

8. Some of these omissions—David Salle's and Matt Mullican's in particular—can be explained by a policy Artists Space established at its inception, holding that artists could only be featured in an exhibition once. On the other hand, Philip Smith had had a one-person exhibition there in December 1975. See Eklund, *Pictures Generation*, and the Artists Space Archive, 1973–2009, Fales Library and Special Collections, New York University, http://dlib.nyu.edu/findingaids/html/fales/artistsspace/dscaspace_ref4.html.

9. While adding Cindy Sherman, Douglas Crimp erased Philip Smith, something he discusses at length in his memoir of his early years in New York; Douglas Crimp, *Before Pictures* (Chicago: Dancing Foxes Press/University of Chicago Press, 2016). At the same time, he takes to task the decision of the curator of the Metropolitan Museum's 2009 *The Pictures Generation*, Douglas Eklund, for leaving Smith out of that show entirely, saying that Smith continued to be an artist of interest after leaving New York for Miami shortly after the *Pictures* show happened. Crimp, *Before Pictures*, 253–254 and 260–263.

10. Douglas Crimp, "Pictures," *October* 8 (spring 1979): 87

11. "But if *postmodernism* [italics his] is to have theoretical value, it cannot be used merely as another chronological term; rather it must disclose the particular nature of a breach with modernism." Ibid., 87. Crimp avoids the term *deconstruction*, however, or mention of its primary proponent and practitioner, Jacques Derrida, which has turned out to be a good thing, given how abused the term has become in more recent criticism.

12. The tour included venues at the Institute of Contemporary Art, Los Angeles; the Allen Memorial Art Museum at Oberlin College; and the University of Colorado Art Museum.

13. Crimp, *Before Pictures*, 270–272.

14. Telephone conversation with Michael Klein, September 11, 2018.

15. The show, *Photo 12*, also included artists from outside the early group of Metro Pictures regulars, including Ellen Carey, Sarah Charlesworth, Louise Lawler, and Brian Weil. "Metro Pictures Exhibitions, 1980–1981 Season," typescript, Metro Pictures Gallery.

16. Richard Prince's picture of Gary Gross's picture of Brooke Shields continues to resonate; it was removed by police from a show at the Tate Modern in Britain in 2009. See, for reaction, Florence Waters, "Brooke Shields Photograph at Tate: Art Belongs in an Art Gallery," *Telegraph* (London), Oct. 1, 2009, https://www.telegraph.co.uk/culture/art/6251481/Brooke-Shields-photograph-at-Tate-art-belongs-in-an-art-gallery.html.

17. Marvin Heiferman would recall the resistance to Postmodernist art in a conversation thirty years later with Laurie Simmons that was published in *Art in America*: "'Pictures' work, when it surfaced . . . in the 1970s, created wisecracks, then confusion, then resentment in the art photography world. . . . Work that thumbed its nose at art photography's hard-won status and standards—that questioned how photography shapes us, instead of celebrating how we shape it—was the center of attention." "Laurie Simmons and Marvin Heiferman," *Art in America* online, March 18, 2009, https://www.artinamericamagazine.com/news-features/magazines/laurie-simmons-and-marvin-heiferman/.

18. Douglas Crimp, "The Photographic Activity of Postmodernism," *October* 15 (winter 1980): 91–101. His discussion of Levine's work in the Metro Pictures show is on pages 98–99.

19. Cindy Sherman, speaking about her *Untitled Film Stills*: "I know I was not consciously aware of this thing the 'male gaze.' It was the way I was shooting, the mimicry of the style of grade-Z motion pictures that produced the self-consciousness of these characters." Cited by Eva Respini in her essay "Will the Real Cindy Sherman Please Stand Up?," in the catalog to *Cindy Sherman*, MoMA's 2012 retrospective exhibition (New York: Museum of Modern Art, 2012), 30. Laurie Simmons, while citing Sarah Charlesworth, Barbara Kruger, and Louise Lawler as artists who were engaged with theory, has said, "A number of artists I admired had zero interest in theory though their work was being firmly attached to it. I always felt that the art led me to places where I had no intention of going. Art, eventually, made me read some theory; I didn't read [Roland] Barthes and then make a picture." Conversation with Marvin Heiferman, *Art in America*.

20. Images from these and other series of Sarah Charlesworth's work can be found on the late artist's website, http://www.sarahcharlesworth.net/index.php. The site is also the source for my account of her career. Curiously, the show at C Space was curated by Annina Nosei, who later opened an eponymous gallery and famously showed and represented Barbara Kruger and Jean-Michel Basquiat—but not Charlesworth.

21. Andy Grundberg, "Photography View: Post-Modernists in the Mainstream," *New York Times*, Nov. 20, 1983, https://www.nytimes.com/1983/11/20/arts/photography-view-postmodernists-in-the-mainstream.html.

22. Irving Sandler, *Art of the Postmodern Era: From the Late 1960s to the Early 1990s* (Boulder, Colo.: Westview Press, 1997), 446–452.

23. The journal *October*'s reaction to the transnational appearance of Neo-Expressionism can be judged from Benjamin Buchloh's "Figures of Authority, Ciphers of Regression: Notes on the Return of Representation in European Painting" and Douglas Crimp's "The End of Painting," both in *October* 16 (spring 1981).

24. Richard Hennessy, "What's All This about Photography," *Artforum* 17, no. 9 (May 1979): 23.

25. Carlo McCormick, "Art Seen," *East Village Eye*, Oct. 1983. See https://ephemeralnewyork.wordpress.com/tag/east-village-art-scene/.

26. Yve-Alain Bois and Hal Foster were writing in the catalog for the show *Endgame*, at the ICA in Boston (Cambridge, Mass.: MIT Press, 1986). See my "When Outs Are In, What's Up?," *New York Times*, July 26, 1987, https://www.nytimes.com/1987/07/26/arts/when-outs-are-in-what-s-up.html.

CHAPTER 11
ESSENTIALS FOR THE EIGHTIES

1. Andy Grundberg, "Arbitrariness Is the Enemy," *New York Times*, May 10, 1981, https://www.nytimes.com/1981/05/10/arts/photography-view-arbitrariness-is-the-enemy.html.

2. David Rimanelli, "Time Capsules: 1980–1985," *Artforum* 41, no. 7 (November 2003): 112.

3. Andy Grundberg, "Cindy Sherman: A Playful and Political Post-Modernist," *New York Times*, Nov. 22, 1981, www.nytimes.com/1981/11/22/arts/photography-view-cindy-sherman-a-playful-and-political-post-modernist.html.

4. Eva Respini, "Will the Real Cindy Sherman Please Stand Up?," *Cindy Sherman* (New York: Museum of Modern Art, 2012), 30–31.

5. Andy Grundberg, "The Point of Photographs," *New York Times*, Nov. 29, 1981, https://www.nytimes.com/1981/11/29/books/the-point-of-photographs.html.

6. Andy Grundberg, "Should Photography Galleries Exhibit Paintings?" *New York Times*, Aug. 9, 1981, http://www.nytimes.com/1981/08/09/arts/photography-view-should-photography-galleries-exhibit-paintings.html.

7. Andy Grundberg, "A Renewed Vitality in the Face of Economic Hard Times," *New York Times*, April 11, 1982, https://www.nytimes.com/1982/04/11/arts/photography-view-a-renewed-vitality-in-the-face-of-economic-hard-times.html. In the short term my photo-gallery obituary may have been premature, since new photography galleries would soon appear—Howard Greenberg in 1981, Pace/MacGill in 1983, Laurence Miller in 1984, Benrubi in 1987—and Light would linger on until 1987.

8. The lecture was the first attempt at what ultimately became my essay "Crisis of the Real," which is the title piece of my collected writings published by Aperture in 1990. The essay basically tries to explain Pictures Generation art and theory to a skeptical audience of photographers, but it also argues that some photographers introduced ideas about the "image world" years earlier. It was first published in *Views*, the journal of the Photographic Resource Center, Boston, in 1986, after it won the organization's Ruttenberg Prize for writing on photography. Later it was anthologized in *The Photography Reader*, ed. Liz Wells (London: Routledge, 2003).

9. The coincidence in New York in the spring of 2012 of large retrospective exhibitions of the work of Cindy Sherman and Francesca Woodman, at the Museum of Modern Art and the Guggenheim Museum, respectively, made obvious a broader and historically important coincidence: both artists, using the camera as a means of intentionally staging tableaux (and themselves as central figures within), did important breakthrough work at precisely the same time—roughly, the last three years of the seventies. As for Nan Goldin, her importance was emphasized when MoMA put *The Ballad of Sexual Dependency* on view, as a slide show, for ten months in 2016–17.

10. Andy Grundberg, "Nan Goldin's Bleak Diary of the Urban Subculture," *New York Times*, Dec. 21, 1986, https://www.nytimes.com/1986/12/21/arts/photography-view-nan-goldin-s-bleak-diary-of-the-urban-subculture.html.

11. *The Ballad of Sexual Dependency* is best seen performed live, with the artist changing the slide trays and the projector making its trademark clicking noises; that's how I experienced it the first three or four times I saw it. It has since been recorded as a video, in an edition; MoMA and the Whitney own the work in its original slide form (albeit with duplicate slides).

12. Anyone wanting details of Francesca Woodman's brief but incredible life should try to see Scott Willis's remarkable film *The Woodmans* (2010), which features interviews with her mother, father, and brother, among others. Spoiler alert: the film ends with George Woodman, after the deaths of his wife and his daughter, taking up the camera to produce quasi-facsimiles of his daughter's work.

13. These were shown at Marian Goodman Gallery in February–March 2015, with the title *I'm trying my hand at fashion photography*, an excerpt from Woodman's journal.

14. Abigail Solomon-Godeau, "Just Like a Woman," in *Francesca Woodman: Photographic Work*, by Ann Gabhart (Wellesley, Mass.: Wellesley College, 1986), reprinted in Abigail Solomon-Godeau, *Photography at the Dock* (Minneapolis: University of Minnesota Press, 1991), 255.

15. Ibid., 252.

CHAPTER 12
INVENTIONS OF PURE IMAGINATION

1. How obviously fake the photographs of *Hitler Moves East* appear apparently continues to be an issue, especially when it comes to librarians. I found the book at the George Washington University's Gelman Library filed not in the art stacks, among the "TR" cataloging codes common to art and photography books, but in the history stacks coded "D." It was next to an English translation of a 1963 scholarly volume, also titled *Hitler Moves East*, by a German historian. This is an amusing repeat of what happened to Edward Ruscha's *Twentysix Gasoline Stations*, which often ended up in stacks devoted to architecture or fossil fuels.

2. Roland Barthes, "The Death of the Author," *Image-Music-Text*, trans. Stephen Heath (New York: Hill and Wang, 1977), 142–148.

3. Hilton Kramer, "The Paradoxical Museumization of Photography," *New York Times*, Nov. 13, 1977, https://www.nytimes.com/1977/11/13/archives/art-view-the-paradoxical-museumization-of-photography.html. This reference to Kramer's article in relation to *Evidence* comes from Sandra S. Phillips's essay, "A History of the Evidence," in a 2003 reprint of the book (New York: D.A.P.).

4. Tom Wolfe's book using that cutting phrase, *The Painted Word* (New York: Farrar, Straus and Giroux, 1975), published to a chorus of bad reviews, was in advance of Postmodernism's linkage with poststructuralism and other theories derived from language. Its focus was on painting and its supposed obeisance to the critics Clement Greenberg, Harold Rosenberg, and Leo Steinberg.

5. A. D. Coleman, "The Directorial Mode: Notes toward a Definition," *Artforum* 15, no. 1 (September 1976): 55–61. Reprinted in A. D. Coleman, *Light Readings: A Photography Critic's Writings, 1968–1978* (New York: Oxford University Press, 1979).

6. Van Deren Coke, *Fabricated to Be Photographed* (San Francisco: San Francisco

Museum of Modern Art, 1979), 2–12. The exhibition traveled from San Francisco to the University of New Mexico Art Museum, the Albright-Knox Art Gallery in Buffalo, and the Newport Harbor Art Museum in 1980.

7. David Boss, ed., "Tableau Photography," *Picture*, special issue 18 (September 1981).

8. Ironically, Ansel Adams played a major role in *Picture*'s existence; the magazine's publisher, David Gardner of Gardner/Fulmer Lithograph, was Adams's friend and patron and the printer of most of his books. This apparently did not prevent the magazine from featuring William Mortensen's work, about which Adams had once penned a scathing critique.

9. "1973 Biennial Exhibition," Internet Archive, 2013, https://archive.org/stream/1973biennialexhi/1973biennialexhi_djvu.txt. See also Roberta Smith, "A Remembrance of Whitney Biennials Past," *New York Times*, Feb. 28, 1993, https://www.nytimes.com/1993/02/28/arts/art-view-a-remembrance-of-whitney-biennials-past.html.

10. David Haxton made a repeat appearance in the 1983 Biennial, along with Pictures artists Cindy Sherman and Barbara Kruger and tableau photographers Ellen Brooks, Eileen Cowin, and Nic Nicosia, a Texas artist who produced *Domestic Dramas,* a series of wry scenes created within the confines of his studio. In the 1985 Biennial, one of the largest and most widely pilloried of them all, Postmodernists were a counterpoint to the slapdash, graffiti-inspired styles of the new East Village art. James Casebere, Sarah Charlesworth, Sherrie Levine, Frank Majore, Richard Prince, Cindy Sherman, and Laurie Simmons were there, as was Joel-Peter Witkin, producer of grotesque tableaux modeled on classic paintings.

11. Andy Grundberg, "Art Breakers: New York's Emerging Artists," *Soho Weekly News*, September 17, 1980.

12. Gene Thornton, "A Mixed Bag of Exhibitions," *New York Times*, Jan. 18, 1981, https://www.nytimes.com/1981/01/18/arts/photography-view-a-mixed-bag-of-exhibitons.html.

13. Andy Grundberg, "Big Pictures That Say Little," *New York Times*, May 8, 1983, https://www.nytimes.com/1983/05/08/arts/photogtaphy-view-big-pictures-that-say-little.html.

14. Marvin Heiferman, "Essay," in the exhibition brochure of *The Real Big Picture*, the Queens Museum, 1986. The fold-out brochure has the essay, a checklist, and illustrations of some of the works on view on one side and on the other a poster featuring Chuck Close's 1980 large Polaroid self-portrait.

15. Kathleen McCarthy Gauss and Andy Grundberg, *Photography and Art: Interactions Since 1946* (New York: Abbeville Press, 1987).

16. Only a few months before the National Museum of American Art opened *The Photography of Invention* it showed a comprehensive retrospective of the art of Man Ray, an artist whose use of photography in the twenties and thirties in Paris made him a harbinger of what was to come in the seventies and eighties. Organized by Merry Foresta, *Perpetual Motif: The Art of Man Ray* attracted more than a few New York artists and critics to Washington, D.C., including Roberta Smith and myself from the *Times*. In my review of the exhibition I specifically called out the artist's affinity to the current mode of tableau photography: "The connection is not merely one of approach to the medium—Man Ray was not the first to arrange subject matter for the camera, after all—but also one of attitude toward what is photographed. Like Man Ray, today's photographers are less interested in reflecting reality than in rendering it inscrutable." Notably, my review was slugged "Art View" instead of the usual "Photography View." "A Revival of Interest in a World Gone Awry," *New York Times*, Dec. 4, 1988, https://www.nytimes.com/1988/12/04/arts/art-view-a-revival-of-interest-in-a-world-gone-awry.html.

17. Although artists associated with Neo-Expressionism were known for their paintings, several employed photography—either in their work or to provide models for paintings. For example, Anselm Kiefer produced photo-based artist books and stuck black-and-white prints on his canvases before painting over them; Eric Fischl used his own photographs to paint from and later showed the photographs as his work.

18. Irving Sandler, *Art of the Postmodern Era: From the Late 1960s to the Early 1990s* (Boulder, Colo.: Westview Press, 1998), 499–500.

19. Gary Indiana, *Village Voice*, April 22, 1986, 71. For a full account of the Starns' early critical reception, from which this quote is drawn, see my essay "Mike and Doug Starn" in *Mike and Doug Starn*, by Andy Grundberg (New York: Harry N. Abrams, 1990), with an introduction by Robert Rosenblum.

20. As I noted in my review of the Starns' Castelli and Stux shows for the *Times* ("A Pair of Shows for a Pair of Trendy Twins," Oct. 2, 1988), since the start of that year the Starns had had museum shows at the Museum of Contemporary Art Chicago, the Wadsworth Athenaeum in Hartford, and the San Francisco Museum of Modern Art.

CHAPTER 13
EXPANDED TERRAIN

1. Readers attempting to retrieve this review by searching on the *Times*'s website using my name may be disappointed, since my byline is misspelled as "Andy Grudenberg"—an error apparently introduced by whomever typed the newsprint version into a digital file. With my agreement, the paper has catalogued all my reviews and essays, not to mention the obituaries and camera columns I churned out over the years, and made them available to subscribers in full-text form. When I started writing for the *Times* it was still a couple of years away from receiving and editing stories electronically, but the paper has since digitally reentered all of my and most everyone else's articles from back in the glamorous days of typewriters.

2. I had a front-row seat for Mike Disfarmer's auspicious debut, since it was the result of years of research by my boss, Julia Scully, the editor of *Modern Photography*. I became her sounding board during the process of shaping and editing the book and, not long after its publication, her partner.

3. Examples of such canon-busting exhibitions include *The Indelible Image: Photographs of War, 1846 to the Present*, a show organized by Corcoran Gallery of Art curator Frances Fralin that opened at New York University's Grey Art Gallery

in 1985, and a much smaller presentation at MoMA in 1986 of the work of W. Grancel Fitz, a nearly forgotten midcentury New York photographer who created confectionary studio concoctions showing products such as gleaming white refrigerators being admired by gleaming white middle-class women. I reviewed both shows in the Arts and Leisure section: "Recording the Brutal, Fascinating Faces of Warfare," *New York Times,* Sept. 29, 1985, and "His Pictures Sold Prosperity During the Depression," *New York Times*, April 6, 1986: respectively, https://www.nytimes.com/1985/09/29/arts/photography-view-recording-the-brutal-fascinating-faces-of-warfare.html and https://www.nytimes.com/1986/04/06/arts/photography-view-his-pictures-sold-prosperity-during-the-depression.html. The Fitz exhibition was organized by Sarah McNear, a Beaumont and Nancy Newhall Fellow in MoMA's Photography Department. To quote in full a paragraph of that review that applies to my subject here, "The Museum of Modern Art's attention to W. Grancel Fitz's pictures focuses our attention on two ongoing tendencies in the art of today. One is the expansion of the arena of what can be called art, a tendency that has the function not only of creating a broader marketplace for art but also of decreasing the perceived distance between what we call high culture and popular culture. The second tendency, which is especially germane to photography, is the examination of advertising imagery as an element of cultural persuasion—as a major means by which we learn to see, believe and behave."

4. Installation views of the show can be found on the Richard Avedon Foundation website, https://www.avedonfoundation.org/exhibitions/.

5. Press release, "Recent Work by Irving Penn on View at Museum of Modern Art," Museum of Modern Art, May 23, 1975, https://www.moma.org/documents/moma_press-release_326947.pdf.

6. Gene Thornton, reviewing the show for the *New York Times*, sagely wrote, "Mr. Penn does not have to make this kind of picture to prove that he is a photographer whose pictures are worthy of hanging in a museum." Gene Thornton, "Penn Transforms Cigarette Butts into Works of Art," *New York Times*, July 6, 1975, https://www.nytimes.com/1975/07/06/archives/photography-view-penn-transforms-cigarette-butts-into-works-of-art.html.

7. The fall 1980 show, *Earthly Bodies*, was accompanied by a small catalog with a mostly admiring essay by Rosalind Krauss. Three years later, in an essay "A Note on Photography and the Simulacral," derived from her keynote talk at the Society for Photographic Education national conference in Philadelphia in March 1983, she would write less complimentarily about Irving Penn's latest platinum still-life images. Rosalind Krauss, "A Note on Photography and the Simulacral," *October* 31 (winter 1984): 49–68.

8. Andy Grundberg, "The 'Fashionable' Figure," *New York Times*, March 14, 1982, https://www.nytimes.com/1982/03/14/arts/photography-view-the-fashionable-figure.html.

9. Andy Grundberg, "Images That Represent Deep Bites of Forbidden Fruit," *New York Times*, Jan. 26, 1986, https://www.nytimes.com/1986/01/26/arts/photography-view-images-that-represent-deep-bites-of-forbidden-fruit.html.

10. Andy Grundberg, "Two Camps Battle over the Nature of the Medium," *New York Times*, Aug. 14, 1983, https://www.nytimes.com/1983/08/14/arts/photography-view-two-camps-battle-over-the-nature-of-the-medium.html.

11. Allan Sekula's "Photography Between Labor and Capital" appears in *Mining Photographs and Other Pictures, 1948–1968: A Selection from the Negative Archives of Shedden Studio, Glace Bay, Cape Breton*, ed. Benjamin H. D. Buchloh and Robert Wilkie (Halifax, Canada: Press of the Nova Scotia College of Art and Design, 1983).

12. Andy Grundberg, "Pictures of Change," *New York Times Book Review*, June 14, 1981, https://www.nytimes.com/1981/06/14/books/pictures-of-change.html.

13. Adam Weinberg, "On the Line: The New Color Photojournalism," in *On the Line: The New Color Photojournalism*, by Adam Weinberg (Minneapolis: Walker Art Center, 1986), 16.

CHAPTER 14
CULTURE WARS

1. In the course of the trial the two pictures of children were dropped from the charges, after the children's parents attested that they had agreed to the photo sessions and approved of the photographs that resulted.

2. In 1973 the U.S. Supreme Court ruled, in Miller v. California, that for a work to be considered obscene in a legal sense it must meet three standards: be patently offensive in its portrayal of sexual activity, appeal to a prurient interest, and be without literary, artistic, political, or scientific value. If Robert Mapplethorpe's (or anyone's, for that matter) photographs were to be judged obscene, they would have to lack artistry, the issue that consumed much of the trial.

3. The selection of the jury was a process I sat through for much of two days, and I came away mightily impressed. The prosecution, hoping to fill the panel with people who had little to no experience of the arts, asked the first question of every prospective juror, "Have you ever been to a museum?" Every one of them answered yes. Most only had been to one, and it had happened when they were children on a school-sponsored trip, but that seemed to be enough to impress them—even if the museum's focus was natural history, not art. It also seemed to be enough for the defense team, which rarely had to challenge a prospect. I remember thinking, thank God for the Cincinnati school system, and I hope it still funds field trips to the city's many cultural centers. For all of my reaction to the trial, see Andy Grundberg, "Critics Notebook: Cincinnati Trial's Unanswered Question," Oct. 18, 1990, https://www.nytimes.com/1990/10/18/arts/critic-s-notebook-cincinnati-trial-s-unanswered-question.html. For more about jury selection and the testimony delivered by Janet Kardon and others, see Elizabeth Hess, "Art on Trial: Cincinnati's Dangerous Theater of the Ridiculous," *Village Voice*, October 23, 1990, reprinted in *Culture Wars*, ed. Richard Bolton (New York: New Press, 1992), 269–282.

4. Founded by Donald Wildmon in 1977 as the National Federation for Decency,

the American Family Association is listed by the Southern Poverty Law Center as a Designated Hate Group. While the NFD initially focused its attacks on television, films, and magazines that it saw as pornographic, AFA is now focused almost exclusively on an anti-LGBTQ crusade. Jerry Falwell's Moral Majority took on similar issues starting in 1979. Pat Robertson, best known as a televangelist entrepreneur, formed the Christian Coalition at the time of the Mapplethorpe controversy and sent a membership-solicitation letter that blithely described the images in the *X Portfolio*: "A photo showing one man holding another man's genitals," and so forth.

5. For details on this and a much wider picture of Reagan-era attacks on the arts and culture as a whole, see Bolton, *Culture Wars*.

6. Andy Grundberg, "Art Under Attack: Who Dares Say That It's No Good?," *New York Times*, Nov. 25, 1990, https://www.nytimes.com/1990/11/25/arts/art-view-art-under-attack-who-dares-say-that-it-s-no-good.html.

7. Andy Grundberg, "Lost Causes," *Soho Weekly News*, April 5, 1979, 31.

8. Here is the exact text: "Unfortunately, the argument for Mr. Mapplethorpe as a Postmodernist artist quickly breaks down, because any evidence of a critical distance from his material is lacking in this for-adults-only exhibition. He seems to be more fascinated with the explicit depiction of the sexual parts and acts of men and women than with the cultural biases by which we know them. It may not be his intention to reinforce existing stereotypes (of black male virility and white female voracity, for instance), but this is the effect nonetheless. Rather than educate, these pictures titillate; rather than addressing the conventions of pornography, they are pornography—by the standards of this writer, if not by the standards of their intended audience." Based on this, I have long been mystified that I would have been considered a defense witness for the work in an obscenity trial. Andy Grundberg, "Is Mapplethorpe Only Out to Shock?," *New York Times*, March 13, 1983, https://www.nytimes.com/1983/03/13/arts/photography-view-is-mapplethorpe-only-out-to-shock.html.

9. For a comprehensive account of the traumatic damage the obsession with child pornography can do to a family, see Lynn Powell's sympathetic book *Framing Innocence: A Mother's Photographs, a Prosecutor's Zeal, and a Small Town's Response* (New York: New Press, 2010), which focuses on the case of Cynthia Stewart of Oberlin, Ohio, which began in 1999. The author also mentions the case of Kate Myers, an Ohio mother who was arrested in 1993 in Akron because of nude photographs her young daughter had taken with her camera. These examples happened years after the case of Alice Sims, an artist in Arlington, Virginia, who in 1988 had her children removed from her home because she had sent film off for processing that contained nude studies of them. See Bolton, *Culture Wars*, 341. There are other examples equally egregious.

10. Powell, *Framing Innocence*, 267–268.

11. Andy Grundberg, "Blaming a Medium for Its Message," *New York Times*, August 6, 1989, https://www.nytimes.com/1989/08/06/arts/photography-view-blaming-the-medium-for-its-message.html.

12. Another irony worth noting: the National Gallery's celebration of photography happened a year before the museum announced the formation of a department of photography; the National Gallery's Sarah Greenough, a contributor to the exhibition and its catalog, is listed as "research curator." The Art Institute of Chicago and the Museum of Fine Arts, Houston, established their photography departments in the midseventies.

13. The idea that contemporary art itself was the target of the Culture Wars was clearly voiced by the drama critic Robert Brustein in his essay "Art Wars," in *Reimagining American Theatre*, by Robert Brustein (New York: Hill and Wang, 1991), 257–271.

14. Contemporary artists outside of photography did not entirely escape the antiporn, anti-NEA crusaders. Eric Fischl's paintings, for example, were attacked as pornographic, as were those of David Salle, mostly by feminists objecting to the representation of women as subjects. Both painters worked from photographs and painted in realist styles. More problematic was performance, which arguably has a greater immediacy than photography because it happens in front of you. Karen Finley, Holly Hughes, and Annie Sprinkle were transgressive female performance artists whose support by the NEA became a cause célèbre in Congress.

CHAPTER 15
MOVING ON

1. "Two of the perceived shortcomings of photography as a modern art had been its excessive factuality and its insufficient self-absorption. These two objections were met with one stroke by the fictionalized self-portrait, which has proven one of the most rewarding single subject-genres for photographers working within the gallery system." John Szarkowski, *Photography Until Now* (New York: Museum of Modern Art, 1989), 276, 281.

2. Peter Galassi served as head of MoMA's photography department from 1991 to 2011. He was appointed Director of Photography, like John Szarkowski, but in 1995 his title became Chief Curator of Photography in a museum-wide change instigated by the museum's director, Glenn Lowry. The switch in titles was never publicly announced, as best I can ascertain. Press release, "Peter Galassi Appointed Director of Photography at the Museum of Modern Art; John Szarkowski Named Director Emeritus," Museum of Modern Art, October 11, 1991, https://www.moma.org/momaorg/shared/pdfs/docs/press_archives/6977/releases/MOMA_1991_0106_76.pdf?2010, and email from Galassi to the author, Dec. 3, 2019.

3. Hal Foster, *The Return of the Real* (Cambridge, Mass.: October Books/MIT Press, 1996), 206.

4. *The Indomitable Spirit* was a multipronged enterprise. Heiferman asked more than ninety photographers to submit a picture that represented their idea of strength in the face of adversity; ten of the pictures were assembled into a portfolio that was sold to raise money, and all of the pictures were sold in a charity auction at Sotheby's in the fall. The show was assembled by Lisa Cremin and Associates and after appearing at ICP traveled to the Los Angeles Municipal Art Gallery. There also was a catalog,

distributed by Harry N. Abrams, for which I wrote an essay. The exhibition was well received; see, for example, Christopher Knight's review in the *Los Angeles Times*, "Two Views of AIDS: One a Triumph, the Other a Failure," May 18, 1990, https://www.latimes.com/archives/la-xpm-1990-05-18-ca-59-story.html.

5. *Image of Desire: Portrayals in Recent Advertising Photography* was shown at Moore College's Goldie Paley Gallery in the winter of 1989; a small catalog also was produced. Reaction was mixed at best: I was booed by the student audience at the opening panel discussion for promoting images that presented women as sex objects. I think they got my point.

6. *Alexey Brodovitch*, by Andy Grundberg, was published by Harry N. Abrams in 1989. *Mike and Doug Starn*, by Andy Grundberg with an introduction by Robert Rosenblum, was published by Abrams in 1990.

7. *The Art of Paul Strand*, National Gallery of Art, December 2, 1990–February 3, 1991, https://www.nga.gov/exhibitions/1990/strand.html.

8. The Louis Agassiz daguerreotypes, as they are known, recently became the focus of a lawsuit by an African American woman who claims a right to their ownership based on her belief that she is descended from two of the subjects. See Scott Jaschik, "Harvard Sued over 19th-Century Biologist's Racism," *Inside Higher Ed,* March 21, 2019, https://www.insidehighered.com/news/2019/03/21/lawsuit-against-harvard-focuses-actions-19th-century-biologist. They were obviously also controversial when Carrie Mae Weems used them; Harvard claimed that she violated its copyright on the images and in a settlement won the right to a fee from Weems's sales. Harvard then purchased a set of the series for the university's art museum. Jasmine Weber, "Descendant of Slaves Sues Harvard for Rights to Daguerreotypes of Her Ancestors," *Hyperallergic,* March 20, 2019, https://hyperallergic.com/490797/descendant-of-slaves-sues-harvard-for-rights-to-daguerreotypes-of-her-ancestors/.

9. These pictures were collected in Adam Fuss, *My Ghost* (Santa Fe: Twin Palms Press, 2002).

10. My list leaves off Axel Hütte and several others of note, including Düsseldorf students who arrived later, such as Thomas Demand.

11. Thomas Struth's rollout of the new images in his *Museum Pictures* series was an international venture: Marion Goodman's show was but one of five exhibitions staged that year. Other venues were at galleries in Amsterdam, Brussels, Cologne, and Paris. See "Museum Photographs 1," *Thomas Struth: Photographs, 1978–2010,* http://www.thomasstruth32.com/bigsize/photographs/museum_photographs_1/index.html# for details.

12. For details about Nancy Burson's process and early career, as well as the story of the *National Geographic*'s infamous pyramid cover, see Fred Ritchin's early and eye-opening article in the *New York Times*, "Photography's New Bag of Tricks," Nov. 4, 1984, https://www.nytimes.com/1984/11/04/magazine/photography-s-new-bag-of-tricks.html.

13. See Peter Buse, *The Camera Does the Rest: How Polaroid Changed Photography* (Chicago: University of Chicago Press, 2016), 81–84.

EPILOGUE

1. Press release, "Cruel and Tender: The Real in the Twentieth-Century Photograph," Tate, June 2, 2003, http://www.tate.org.uk/press/press-releases/cruel-and-tender-real-twentieth-century-photograph.

2. The Tate was not *that* late to the party. The Guggenheim Museum treaded lightly into photography, starting with a gift of Robert Mapplethorpe photographs by the Mapplethorpe Foundation in 1992. The Whitney Museum of American Art established a photography support group in 1991 but its photography department was not created until 1998, and it hired its first photography curator, Sylvia Wolf, in 1999—just making the deadline for the twentieth century.

3. Carter Ratcliff, "Cruel and Tender," *Tate Magazine*, no. 5 (May/June 2003), http://www.tate.org.uk/context-comment/cruel-and-tender.

Index

Photo Credits

Page 12. © 2020 The Andy Warhol Foundation for the Visual Arts, Inc. / Licensed by Artists Rights Society (ARS), New York

Pages 14, 15. © 2020 Robert Rauschenberg Foundation / Licensed by VAGA at Artists Rights Society (ARS), New York

Page 18. © Ed Ruscha, courtesy of the artist and Gagosian

Page 20. © Lee Friedlander, courtesy Fraenkel Gallery, San Francisco, and Luhring Augustine, New York

Page 24. © 2020 Estate of Gordon Matta-Clark / Artists Rights Society (ARS), New York / Courtesy the Estate of Gordon Matta-Clark and David Zwirner

Page 28. Photo: Andy Grundberg / © 2020 Estate of Gordon Matta-Clark / Artists Rights Society (ARS), New York

Pages 29, 30. Photographs by Andy Grundberg

Pages 31, 33. © 2020 Estate of Gordon Matta-Clark / Artists Rights Society (ARS), New York / Courtesy The Estate of Gordon Matta-Clark and David Zwirner

Page 35. © William Wegman, courtesy Sperone Westwater, New York

Pages 37, 38. Photographs by Andy Grundberg

Page 40. © Michael Heizer / Photo: John Weber

Page 42. © Hans Haacke / Artists Rights Society (ARS), New York / VG Bild-Kunst, Bonn / Photo: Ron Amstutz / Digital image: © Whitney Museum of American Art / Licensed by Scala / Art Resource, New York

Page 44. Cornell University News Service records, #4-3-15. Division of Rare and Manuscript Collections, Cornell University Library

Page 46. Cornell University News Service records, #4-3-15. Division of Rare and Manuscript Collections, Cornell University Library / © Hans Haacke / Artists Rights Society (ARS), New York / VG Bild-Kunst, Bonn

Page 47. Photo: Richard Clark, courtesy Herbert F. Johnson Museum of Art at Cornell University / © Dennis Oppenheim Estate

Page 48. Photo: Gianfranco Gorgoni, courtesy James Cohan Gallery, New York and Shanghai / Art: © 2020 Holt/Smithson Foundation and Dia Art Foundation / Licensed by VAGA at Artists Rights Society (ARS), New York

Page 49. © 2020 Holt/Smithson Foundation / Licensed by VAGA at Artists Rights Society (ARS), New York

Page 50. Courtesy the artist and Peter Freeman, Inc. / Photograph by Nicholas Knight / © 2020 Jan Dibbets / Artists Rights Society (ARS), New York

Page 52. Courtesy of Marian Goodman Gallery and the Estate of John Baldessari / Copyright: The Estate of John Baldessari

Page 55. © 2020 Douglas Huebler, courtesy Darcy Huebler / Artists Rights Society (ARS), New York / Digital Image: © The Museum of Modern Art / Licensed by Scala / Art Resource, New York

Page 59. © 2020 The LeWitt Estate / Artists Rights Society (ARS), New York / Photo: Albright-Knox Art Gallery / Art Resource, New York

Page 60. Courtesy of the artist and Marian Goodman Gallery, Paris / Copyright: Dan Graham

Page 61. © Estate Bernd & Hilla Becher, represented by Max Becher, 2020

Page 64. Courtesy of Marian Goodman Gallery and the Estate of John Baldessari / Copyright: The Estate of John Baldessari

Page 66. © 2020 The Estate of Ana Mendieta Collection, LLC. Courtesy Galerie Lelong & Co. / Licensed by Artists Rights Society (ARS), New York

Page 68. © 2020 Chris Burden / Licensed by The Chris Burden Estate and Artists Rights Society (ARS), New York. Courtesy Gagosian

Page 70. Photo: Erró / © 2020 The Carolee Schneemann Foundation / Courtesy the Carolee Schneemann Foundation, Galerie Lelong & Co., and P.P.O.W., New York / Artists Rights Society (ARS), New York

Page 72. © 2020 Vito Acconci / Artists Rights Society (ARS), New York

Page 74. Photo: Rosemary Mayer. © Adrian Piper Research Archive Foundation Berlin and Generali Foundation

Page 75. © 2020 Marsie, Emanuelle, Damon, and Andrew Scharlatt, Hannah Wilke Collection & Archive, Los Angeles / Licensed by VAGA at Artists Rights Society (ARS), New York

Page 76. © 2020 The Estate of Robert Morris / Artists Rights Society (ARS), New York / Courtesy Castelli Gallery, New York

Page 77. Photograph by Chris Burnside, courtesy of the artist and Pace Gallery / © 2020 Lynda Benglis / Licensed by VAGA at Artists Rights Society (ARS), New York

Page 79. © 2020 The Estate of Ana Mendieta Collection, LLC. Courtesy Galerie Lelong & Co. / Licensed by Artists Rights Society (ARS), New York

Page 82. Courtesy of the artist

Page 88. © Duane Michals. Courtesy of DC Moore Gallery, New York

Page 89. © Copyright Jerry N. Uelsmann

Page 90. © Mark Cohen

Page 96. © Estate of Ray K. Metzker, courtesy Howard Greenberg Gallery, New York

Page 97. Copyright Kenneth Josephson. Courtesy of Stephen Daiter Gallery

Page 98. The Robert Heinecken Trust

Page 99. Copyright Sally Larson, courtesy Gitterman Gallery

Page 100 top. Courtesy of the artist and Derek Eller Gallery

Page 100 bottom. Hood Museum of Art, Dartmouth: Gift of the artist

Page 102. © Estate of Jan Groover, courtesy Janet Borden, Inc., NY

Page 105. Courtesy of Marian Goodman Gallery and the Estate of John Baldessari

/ Copyright: The Estate of John Baldessari

Page 106. © William Wegman, courtesy Sperone Westwater, New York

Page 107. © 2020 Robert Cumming, courtesy Janet Borden, Inc., NY / Licensed by VAGA at Artists Rights Society (ARS), New York

Page 109. © Robert Adams, courtesy Fraenkel Gallery, San Francisco

Page 110. © 2020 Estate of Lewis Baltz. Used by permission

Page 111. © Stephen Shore. Courtesy 303 Gallery, New York

Page 114. © Eggleston Artistic Trust / Courtesy Eggleston Artistic Trust and David Zwirner

Page 117. Copyright Joel Meyerowitz, courtesy Howard Greenberg Gallery

Page 118. Photograph by Ellen Page Wilson, courtesy Pace Gallery / © Lucas Samaras, courtesy Pace Gallery

Page 120. © William Wegman, courtesy Sperone Westwater, New York

Page 121. © William Christenberry; courtesy Pace/MacGill Gallery, New York

Page 122. © 2020 Bruce Nauman / Artists Rights Society (ARS), New York, courtesy Sperone Westwater, New York

Page 124. Courtesy of the Artist and Cristin Tierney Gallery, New York

Page 129. © Nam June Paik Estate / Digital Image © Whitney Museum of American Art / Licensed by Scala / Art Resource, New York

Page 132. © 2020 Joan Jonas / Artists Rights Society (ARS), New York / Courtesy Electronic Arts Intermix (EAI), New York

Page 134. © 2020 Bruce Nauman / Artists Rights Society (ARS), New York, courtesy Sperone Westwater, New York

Page 135. © William Wegman, courtesy Sperone Westwater, New York

Page 136. ©PhilipMakanna/GHOSTS

Page 138. Courtesy of the artist and Marian Goodman Gallery / Copyright: Dara Birnbaum

Pages 140–141 top. Courtesy of Mary Lucier

Page 141 bottom. Photo: Kira Perov

Page 142. © Tina Barney / Image courtesy of the artist and Kasmin Gallery

Page 144. © 1987 The Peter Hujar Archive LLC; courtesy Pace/MacGill Gallery, New York, and Fraenkel Gallery, San Francisco

Page 153. Photograph by Andy Grundberg

Page 158. Courtesy of the artist and Metro Pictures, New York

Page 163. Courtesy of the artist and Petzel, New York

Page 165. © 2020 Laurie Simmons, courtesy of the artist and Salon 94, New York

Page 166. © James Casebere / Courtesy: the artist and Sean Kelly, New York

Page 167. © Sherrie Levine / Courtesy the artist and David Zwirner

Page 168. © Richard Prince

Page 169. Courtesy of the artist and Metro Pictures, New York

Page 171. © The Estate of Sarah Charlesworth. Courtesy Paula Cooper Gallery, New York

Page 173. Courtesy of the artist. Photo: Tim Nighswander / Imaging4Art.com

Page 178. Courtesy of the artist

Page 181. Courtesy of the artist and Metro Pictures, New York

Page 185. Courtesy of the Akron Art Museum Archive

Page 187. © 2020 Estate of Francesca Woodman / Charles Woodman / Artists Rights Society (ARS), New York

Page 190. © 1981, Sandy Skoglund

Page 192. Courtesy of David Levinthal

Page 193. © Mike Mandel, © Larry Sultan / Courtesy of Mike Mandel and Estate of Larry Sultan

Page 196. © John Pfahl, courtesy Janet Borden, Inc., NY / Courtesy of the George Eastman Museum

Pages 197, 198, 199. Courtesy of the artist

Page 201. Copyright David Haxton 1980

Page 205. © Joel Sternfeld

Page 207. © 2020 Mike and Doug Starn / Artists Rights Society (ARS), New York

Page 208. Courtesy of the artist

Page 210. © Susan Meiselas / Magnum Photos

Page 212. Photo: Mary Ellen Mark

Page 215. Photographs by Richard Avedon, © The Richard Avedon Foundation

Page 216. © The Irving Penn Foundation

Pages 218, 219. Courtesy of the artist

Page 221. © Neil Winokur, courtesy Janet Borden, Inc., NY

Page 226. Courtesy of the artist and Nathalie Obadia gallery

Page 228. © Robert Mapplethorpe Foundation. Used by permission

Page 231. Courtesy of the Estate of David Wojnarowicz and P.P.O.W., New York

Page 238. © Thomas Struth, courtesy Marian Goodman Gallery

Page 244. © Muna Tseng Dance Projects, Inc.

Page 245. © Lorna Simpson. Courtesy the artist and Hauser & Wirth

Page 246. © Carrie Mae Weems. Courtesy of the artist and Jack Shainman Gallery, New York

Page 247. © 2020 Vik Muniz / Licensed by VAGA at Artists Rights Society (ARS), New York

Page 249. Courtesy of the artist Adam Fuss

Page 250. © 1995 Ellen Carey. All rights reserved / Courtesy of the Artist, Jayne H. Baum (NY, NY), Galerie Miranda (Paris, FR), M+B (LA, CA)

Page 251. Abelardo Morell / Courtesy Edwynn Houk Gallery

Page 253. © 2020 Artists Rights Society (ARS), New York / VG Bild-Kunst, Bonn / Courtesy of the artist and David Zwirner

Page 255. © Andreas Gursky / Courtesy Sprüth Magers / Artists Rights Society (ARS), New York / VG Bild-Kunst, Bonn

Page 256. © Nancy Burson

Page 260. © Estate of Martin Kippenberger, Galerie Gisela Capitain, Cologne